THE
ROOTS
OF
TREASON

EZRA POUND AND THE SECRET OF ST. ELIZABETHS

E. FULLER TORREY

HBJ

A HARVEST/HBJ BOOK
HARCOURT BRACE JOVANOVICH, PUBLISHERS
SAN DIEGO   NEW YORK   LONDON

LIBRARY OF CONGRESS CATALOGING IN PUBLICATION DATA

Torrey, E. Fuller (Edwin Fuller), 1927–
The roots of treason.

Includes index.

1. Pound, Ezra, 1885-1972.   2. Saint Elizabeths
Hospital (Washington, D.C.)   3. Poets, America—
20th century—Biography. I. Title.
[PS3531.082Z867   1984b]   811'.52   84-10727
ISBN 0-15-679015-7 (pbk.)

Printed in the United States of America

First Harvest/HBJ edition 1984

A B C D E F G H I J

ARTICLES AND BOOKS cited in the text under fair usage allowance are acknowledged in the notes. I wish to thank the following for permission to quote more extensively and for permission to use unpublished and interview material:

The Trustees of the Ezra Pound Literary Property Trust and the New Directions Publishing Corporation for permission to quote and reprint excerpts from the works of Ezra Pound as follows:

Ezra Pound, previously unpublished works. Copyright © 1983 by the Trustees of the Ezra Pound Literary Property Trust. Used by permission of New Directions Publishing Corporation, agents for the Trust.

Ezra Pound, *The Cantos of Ezra Pound.* Copyright 1934, 1937, 1940, 1948, © 1956, 1959, 1962, 1963, 1966, 1968 by Ezra Pound. Copyright © 1972 by the Estate of Ezra Pound.

Ezra Pound, *Collected Early Poems.* Copyright © 1976 by the Trustees of the Ezra Pound Literary Property Trust. All rights reserved.

Ezra Pound, *Ezra Pound Speaking.* Copyright © 1978 by the Ezra Pound Literary Property Trust.

Ezra Pound, *Gaudier-Brzeska.* Copyright © 1970 by Ezra Pound. All rights reserved.

Ezra Pound, *Guide to Kulchur.* Copyright © 1970 by Ezra Pound. All rights reserved.

Ezra Pound, *Literary Essays of Ezra Pound.* Copyright 1918, 1920, 1935 by Ezra Pound.

Ezra Pound, *Pavannes and Divagations.* Copyright © 1958 by Ezra Pound.

Ezra Pound, *Personae.* Copyright 1926 by Ezra Pound.

Ezra Pound, *Selected Letters.* Copyright 1950 by Ezra Pound.

Ezra Pound, *Selected Prose.* Copyright © 1973 by the Estate of Ezra Pound.

Ezra Pound, *Spirit of Romance.* Copyright © 1968 by Ezra Pound. All rights reserved.

Acknowledgment is given to the following journals where articles by Ezra Pound, quoted herein, first appeared: *Criterion, Dial, The Drama, Egoist, English Journal, Exile, Front, Little Review, New Age, The New English Weekly, The New Freewoman, New Review, Poetry, Townsman,* and *Blast.*

W. W. Norton and Company, Inc., for permission to reprint excerpts from *Jefferson and/or Mussolini* by Ezra Pound. Copyright 1935, 1956 by Ezra Pound.

Greenwood Press, a division of Congressional Information Service, Inc., for permission to quote from *Ezra Pound Speaking* by Leonard Doob.

The Trustees of the Ezra Pound Literary Property Trust for permission to quote from Louis Dudek, *Dk/Some Letters of Ezra Pound.* Copyright © 1974 by the Trustees of the Ezra Pound Literary Property Trust.

New Directions Publishing Corporation for permission to reprint excerpts from *End to Torment* by Hilda Doolittle. Copyright © 1979 by New Directions Publishing Corporation.

Omar Pound and The Wyndham Lewis Memorial Trust for permission to reprint excerpts from "Doppelgänger" in *Unlucky for Pringle: Unpublished and Other Stories* by Wyndham Lewis, copyright © by the Wyndham Lewis Memorial Trust, and for permission to quote from a previously unpublished letter of Wyndham Lewis, copyright © 1983 by The Wyndham Lewis Memorial Trust.

New Directions Publishing Corporation for permission to quote and reprint excerpts from the works of William Carlos Williams as follows:

William Carlos Williams, previously unpublished material. Copyright © 1983 by William Eric Williams and Paul H. Williams. Used by permission of New Directions Publishing Corporation, Agents.

Timothy Materer for permission to reprint excerpts from his book *Vortex: Pound, Eliot and Lewis*.

John H. Edwards for permission to reprint excerpts from his doctoral dissertation, "A Critical Biography of Ezra Pound: 1885–1922."

The Hamilton Literary Magazine for permission to reprint excerpts from an article by John L. Brown.

William Heinemann Ltd. for permission to reprint excerpts from *My Friends When Young* by Brigit Patmore.

American Journal of Psychotherapy for permission to reprint excerpts from an article by Fredric Wertham.

Charles Norman for permission to reprint excerpts from his books *Ezra Pound* and *The Case of Ezra Pound*.

Stanford University Press for permission to reprint excerpts from *The Political Identities of Ezra Pound and T. S. Eliot* by William M. Chace.

The Wabash Review for permission to reprint excerpts from an article by James E. Rader, Viola Wildman, and Fred H. Rhodes.

Quarterly Review of Literature for permission to reprint excerpts from an article by Wyndham Lewis.

Carroll F. Terrell and *Paideuma* for permission to reprint excerpts from articles by Carroll F. Terrell, Eric Homberger, Tim Redman, Romano Bilenchi, Brita Lindberg-Seyersted, and Evelyn Bates Doob.

W. W. Norton and Company for permission to reprint excerpts from *The Greek Way to Western Civilization* by Edith Hamilton.

Horizon Press, New York, for permission to reprint excerpts from *My Thirty Years' War* by Margaret Anderson. Copyright 1969.

Liveright Publishing Corporation and W. W. Norton and Company, Inc. for permission to reprint excerpts from *Return to Yesterday* by Ford Madox Ford.

Dodd, Mead and Company for permission to reprint excerpts from *American Aristocracy* by C. David Heymann.

Pantheon Books, a Division of Random House, Inc., for permission to reprint excerpts from *The Life of Ezra Pound* by Noel Stock. Copyright 1970.

Viking Penguin Inc. for permission to reprint excerpts from *Paris Was Our Mistress* by Samuel Putnam. Copyright 1947 by Samuel Putnam. Copyright renewed 1975 by Hilary Putnam.

Leon Surette for permission to reprint excerpts from his book *A Light From Eleusis*.

Robert A. Corrigan for permission to reprint excerpts from his article in *Prospects: An Annual of American Cultural Studies*.

University of Texas Press for permission to reprint excerpts from Michael King, "Ezra Pound at Pisa: an interview with John L. Steele" in *Texas Quarterly*.

Ms. Catherine Guillaume for permission to reprint excerpts from *Life for Life's Sake* by Richard Aldington.

Methuen and Company, Ltd., for permission to reprint excerpts from *Time and Western Man* by Wyndham Lewis.

Carlos Baker and Charles Scribner's Sons for permission to reprint excerpts from *Ernest Hemingway: Selected Letters* and *Ernest Hemingway: A Life Story*.

Julien Cornell for permission to reprint excerpts from his book *The Trial of Ezra Pound*, and from an unpublished letter.

Esquire for permission to reprint excerpts from an article by Robert L. Allen, "The Cage," February 1958. Copyright © 1958 by Esquire Publishing Inc.

Princeton University Press for permission to reprint excerpts from *Letters of Ford Madox Ford* by Richard M. Ludwig. Copyright © 1965 by Princeton University Press.

Victor Gollancz Ltd. for permission to reprint excerpts from *The Reactionaries: A Study of Anti-Democratic Intelligentsia* by John R. Harrison.

University of Chicago Press for permission to reprint excerpts from *Florence Ayscough and Amy Lowell: Correspondence of a Friendship*, edited by Harley F. MacNair. Copyright © 1945 by the University of Chicago.

The New York Times Magazine for permission to reprint excerpts from Alan Levy, "Ezra Pound's Voice of Silence," January 9, 1972. Copyright © 1972 by the New York Times Company.

Janice Biala for permission to reprint excerpts from *It Was The Nightingale* by Ford Madox Ford.

Doubleday and Company for permission to reprint excerpts from *Life and the Dream* by Mary Colum and from *Golden Friends I Had* by Margaret Widdemer.

Michael Reck for permission to reprint excerpts from his book *Ezra Pound: A Close-Up*. Copyright © 1967 by Michael Reck.

Charles Scribner's Sons for permission to reprint excerpts from *A Moveable Feast* by Ernest Hemingway. Copyright © 1964 by Ernest Hemingway Ltd.

Holt, Rinehart and Winston, Publishers, for permission to quote from *Selected Letters of Robert Frost* edited by Lawrance Thompson, copyright © 1964 by Lawrance Thompson and Holt, Rinehart and Winston. And from *Life Is My Song* by John G. Fletcher, copyright 1937 by John Gould Fletcher, copyright © 1965 by Charles May Fletcher.

Colin Smythe Ltd. for permission to reprint excerpts from *Yeats and Magic: The Earlier Works* by Mary Catherine Flannery.

Duke University Press for permission to reprint excerpts from an article in *American Literature* by Ben D. Kimpel and T. C. Duncan Eaves. Copyright © 1981, Duke University Press, Durham, North Carolina.

New Republic for permission to reprint excerpts from an article by Jack LaZebnik.

Malcolm Cowley for permission to reprint excerpts from his article in *New Republic*.

Wittenborn Art Books, Inc. for permission to reprint excerpts from *The Dada Painters and Poets: An Anthology* edited by Robert Motherwell.

Ruth Limmer, Literary Executor, Estate of Louise Bogan, for permission to reprint excerpts from "A Poet's Alphabet" by Louise Bogan; originally published in *The New Yorker*, October 30, 1948.

The New Yorker for permission to reprint excerpts from "A Day with Ezra Pound" by Elizabeth Delehanty, copyright © 1940, 1968 by The New Yorker Magazine, Inc. and from The Talk of the Town copyright © 1943, 1971 by The New Yorker Magazine, Inc.

Harper and Row, Publishers, Inc. for permission to reprint excerpts from *Remembering Poets* by Donald Hall. Copyright 1977, 1978 by Donald Hall.

Alfred A. Knopf, Inc. for permission to reprint excerpts from *Letters of H. L. Mencken* edited by Guy J. Forge. Copyright 1961 by Alfred A. Knopf, Inc.

Faber and Faber, Publishers, for permission to reprint excerpts from *Henri Gaudier-Brzeska, 1891–1915* by Horace Brodsky.

Curtis Brown, Ltd. for permission to reprint excerpts from *Balcony Empire* by Reynolds and Eleanor Packard. Copyright © 1942 by Reynolds and Eleanor Packard.

James Laughlin for permission to reprint excerpts from his articles in *University Review* and *Poetry*.

David Hingham Associates Ltd. for permission to reprint excerpts from *From The Life* by Phyllis Bottome.

Robert Payne for permission to reprint excerpts from his book *Hubris: A Study of Pride*.

Routledge and Kegan Paul Ltd. for permission to reprint excerpts from *The Enemy* by Jeffrey Meyers.

Farrar, Straus, and Giroux, Inc. for permission to reprint "Visits to St. Elizabeths" from *The Complete Poems* by Elizabeth Bishop. Copyright © 1957, 1969 by Elizabeth Bishop.

Allen Ginsberg for permission to reprint excerpts from his book *Composed on the Tongue* and from Michael Reck's "A conversation between Ezra Pound and Allen Ginsberg" in *Evergreen Review*.

Arthur Miller for permission to reprint excerpts from his article in *New Masses*.

The Watkins/Loomis Agency for permission to reprint excerpts from *Being Geniuses Together* by Robert McAlmon.

Twayne Publishers, a Division of G. K. Hall and Co., Boston, for permission to reprint excerpts from *The Caged Panther: Ezra Pound at St. Elizabeths* by Harry M. Meacham. Copyright 1967.

Constable and Company, Ltd., for permission to reprint excerpts from *South Lodge* by Douglas Goldring.

George F. Butterick, Literary Executor, Estate of Charles Olson, for permission to reprint excerpts from *Charles Olson and Ezra Pound* edited by Catherine Seelye.

J. P. Lippincott and Company for permission to reprint excerpts from *Handbook of Psychiatry*, by Winfred Overholser and Winifred V. Richmond.

Chilton Book Company for permission to reprint excerpts from *Nancy Cunard: Brave Poet, Indomitable Rebel 1895–1965* by Hugh D. Ford.

The Poetry/Rare Books Collection of the University Libraries, State University of New York at Buffalo, for permission to quote from unpublished letters of Ezra Pound and William Carlos Williams.

The Lilly Library, Indiana University, for permission to quote from unpublished letters of Wyndham Lewis and William Carlos Williams.

The Humanities Research Center, The University of Texas at Austin for permission to quote from unpublished letters of Ezra Pound, John Drummond, and Mario Praz.

The Yale Collection of American Literature, Beinecke Rare Book and Manuscript Library, Yale University, for permission to quote from unpublished letters of Ezra Pound and William Carlos Williams.

The George Arents Research Library, Syracuse University, for permission to quote from unpublished letters of Ezra Pound.

The Manuscripts Division, Library of Congress, for permission to quote from unpublished notes and letters of Ezra Pound, T. S. Eliot, Archibald MacLeish, and Huntington Cairns.

The Department of Rare Books, Cornell University Library, for permission to quote from unpublished letters of Ezra Pound.

Valerie Eliot for permission to quote unpublished letters of T. S. Eliot.

Huntington Cairns for permission to quote his unpublished notes of interviews with Ezra Pound.

John Drummond for permission to quote his unpublished letters.

Wendell S. Muncie, Addison Duval, Harold Stevens, Fredric C. Porten, Mauris Platkin, Jerome Kavka, Ms. Myrtle Istvan, and José Vasquez-Amaral for permission to quote from interviews, telephone interviews, and letters to the author.

Mrs. Merrill Moore for permission to quote from her late husband's unpublished letters and from her letter to the author.

Mrs. Carlos Dalmau for permission to quote from telephone interviews with her late husband.

FOR BARBARA, WHO TAUGHT ME MUCH OF WHAT I KNOW,

AND SOME OF WHAT I DON'T KNOW.

God damn it one lives so long to learn so little.
> Ezra Pound, letter to Wyndham Lewis,
> December 3, 1936

Whom God would destroy He first sends to the bughouse.
> Ezra Pound, speaking on Rome Radio,
> January 29, 1942

Time passes and pisses on us all.
> William Carlos Williams, letter to
> Ezra Pound, August 23, 1946

ACKNOWLEDGMENTS

I AM INDEBTED to the many people who searched their memory for events of thirty and more years ago and patiently answered my questions. The staff members of the Manuscript Division of the Library of Congress, the Humanities Research Center at the University of Texas at Austin, the Department of Rare Books at Cornell University, the George Arents Research Library at Syracuse University, the Beinecke Rare Book and Manuscript Library at Yale University, the Poetry/Rare Books Collection at the State University of New York at Buffalo, the Lilly Library at the University of Indiana, the Van Pelt Library at the University of Pennsylvania, and the Hamilton College Library were invariably helpful. The overworked staffs in the Freedom of Information offices in the Department of Justice, Federal Bureau of Investigation, and U.S. Army searched admirably for missing documents, and without the FOI law this book could not have been written. Drs. Addison Duval, Harold Stevens, Daniel Weinberger, Roger Peele, and the late Carlos Dalmau provided useful psychiatric and neurological consultations, and Carlos Baker, William French, Stanley Kutler, and the late Archibald MacLeish helped sharpen my understanding of specific events. Al Prettyman and Elsa Dixler at McGraw-Hill skillfully shepherded the book into its final form. Mary Adams, Carolyn Dudley, and Kathy McCollum helped with typing, and Karin Thomas provided invaluable assistance in all stages of manuscript preparation.

The opinions expressed herein are the views of the author and do not necessarily reflect the official position of St. Elizabeths Hospital, the National Institute of Mental Health, or the U.S. Department of Health and Human Services.

CONTENTS

PREFACE

OLGA RUDGE, Ezra Pound's friend of over fifty years, once complained about self-appointed Pound biographers. "They ring my bell and announce they are writing books that 'will tell both sides.' *Both* sides? Both sides! What do they think we are? Ezra Pound is no pancake!"[1]

There was only one Ezra Pound. He was charming and learned, creative and lusty, vicious and bigoted. His cerebral fault lines coexisted uneasily with the overlying terrain, producing prize-winning poetry in the morning and racist tracts in the afternoon. He helped T. S. Eliot and James Joyce, Benito Mussolini and Adolf Hitler. As a wordmaster he evoked both a revolution in poetry and an indictment for treason. He was a man easy to hate yet difficult to dislike. "Is the proper comparison with Dante, Judas, or Don Quixote?" one critic asked.[2] It is with all three.

Ezra Pound is not an easy man to find. Although he wrote prolifically he revealed very little about himself. His published and unpublished letters have been heavily edited, and passages have been deleted from later editions of his poetry and prose works.[3] Biographers and friends have woven a multitude of myths around him in their efforts to refurbish his reputation. They have said that he was like George Washington and his "only crime was his unswerving and uncompromising patriotism,"[4] that he was not guilty of treason, that he was not a Fascist, that he was not anti-Semitic, that he was deprived of his rights to a fair trial, and that he was held as a political prisoner. The biggest myth, however, was that he was insane.

Reconstruction of the historical record, aided by recent release of files in the Department of Justice and his psychiatric hospital, has made it possible to understand Ezra Pound. This understanding in turn permits an understanding of his poetry, for the man and his poems are one. The true story is better than the myths, but raises disturbing questions about the influence of the literati, the role of psychiatrists, and the performance of justice in our society.

My interest in Pound began when I noticed that I was following him around. I grew up in the town where he went to college, helped build a road through his grandmother's homestead in Nine Mile Swamp, and as a student focused on the work of his protégé T. S. Eliot. Two decades later I began work in the asylum he had called home for over twelve years. It was then that I became intrigued with the myths Pound's friends had created, and I began playing hide-and-seek with him in the stacks of the Library of Congress.

I believe Ezra Pound would want his story told. At the end of his life he realized that he had deceived himself even more effectively than he had deceived others. "Do what you can to save innocence," he told a friend. "Stop this Pound influence from spreading."[5] And to another friend he wrote: "Whether my errors can be useful to others, God knows."[6]

CHAPTER 1

THE GORILLA CAGE

[PISA: 1945]

"CAT PISS AND PORCUPINES" railed the prisoner at no one in particular.[1] The man in the adjoining cage was vaguely interested in his newest neighbor but had his own problems. He was scheduled to be hanged. And the guards, curious about the prisoner for whom such extraordinary precautions had been taken, were not allowed to speak to him. He certainly didn't *look* that dangerous.

Thirty years earlier Carl Sandburg had written of him:

> If I were driven to name one individual who in the English language, by means of his own examples of creative art in poetry, has done most of living men to incite new impulses in poetry, the chances are I would name Ezra Pound.[2]

Now he was on display for the three thousand inmates of the Disciplinary Training Center.[3] All day "trainees" (as they were called) stole glances at him, circumambulating the stockade so as to pass near his cage. The night before the prisoner arrived, the cage had been reinforced with the kind of steel mats used for airplane runways, making it stronger than the other cages that held mere rapists and murderers. The blue light of acetylene torches rent the night air, leading to much speculation about whom it was being prepared for. A poet, somebody said. The late spring night had given way to a cool day on the Italian plain. It was May 24, 1945. Ezra Pound was fifty-nine.

He was lucky to be alive at all, for partisans had executed many

1

of the Fascists they had captured. Being an American had probably helped, and the two partisans who came for him had turned him over to the American army after questioning. The army had kept him for three weeks at the Counter Intelligence Center in Genoa, where he was questioned and allowed an interview with a reporter from the *Chicago Sun*. Nobody was certain what to do with him next, and there was no word from Washington. Army regulations covered most contingencies, but they did not mention poets charged with treason.

The cage measured six by six and one-half feet and was ten feet high. He could extend his arms horizontally when he stood up, but exercise was difficult. Pound later described the cage as "big enough for a puma but it was a matter of relativity . . . he was larger than a puma."[4] There was a cement floor and a tar-paper roof. All body wastes had to be deposited into a tin can. Once a day he was given something to eat. The cage was open to view on all sides, and at night a special reflector poured light into it. A guard was posted twenty-four hours a day.

Ezra Pound had been one of the best-known poets in the earlier years of the century. In 1909 he had been acclaimed as "the most remarkable thing in poetry since Robert Browning."[5] Rudyard Kipling had called him one of the world's great poets.[6] Later he would be described as "the writer most responsible for making 'modernism' in literature part of our lives" and as being "to modern poetry what Picasso is to modern painting."[7] Sandburg had added:

> I like the pages of Ezra Pound. He stains darkly and touches softly. The flair of great loneliness is there. He is utter as a prairie horseman, a biplane in the azure, a Norse crag, or any symbol of the isolate, contemplative spirit of man unafraid and searching. He is worth having.[8]

The cable from the Commanding General, Mediterranean Theater of Operations, had been brief and specific: "Exercise utmost security measures to prevent escape or suicide. No press interviews authorized. Accord no preferential treatment."[9] The cable had even been sent in code, necessitating a trip to a nearby army base to get it deciphered. For those in charge of the camp it had all been most unusual. The commanding officer of the DTC, Lieutenant Colonel John L. Steele, was on leave in the United States when the cable arrived. His deputy was young and inexperienced, and "there was a certain amount of apprehension that we didn't get caught unawares or that this very important person didn't disappear, or anything happen to him."[10] The result was the reinforced cage. Pound called it his "gorilla cage."

It had all begun with promise, an Odyssean voyage to greatness.

Now it lay wrecked, caught up by the vortex of his ego. On Philadelphia's Main Line, where Pound had had a genteel upbringing, gracious ladies and gentlemen did not give names to the things he was supposed to deposit into the can. He looked out of the cage at his captors and the other prisoners. He had been driven the two hundred miles from Genoa that day in a jeep, handcuffed to a black soldier who was charged with rape and murder. For Pound, who commonly referred to blacks as "coons," it must have been a very long trip. The jeep had passed directly through Rapallo, where he had been living for twenty-one years. His mother, wife, mistress and daughter were all in the town, not knowing where he was, not sure if he was dead or alive.[11]

Treason was the charge against him, and execution the possible penalty. Two years earlier a grand jury in the District of Columbia had handed down the indictment:

> . . . then and there being a citizen of the United States, and a person owing allegiance to the United States, in violation of his said duty of allegiance, knowingly, intentionally, willfully, unlawfully, feloniously, traitorously, and treasonably did adhere to the enemies of the United States to wit, the Kingdom of Italy, its counsellors, armies, navies, secret agents, representatives, and subjects, and the military allies of the said Kingdom of Italy, including the government of the German Reich and the Imperial Government of Japan, with which the United States at all times since December 11, 1941, have been at war, giving to the said enemies of the United States aid and comfort within the United States and elsewhere.[12]

The erstwhile man of lyricism and letters had assailed the airwaves with invective, reviling Churchill and Roosevelt, extolling Hitler and Mussolini. In broadcasts from Rome beamed to American troops in the field he had said:

> You are at war for the duration of the German's pleasure. You are at war for the duration of Japan's pleasure. Nothing in the Western world, nothing in the whole of our Occident, can help you to dodge that. Nothing can help you dodge it. (February 3, 1942)

> You are not going to win this war. None of our best minds ever thought you could win it. You have never had a chance in this war. (June 28, 1942)[13]

Even after he had been taken into custody by the American army, Pound had told the reporter in Genoa that he strongly preferred Mussolini over Roosevelt, called Hitler "a Jeanne d'Arc, a saint . . . a martyr" and volunteered that "Stalin is the best brain in politics today."[14] Pound made these remarks on V-E Day, when the German surrender was being finalized.

In earlier years he had been described by friends as a "really simple charming creature" and "one of the kindest men that ever lived."[15] Yet in his radio broadcasts he had excoriated the "Jew in the White House" and "the 60 kikes who started this war." As Jews were being led to their deaths in Auschwitz and Buchenwald, Ezra Pound was broadcasting:

> Don't start a pogrom. This is, not an old-style killing of small jews. That system is no good, whatever. Of course, if some man had a stroke of genius, and could start a pogrom up at the top. I repeat . . . if some man had a stroke of genius, and could start a pogrom up at the top, there might be something to say for it. (April 30, 1942)

As Pound sat in the cage contemplating his fate, agents of the American government were assiduously building the legal case against him. His apartment in Rapallo had already been searched twice and large quantities of papers confiscated. Even his typewriter had been taken as evidence, presumably to prove that it had been used to type his broadcast speeches.[16] Records from the Italian Ministry of Popular Culture on the Via Veneto in Rome were being sent to the Federal Bureau of Investigation, as were receipts proving that Pound had been paid for his propaganda efforts. The Fascist government archives were turning up letters from Pound to Mussolini. All were carefully catalogued and forwarded by J. Edgar Hoover to the Department of Justice. They would be used to obtain a second indictment against Pound, this time specifying nineteen acts of treason.

As representatives of the American government collected evidence to bring Pound to trial, his friends in America and England proceeded with plans to help him. While Pound was still being held in Genoa, T. S. Eliot had cabled Archibald MacLeish: "Anxious do everything possible mitigate treatment of Ezra Pound stop please advise me."[17] Eliot had known Pound for over thirty years and was indebted to him for getting his early poetry published and for editing The Waste Land; Eliot had even dedicated the poem to Pound. Eliot's work eventually led to a Nobel Prize, as did the work of Bengali poet Rabindranath Tagore, William Butler Yeats, and Ernest Hemingway; all had been helped by Pound. Hemingway claimed that Pound had taught him more about how to write and how not to write than anyone else.[18]

MacLeish had known Pound for over twenty years and had also been influenced by Pound's style and advice. So had William Carlos Williams, Robert Frost, E. E. Cummings, Hart Crane, Marianne Moore, Wyndham Lewis, D. H. Lawrence, Katherine Anne Porter, James Joyce, and a host of lesser-known poets and novelists. Pound's friends extended beyond literature, for he had launched the career of French sculptor

Henri Gaudier-Brzeska and had assisted Rumanian sculptor Constantin Brancusi. In music he had promoted American composer George Antheil and had helped revive interest in the music of Antonio Vivaldi. Pound had been a one-man literati band; he had been called a minister to the arts without portfolio.[19]

THE DTC

The Disciplinary Training Center was an army prison located just north of Pisa. It housed an assortment of AWOLs, social misfits, soldiers who had turned their guns on their commanding officers, thieves, rapists and murderers. Almost half the inmates were said to be alcoholics, and a large number were black and poorly educated. Those with lesser charges were given an opportunity to "soldier out" and back to duty if they could withstand several months of unbroken regimentation, fourteen-hour days, moonlight drills, and strict discipline. The camp was surrounded by barbed wire and fourteen sentry boxes. Guards in the corner boxes carried Browning automatic rifles, known for their accuracy. The others carried Thompson submachine guns. The camp had been built to hold "the slime and filth of the whole Mediterranean Theater of Operations."[20]

Most of the inmates in the DTC lived in tents, but at one end of the compound ten cages had been built. They were officially called "observation cells" but were widely known as "death cells," for they housed the worst criminals in the camp—many under sentence of death, waiting to be transferred to Naples for execution. During Pound's stay in the DTC there was an attempted escape; several inmates were shot and at least two were killed. Occasionally an inmate poured lye on his feet in order to get transferred to the hospital in Pisa. Pound was assigned to one of the "death cells," specially reinforced to make it escape-proof. It was as if he were the most dangerous of them all.

For twenty-five days he lived in his cage. He wore army fatigues with the trousers hanging loosely because he was not allowed to have a belt. He had no laces in his shoes—they too were not allowed, because he might use them to hang himself. And yet they had cut off the old steel netting about ten inches from the ground when they had added the reinforced mats, forming a low hedge of spikes. Pound interpreted it as an invitation to slash his wrists. Perhaps they wanted him to commit suicide after all.[21] His red beard, once the talk of the literary salons of London and Paris, had faded into a scraggy amber Vandyke, giving him, according to one observer, a "somewhat bizarre" appearance.[22]

At twilight he looked out at the hills and remembered when he had first come to Pisa. It had been in 1898, when he was only twelve, in the company of his maternal aunt.[23] He had also come this way in 1923, when he had taken Ernest Hemingway and his wife on a walking tour of Italy, lunching on cheese and wine under the olive trees, showing "Hem" the fifteenth-century battlegrounds where the campaigns of Malatesta had been fought.[24] They had probably walked down the very road that passed in front of the camp, the Via Aurelia. The road had been named for Marcus Aurelius, who had traveled this way eighteen hundred years earlier in his quest to restore the glories of the Roman Empire. Aurelius had written: "If anyone can show me, and prove to me, that I am wrong in thought or deed, I will gladly change. I seek the truth, which never yet hurt anybody. It is only persistence in self-delusion and ignorance which does harm."[25] Pound had discarded Aurelius as "a dilettante who liked intellectual toys."[26]

Years later Pound would joke about his days in the cage:

Ha, I was a dangerous criminal . . . They thought I was a dangerous wild man and were scared of me. I had a guard night and day and when they built a cage out of iron mats from airplane runways and put me in the cage for the merriment of all, they posted a guard outside. Soldiers used to come up to the cage and look at me. Some of them brought me food. Old Ez was a prize exhibit.[27]

But in May 1945 he could not joke about it. Just four days before Pound was taken into custody, Benito Mussolini had been killed by Italian partisans and his body publicly displayed hanging by its heels in Milan. Next to him hung his mistress, Claretta Petacci. Mussolini had been Pound's idol for twenty years. Pound had kept a scrapbook of Il Duce's life and work, had written to him frequently, and had published a book comparing him with Thomas Jefferson. He met Mussolini once, and had been so pleased with the meeting that he hung the official notice granting the interview on the wall of his apartment in Rapallo.[28] For over thirteen years Pound had even dated his letters according to the Fascist calendar, which began with the 1922 Black Shirt march on Rome. Mussolini was going to restore the world to greatness, restore the arts to greatness, restore Pound himself to greatness.

The depth of Pound's despair is reflected in the opening lines of Canto 74, begun while he was in the cage:

> The enormous tragedy of the dream in the peasant's bent shoulders
> Manes! Manes was tanned and stuffed,
> Thus Ben and la Clara a Milano
>
> by the heels at Milano

Three times in the poem Pound refers to "a man on whom the sun has gone down," apparently referring to himself as well as to Mussolini. In later years he frequently summarized his Pisan prison experience by saying, "The world fell on me."[29]

In addition to being disconsolate, Ezra Pound was also frightened. He understood the severity of the charges against him and their possible consequences. When interviewed by the reporter in Genoa he had twice made reference to the possibility of execution: "I do not believe that I will be shot for treason. I rely on the American sense of justice . . . If I am not shot for treason, I think my chances of seeing Truman are good."[30] His imprisonment in one of the "death cages" at Pisa and his special treatment as a dangerous inmate suggested otherwise. As he sat writing in the cage he wondered how much longer he would live:

> *we will see those old roads again, question,*
> *   possibly*
>
> *but nothing appears much less likely*

And he thought he knew how it would end:

> *yet say this to the Possum: a bang, not a whimper,*
> *   with a bang not with a whimper,*
>
> *To build the city of Dioce whose terraces are the colour of stars.*
>
> *(Canto 74)*

The Possum was Pound's name for his friend T. S. Eliot, who had previously written in "The Hollow Men" that "This is the way the world ends / Not with a bang but a whimper."

THE FIRST PSYCHIATRISTS

After Ezra Pound had been in the cage for two weeks he had a "spell." According to one of the guards in the DTC, "he appeared to have lost weight and stopped all activity . . . A good friend in the dispensary informed me that 'he cracked!' The truth is that he became hysterical, lost his memory, and was having nightmares."[31] Pound's own explanation to his daughter four months later was that he had suffered from sunstroke.[32] When Pound described the episode to a psychiatrist at St. Elizabeths Hospital six months after its occurrence, the psychiatrist recorded that "he fell ill and was stricken with violent terror. His memory failed and he became thin and weak."[33]

Because of his "spell" Pound was examined by the two camp psychiatrists, Richard W. Finner and Walter H. Baer. Dr. Finner described the

episode as "a period of several minutes during which he had great difficulty in collecting his thoughts . . . This occurred while he was sitting
in the sun."[34] Dr. Baer called it a "recent spell of confusion and complaints of 'claustrophobia' " and added that Pound was presently complaining of "temporary periods of confusion, anxiety, feelings of frustration, and excessive fatiguability."[35] Given Pound's age, his confinement
in a small cage, exposure to the June Italian sun with possible dehydra-
tion, isolation, depression over Mussolini's death, and anxiety about
his own fate, Pound's complaints and his "spell" would not be unex-
pected. The episode would prove to be crucial in determining Pound's
fate, for five months later Pound's lawyer would publicly represent the
events as a "period of violent insanity [which] apparently began about
mid-June, to endure for three months or more."[36]

Both psychiatrists judged Pound to be normal. Dr. Baer added that
Pound "does, however, lack personality resilience," and "due to his
age and loss of personality resilience, prolonged exposure in present
environment may precipitate a mental breakdown, of which premonitory
symptoms are discernible. Early transfer to the United States or to an
institution in this theatre with more adequate facilities for care is recommended." In short, Dr. Baer recommended that Pound be moved out
of the cage to more humane living conditions. Lieutenant Colonel Steele
accepted Dr. Baer's recommendation and on June 18, 1945, moved
Pound to a tent in the medical compound.

Pound had never thought highly of psychiatrists as a group and
in later years would express supreme contempt for them. During his
confinement in the DTC he attacked "the germy epoch of Freud"[37]
and said that "Proust and Freud are unmitigated shit / they pass for
intelligentzia because their shit is laid out in most elaborate
arabesques."[38] He attacked Freud's theories as the "flower of a deliques-
cent society going to pot . . . The general results of Freud are Dostoives-
kian duds worrying about their own unimportant innards . . .[39]

Immediately following his psychiatric interviews, word spread
around the DTC that Pound had "made a dummy of the psychiatrist,"
turning the questions around so that the psychiatrist himself became
confused. The story originated with a trainee who had been present
during the interview.[40] The psychiatrists had, however, helped Pound
get out of his gorilla cage.

THE SUMMER OF '45

Pound's new quarters were comparatively luxurious. His tent was
furnished with an army cot, a table, and two wooden packing crates.

During the mornings he rested, a habit which he had maintained most of his life.[41] For exercise "he found an old broom handle that became a tennis racquet, a billiard cue, a rapier, a baseball bat to hit small stones and a stick which he swung out smartly to match his long stride. His constitutionals wore a circular path in the compound grass . . . He was granted permission to use the dispensary typewriter in the evening and it was not unusual to see him typing a letter to some trainee's girl or mother with the trainee dictating at his shoulder and Pound interpreting for him. After taps, when all trainees were in their tents, Pound worked on his epic Cantos and Chinese translations. The constant clanging and banging of the typewriter, which he punched angrily with his index fingers, were always accompanied by a high-pitched humming sound he made as the carriage raced the bell. He swore well and profusely over typing errors."[42] The use of a typewriter and supply of paper were privileges not given to other inmates, who were allowed to write only one letter a week. Lieutenant Colonel Steele rationalized Pound's special prerogatives as being good for his mental health and said that because "he was a very significant person in the literary world . . . I did sort of go out of my way to do things that were not required in order to help him get on with the writing."[43]

"Throughout the summer of 1945," according to one of the DTC guards, "Pound was in excellent spirits."[44] Because of the question about Pound's psychiatric condition which had been raised by his "spell" in the cage, Steele's superiors ordered him to have Pound re-examined a month later to ensure that he was still healthy. Therefore on July 17, 1945, Dr. William Weisdorf, the new DTC psychiatrist, examined Pound. Dr. Weisdorf described Pound's previous "spell" as a "transitory anxiety state as the culmination of several weeks in close confinement . . . These manifestations cleared up rapidly as the prisoner was made more comfortable physically." He found him to be psychiatrically normal.[45] Based upon these findings Lieutenant Colonel Steele filed an updated report on Pound's psychiatric status, with the "Commanding General, The Replacement and Training Command," reassuring his superiors that "Pound has made a satisfactory mental adjustment to his present situation and is mentally competent."[46] Steele himself had independently come to the conclusion that Pound was perfectly sane.[47]

Pound occupied himself throughout the summer with continuing work on his Cantos, originally begun in 1915. The newest ones would later be published as *The Pisan Cantos*. One critic noted that in these Cantos "Pound appears more sane at that time, less driven by obsessions, than at any other time since the First World War."[48] Another reviewer said of them:

Pound's imprisonment in Pisa seems to have brought him back to art and to life. *The Pisan Cantos* shows a new sense of proportion. He begins to feel pity and gratitude, and he begins to smile wryly, even at himself. I cannot think of any other record by an artist or a man of letters, in or out of prison, so filled with a combination of sharp day-to-day observation, erudition, and humorous insight.[49]

Within the DTC Pound was regarded with bemused affection and was commonly referred to as "Uncle Ezra." He was a standard camp fixture as he hunched over his typewriter, swearing at errors. One guard was impressed by how patient and appreciative Pound was and recalled that "Uncle Ezra" invariably thanked his captors for small kindnesses.[50]

Pound lost no opportunity in promoting his ideas with the staff of the DTC. Lieutenant Colonel Steele had taught economics at Boston University before the war, and according to his recollections, Pound "wanted to talk only about economics and the fact that he needed to go straighten out Truman."[51] Pound also gave impromptu economics lectures to the guards and inspired one guard to write his mother that he had found a great man who had taught him how to correct the economic problems of America.[52]

Pound also talked freely about the treason charges against him and his belief that he would not be brought to trial. He claimed he "had too much on several people in Washington for the Government to allow him to testify in court."[53] He acknowledged that he had made broadcasts from Rome but claimed they were in no way treasonable. He denied ever supporting the Fascists. "His connection with Mussolini was brushed off lightly with a laugh. He said that he had seen 'Muss' (or 'Ben') once and then they had talked only for a short time about non-political matters."[54] As the summer wore on and no movement toward trial was visible, Pound became more convinced that he would be released. On August 17, 1945, when he was summoned to an office in the DTC, he even gave the Fascist salute upon entering.[55]

The Cantos he worked on throughout the summer reflected the beliefs and biases which had preoccupied Pound for almost three decades. He wrote of "the little coon" (Canto 74), "the nigger murderer" (Canto 76), "a good nigger" (Canto 79), and a "young nigger" (Canto 80). He accused Jews of causing the war and of profiting from it:

> The yidd is a stimulant, and the goyim are cattle
> in gt / proportion and go to saleable slaughter
> with the maximum of docility.

(*Canto 74*)

And his contempt for people other than the aristocracy continued un-
abated, e.g., "Fear god and the stupidity of the populace" (Canto 74).

The Pisan Cantos are also remarkable in that they reflect no regret,
no remorse, no self-doubt. Pound's faith in himself and in the validity of
his ideas was as strong as ever. Some scholars have claimed that he was
expressing repentance in his oft-quoted passage on vanity in Canto 81:

> Pull down thy vanity
>> How mean thy hates
>
> Fostered in falsity,
>> Pull down thy vanity,
>
> Rathe to destroy, niggard in charity,
>> Pull down thy vanity,
>>> I say pull down.

Pound himself vehemently denied any such intent and said the vanity
he referred to was that of his American captors.[56] The Canto continues
in the same vein:

> But to have done instead of not doing
>> This is not vanity
>
> To have, with decency, knocked
> That a Blunt should open
>> To have gathered from the air a live tradition
>
> or from a fine old eye the unconquered flame
> This is not vanity.
>> Here error is all in the not done,
>
> all in the diffidence that faltered . . .
>
>   (Canto 81)

His actions justified themselves, Pound claimed; those who failed to
act are the blameworthy ones. He compared himself with Wilfred Blunt,
renowned in England for his independence of mind, his dislike of democracy, and his myriad mistresses (thus "the unconquered flame," Pound's
symbol for passion and sex).[57] In another Pisan Canto (number 74)
Pound compared himself with Barabbas "and two thieves lay beside
him . . . minus Hemingway, minus Antheil, ebullient," having apparently
taken Christ's place on the cross. Later in the same Canto he had become
Christ, "with Barabbas and 2 thieves beside me." Ezra Pound saw himself
as a martyr whose actions history would justify. Narcissus had been
untouched by the events of the war.

QUISLING AND LAVAL

The bombs that dropped on Hiroshima and Nagasaki in early August ended Ezra Pound's peaceful summer. While in the camp latrine he heard the news of the Japanese surrender, perhaps an augury of things to come. In Europe and America there was euphoria at having won, but also a desire to settle accounts with those who were seen as responsible for the war.

The first account to come due was that of Marshal Pétain, head of the French Vichy government, who had collaborated with the Nazi army of occupation during the war. Pound was sympathetic to Pétain, noting in Canto 80 that "Pétain defended Verdun while Blum / was defending a bidet." On August 15, 1945, the day on which the final surrender of Japan was being trumpeted around the world, Pétain was condemned to death by a French court. Because he was an old man, a French appeals court in a close vote commuted his sentence to life imprisonment. Pound recorded the outcome in Canto 79: "And Pétain not to be murdered 14 to 13 / after six hours' discussion."

Pound had daily access to the army newspaper, the *Stars and Stripes*, as well as to *Time* and *Newsweek*. He read them avidly.[58] On August 20 the *Stars and Stripes* reported that Archibald MacLeish, Pound's old and close friend, had resigned as assistant secretary of state. MacLeish and T. S. Eliot had continued to correspond during the summer in an attempt to help their friend. On May 18 MacLeish had written: "According to the same newspaper account, Pound admits having broadcast for the Fascists and the Nazis for pay. If he takes that position on trial here, I assume the only defensive position will be a defense based upon some mitigating circumstance."[59] Eliot replied that he had "not heard a single voice express any desire except that Pound should be let off as lightly as possible and that the whole affair might be forgotten as quickly as possible."[60] By early August Eliot had made inquiries about the best legal counsel for Pound,[61] and MacLeish informed Eliot that Pound had undergone psychiatric examination at the DTC but to date "no report has been received by the Department of Justice as to the results of the examination."[62] Since MacLeish was a poet as well as a friend, his resignation from an influential position in the Truman administration was a setback for Pound.

On August 21 a front-page story discussed the opening of Vidkun Quisling's treason trial in Norway. Quisling had been extolled by Pound during his wartime broadcasts, and Pound identified with him; both had warned of excessive Jewish influence in international affairs, both had opposed the League of Nations, and both claimed that their wartime activity was aimed at averting further war and therefore was not treasonous.[63] In Canto 84 Pound would praise Quisling as "full of humanitas." Now Quisling's somber eyes looked out from the front page of the *Stars and Stripes*. He had read a long treatise in court defending his actions, arguing that he had worked in the best interests of Norway, and bemoaning his fate: " 'All asses give the dying lion its kick,' he lamented."[64]

In the days that followed, the prosecution demonstrated that Quisling had urged Hitler to invade Norway, had promoted the development of the hated secret police, had sanctioned the deportation of Norwegian Jews to Nazi concentration camps, and had even stolen money and property from the state. Quisling's comportment during the proceedings was shameful, with frequent claims of memory lapses; on August 24 the coverage was headlined: "Quisling denies, cries, forgets—and squirms." When asked why he had stolen marble statues from the grounds of the government palace and placed them in his own home, Quisling replied that he was just protecting them from the wind and rain. Years later Pound would call him "the smeared Vidkun."[65]

Especially interesting to Pound was the account of the trial on August 25, when tapes of Quisling's wartime broadcasts were played in court; apparently his exhortations to his countrymen to surrender to the Nazis were not covered by the freedom of speech. Senator Wiley of the United States Senate Judiciary Committee proclaimed that the Quisling trial would be a test case for all future war crimes trials, and Supreme Court Justice Robert Jackson assisted the Norwegian government in planning the prosecution. On August 28 Quisling was ordered to have a psychiatric examination to ensure that he was not "suffering from some disease that might account for the tremendous difference between witnesses' descriptions of his character during youth and early manhood and his subsequent actions and utterances." Two days later the court received the report: Quisling was perfectly sane except for "a slight nervous strain which would have no effect on his mental activities."

The outcome of the trial was never in doubt. On September 11, 1945, the *Stars and Stripes* reported on page one: "Quisling guilty of treason; court passes death sentence." The Norwegian parliament had passed a special bill restoring the death penalty, which had previously been abolished. Everyone at the DTC was excitedly discussing Dick Fowler's no-hitter for the Philadelphia Athletics the previous day, and whether the Tigers and Cubs could retain their diminishing leads in the closing days of the baseball season, but Pound's mind was elsewhere. He was beginning to realize how vengeful the public could be. America had lost over 400,000 young men in the war, with another 671,000 wounded; it wanted to hold people responsible. Pound realized that America wanted its pound of flesh.

Quisling's fate was not the only bad news in September. On September 17 William Joyce went on trial in London, charged with three counts of treason. Joyce and Pound shared many interests. Both had been born in America but had spent many years in England; Joyce had become an English citizen. Both were well educated, outspokenly critical of the economic system in England, and had supported Oswald Mosley and the British Fascists in the 1930s. During the war while Pound was broadcasting over Radio Rome for Mussolini, Joyce was broadcasting on Radio Berlin for Hitler and had become known in England as Lord Haw-Haw. Pound and Joyce had also corresponded in 1941, exchanging ideas for effective propaganda; Pound had signed one letter with "Heil Hitler."[66]

One of the reporters covering William Joyce's trial was Pound's friend from his early London days, Rebecca West. She wrote that Joyce "had wanted glory, and his trial gave him the chance to wrestle with reality, to argue with the universe, to defend the revelations which he believed had been made to him; and that is about as much glory as comes to any man." Joyce used his public forum skillfully and carried the courtroom with grace; when finally sentenced to hang, he bowed politely to the judge, then waved to his brother. In summarizing her impressions of Joyce and other traitors, West concluded: "The trouble about man is twofold. He cannot learn truths which are too complicated; he forgets truths which are too simple."[67]

The death sentences meted out to Quisling and Joyce changed Pound's mood perceptibly. "The rainy, grey fall weather came and Pound's tent was anything but comfortable . . . He became extremely depressed . . . in that cold, wet fall, with no indication of when the occupation of Italy would be terminated, he almost despaired of ever leaving Pisa."[68] Perhaps because of his depression, DTC officials finally gave Pound permission to write to his family and allowed them to visit. Up to this time Pound had been allowed only a single visitor, elderly philosopher George Santayana, who had come from Rome. After trying vainly for ten days to get transportation to Pisa, Dorothy Pound finally arrived at the DTC on October 3. She identified herself to the guard at the gate, who telephoned ahead: "Tell Uncle Ez his wife is here to see him."[69]

Dorothy's visit briefly revived Pound's flagging spirit. The following day in Paris, the treason trial of Pierre Laval opened. Laval had been vice president of the Vichy government under Pétain and was highly esteemed by Pound. In the 1930s Laval had favored partitioning Ethiopia in Mussolini's favor. During the war Laval had criticized the English, President Roosevelt, and the Jews. Pound praised him in Canto 84 as a man who, like Quisling, was "full of humanitas."

Laval's courtroom performance was dramatically different from Quisling's. On the trial's opening day Laval "dominated the courtroom with his impressive arguments." Turning to the foreign press section he told the reporters: "I beg you to report my words exactly, for from them history will give justice." He denied all the specific allegations against him and "charged that pre-trial examination was 'ended abruptly' because of fears of examining France's entry into World War II about which 'none of you know what happened.' He said he would show who was 'truly responsible' for France's predicament. 'I knew the danger was coming from Hitler,' he said. 'If France had followed my policies, we would have had no Munich, no German-Soviet accord.' "[70] A shouting match ensued between Laval and the judge, with Laval eventually being expelled from the courtroom.

The *Stars and Stripes* reported the Laval trial proceedings under page-one headlines on October 5. That same day Pound wrote to his father-in-law's law firm in London and outlined his defense. He wished to represent himself in court, he said, but planned to discuss his case with Archibald MacLeish before making a final decision. If he had to get a lawyer, then Lloyd Stryker would be his choice; Stryker was a well-known criminal lawyer whose father had been president of Hamilton College when Pound was a student there. Pound's main defense would be the issue of freedom of speech, and he suggested a contact "with Roger Baldwin of the Civil Liberties Union" to explore this.[71] Like Laval, Pound would deny all charges, stand on principle, and put the court on trial rather than the other way around. He would publicly defend himself and his actions. As he had told the Americans when he was taken into custody: "If a man isn't willing to take some risk for his opinions, either his opinions are no good or he's no good."[72]

For each of the next five days there was a page-one account of the Laval trial. The defendant was said to have delivered "a brilliant three-hour-long monologue" in which he pictured himself as a superpatriot: "I have nothing to hide. I have served my country." The judge and jury repeatedly violated courtroom decorum and even shouted Laval down on occasion. The *Stars and Stripes* noted that "the wily, eloquent Laval has improved his own position immeasurably by his deft handling of his own defense . . . he has remained constantly master of his own trial, has handled it with consummate skill, and has—at least thus far—made a more convincing case in the hearings than has the prosecution." "To judge me," said Laval, "you must examine the whole of my policies,

not isolated facts. I acted not to betray France, but to protect her."
Here indeed was a man with whom Pound could enthusiastically identify;
he had a model for his own defense if they brought him to trial.

The only problem with Laval's defense was that, however eloquent,
it failed. The jury took just fifty-eight minutes to find him guilty, and
he was sentenced to death. Five days later the sentence was carried
out by a firing squad. Laval was heroic to the end, refusing the proffered
blindfold and asking permission to give the command to the firing squad
for his own execution. As the shots rang out he cried defiantly, "Vive
la France!" It had been a Demosthenic performance, evoking admiration
from Pound and much of the world. But Laval, like Quisling and Joyce,
had been sentenced to death. Neither fearlessness nor eloquence could
reverse that ultimate fact.

On October 17, the day following the report of Laval's death, Olga
Rudge, Pound's friend and mistress of twenty-five years, came to visit
with their daughter, Mary. According to Mary her father had aged considerably during his four-month imprisonment and appeared both unkempt
and despondent.[73] She quoted Pound's lines from Canto 83: "Nothing.
Nothing that you can do . . ." Pound undoubtedly reflected on happier
times when Mary would visit her mother and father in Venice, and in
the same Canto he asks, "Will I ever see the Guidecca again?"

The events of the ensuing days did not increase Pound's optimism
about the future. On the day following Olga and Mary's visit, twenty-
four Nazis were indicted for war crimes and preparations were accelerated for their trial at Nuremberg; three days later it was announced
that the trials of "forty to fifty" administrators and guards of the Dachau
concentration camp would begin. On October 23 the *Stars and Stripes*
carried an account of the forthcoming treason trial of Norman Baillie-
Stuart, another Englishman who had broadcast propaganda for Hitler
during the war.[74] Two days later Vidkun Quisling's delayed execution
by a firing squad was announced. Pound's sixtieth birthday came and
went on October 30, and he was not at all certain that he would see
his sixty-first.

Pound's last two weeks at the DTC were the most difficult. A story
in the *Stars and Stripes* said that six Italian radio technicians were being
flown to Washington to testify against him at his forthcoming trial. There
was no longer any doubt about what he was facing, and his mood, which
had been somber, became fatalistic: "His tone of conversation changed
and occasionally he spoke of himself in the past tense. Several times
he said, 'If I go down, someone must carry on.' "[75] His wife visited
again on November 3. Three days later there was a picture in the *Stars
and Stripes* of Tokyo Rose in prison awaiting her treason trial; she had

become a household name in America, and often linked with her were other names like Axis Sally and Ezra Pound.

Finally, on the evening of November 16, 1945, the waiting came to an end. "Pound was sitting in the dispensary reading Joseph E. Davies' *Mission to Moscow.* The Charge of Quarters sat at the desk next to him. From time to time Pound commented on the book. Suddenly the door opened and two young lieutenants entered. They told Pound that he would be flown to Washington in one hour and to get his personal effects together. They turned and left. Pound handed the book to the CQ. He asked him to thank all of the medical personnel for their kindness. He then walked to the door of the prefab, turned, and with a half-smile, put both hands around his neck to form a noose and jerked up his chin."[76]

CHAPTER 2

BAPTISM IN
A LILY POND

[PHILADELPHIA: 1885–1907]

THE ROAD TO THE GORILLA CAGE began in Hailey, Idaho, where Ezra
Pound was born on October 30, 1885. His forebears included an eminent
poet, a Civil War cavalry officer, a congressman, and a famous horse
thief. It was an interesting assortment of genetic baggage with which
to set forth.

New England aristocracy was well represented in the Pound family
tree on his maternal side. His grandmother was a Wadsworth and was
related both to poet Henry Wadsworth Longfellow and to Captain Joseph
Wadsworth, who in 1687 had saved the Connecticut charter (and thereby
thwarted English intervention) by hiding it in an oak tree. As a child
Pound was taken to Hartford to see what had become known as the
Charter Oak. Pound's grandfather was a Weston, another venerable New
England name, and had fought as a cavalry captain for the North during
the Civil War.

The genetic stock on his father's side was less predictable and therefore more interesting. Thaddeus Pound, his grandfather, came from a
family of whalers who had settled in New Jersey and, later, Pennsylvania.
He took his bride, Sarah Angevine Loomis, west to the Wisconsin frontier
in search of his fortune. He was interested in spiritualism, "and performed, I believe, in company with his brother Albert, a tour of spiritual
or magnetic healing and demonstration."[1] After giving up the traveling
medicine show, Thaddeus ran a general store and then went into the
lumbering business. It prospered, and he branched out into silver min-

18

ing, railroading, and eventually politics. He moved from the state assembly to become lieutenant governor, acting governor, and three-term
United States congressman from 1872 to 1878.[2] His career reached its
apex when he was promised a seat in President Garfield's cabinet. However, in Washington Thaddeus had succumbed to the Sirens of the Potomac and had taken "to himself a second feminine adjunct, without sanc-
tion of clergy." This was discountenanced by another Garfield nominee
who refused "to sit in the same cabinet with a man who was not living
with his wife."[3] Morality won out, and Thaddeus's professional career
came to rest on the shoals of his personal life.

Thaddeus Pound was an important influence on his grandson in
several areas. While living in Rapallo Ezra was given newspaper articles
which his grandfather had written on political and economic topics; Ezra
claimed that Thaddeus's writing style was similar to his own. On another
occasion Pound recalled that Thaddeus "was asking for the same things
I am asking for in very much the same style."[4] Pound invoked his grandfather as justification for his bigotry and for his economic theories. For
example, on his broadcast over Radio Rome on May 5, 1942, Pound
said that "the Kike" was "against all that is decent in America, against
the total American heritage. This is my war all right. I've been in it
for twenty years—my granddad was in it before me."[5] Thaddeus Pound
had apparently been interested in ideas of monetary reform, and had
issued his own scrip money when he was running the lumber camps;
monetary reform was to become a dominant influence in Ezra Pound's
adult life, and he frequently cited his grandfather to justify his theories.
How much of this familial legitimization was fact and how much was
romantic rationalization is unknown. It *is* known that Thaddeus made
and lost a lot of money more than once. Ezra claimed that Thaddeus
accumulated and lost three fortunes during his lifetime, and that one
of them was lost during his years in Congress.[6] Since it was the American
custom in those days to acquire rather than lose a fortune during time
spent as a congressman, it is unclear what happened to it.

Sarah Angevine Loomis, Pound's paternal grandmother, was a descendant of an esteemed New England family, which had founded the
Loomis School in Connecticut. However Sarah was from a branch of
the family that had chosen to make its fortune disreputably. Sarah's
grandfather had settled in upstate New York and, with the help of a
rapacious wife and several willing progeny, had led a band of horse
thieves. These thieves terrorized the surrounding countryside from their
ranch in Nine Mile Swamp and were known as the Loomis Gang. As
detailed by their biographer, "the Loomises made crime a big business
and used highway robbery, counterfeiting, arson and murder as their

weapons of terrorism."[7] Their outlaw empire continued for several decades "until it became an international scandal," and was sustained by bribery of both local officials and New York State assemblymen. The women in the family—Sarah's grandmother, mother, and aunts—played major roles in the family's brigandage. Finally, in the waning years of the nineteenth century the gang was dispersed by a posse and its various members killed, imprisoned, or forced to flee to Canada. Sarah and one of her sisters had already left to marry Thaddeus Pound and his brother.

Ezra learned of his grandmother's infamous origins early in life but chose to minimize them. In a biographical note written when he was thirty-five, Pound said that "an old lady whom I met in Oneida County said they [the Loomis family] were horse-thieves, charming people, in fact the 'nicest' people in the county, but horse-thieves, never, I think, brought to book."[8] This information was presumably received while Pound was at Hamilton College, which is in Oneida County and only ten miles from the old Loomis homestead at Nine Mile Swamp. It was also while at Hamilton that Pound permanently dropped Loomis as his middle name and adopted Weston instead.[9]

In later years Pound painted this branch of the family with a veneer of respectability. In 1944 he alluded to his great-grandfather as a "Justice of the Peace in New York State" and two years later described Sarah simply as "a progenitor of one of the oldest homesteads in America," making no mention whatsoever of her more immediate origins. Pound claimed to have known her well and considered her a "model of commonsense" and a "solid frontier type." He assured the interviewer that "you could put that grandmother down as no fuss—no fuss about anything."[10] In view of Pound's fanatic insistence on proper genetic roots and his later derision of people whose pedigree did not match the theoretical purity of his own, it is ironic that the black sheep in his family background were bigger and blacker than those in most families. His selective memory also illustrates a lifelong propensity for reconstructing facts to meet the standards of personal mythology.

EARLY YEARS

Ezra was the first and only child of Isabel and Homer Pound. Isabel was herself an only child, had been raised in New York, and was later described by her son as "spoiled" and a person who "liked pretty things."[11] She was "a beautiful woman, well-bred, somewhat affected in manner," had a "high society voice" and "was often regarded as uppish." She is said to have conferred on Ezra "an occasional willfulness in not admitting or even seeing the other side," and in later years it was said that "she held herself like Queen Mary."[12] She had arrived in Idaho with a servant retinue of "stylish New York niggers,"[13] a debut which surely evoked commentary from the local denizens.

Homer Pound had moved to Hailey two years previously to establish a United States government land office. It was a frontier town consisting mostly of saloons and surrounded by silver mines. Thaddeus owned several of the mines and, through his political connections, arranged for his son to get the job so that they would be protected. There is evidence that Homer did not do very well at this, for Thaddeus's mine claims were violated on the very day he arrived for a visit.[14] Homer had not accomplished much on his own prior to this job, nor was he to do so in the future. He had been "probably the first white male child born in the northern part of Wisconsin" and had "an aborigine for [a] nurse."[15] He ran away from one school to which he had been sent and eventually graduated from a military school in Minnesota. Thaddeus then obtained a congressional appointment to West Point for his son, but Homer changed his mind while traveling there, returned home, and took a job in a butcher shop instead. Following Homer's stay in Idaho, Thaddeus arranged for a job for his son in the United States Mint in Philadelphia,[16] and Homer worked there as a civil servant until his retirement. He is described as "hearty, informal, very kind," with a complete "lack of guile."[17] Ezra described his father as "the naivest man who ever possessed sound sense, and whose virtues have more than once served him as well, or possibly better, than other men are served by intellectual subtlety," and as "my best and most faithful reader, but was no intellectual by a long shot."[18] Homer clearly never lived up to the economic, social, or intellectual standards of his successful father.

Hailey, Idaho, was no place for a dignified lady of Isabel's pretentions, and she persuaded Homer to give up his job there a year and a half after Ezra's birth.[19] They went to New York, where they lived with Isabel's family. From there they moved to Philadelphia just prior to Ezra's fourth birthday, and Homer began his job at the mint. They lived in West Philadelphia, then in Jenkintown, and finally moved to genteel Wyncote on the Main Line when Ezra was six. Isabel's mother bought the house for them, so Homer was indebted for his job to his father and for his house to his mother-in-law.[20]

Ezra's early years were dominated by a dual matriarchy. His maternal grandmother, affectionately known to the family as "Ma Weston," was a frequent visitor. She read Charles Dickens, Sir Walter Scott, and colonial history to her grandson, wrote him verse and prose, and generally left a "deep impression" on him. According to Ezra, "Ma Weston was proud of the Wadsworth blood and was responsible for maintaining the cultural heritage of the family."[21] Similarly, Ezra's mother was reading him the classics by age five before his afternoon nap, and throughout her life she continued to affirm her aristocratic origins by demanding cultivated colloquy from those around her; even at age eighty she is described as determined "never to allow the conversation to drop below a cultural level."[22] Grandmother and mother were true Brahmin matrons.

The consequences for Ezra were predictable. He later recalled having protested at age four because "my damned mother made me wear my hair in curls." By age six he was known as "professor" to his playmates because "I wore glasses and used polysyllables, in the wake of my mother."[23] It was perhaps these early years he had in mind when he wrote in "Plotinus":

> But I was lonely as a lonely child.
> I cried amid the void and heard no cry,
> And then for utter loneliness, made I
> New thoughts as crescent images of me.
> And with them was my essence reconciled
> While fear went forth from mine eternity.[24]

He was badly spoiled not only by his mother and grandmother, but also by a maid whom the family employed, as was the custom among their more affluent neighbors. By the time Pound reached college his closest friend, William Carlos Williams, called him "a spoiled brat."[25] In later years others would also perceive the consequences of his having been "a beloved, an only, and a spoilt child . . . he felt that he should be affectionately accepted by all intelligent people, however badly he behaved; and he was *not* so accepted. He thought all his ideas were equally valuable, even when they were little more than irritated yells."[26]

His mother and father appear to have indulged him excessively throughout his life. They continued to provide money for his support, and although they encouraged him to get a paying job and support himself, they never required it.[27] After Homer retired from the mint in 1928, he and Isabel went to Rapallo to live close to their son; both eventually died in Italy. A measure of the father's uncritical devotion is provided by a vignette:

It was in Rapallo in the 1930s and Homer and his son were in attendance on Max Beerbohm at his home on the road to Zoagli. Most of the time Ezra Pound talked, a barrage of historical detail and proposals for monetary reform. During a lull in which he was absent from the room, Homer leant across, and, shaking his head in wonderment, said, "You know Mr. Beerbohm, there isn't a darn thing that boy of mine don't know."[28]

Pound completely incorporated his family's beliefs about its membership in the aristocracy. As he expressed it when he was thirty-five years old: "I am American in so far as all my progenitors of whom I know anything what-soever arrived in that country between 1630 and 1650; this means that I am racially alien to the mass of the population in the Central States of America, wherein I passed most of my youth, for I take it that the mass of this population is either of continental or of mixed origins."[29]

The unwritten creed of any aristocracy is that genteel genes will be ruined if allowed to mix with the genes of nonaristocrats. Pound voiced this fear in his radio broadcasts during World War II:

. . . what races can mix in America without ruin of the American stock, the American brain?
The melting pot in America may have been a noble experiment, though I very much doubt it.[30]

In fact, however, the Americans who landed in 1650 were just as heterogenous a genetic collection as those who landed in 1850 and 1950. The "Angle-Saxons" to which Pound frequently refers as the preferred species were actually a genetic assortment of Celtic and Iberian origins, washed over by several centuries of invasions by Romans, Anglo-Saxons, Danes, and Normans. Many of the later immigrant groups whose arrival Pound deplored came originally from this same genetic pool.

Pound's family was particularly susceptible to the myth of the aristocracy and its inevitable handmaiden, bigotry. Newly arriving immigrants are always most threatening to families whose social and economic status is marginal. W. M. Chace, in his analysis of Pound's political ideas, has pointed this out clearly:

Ezra Pound's family could be described as nouveau poor: refined, with pretensions to gentility, with a memory of rather better times, with little room for social mobility. Such families contrasted sharply with those alien or immigrant families who were arriving by the thousands on America's Eastern shores during Pound's formative years and were rapidly transfiguring American life. It was this process, of course, that so repelled Pound when he came home to the United States in 1910. The process was to become more intense as the "strangers" achieved greater vertical mobility in the nation's economy and displaced people who could trace their American lineage back to the early years of the republic.[31]

"Nouveau poor" is an apt description of the Pound family, and many of Ezra's beliefs were spawned in the turbulence of his family's social frustration. When he described the immigrants "sweeping along Eighth Avenue in the splendor of their vigorous unwashed animality," or when he talked about the Civil War having led to "extermination of the Anglo-Saxon race in America in order that the Czecho-Slovaks might inherit the Boston Common," Pound was speaking for his family and their friends.[32] He merely said publicly what was said privately across the dinner table at home, loudly what was usually whispered on Wyncote's shaded streets.

"O, EZRA POUND'S CRAZY"

Pound apparently did well academically in primary and secondary school. He later claimed that he "cleaned up medals for everything except conduct, being a non-conformist." He skipped two grades and entered the University of Pennsylvania at age fifteen. His mother strongly encouraged this precocious advancement, which Pound claimed was "a tremendous saving of time."[33]

As a freshman at the university Pound studied German, Latin, American history, government, English, public speaking, and algebra. He did not work hard, recalling later "having done little more than play chess throughout the period."[34] One of his freshman-year teachers recalled him "as being abrupt, desirous of recognition, and frequently out of hand, a boy disliked both by his teachers and his classmates for what seemed like unnecessary eccentricities." Another remembered him "as being quick and very sensitive." On one occasion Pound defended the merits of a poem being discussed and came to the front of the class to read it. "After reading only the first few lines, however, he became so overcome by the poem that he broke down in tears and was unable to go on."[35] His academic record for his freshman and sophomore years was undistinguished, with three course failures, one incomplete, and mostly C's in the others.[36]

It was during this period that Pound began writing occasional poems and became interested in the arts in general. For friendship he sought out those with like interests. His "first friend" according to his own account was William Brooke Smith, a student artist at the Philadelphia College of Art, and he often visited his friend's studio.[37] Six years later Smith died of tuberculosis, and Pound dedicated a book of poems to him.

It was also during his freshman year at college that Pound's friendship with William Carlos Williams began. Williams was studying dentistry at the university and was to change the following year to medicine; he was very interested in poetry and was destined to become one of America's best-known poets. Williams clearly liked Pound, calling him a "fine fellow" and "the livest, most intelligent and unexplainable thing I'd ever seen." They became good friends, with Williams visiting the Pound home in Wyncote. Following one such visit Williams wrote to his mother a description of Pound which would be as accurate a description of him as anyone would ever pen:

> If he ever does get blue nobody knows it, so he is just the man for me. But not one person in a thousand likes him, and a great many people detest him and why? Because he is so darned full of conceits and affectation. He is really a brilliant talker and thinker but delights in making himself just exactly what he is not: a laughing boor. His friends must be all patience in order to find him out and even then you must not let him know it, for he will immediately put on some artificial mood and be really unbearable. It is too bad, for he loves to be liked, but there is some quality in him which makes him too proud to try to please people.[38]

The Pound-Williams friendship was to last for sixty years, until Williams's death, and involved an extended correspondence on literary matters and the arts. The warmth and affection were mutual, with Pound addressing his friend as "Willyum the Wumpus" and "Old Sawbuck von Grump." According to Williams's biographer, the two were attracted to each other by "their common mixture of private ambition and worldly unease," and they "reinforced each other as loners by passing back and forth between themselves images of an enemy to whom one *could* say, tirelessly, nuts and decorated nuts again."[39] Williams saw his young friend's assets and liabilities with uncanny accuracy. Many years later in his autobiography Williams captured the bittersweet quality that underlay Ezra Pound's personality:

> As an occasional companion over the years he was delightful, but one did not want to see him often or for any length of time. Usually I got fed to the gills with him after a few days. He, too, with me, I have no doubt.
> I could never take him as a steady diet. Never. He was often brilliant but an ass. But I never (so long as I kept away) got tired of him, or, for a fact, ceased to love him. He had to be loved, even if he kicked you in the teeth for it (but that he never did); he looked as if he might, but he was, at heart, much too gentle, much too good a friend for that. And he had, at bottom, an inexhaustible patience, an infinite depth of human imagination and sympathy. Vicious, catty at times, neglectful, if he trusted you not to mind, but warm and devoted—funny too as I have said.[40]

Most of his fellow students at the University of Pennsylvania saw only the negative aspects of Pound's personality. He was viewed as "a person aloof from his classmates and indifferent to them." "In class, Ezra was very shy—a dreamer, 'lone wolf,' and didn't appear to have or care to have any particular friends." Another described him "as a sort of screwball very easily duped and the basis of many practical jokes." One such joke, involving a group of his male acquaintances, was described by a classmate:

> It soon became evident, that Ezra was of a naive disposition, so guileless as to be the butt of numerous college pranks, usually harmless but sometimes cruel and thoughtless, so characteristic of unthinking youngsters. There was the night, for example, we were assembled in his room, eating his sweets and crackers which he always brought back with him at weekends. By prearrangement with Brooke (one of the mixed lot) I was to crawl into Pound's bed in my "nightie"—I wore the old-fashioned kind—and Brooke would then unexpectedly douse me with the contents of Pound's water-pitcher. This he did, to Pound's delight, especially as in my righteous indignation, I appeared ready to fight Brooke (who could have tossed me over his shoulder with one hand). A towel and a dry "nightie" of course restored me to status quo but Pound's bed was wet through and through. Ezra never "caught on." The next morning, I asked him how he managed to sleep in that wet bed. "Oh," said he, "I didn't sleep in the bed, I slept on the floor." And then with a laugh—"But I will never forget the look on your face when Brooke threw that water on you."[41]

On another occasion Pound was awakened by his colleagues in the middle of the night and, as a joke, told to find a doctor for a "sick" friend. This Pound faithfully did, returning two hours later with a doctor, much to the students' surprise and embarrassment.[42] The story illustrates Pound's generosity toward friends as well as his willingness to do whatever was necessary in an attempt to make friends.

Such efforts were usually canceled out by other aspects of Pound's personality, however. His aristocratic upbringing betrayed him from the beginning, and as an undergraduate at Pennsylvania he "rendered himself unpopular by defending the Southern slaveholders' side in the Civil War."[43] Pound also showed nonconformist tendencies at the university. He affected "from time to time noticeable accouterments like a gold-headed cane or a broad brimmed hat with a sweeping feather" and "set off his naturally bright color with loud vests and socks. He wore horn-rimmed glasses. At that time they were 'new': Yeats wore them . . . Ezra's non-conformist tendencies manifested themselves on the intellectual plane as well. He was once heard to say out loud to one of the most important professors at the University 'Shaw is greater than

Shakespeare.' Shaw was then considered 'daring' and was anathema in academic circles."[44]

Young Ezra Pound was developing methods of drawing attention to himself. He probably did this as a reaction to what Williams described as his "painful self-consciousness." Pound decided early in life that when unsure of himself, simulated expertise was his best gambit. For example, although he never learned to play the piano, he did not hesitate to "play," as on one occasion at Williams's home:

> I remember my mother's astonishment when he sat down at the keyboard and let fly for us—seriously. Everything, you might say, resulted except music. He took mastership at one leap; played Liszt, Chopin—or anyone else you could name—up and down the scales, coherently to his own mind, any old sequence.[45]

Athletics was another area in which Pound failed to achieve the level to which he aspired. As a child he was rejected for most sports activities because he was "too young and too light."[46] Later he took up tennis, at which he did become competent. At the University of Pennsylvania he went out for the fencing team but then quit. He joined the lacrosse team, "but that didn't last long either." Pound became frustrated by such failures and often turned his rage upon his friends. William Carlos Williams described such an episode:

> But this day, late in the afternoon—I had been fencing regularly with the Penn squad long after Ez had resigned—as I entered the front door he greeted me with an offer for a friendly bout with two of his father's walking sticks. I took one, made a few formal flourishes and placed myself en garde. But he, before I could do more than laughingly provoke him, came plunging wildly in without restraint, and hit me with the point of the cane above my right eye to fairly lay me out. I imagine I told him what I thought of him and threw down my stick. He felt triumphant that he had put the whole team of the University of Pennsylvania behind him with that single stroke. You can't trust a guy like that![47]

The episode which best captures Ezra Pound during his two years at the University of Pennsylvania occurred in the spring of his freshman year. At the time it was customary on American college campuses for upperclassmen to dictate appropriate dress standards for the lower classes. One day Pound wore "lurid, bright socks that the older students ruled out for freshmen. The sophomores threw him in the lily pond," despite the fact that the temperature outside was only about forty degrees. "It is recorded that he cursed his classmates in seven languages and returned the next day wearing the offending socks."[48] Thereafter they called him Lily Pound. Hilda Doolittle, who knew Pound at the

time and who later became a well-known poet, recorded in her memoirs
the reaction of her friends to this incident: " 'O, Ezra Pound's crazy'
was the verdict of my schoolgirl contemporaries. 'He wanted them to
throw him in the pond.' "[49] Here was sixteen-year-old Pound as nonconformist and social outcast raging against his fellows for mistreating him.
At the same time he had apparently invited the mistreatment by wearing
proscribed attire. Being thrown in the pond made Pound an instant
celebrity among his peers, and he thus achieved the recognition that
he so much wanted.

HAMILTON COLLEGE

Following two undistinguished years at the University of Pennsylvania, Pound's parents withdrew him and sent him to Hamilton College
in Clinton, New York, for his junior and senior years. William Carlos
Williams speculated that Pound "was banished by his father to the sticks
for general insubordination of what quality I don't know, probably nothing more than refusing to do anything but what he pleased to do in
his classes, perhaps spending more cash than the old man could give
him."[50] Given the high aspirations which Pound's parents held for their
son, his mediocre academic record must have been a cause for concern.
Another contributing factor may have been Pound's failure to become
part of the social life at Pennsylvania, where "he was frustrated in his
desire to pledge a fraternity."[51] According to a story published in *The
New Yorker,* Pound had been asked to join one but "he bit one of the
brothers during an undignified part of his initiation and left the fraternity
house in a huff, never to return."[52]

Hamilton College was bucolically set in upstate New York's rolling
hills, ten miles south of the homestead from which Pound's great-grandfather had once led the Loomis gang on raids. The transfer to Hamilton,
however, produced no improvement in Pound's social circumstances.
Upon arrival he was pledged to the local Delta Kappa Epsilon fraternity.
The Hamilton "Dekes" inquired routinely of their Pennsylvania counter-
parts about Pound's social desirability and elicited a telegram warning
that "under no considerations pledge Ezra Pound"; the invitation was
immediately withdrawn.[53]

At the time fraternities completely dominated the social life at Hamilton. Only two other students in his class were not pledged; one lived
with his family in the village and the other became Pound's roommate.
Pound was therefore "driven into being a campus exile . . . He had
little to do with his classmates, and they, though admitting his quick
wit, and perhaps in fear of it, would have little to do with him. 'He

was unpopular because he was eccentric,' one of his classmates remembers. 'We didn't know what to do with him.' Pale, slender, not very healthy looking, Pound struck his classmates as unnecessarily self-conscious and too tense for comfort, quite obviously a social misfit, one who by trying to compensate for his 'difference' by an assumed sophistication merely drove them further from him."[54] Other classmates remembered him as a "lone wolf" who "kept strictly to himself" and who "had very little connection with the college" except for playing on the chess team.[55] Because many of these recollections were elicited after World War II when Pound had attained notoriety by his treason indictment, it is worth noting that prewar recollections by a faculty member were virtually identical:

> He was always walking about the campus, and of the hundreds of times I have seen him passing my house, he was always walking alone . . . He lacked companionship, understanding, appreciation. He was lonely and out of his element . . . And there are tales of more than a quiet dislike of this brilliant boy, proud and conscious of his own superiority, tales of his being hazed and his room being torn up by college mates in search of sport.[56]

As he had been at Pennsylvania, Pound continued to be the butt of his classmates' practical jokes. On one occasion when Pound was meeting his parents at the railroad station, his classmates, according to an account in *The New Yorker,* moved "all his furniture and personal effects from his room to the campus, where they left them with the bed neatly turned down and a pair of pajamas laid out on top." William Carlos Williams was under the impression that Pound was "the laughing stock of the place" while at Hamilton.[57]

Much of Pound's difficulty with his peers was due to his self-centeredness, a personality trait which was clearly in evidence by his college days. Claudius A. Hand, one of Pound's roommates at Hamilton, recalled being awakened by him in the middle of the night so that Pound could read him the poems he had just written. "He'd shove a glass of beer at Hand, who was the son of a Methodist minister and didn't drink, and declare sonorously for as much as an hour or so. When he stopped Hand would nervously say, 'That's wonderful, Ezra, wonderful!' Ezra would invariably look at him and, without a word, tear the manuscript into long strips and throw it into the wastebasket. Then he would take back the beer he had offered Hand, drink it, and go to bed." On another occasion Pound called on a faculty member one evening, "and after chatting for a few moments inquired if he might use the bathroom. He went above and for the next hour was engaged in taking a bath."[58]

If Hamilton failed to improve Pound's lot socially, it did ameliorate it academically. He studied economics, religion, mathematics, and parliamentary law, as required by the curriculum, but two-thirds of the courses he took during the two years were in languages and literature. He was a good but not brilliant student, with grades averaging between B and C. His roommate remembers him as not working very hard and seldom spending his evenings at study. In a course on Job, who was afflicted by God with sufferings to test his faith, Pound received an E.[59]

In his area of concentration Pound did better. He studied Old English, German, Italian, Spanish, and French; in the last he received second prize at graduation. During his junior year he was introduced to the works of Dante. "He would talk at any time, at any length, about the beauties, the grandeur of language, the sublimity of the *Divine Comedy* . . . many a professor can relate of early morning hours spent in wishing that Ezra Pound would stop talking about Dante and go home."[60] He wrote his mother: "I praise Messire Dante Alighieri merely because he wrote a book most people are too lazy to read and nearly all the rest to understand . . . He was incidently a poet, a lover and a scholar and several other trifles served to round out his character although it is not recorded that he was President of a U.S. steel trust or the inventor of pin wheels." Pound was impressed by the cantos which comprise the *Divine Comedy* and began considering writing some cantos of his own.[61]

During the two years at Hamilton Pound was introduced to another literary resource which would become seminal to the development of his thought. William P. Shepard, a young professor of Romance languages and literature, had studied in Grenoble in southern France and was an expert in Provençal literature. Provençal poetry of the twelfth and thirteenth centuries celebrated the feats of the troubadours and was a landmark in the development of the lyric poem. Shepard provided Pound with two hours a week of special tutoring in Provençal, lent him books, and awakened in him an interest in medievalism which would be lifelong. In a letter to his mother written during his senior year Pound described the "comfort to go back to some quiet old cuss of the dark, so-called silent centuries and find written down the sum and substance of what's worthwhile in your present day frothiness."[62]

Pound's interest in Provençal proved crucial to his plans about his future. During his junior year at Hamilton he had decided on a career in the diplomatic service (he told one classmate facetiously that "I think I'd like to lie for my country"), preferring it over the alternative careers which he had considered—law or selling bonds.[63] By his senior year Professor Shepard had strongly encouraged him to go on to graduate school and pursue studies in Provençal, and that is what Pound decided to do. In 1905 working toward an advanced degree after college was unusual; only two other members of his graduating class did so, and both were preparing for the ministry.

In June 1905, Ezra Pound received his degree from Hamilton. That was the essential thing his parents had sent him to college for, and he was ready to leave. Following the graduation ceremonies he walked with his roommate down the long hill to Clinton. As he passed the fraternity house from which he had been excluded, "he paused for a moment, turned to his friend to swear that he would never return to the school again, and walked on to the station."[64]

GRADUATE SCHOOL AND THE TROUBADOUR LOVE CULT

Pound returned to Philadelphia to pursue graduate studies at the University of Pennsylvania, and during the 1905–1906 academic year was enrolled in courses to lead to a masters degree. He studied Latin, Italian, Old French, and Spanish literature and drama as well as Provençal.

During this period Pound delved deeply into the literature of the poet-musician troubadours and made what he believed were important discoveries. Provençal poetry had always been known for its sensual quality and celebration of physical love. Pound decided that the troubadours had been connected with the Albigenses, a religious sect active in southern France at the time the troubadours flourished, and that the Albigenses had been "adepts of a pagan love cult." This "cult of amor," furthermore, was not unique to the Albigenses and troubadours, but had originated in the Eleusinian rituals of ancient Greece and had been passed down over the centuries. According to Leon Surette, who has studied the development of Pound's thinking in detail, "the notion of some connection between the Provençal singers of 'gay savoir' and the Albigenses is, as we have seen, a persistent if minority view . . . But the further identification of this late-medieval complex of associations with the [Eleusinian] Mysteries is, so far as I can determine, peculiar to Pound."[65] Surette suspects that Pound derived many of these ideas from a book by Péladan which he read during the 1905–1906 period.

All of this would be merely esoterica except for one central fact: Ezra Pound believed that the sacrament of Eleusis was coitus.[66] The ritual sexual union of priests with young women produced knowledge, symbolized as light, which was then carried forward through the ages. When in later years Pound put forth his "Credo" he said: "I believe that a light from Eleusis persisted throughout the middle ages and set beauty in the song of Provence and of Italy."[67] Pound, as Surette notes, "is quite explicit about the role of sexuality in his highly syncretic version of Eleusis."[68] A decade later Pound would elucidate the relationship of coitus and knowledge in greater detail, but the origin of his ideas appears to date from his graduate-school days.

At the same time that Pound was delving into the Eleusinian Mysteries he was also discovering the felicity of female companionship. He had shown a liking for women since his early college days, and William Carlos Williams recalled early forays together:

> Once Ez asked me to go on a secret mission with him—to pick up one girl, yes, *one* girl, though why he wanted *me* along was more than I could figure. He had noted that a particularly lovely thing in her early teens, surely, would pass up Chestnut Street daily, at a certain hour, on her way home from school toward evening. I say school because her arms, when I saw her, were full of books. I acknowledged it, she was exceptional.
>
> As she came along we drew beside her, one to the left, one to the right. I was not interested and found the goings on ridiculous. Ezra was Ronsard. The poor child was all but paralyzed with fear, panting to the point of speechlessness as she just managed to say in a husky voice, "Go away! Please go away! Please! Please!" I dropped back. Ezra continued for another twenty paces and then quit also—to bawl me out for not persisting. I told him what I thought of him. After all, what was there in it for me?[69]

Most such attempts in the early college years ended equally futilely according to Williams, who claims that if Pound "ever got under a gal's skirts it must have been mainly in his imagination."[70]

While at Hamilton Pound had met two women who had interested him. Viola Baxter was one and, according to Pound, had "made hell homelike for me during my exile in upper New York. One of the few girls I have fallen in love with . . ."[71] He continued to remain in contact with her for many years, and stayed with her and her family for three weeks in 1939 when he returned from Italy. The other was Katherine Heyman, a concert pianist who was eleven years his senior.[72] Pound also retained contact with her over many years. She was in Venice when he was there in 1908, and he even announced to his friends that he was going to become her concert manager. When he returned to America in 1939 she was one of the friends whom he visited.

As a graduate student his relationships became more serious. Foremost among these was Hilda Doolittle, whom he had known since his first undergraduate year and who would become a published poet as "H.D." Hilda was "tall, blond and with a long jaw but gay blue eyes."

According to Williams, "Ezra was wonderfully in love with her and I think exaggerated her beauty ridiculously." She had "a provocative indifference to rule and order" to which Ezra probably was attracted. Her father, a professor of astronomy at nearby Bryn Mawr College, was "a tall gaunt man who seldom even at the table focused upon anything nearer, literally, than the moon."[73] Hilda saw Ezra as "immensely sophisticated, immensely superior, immensely rough-and-ready, a product not like any of the brothers and brothers' friends." He was nineteen, she was one year younger, and together they explored the perimeters of young passion. Some of their trysts took place in a tree house in Hilda's backyard, and Ezra was frequently in danger of missing the last train home: "He snatches me back. We sway with the wind. There is no wind. We sway with the stars. They are not far . . ." On another occasion they met in a friend's house: "There was a couch. There were fiery kisses."[74]

Ezra and Hilda shared an interest in both the occult and in poetry. Pound introduced her to Eastern religions and yoga in 1905 and later to theosophy and astrology. He also memorialized their meetings in lyrics, collected these poems, bound them, and presented them to her in 1907 as *Hilda's Book*. In them their moments of shared passion are exalted, their love becomes transcendent, and he calls her "Saint Hilda":

> *A wondrous holiness hath touched me*
> *And I have felt the whirring of its wings*
> *Above me, Lifting me above all terrene things*
> *As her fingers fluttered into mine*
> *Its wings whirring above me as it passed*
> *I know no thing therelike, lest it be*
> *A lapping wind among the pines*
>
> . . . .
>
> *Her fingers layed on mine in fluttering benediction*
> *And above the whirring of all-holy wings.*[75]

And in "Ver Novum":

> *Holy, as beneath all-holy wings*
> *Some sacred covenant had passed thereby*
> *Wondrous as wind murmurings*
> *That night thy fingers laid on mine their benediction*
> *When thru the interfoliate strings*
> *Joy sang among God's earthly trees*[76]

The tree house is empyrean, and appears to have been the locale of a special insight gained by Pound with Hilda's assistance:

That wind-swept castle hight with thee alone
Above the dust and rumble of the earth:
It seemeth to mine heart another birth
To date the mystic time, whence I have grown
Unto new mastery of dreams and thrown
Old shadows from me as of lesser worth.
For 'neath the arches where the winds make mirth
We two may drink a lordship all our own. [77]

Because of this Ezra nicknamed Hilda "Dryad," after the Greek deity of trees:

She hath some tree-born spirit of the wood
About her, and the wind is in her hair
Meseems he whisp'reth and awaiteth there
As if somewise he also understood.
The moss-grown kindly trees, meseems, she could
As kindred claim, for tho to some they wear
A harsh dumb semblance, unto us that care
They guard a marvelous sweet brotherhood [78]

As Dryad she appears frequently in his poetry, most notably in *The Pisan Cantos,* and she signed her letters to him as Dryad until the end of her life. [79]

Given Pound's later writings, it is not difficult to guess what insight he achieved with Hilda in the tree house. He discovered that passion, sexual or otherwise, was the mother of poetic inspiration, and it is significant that Pound's initial excursions into passion coincided temporally with his earliest attempts at serious poetry. Ezra Pound became convinced that such experiences were requisite for creative inspiration, and that that was the secret of Eleusis. He believed the troubadour cult of amor was a direct descendant of Eleusis, and that the cult had been passed down through Cavalcanti, Dante, François Villon, and other poets to the present.

Pound acknowledged his debt to Hilda more explicitly in "Praise of Ysolt," published in 1910 but written earlier. "Ysolt" was another nickname he used for Hilda. [80] In reading the poem it should be noted that "songs" were often used by Pound as a euphemism for poems, and flames symbolized passion and coitus:

But my soul sent a woman, a woman of the wonderfolk,
A woman as fire upon the pine woods
    crying "Song, a song."

As the flame crieth unto the sap.
My song was ablaze with her and she went from me

As flame leaveth the embers so went she unto new forests
And the words were with me
      crying ever "Song, a song."

And I "I have no song,"
Till my soul sent a woman as the sun:
Yea as the sun calleth to the seed,
As the spring upon the bough
So is she that cometh, the mother of songs,
She that holdeth the wonder words within her eyes
The words, little elf words
      that call ever unto me,

                                        "Song, a song."[81]

Hilda had provided Ezra with the inspiration for his "songs," and in so doing had carried on the cult of amor. The moment in the tree house was a re-enactment of Eleusis, divinely sanctioned and timeless. Surette comes to a similar conclusion: "In the familiar lyric impulse of sexual love Pound pretends to find the source of the beauties of Provence, of the 'dolce stil nuovo,' and even of Dante. It seems to me not to matter very much whether we find this supposition plausible or bizarre. If Pound thinks it true of the poets he most admires, it is probably true of himself."[82]

Ezra and Hilda became officially engaged in 1905; it was a tumultuous betrothal which lasted intermittently until 1911. Hilda apparently both loved and pitied her friend, confiding to William Carlos Williams that she wanted to help Pound who was "beyond all others, torn and lonely."[83] Hilda's parents, however, had other ideas. On one occasion Professor Doolittle caught Ezra and Hilda "curled up together in an armchair" and suspected that their mutual interests extended beyond poetry. Pound was asked to visit less often, and Hilda was forbidden to marry him.[84]

During 1906 and 1907 the relationship between Ezra and Hilda became more complicated. There were other women in Ezra's life, including Bessie Elliot, Louise Skidmore, and Mary Moore. He became engaged to Mary Moore in 1907 and later dedicated *Personae* to her; she visited him in London in 1912, and they maintained a correspondence for over forty years. There were also other women in Hilda's life. Frances Gregg, a girlhood friend and writer, appeared in Hilda's autobiographical novel *HERmione* as a young woman whom the heroine turns to in times of crisis, and according to one reviewer, "there are dark hints that the girls' attraction for each other is not exclusively spiritual."[85] Ezra also began a friendship with Frances at this time. Margaret Widdemer even claims they became engaged, but "it broke off because she demanded a 'mariage blanc' till she felt otherwise, and Pound wasn't willing."[86] During 1906 Hilda withdrew from Bryn Mawr "for reasons of health"; according to her own notes Pound had engineered the termination of her relationship with Frances.[87]

Pound was awarded a masters degree in June 1906, and a fellowship to begin work on a doctorate. He went to Europe for the summer to begin research on Lope de Vega, a medieval Spanish poet, playwright, and philanderer whom Pound chose as the subject of his doctoral dissertation. He returned to Philadelphia in August to resume his studies.

The graduate studies formal courses, however, were not going well for Pound. One of his professors remembered him "as a remarkably idle student, absolutely evading all work to such an extent that I recall saying to him, 'Mr. Pound, you are either a humbug or a genius.' " Another professor characterized him as "a weed" in a "grove of giant growth."[88] Pound's intellectual reputation fell still further when he failed a course entitled "History of Literary Criticism"; the failure placed him in double jeopardy since it was taught by the dean of the faculty. Even more serious was the fact that he could not get along with the faculty. He later acknowledged that he had ridiculed and vilified faculty members, attributing this to "an unusual agility of mind and a misplaced sense of humor." On at least one occasion "he composed and distributed poetry of a critical nature which resulted in 'acrimonious' retorts from the victims but not in disciplinary action."[89] In a letter written at that time Pound acknowledged that "I have spatted with nearly everybody," and according to one of his biographers Pound "rather prided himself on his self-assumed role as gadfly among the professoriate."[90]

Among his peers he continued to have problems making friends. Hilda Doolittle, William Carlos Williams, and his small circle of artistically oriented acquaintances understood him and were willing to overlook his peccadillos, but others were less tolerant. When one young woman asked him why he was translating Provençal poetry he replied: "I'm picking out something other people haven't heard about. If you do that, you get a reputation for being scholarly. I'm going to put myself across with Provençal." Librarians at the University of Pennsylvania library said that "he always talked to us like dogs" and "he even tried to make us bring his hat and coat."[91]

For reasons which are not known, the patience of the faculty expired during Pound's 1906–1907 graduate year and his fellowship was abruptly withdrawn. Pound protested and even sought out the founder of the fellowship program for a clarification of its purpose, but to no avail; the University of Pennsylvania had had enough. The dismissal was a blow to his academic aspirations and would become a festering sore on his ego. He attempted to be readmitted to the program in 1910 and again in 1911 but was refused. In 1920 Pound's father sounded out the university about the possibility of an honorary doctorate for his son; in 1932 Pound submitted his translations of Cavalcanti in lieu of a thesis, but the university refused to consider either.[92] Pound's bitterness was visible many years later when he wrote to the university alumni secretary: "In other words what the HELL is the grad. school doing and what the HELL does it think it is there for and when the hell did it do anything but try to perpetuate the routine and stupidity that it was already perpetuating in 1873? P.S. All the U. of P. or your damn college or any other god damn American college does or will do for a man of letters is to ask him to go away without breaking the silence."[93]

Pound had no plans for his immediate future and contemplated how he might achieve a life of leisure. While at Hamilton he had defined independence as having a "sufficient income to live on, so that a man can do what he liked." After his dismissal from the university he dreamed of "retiring to Venice to live and loaf as he pleased."[94] At this time he was just twenty-two years old. He lived with his family in Wyncote for several months in 1907, reading, writing, and trying to find a teaching job. Finally, with the help of a Hamilton College professor,[95] he located an opening teaching Romance languages at Wabash College, a small Presbyterian institution in Crawfordsville, Indiana.

WABASH COLLEGE

In September 1907, when Ezra Pound joined the faculty as an instructor, Wabash College was very similar to Hamilton College. Both were Protestant-oriented schools with approximately one hundred fifty students, offered a traditional curriculum, and were situated in small, conservative villages. Thus Pound should have known what was expected of him as a fledgling faculty member.

From the start Pound and Wabash did not mix. He flaunted tradition by refusing to wear "the professorial uniform of grey trousers, white shirt with stiff white collar, and frock coat." Instead his wardrobe was comprised of "a most informal hodge-podge that caused much snide comment," including "a black velveteen jacket, soft-collared shirt with flowing bow tie, patent leather pumps, a floppy, wide brimmed felt hat and an ever-present Malacca cane." And there were the socks—the same hosiery that had landed him in the lily pond—lavender, purple, green, and orange according to the recollections of one of his students.[96] It was as if he were inviting the world to throw him in again. He kissed the hands of ladies and poured rum into his hot tea to make "ambrosial nectar—food fit for the gods." As he discreetly stashed his flask he added: "The Indiana natives would never condone my continental appetite."

Rhythmics, graphology, palmistry, and spiritualism were subjects of great interest to him; "never was there a dull moment in this young man's company." One fellow faculty member remarked that "the trace of showman and charlatan in him was very strong at the time. He was half a brilliant—at least superficially brilliant—and interesting man. Sometimes when he came to our house I was exceedingly glad to see him. But by the time he had stayed from four on Sunday afternoon till twelve or one at night, and had crawled all over the sofa and stuck his feet up against the wall and otherwise engaged in unnecessary contortions, I was at least glad to see him go."[97] To another faculty member Pound observed: "The most beautiful thing that the mind of man can conceive is a strawberry in the bowl of a spoon—covered with olive oil"; it was early Dada come to Crawfordsville.[98]

Many students and faculty members found Pound refreshing. One freshman recalled him as "intensely stimulating, intellectually and emotionally. I believe he was a pretty good teacher in an unorthodox sort of way." On visits to his "Bohemian" quarters "he regaled us goggle-eyed youngsters with the reading of poetry—his own and Blake's." Others were antagonized by "his affectations and precious pretensions" and recall him as "exhibitionist, egotistic, self-centered and self-indulgent. He viewed the world through the blurred and wavy glass of his own imaginings." A student in one of his French classes described his teaching method as effective, while a faculty member claimed that he "took an elementary French class and turned it into a lecture course on Dante. He wasn't doing any good." The inhabitants of Crawfordsville were both intrigued and polarized by this Muse from the Main Line.

Pound's closest friends during his Wabash months were a local painter and an undertaker. The inclusion of the latter in this small circle was due to the fact he admired Pound, "had some money," and "owned an automobile of considerable utility to the trio in their amorous and convivial undertakings." Pound organized literary soirées in his room, to which his friends and selected students were invited. One student, not sympathetic to the forced cultural infusion, remembered it as follows:

After the preliminary formalities, Pound seated himself on a chair, while his disciples and satellites disposed themselves gracefully, but uncomfortably, cross-legged on the floor at the feet of the master. The leader then began a spirited but disconnected discourse on many topics, leaping with capric abandon from subject to subject. The dissertation was, at appropriate intervals, punctuated but not interrupted by interjections of agreement from the artist and by the hearty applause of the undertaker. The subordinate satellites listened with rapt attention and numbing legs.

I do not now recall fully the message of the master, although I do remember that he was disdainfully critical of the current trends in social and political life, in art, in economics, in education, and in other fields in which he was equally an authority.

He was vehement in voicing his dislike of all things British—so vehement, in fact, that I gained the apparently false impression that he had lived for some time in England. It seemed probable that so intense a dislike could have been acquired only by close association for considerable time . . . He discoursed at length and with vehemence on many topics. He was especially critical of the doltish and moronic crudity of the Philistines, to which despised class all members of the human race, with the exception of those present, apparently belonged. The future of civilization rested in the hands of a few especially gifted individuals, of which small group he was, by definition, one.[99]

The most remarkable thing about this description is its similarity to descriptions of Pound's afternoon "soirées" at St. Elizabeths Hospital fifty years later. Why Pound was so decidedly anti-British at this time, when he had visited there only briefly on his European sojourns, is not known.

Another subject which almost certainly came up for discussion between Pound and his friends was sexual passion and its relationship to art. On October 24, 1907, Pound wrote to Viola Baxter, whom he had fallen in love with while at Hamilton: "I am interested in art and ecstasy, ecstasy which I would define as the sensation of the soul in ascent, art as the expression and sole means of transmuting, of passing on that ecstasy to others."[100] During the early weeks at Wabash Pound was also engaged to Mary Moore of Trenton, New Jersey, writing to her almost daily with a clear expectation that they would become man and wife. These letters, with salutations such as "Dear Furry Little Rabbit," reveal a softness in Pound rarely seen later in his life, but they also discuss his belief that love and marriage were incompatible—proven, Pound asserted, centuries before in Provence.[101]

Many of the poems Pound wrote at Wabash would later be included in *A Lume Spento* and *A Quinzaine for this Yule*, including "Salve O Pontiflex" in which he celebrates the sacred sexual coupling of a high priest with Persephone. He also composed "Piere Vidal Old" at this time, writing to a friend that Vidal represented sexual passion:

> *God! she was white then, splendid as some tomb*
> *High wrought of marble, and the panting breath*
> *Ceased utterly. Well, then I waited, drew,*

Half-sheathed, then naked from its saffron sheath
Drew full this dagger that doth tremble here. [102]

Pound appears to be refining the ideas which had preoccupied Hilda and himself in the previous months, searching for the source of the light from Eleusis.

In early November 1907, Mary Moore decided that marriage to Pound was not in her best interest, and she wrote and told him so. Pound protested vigorously but to no avail. In Crawfordsville there were "few personable young ladies compared to the number of Wabash students;"[103] in a letter to a friend in November or December Pound yearned for "degenerate decadent civilization, as represented by cocktails, chartreuse and kissable girls."[104] Shortly thereafter an opportunity presented itself. A visiting burlesque troupe was left stranded when the manager absconded with its receipts, and the young ladies had nowhere to go. Taking pity, "Ezra invited the 'première danseuse' of the company to be his house guest for a few days. The lady graciously accepted his invitation in the spirit in which it was intended."[105]

Unfortunately for Pound, Crawfordsville, Indiana, in 1907 was a long way from Paris, and his room was in the boardinghouse of the elderly spinster Hall sisters. These ladies lived in a world of "refinement and cameo-studded velvet dog-collars," and when they found the young lady in Pound's room they were properly horrified. Pound protested that he had only offered the lady shelter from a snowstorm, that he had heated water for tea "to bring warmth to her frozen body," and that he gave her his bed where she slept "safe as in her mother's arms" while he slept on the floor in his topcoat.[106] They were unmoved by his imaginative story and went directly to the president of the college. In later years Pound privately acknowledged that he had indeed had an affair with the woman, and one Pound scholar even claims that the lady in question was another resident of the boardinghouse and that "this particular incident had been the last in a series of nocturnal events."[107] Support for this thesis can be found in a letter Pound wrote to a friend in November 1907, in which he said: "Two students found me sharing my meagre repast with the lady-gent impersonator in my privut apartments. Keep it dark and find me a soft immoral place to light in when the she-faculty-wives get hold of that jewcy [sic] morsel . . . For to this house come all the traveling show folk and I must hie me to a nunnery eer I disrupt the college."[108]

Ezra Pound had once again exceeded the tolerance of his superiors and provoked their wrath. His accumulated reputation with the faculty and administration was put on the balance, and the president of the college decided it was time to excise this periculous and vice-prone presence from Crawfordsville's midst. In a brief meeting in the president's office in late January 1908, Pound was given the news that he was fired and was paid the remainder of his year's wage. According to a student who chanced upon him, Pound left the office with tears streaming down his cheeks.[109]

He had been dismissed by two academic institutions within less than a year. His doctorate had been aborted, and his pretensions toward a professorship were stillborn after only four months. For the rest of his life he castigated and excoriated American colleges and universities. "The American University system," he said, "is run by hirelings and by boors in great part. The modern and typical prof holds his job . . . because he crawls under the buggy rug of a motheaten curriculum in sheer craven terror of known fact and active discovery. That is what the half-louse is paid for."[110]

The abrupt termination of his brief and inglorious career was well known to his friends in Wyncote.[111] What Pound told his parents, or what they told him, can only be guessed. The feelings engendered in the young man by his succession of social failures in college, by his academic failure, and then by his professional failure were bitter indeed. His classmates, professors, and the college officials with whom he had had so much trouble eventually merged into one in Pound's mind and became symbolic of the entire United States. His bitterness smoldered and in later years would break into flame with bitter rantings against his native land.

He was jobless, without prospects, and dependent on his parents for support. He tried to resume his engagement to Hilda and asked her to elope with him; his father, he promised, "would scrape up enough for him to live on."[112] After the Wabash fiasco Hilda's parents were more firmly set against him than ever, and she declined his offer. He left home in less than a month, bound for Europe. His friends in Philadelphia believed he was leaving the United States because he had been fired and had failed professionally.[113] Except for two brief visits, he would not return again for over thirty-seven years, and then it would be in the company of FBI agents.

CHAPTER 3

MIXED REVIEWS

[LONDON: 1908–1920]

WHEN EZRA POUND landed at Gibraltar in 1908 he was returning to a continent that was familiar to him. He had first been taken abroad at age twelve by his maternal Aunt Frank, a charming lady who had once danced with President Grant and who packed an individual tea bag in her luggage for each day of the trip. Aunt Frank had dutifully introduced young Ezra to the sights of London, Paris, Venice, and the Swiss Alps.[1] At age sixteen he returned to Europe with his father and again visited London and Venice. Most recently he had spent the summer of 1906 in London, Paris, and Spain, beginning work on his planned doctorate dissertation.

Pound felt comfortable in Europe. He spoke French, Spanish, Italian, and some German and enjoyed the tolerance offered to artists. Living was also less expensive in Europe, which was important since he had only eighty dollars with him. For two weeks he remained in Gibraltar working as a guide, then left and continued to his planned destination, Venice.[2]

As Pound later wrote, Venice was "an excellent place to come to from Crawfordsville, Indiana."[3] It provided refuge from the embarrassments of Philadelphia and allowed him to work on his poems in comparative peace. During his three months there he wrote several short stories and part of a novel which he finally abandoned. As his finances dwindled he considered getting a job and even visited an employment agency; they offered only full-time jobs, however, and he did not want that.

He also found time to make new acquaintances; Katherine Heyman, who was in Venice at the time, recalled chaperoning "for the copulating pair" of Ezra and a lady friend.[4]

The principal goal of his stay in Venice was to complete a group of poems and to get them published. He had brought with him those that he had written in Philadelphia and Crawfordsville, and he set to work writing others. He was convinced of his talent, but finding a publisher who could also be convinced was another matter. An old family friend, the Reverend Alex Robertson, who was the pastor of the Presbyterian Church in Venice, came to his assistance and arranged for Pound to use the printing equipment at an orphanage.[5] By August one hundred copies of *A Lume Spento* were ready. The title was taken from Dante's *Inferno* and means "with tapers quenched"; the book was dedicated to William Brooke Smith, his friend from undergraduate days at the University of Pennsylvania.

Pound's next task was to get the book noticed and reprinted in America. In a letter to his mother he outlined his strategy: "The American reprint has got to be worked by kicking up such a hell of a row with genuine and faked reviews that Scribner or somebody can be brought to see the sense of making a reprint. I shall write a few myself and get some one to sign 'em."[6] According to John Edwards, "one Venetian critic reviewed the book in such a manner that one is tempted—although without evidence—to think that the critic's name was Ezra Pound." The review described the poems of *A Lume Spento* as "wild and haunting stuff, absolutely poetic, original, imaginative, passionate, and spiritual . . . Coming after the trite and decorous verse of most of our decorous poets, this poet seems like a minstrel of Provence at a suburban musical evening."[7] Like grandfather Thaddeus, Ezra Pound now had his traveling show ready for the road. He packed his poems and the review and departed for London.

Pound traveled from Venice to London by way of Paris, an itinerary he was destined to slowly retrace during the rest of his lifetime. He had no intention of remaining in London for long. Before leaving Venice he had written his mother that he merely wanted "to have a month up the Thames somewhere and meet Bill Yeats and one or two others" as well as to elicit some London reviews of *A Lume Spento* which could be "sent to American publishers as an index of fame." The letter was signed "Modest Violet."[8] London, then, was a stop en route back to the United States; the ultimate goal was to get his poems printed at home.

Pound spent his initial weeks in London working assiduously to get the literary set to take notice of him. He distributed copies of *A*

Lume Spento to bookstores, continued writing poems, and in October successfully got "Histrion" published in the *Evening Standard and St. James's Gazette*. He stayed at a series of boardinghouses since he was virtually penniless, and in September turned to a family friend, who arranged for Pound to give a short series of lectures at the London Polytechnic Institute the following January. During these weeks he also sent poems to several American magazines including *Century, Harper's, Scribner's*, and *American Magazine*. For reasons which are not clear he sent them under a pseudonym, "John Vore." All of the poems were rejected for publication.[9]

His twenty-third birthday was approaching and he was undecided what to do next. His family was urging him to return home, but he was not ready; he considered returning to northern Italy, where he felt he really belonged.[10] Besides, he had made a commitment to do the lecture series in January. He felt out of place in London, yet he did not know where he did belong. In *A Lume Spento* he had described himself as follows:

> For I am a weird untaméd
> That eat of no man's meat.
> My house is the rain ye wail against
> My drink is the wine of sleet.[11]

The one thing Pound was certain of was his ability as a poet, his genius, and his destiny. On October 21, 1908, he wrote to William Carlos Williams: "But, mon cher, would a collection of mild pretty verses convince any publisher or critic that *I* happen to be a genius and deserve audience? I have written bushels of verse that could offend no one except a person as well-read as I am who knows that it has all been said just as prettily before."[12] A few months later he added in a letter to another friend: "Art is long. I am only on the threshold."[13]

By December 1908, Pound's prospects were improving. Elkin Mathews, owner of a bookshop in which Pound had deposited his initial book of verse, offered to publish another Pound collection to be called *A Quinzaine for this Yule*. Shortly thereafter Mathews also agreed to publish *Personae*, which would come out the following spring. He was convinced of Pound's ability as a poet and began introducing him to influential figures in London's literary circles.

FAVORABLE REVIEWS

The year 1909 was a successful one for Ezra Pound. "Tis the white stag, Fame, we're a-hunting / Bid the world's hounds come to horn!"[14] he wrote, and for a few months it appeared that they would do so.

It began in January when Pound met Australian writers James G. Fairfax and Frederic Manning, with whom he became friends. Shortly thereafter Pound wrote to Fairfax with warmth but prophetic irony: "Are you never coming up to London again, even if it is only to be filled with deep doubts of my sanity?"[15] The Australians, meanwhile, had introduced Pound to Olivia Shakespear, whom he described in a January 31 letter to his mother as "undoubtedly the most charming woman in London."[16] Pound failed to mention to his mother that Olivia was a close friend of Yeats's, with whom she had had an adulterous affair in 1896, and had been immortalized in Yeats's diary as "Diana Vernon," or that Olivia had a beautiful daughter, Dorothy, just one year younger than himself. Pound had not yet met Yeats but still hoped to, as it had been his principal reason for going to London.

By February Pound had embarked upon a round of "teas" and "evenings" which would occupy him for the next several months, meeting the poets, writers, critics, and publishers of London's literary scene. Elkin Mathews and Olivia Shakespear were especially helpful in facilitating these introductions and in guiding him toward the élite of the literati. On February 23 Mathews introduced him to the Poets' Club, a select dinner group which met monthly. George Bernard Shaw was entertaining that evening, and T. E. Hulme, Sturge Moore, Hillaire Belloc, and F. S. Flint among others were present. Pound's lectures at the Polytechnic Institute were underway by this time but were apparently of limited success. Discouraged, he wrote to his parents that he might return home in March and try to get a job teaching at the Princeton Summer School and then at Temple University.[17]

Further introductions and the publication of *Personae* in March improved his spirits. He met Padraic Colum and Ernest Rhys, who with other members of the Poets' Club were attempting to modernize English poetry. An introduction to Yeats was finally arranged in May, and by the summer Pound was a regular at Yeats's Monday evening soirées. Selwyn Image and Laurence Binyon, both well known in London literary circles, became acquaintances. He was introduced to May Sinclair, novelist and feminist, and through her met Ford Madox Hueffer (who later changed his name to Ford Madox Ford), Violet Hunt, and Wyndham Lewis, all of whom would become his close friends. Later in the year he also met D. H. Lawrence, who was impressed by Pound, describing him in a letter to a friend as "a well-known American poet—a good one. He is 24, like me—but his god is beauty, mine life. He is jolly nice . . . a good bit of a genius." Lawrence and Pound saw each other again; on December 11, Lawrence spent the night with him after apparently missing the last train home.[18]

The publication of *Personae,* a collection of thirty-three poems, ushered in an era of good reviews for Pound. "No new book of poems for years past has had such a freshness of inspiration, such a strongly individual note, or been more alive with undoubtable promise," sang one critic. *Exultations of Ezra Pound,* a collection of twenty-seven more poems, was published by Mathews in September, and that too was warmly greeted. The *Observer* noted that "few new poets have so quickly become known to literary London," and the *Spectator* referred to Pound's "immense virility and passion."[19] Just one year after arriving in London, Ezra Pound was being favorably mentioned in the same sentence with Conrad, Galsworthy, and Henry James and acclaimed as "the most remarkable thing in poetry since Robert Browning."[20]

Although current assessments of Pound's status in the hierarchy of twentieth-century poets vary widely, there was a consensus in 1909 that many of his poems showed unusual promise. Pound wrote in *Personae:*

> I will sing of the white birds
> In the blue waters of heaven,
> the clouds that are spray to its sea.[21]

Donald Hall would later reflect: "For me, poetry is first of all sounds. I discovered early that Pound, who could do other things as well, had the greatest ear among modern poets. For the sheer pleasure of sound— the taste of it in one's mouth—no one comes near him." Another critic later praised Pound's "verbal and metrical expression. His visual and acoustic sensitivity is exquisite. His verse is wonderfully lean, clean-cut, packed, intense."[22] An example of this is his short "Erat Hora," which was included in *Personae:*

> "Thank you, whatever comes." And then she turned
> And, as the ray of sun on hanging flowers
> fades when the wind hath lifted them aside,
> Went swiftly from me.[23]

Riding the crest of his new-found fame, Pound made arrangements in July 1909 to give another course of lectures at the Polytechnic Institute beginning that October. It was to be a "Course of Lectures on Medieval Literature" and would be divided into two terms; the first would focus on the Provençal troubadours and the second on Dante. He spent much of the coming months preparing these and in September obtained a contract to publish them as *The Spirit of Romance.* Pound called it his "history of the world," and in the preface said that he was attempting "to examine certain forces, elements or qualities which were potent in the medieval literature of the Latin tongues and are, as I believe, still potent in our own." These forces had a timeless, mystical quality according to Pound: "All ages are contemporaneous . . . the future stirs already in the minds of the few. This is especially true in literature, where real time is independent of the apparent and where many dead men are our grand-children's contemporaries."[24]

Throughout the fall of 1909 Pound continued to work on *The Spirit of Romance* and to write poems. During these months he also spent increasing amounts of time with Olivia Shakespear and Yeats. Already well known as a poet, Yeats was embarking on one of his most productive literary periods. Despite the fact that he was twenty years Pound's senior, the two shared a remarkable number of interests and rapidly became close friends. Like Pound, Yeats had felt isolated as a child; according to one Yeats scholar, "the loneliness of his early days later crystallized into an awareness of alienation which combined with a sense of cosmic importance to mark his life."[25] Like Pound, Yeats admired Dante, disliked Milton, and was striving to create a new poetry which, although spiritually rooted in the past, would transcend it.

But the strongest bond between Pound and Yeats was their shared interest in mysticism and the occult. Yeats had steeped himself in the writings of hermeticism, theosophy, the cabala, and Indian philosophy, and was an expert on astrology, Tarot cards, telepathy, alchemy, automatic writing, mediums, ghosts, and reincarnation. As early as 1892 Yeats had written to a friend: "The mystical life is the centre of all that I do and all that I think and all that I write"; two years previously he had tried to raise "the ghost of a burnt flower according to the instructions of a seventeenth-century writer on magic."[26]

When Pound was introduced, Yeats was active in a small group which met regularly in London to discuss the acquisition of knowledge by revelation rather than by empiricism. Olivia Shakespear was also an integral member of the group, and Pound was soon included. Yeats's great interest at the time was communicating with spirits of dead persons. He had first experienced possession by a spirit at a séance in 1886: "I was now struggling vainly with this force which compelled me to movements I had not willed, and my movements became so violent that the table was broken." Frightened by this experience, he had avoided séances for many years but had recently returned to them. One Yeats scholar notes that "Yeats's interest in séances and mediumship was largely confined to 1909–1918, and especially to 1911–1916."[27] This coincides with his years of closest friendship with Pound.

Yeats believed that the spirits of the dead could be heard and felt. He was fascinated with ideas of reincarnation found in the folk traditions of western Ireland, and spoke obliquely of "disembodied powers" whom he could call upon. One such power was that of Dante; according to M. C. Flannery, "Yeats saw himself and Dante as similar figures, both of them exiles . . . both of them Magician/poets. Yeats believed he and Dante shared the power in the Western imagination of Christ, the Word Incarnate."[28]

It was also during this period that Yeats clearly perceived his personal métier for the first time: "The role Yeats has assigned himself is that of Druidic prophet poet . . . he is the priest possessed of secret knowledge who provides man with his link to divinity, a divinity which is within all of us but directly accessible to the Druid-Poet." Yeats believed himself to have "that common instinct, that common sense which is genius"; previously he had said that "the creative visionary or man of genius has all the thoughts, symbols, and experiences that enter within his larger circle . . . He who has thus passed into the impersonal portion of his own mind perceives that it is not a mind but all minds." Yeats had begun "to believe in himself as an 'Emmanuel' figure, a semi-divine poet."[29]

Yeats's beliefs, resonating with Pound's as they did, must have impressed Pound profoundly. Here was the man whom Pound had come to England to meet, one of the best-known poets in the world, talking in the same mystical language that Pound himself used. In *A Lume Spento* Pound had explored the "vague borderline between the physical and metaphysical worlds" in his poem "La Fraisne." And just six months before meeting Yeats, Pound had published "Histrion," with echoes of reincarnation, the spirit of Dante, and a semidivine role for poets:

> No man hath dared to write this thing as yet,
> And yet I know, how that the souls of all men great
> At times pass through us,
> And we are melted into them, and are not
> Save reflexions of their souls.
> Thus am I Dante for a space and am
> One François Villon, ballad-lord and thief,
> Or am such holy ones I may not write
> Lest blasphemy be writ against my name;
> This for an instant and the flame is gone.

By October 1909, Pound was publicly writing about Yeats's mystical theories, comparing them favorably with Robert H. Benson's *Light Invisible,* in which the author describes a series of encounters with extracorporal beings.[30] Pound and Yeats had formed a friendship which would continue to deepen and broaden and which, in turn, would profoundly influence each other's ideas and poetry. They had discovered they were, quite literally, kindred spirits.

Yeats and Pound shared an additional area of interest that would become important to their friendship: the relationship of sex to creativity and mysticism. According to M. C. Flannery, Yeats initially "conceived of himself as a poet at the time he became aware of sex . . . For Yeats, to be a poet was to be sexually potent and to be a sage and magician too. Sex, magic and poetry were to be part of the same whole for him . . . Sex was a microcosmic representation of a divine, creative act." Yeats's beliefs about sex were intimately connected to his beliefs about spiritualism, and this remained true throughout his life. In 1927, when he was sixty-two years old, he was still writing to Olivia Shakespear, "I am still of [the] opinion that only two topics can be of the least interest to a serious and studious mind—sex and the dead."[31] By "the dead," Yeats was referring to spiritualism and communications with the dead. The linking of sex, creativity, and mysticism was a fusion which Pound had independently arrived at, the "marvelous sweet brotherhood" discovered with Hilda in the tree house, the mystical flame that burned ever brighter in its primeval act of creation. Pound had finally found a friend who understood the cult of amor.

As Pound turned his attention to mysticism in late 1909, his rapid ascent into the literary stratosphere began to slow perceptibly. Ford Madox Ford had published Pound's "Sestina Altaforte" in the June issue of the *English Review,* and in October Ford published three more of his poems. When *Exultations* was published in September, however, reviews included some reservations. The *English Review* noted "that of our younger poets he is the most alive, as he is the most rugged, the most harsh, and the most wrong-headed." The *Spectator* said that Pound "has in him the capacity for remarkable poetic achievement, but we also feel that at present he is somewhat weighted by his learning." And the Birmingham *Daily Post* found him to be "a really sincere and vigorous artist" but with much "evidence of a highly interesting personality unable to express itself." Pound noted such reviews in a December letter to his mother in which he complained of "several more or less violent attacks" on him in the press.[32]

Pound's talents had clearly been noticed and were being acknowledged. At the same time he appeared to be offending people; the critical parts of the reviews of his work were not directed at Pound the poet as much as at Pound the person. Wyndham Lewis, who knew him from his earliest months in London, described him on their first meeting as "an uncomfortably tensed, nervously straining, jerky, reddish-brown young American . . . The impression he made, socially, was not a good one. He was a drop of oil in a glass of water. The trouble was, I believe, that he had no wish to *mix:* he just wanted to *impress."* And D. H. Lawrence, who had lavishly praised Pound when they met in late 1909, had tired of him by early 1910, calling him "irascible" and describing him as a medieval strolling minstrel, a "sort of latest edition of jongleur."[33]

In February 1910, Pound received another setback and facetiously asked his father to place an advertisement in the newspapers: "Poet. Out of a job. Specialities: incisive speech, sarcasm, meditation, irony (at special rates), ze grande manair (to order)." The most likely impetus for this request was that Pound had been told by the Polytechnic Institute that his job as a lecturer would not be renewed. The series had apparently not gone well, and one scholar has voiced the suspicion that the series was not even concluded, because Pound left England on March 23 although the final talk had been scheduled for March 28.[34]

It was time for Ezra Pound to return home. He had stopped for a month in London and ended up staying for a year and a half. It had been a success insofar as his literary career was concerned: he had published three more volumes of verse and had *The Spirit of Romance* in press. He had garnered many favorable reviews with which he hoped to launch his career at home. But he had gone as far as he could go. According to John Edwards, "the London of letters, traditionally respectful of scholarship and politely ready to receive the latest poet, had given him his trial before the elders and, in the end, had in effect dismissed him . . . It was natural for those in literary circles to take notice, but it was not obligatory that they remain attentive, and when attention died out Pound left."[35] In effect, his show closed in London to return to his hometown for what he hoped would be a long stand.

AMERICA 1910

Pound wandered home slowly, going first to Paris and then to Italy. He had realized some modest financial rewards from his writings but still required regular checks from his parents to sustain him. He paused at Verona, where Dante had written much of his *Divine Comedy,* then went on to the resort town of Sirmione, situated majestically on a peninsula jutting into Lake Garda. Pound was enchanted by the lake and settled into a hotel for an extended stay. He wrote Hilda Doolittle urging her to visit because "I know paradise when I see it," and told his parents to invest money in land at the lake's edge. Olivia and Dorothy Shakespear joined him for a holiday, and Dorothy found it to be a perfect place to paint. "That was the first time I ever saw color," she later recalled.[36]

Pound's stay at Sirmione rekindled in him feelings of kinship with his poetic predecessors. In February 1910, just before leaving London, Pound had written to his mother asking for the exact hour of his birth and proclaiming his belief in "planetary influences." Astrology, he said, would produce important discoveries when subjected to the scientific method, and "in the meantime there is no reason why one should not indulge in private experiment and investigation."[37]

Sirmione, whose ancient name was Sirmio, was an excellent locale for such private experiments. As Pound knew, it had been home to the Roman poet Catullus when he was writing some of his most passionate and sensual lyrics in honor of Lesbia, the wife of another man. It sat astride a major trade route across northern Italy and, as such, had watched Grecian culture pass through to Provence, Florence, Verona, and other medieval centers of learning. In more recent centuries it had been dominated by the Scaligeri, a scholarly Italian family whose thirteenth-century castle still stood guard at the town's entrance. And just four years prior to Pound's stay, the Italian poet Giosuè Carducci, who had spent much time writing in Sirmione, had won the Nobel Prize for literature.

Surrounded by olive, orange, and lemon trees, Pound and the Shakespears enjoyed the Italian sun. The lake is deep and frequently described as translucent; in the spring snow-capped mountains are visible to the north. Pound felt the souls of other centuries close by, and remembered the cult of amor:

> What hast thou, O my soul, with paradise?
> Will we not rather, when our freedom's won,
> Get us to some clear place wherein the sun
> Lets drift in on us through the olive leaves
> A liquid glory? If at Sirmio,
> My soul, I meet thee, when this life's outrun,
> Will we not find some headland consecrated
> By aery apostles of terrene delight,
> Will not our cult be founded on the waves,
> Clear sapphire, cobalt, cyanine,
> On triune azures, the impalpable
> Mirrors unstill of the eternal change?[38]

In "The Flame," also probably written while at Sirmione, Pound was more explicit about his belief that he was a direct descendant of the troubadours, one of "the Ever-living," and that the lake held the secrets of the ages:

'Tis not a game that plays at mates and mating,
Provençe knew;
'Tis not a game of barter, lands and houses,
Provençe knew.
We who are wise beyond your dream of wisdom,
Drink our immortal moments; we "pass through."
We have gone forth beyond your bonds and borders,
Provençe knew;
And all the tales of Oisin say but this:
That man doth pass the net of days and hours.
Where time is shrivelled down to time's seed corn
We of the Ever-living, in that light
Meet through our veils and whisper, and of love.

O smoke and shadow of a darkling world,
These, and the rest, and all the rest we knew.

. . . .

Sapphire Benacus, in thy mists and thee
Nature herself's turned metaphysical,
Who can look on that blue and not believe?

Thou hooded opal, thou eternal pearl,
O thou dark secret with a shimmering floor,
Through all thy various mood I know thee mine;

If I have merged my soul, or utterly
Am solved and bound in, through aught here on earth,
There canst thou find me, O thou anxious thou,
Who call'st about my gates for some lost me;
I say my soul flowed back, became translucent. [39]

The light from Eleusis had come to momentary rest in his soul, and it was his task to carry the flame forward. He would return to his homeland, an American Alighieri.

Although Ezra Pound believed himself to have a date with destiny, he was wise enough to confirm the reservations. From early 1909 onward he had sent the reviews of his work that appeared in the English press home to his father with instructions to take them to American publications for reprinting. His efforts were rewarded when in August 1909, the *Book News Monthly* reprinted one of his poems from *Personae*. In November *The Literary Digest*, a New York literary weekly, reprinted another Pound poem and carried an article about "An American Poet Discovered in England"; it included the opinion published in London that he was "the most remarkable thing in poetry since Robert Browning." On December 2, 1909, the *Philadelphia Bulletin* carried a story describing Pound's "sudden fame" and current activities:

> He is certainly getting a hearing, as he is now delivering a course of lectures on "Medieval Literature" at the London Polytechnic, which is no mean honour for a mere youth. He has published four small books of verse, but he has written much more that has not seen the light for he is said to be his own most unsparing critic, having destroyed the manuscripts of two novels and three hundred sonnets.[40]

One week later the article was reprinted by the *Boston Herald.* Homer Pound was proving to be an effective press agent.

For Pound, however, the publicity was merely a prelude to the most important thing—getting his books reprinted by American publishers. And in that endeavor he had reason for optimism. In November 1909, the English publisher of *The Spirit of Romance* had made arrangements for it to be distributed in the United States by E. P. Dutton. In January 1910, he heard that Small, Maynard and Company, a Boston publisher, was interested in publishing a book of his poems, and by March this agreement had been finalized. *The Literary Digest* had published two more poems in February, and his fame had spread even to Australia, where his friend James G. Fairfax had reviewed his books in glowing terms in the Melbourne *Book Lover:* "It is disgracefully easy to lose critical sobriety in the presence of Mr. Pound. When he reads his own work, he creates an atmosphere which delight and enthusiasm can alone inhabit."[41] Sitting on the shores of Lake Garda, Ezra Pound could take satisfaction in the progress of his career and could reasonably expect it to continue to advance when he returned to his homeland.

After spending over a month in Sirmione, Pound took the Shakespears to Venice for a visit. He returned to Sirmione, then briefly visited Verona, Vicenza, returned to Venice, Paris, and finally London. There he announced to his friends that Sirmione was "the earthly paradise" and, according to D. H. Lawrence, discussed his intention of "writing an account of the mystic cult of love—the dionysian rites and so on—from earliest days to the present."

Pound sailed from London to New York, arriving home on June 25, 1910. There is every indication that he intended to remain in the United States and was not merely returning for a visit. He had told his friends in London that he was going to make money, and D. H. Lawrence had facetiously suggested that he run a movie theater; *The Great Train Robbery* was, after all, playing to packed houses in nickelodeons and there was money to be made. Pound apparently did not tell his friends that in January he had applied to the University of Pennsylvania graduate school for readmission and had been turned down, or that he had applied for a teaching job at Hobart College in Geneva, New York.[42] He was rejected for this too, and no other information is available on whether he tried to get other jobs. Given his record at the University of Pennsylvania and at Wabash College, obtaining admission to a graduate school or finding a teaching job would have been difficult.

Pound spent the summer living with his parents and writing. He had jaundice at this time, probably from viral hepatitis.[43] He dined with various relatives, including his grandmother Loomis, and spent time with friends from his graduate-school days. Much of his energy was taken up working on translations of Guido Cavalcanti, Dante's predecessor, whom Pound had decided had been badly neglected by literary history. In July E. P. Dutton issued the American edition of *The Spirit of Romance*, and in November Small, Maynard and Company brought out *Provença*, a collection of his poems.

The American reviews of these works, Pound's first published books in his native land, were mixed. The *Boston Evening Transcript* noted that *The Spirit of Romance* embodied "a noble ambition" and that "Mr. Pound is a man of clear insight and happy enthusiasm," but added that "within him there is a hunger for publicity which weakens the fiber of his work." *Provença* was praised by the *New York Times* as containing much poetry "of extraordinary beauty." However, the *Boston Evening Transcript* was less impressed: "We began the examination of this book of poems with great expectations and we lay it down with considerable contempt for the bulk of English criticism that has pretended to discover in these erratic utterances the voice of a poet."[44] Clearly Pound's literary reputation had preceded him from London, but his compatriots were going to form their own judgment of his work.

In August Pound went to New York, where he spent much time in the succeeding months; Hilda Doolittle joined him there, and their engagement was rekindled briefly. He still had no means of support and, except for token sums realized from the publication of his poems and books, was dependent upon his parents. While in New York he was offered a "business proposition" by a man selling "odd sorts of insurance" if he could raise the capital; Pound asked his father for it, but Homer refused. At about the same time, Pound concocted a fanciful scheme to make money which he presented to his friend William Carlos Williams, who recalled it as follows:

> It was at this time that Ezra made the proposal, which, when I asked my father about it, caused him only to shake his head. It was as follows: That

we get a big supply of "606," the new anti-syphilitic arsenical which Ehrlich had just announced to the world, and go at once with it to the north coast of Africa and there set up shop. Between us, I with my medical certificate and experience, he with his social proclivities, we might, he thought, clean up a million treating all the wealthy old nabobs there—presumably rotten with the disease—and retire to our literary enjoyments within, at most, a year.[45]

Pound must have found New York City a comfortable environment in late 1910. For a person of artistic inclinations New York consisted exclusively of Greenwich Village, "more alive, frenetic, serious and colorful than ever before, the center of a large, inchoate movement of people out of sympathy with prevailing values, searching for more meaningful ways of living and convinced that American society as a whole needed a thorough renovation." Experimentation in the arts, as in life-styles, was encouraged, and the New Jerusalem was being pursued with alternating thrusts of priestly intent and puckish good humor. Visual and literary arts sought new forms, politics and philosophies were openly debated, and on at least two occasions drunken revelers declared independence from the United States and proclaimed Washington Square to be a separate republic. Already present, or soon to arrive, were poets Edna St. Vincent Millay, Joyce Kilmer, Witter Bynner, Harry Kemp, and Alfred Kreymborg, and a mélange of other creative minds including Eugene O'Neill, Floyd Dell, Walter Lippmann, Max Eastman, John Reed, Van Wyck Brooks, Margaret Sanger, Emma Goldman, and Lincoln Steffens. Eastman and Reed edited *The Masses,* which became the unofficial voice of the Village; it was "a magazine directed against rigidity and dogma wherever it is found; printing what is too naked or true for a moneymaking press; a magazine whose final policy is to do as it pleases and conciliate nobody, not even its readers."[46]

The intellectual ferment was already underway in 1910. Pound met some of these people and inhaled the Village pneuma with enthusiasm. When he called upon Witter Bynner, Pound wore purple trousers, a mauve jacket, a wide-brimmed straw hat with large pink polka dots on its white band, and one black and one blue shoe. W. B. Yeats's father, John Yeats, lived there and liked Pound very much. So did John Quinn, a New York lawyer and patron of the arts who would become an important source of support for Pound. Yeats, Quinn, and Pound went together to Coney Island one night, which Pound described as a "sham fairyland . . . however sordid it is when one is in it, it is marvellous against the night as one approaches or leaves it." Another evening Pound attended a meeting of the Poetry Society of America and traded good-natured witticisms "until the audience was in a gale of laughter most of the evening . . . Surely no one could have been more charming, more boy-ish, more delightfully provocative than Ezra that night."[47]

Others who met Pound during his stay in America did not like him. According to Wyndham Lewis, Pound "had been called the greatest bore in Philadelphia, so ceaselessly had he raved about London and Yeats and myself to uninterested Pennsylvanians." When Pound visited William Carlos Williams in New Jersey, Williams took him to dinner at the home of his fiancée; during the dinner Pound stood on his chair to kill a mosquito on the ceiling and, on this or another occasion, "ate off other people's plates, he ate like a pig." On another visit with Williams they went for a walk around a farm. Williams recalls saying to him: "Look, Ez, there's the winter wheat (it was three or four inches high) coming up to greet you." "It's the first intelligent wheat I've ever seen," Pound replied. Williams adds: "That's the way he felt. Such thoughts were always near the surface of his mind. It seemed to become him."[48]

Nor did Pound endear himself to the New York literary establish-ment. Yeats's father wrote that the "young literary men" found him "surly, supercilious and grumpy." Pound exacerbated his problems by making pronouncements on their work, such as claiming to know of only one American poet (Bliss Carman) who "would not improve by drowning." Overall he was not accepted by the American literati and was disappointed by this reception. Pound corroborated this in a letter to Williams ten years later, when he talked of returning to "a New York which wants me as little now as it did ten and fifteen years ago."[49]

During Pound's stay in New York he recorded his impressions of his fatherland. These were edited and published in a series called *Patria Mia* and *America: Chances and Remedies* in 1912 and 1913. They show Pound's strong identification with and affection for "America, my coun-try" and the great hopes for its future which he held at the time. He described America as "a young nation and a strong one . . . we are, I believe, the most generous people in the world . . ." What America needed was an intellectual awakening, "a Renaissance," "an American Risorgimento."

The forces working against the renaissance were the hordes of im-migrants flooding America's shores. These were Hungarians, Swedes, "Kravats, Slavs, Czecs, Italians, Germans . . . Irish or Russian Jew," who despite their aggressiveness and "animal vigour unlike any Euro-pean crowd I have ever looked at," were debasing America's genetic stock. Mixed marriages of immigrants with Anglo-Saxons were producing a race which was "mongrel" with "one stock neutralizing the forces of the other."

Despite this Pound believed the American Renaissance was "imminent" and that it would be led by artists. "Letters are a nation's foreign office. By the arts, and by them almost alone do nations gain for each other any understanding and intimate respect." Behind the coming American Renaissance, as had been true of the Italian Renaissance, there would be "a body of men, determined, patient, bound together informally by kindred ambitions from which they knew that they personally could reap but little." It would be an élite of artist-leaders which would lead America out of "the Dark Ages" that it was "at present enduring" and into Elysian intellectual fields.

Because of the importance of the arts for America's future, Pound advocated government subsidies for artists. This could be done by setting up "a college of one hundred members, chosen from all the arts, sculptors, painters, dramatists, musical composers, architects, scholars of the art of verse, engravers, etc., and they should be fed there during the impossible years of the artists' life—i.e., the beginning of the creative period." The hundred artists to be so supported should be "chosen with regard to their intentions and their capacities, not by an academic foot rule." This selection might pose problems, Pound admitted: "I would rather have the whole hundred of these artists chosen by one efficient artist than by any staid committee that was not composed of efficient artists." If such a college was not possible, then government pensions to support artists would be a reasonable alternative. "The artist should receive the annuity and agree to pass it on . . . when he no longer needed it . . . to the man who in his opinion was most likely to use his time for the greatest benefit of the art." The benefit of the art was the benefit of the nation, and Pound yearned for the day when "the arts shall cease to be regarded as a dope, a drug, a narcotic, as something akin to disease, and when they shall be regarded as sustenance—as clear channels for the transmission of intelligence, then may America and then even England may be a place wherein it is fitting that man made in the image of the invisible should draw breath into his nostrils."[50]

America was not quite ready for its renaissance, however, so Pound decided to return to Europe. Precisely why he made this decision is not known, but the facts that he had no job, had not gained readmission to graduate school, and that his books had not been as avidly acclaimed as he had hoped all contributed to it. He told friends that he was no longer able to "bear the brunt of America" and on February 22, 1911, sailed for London. He had earned just enough during his eight months in the United States to pay for his boat fare.[51]

IMAGISM

Pound's return to Europe did not mean that he had given up hope for America or that he was forgetting it. He was, instead, waiting for the beginning of the American Renaissance, and going to Europe was an interim arrangement. He had gone abroad in 1908 and had won sufficient recognition to compel attention in his homeland; now as he returned in 1911 perhaps he could do so even more effectively.

Pound paused briefly in London and went on to Paris, where Yeats was staying. The two met "almost daily," and Pound wrote to his father that he liked Yeats very much. At the time Yeats was beginning a study of automatic writing based on the premise that spirits of the dead communicate in this way. It was also during this period that Yeats, "at the house of an American medium, . . . confronted a voice which claimed to be his mask, his other self, with him since childhood. The voice called itself Leo Africanus, on whom Yeats checked and found to be a sixteenth-century Moorish writer and explorer who had been a captive at the court of Pope Leo X."[52] Africanus had been one of Yeats's earlier incarnations.

From Paris Pound went to Sirmione, where he spent several weeks at Lake Garda. It seems likely that Pound was preoccupied with thoughts of spiritualism and reincarnation during this period, for when he returned to London in August he went directly to G. R. S. Mead. Mead was an acknowledged authority on such matters and the editor of *Quest*, a quarterly review of theosophy, gnosticism, and the pagan mystery religions. Pound agreed to give a lecture on the troubadours to Mead's Quest Society and, with Dorothy Shakespear, he became a regular attender. In December he published a series of articles in the *New Age* in which he promoted the method of "luminous detail" for ascertaining wisdom. This method consisted of certain facts which "give one a sudden insight into circumjacent conditions"; the approach was contrasted with that of "multidinous detail," or the scientific method, which was said to be currently prevailing.[53]

The London to which Pound returned in 1911 was not the one he had left a year earlier. King Edward VII had died in May 1910, and young King George V found himself embroiled in escalating conflict between the House of Commons and the House of Lords. At issue were reforms to help the working classes—old-age pensions, minimum wages in certain industries, an eight-hour workday for miners, and a national insurance plan. The power of the aristocracy, symbolized by the reigns of Queen Victoria and King Edward and defended by the House of Lords, was being progressively eroded by a new King who was siding with the House of Commons. In addition to this a bitter controversy raged about Home Rule for Ireland; Victorian England had been unabashedly imperialistic, controlling a quarter of the earth, and now the Irish (of *all* people) were demanding a measure of independence. One could sense the crumbling of the Old Order.

Pound set to work refurbishing his literary reputation. A new collection of his poems, *Canzoni,* had been published in July and was greeted with mixed reviews. He wrote more poems and completed his translation of Guido Cavalcanti's poems, which was accepted for publication in both England and America. He became friends with A. R. Orage who, as editor of the *New Age,* provided him with an outlet for many of his writings. Over the next decade Orage would publish nearly three hundred of Pound's articles and provided him with his most reliable source of earned income.[54]

By the spring of 1912 Ezra Pound had made considerable headway in his attempt to become a leader in literary London. He ceaselessly urged his friends to abandon the romantic writing styles of the nineteenth century and to "make it new." Writing was to be lean and precise, and all adjectives were suspect. He was "the picture of a kind of frenetic energy manifesting itself in several ways at once: the complex picture of an active, urgent man at work. Sometimes the work has to do with starting up a new magazine, sometimes with encouraging a new writer, or shouting down an old one."[55]

In late 1911 Hilda Doolittle arrived in London to join Pound and resume their relationship. She was still trying to find herself, and had earlier in the year traveled for four months with Frances Gregg in Europe. In New York Pound had persuaded her that they still were engaged and had urged her to come to England. When she arrived, however, she found her old friend fully occupied with Dorothy Shakespear and other women. She therefore turned her attention to Richard Aldington, a young English poet and friend of Pound's, and began writing poetry herself. In 1912, sitting in a tea shop with Aldington and Pound, she presented them with two poems ("Priapus" and "Hermes of the Ways"), and Pound thereupon anointed her as an "Imagist." This marked the birth of a new literary movement which stressed sharp images, meticulous precision in the use of words, complete freedom in the choice of subject matter, and the use of colloquial language; it would profoundly shape the emergence of modern poetry.

In August 1912, Pound's career took another important step forward. Harriet Monroe in Chicago was founding a new American literary journal to be called *Poetry.* While in London during the summer of 1910 she had been introduced to Pound's poetry by Elkin Mathews and had been favorably impressed. She therefore wrote to Pound asking if he would help in her new venture. Pound accepted, and was designated foreign correspondent; he wrote to Miss Monroe that her offer was an auspicious sign of the coming American Renaissance, an awakening that would "make the Italian Renaissance look like a tempest in a teapot! The force we have, and the impulse, but the guiding sense, the discrimination in applying the force, we must wait and strive for."[56] Over the coming months Pound delivered to Harriet Monroe the work of Tagore, Yeats, Aldington, Eliot, and many others for her journal. Also in August Pound began to host a regular series of "evenings" at his flat, just as Yeats did; this was a certain sign of literary status.

During the years between 1911 and 1914 Ezra Pound became a moving force in the literary salons. He was distinguishable by "his immense will power, his drive and determination, and his intention to set literature and literary trends in order." He was said to be "everybody's schoolmaster and more—he really bothered as to whether his 'disciples' had enough to eat or read the right books or met the appropriate elders." T. S. Eliot recalled that "no one could have been kinder to younger men, or to writers who, whether younger or not, seemed to him worthy and unrecognized. He liked to be the impresario for younger men, as well as the animator of artistic activity in any milieu in which he found himself. In this role he would go to any lengths of generosity and kindness; from inviting constantly to dinner a struggling author whom he suspected of being under-fed, or giving away clothing (though his shoes and underwear were almost the only garments which resembled those of other men sufficiently to be worn by them), to trying to find jobs, collect subsidies, get work published and then get it criticized and praised." Phyllis Bottome credited Pound for giving her "the first unbiased and objective literary criticism I had ever known . . . He helped to release any, and every artist, young or old, whom he came across, from any shackles that prevented the strength of their artistic impulses." John Quinn noted that "a good half of his energy was being spent in the interest of others," and John Cournos called Pound "one of the kindest men that ever lived . . . the ideal missionary of culture."[57]

One of the distinguishing features of Pound's advocacy for the arts was its amplitude. Not only was he concerned with the artist, his sustenance, and his freedom of expression, but Pound also involved himself in questions of publishers, the price of books, tariffs on book imports, censorship, the support of literary magazines, and the philosophy of artistic ideals. His advocacy was not confined to poets but included other writers, dramatists, painters, sculptors, musicians, composers, and architects as well. In all the arts he promoted the incisive, the lean, the new, and he was powerful in shaping and strengthening the artistic modes of at least two decades.

London was aglow with literary lights during those prewar years, and Pound made the acquaintance of most. George Bernard Shaw was one of the towering figures. Then in his late fifties and at the height of his influence, he was writing *Androcles and The Lion* and *Pygmalion*. In the preceding decade he had successfully transformed the London theater from its late-nineteenth-century melodramatics and histrionics back to its Thespian origin: the theater was for the dramatization of ideas and conflict, not mere entertainment. Political and philosophical ideas had again become legitimate subjects, and Shaw's Fabian leanings were inextricably mixed with his art.

Pound had first met Shaw in early 1909, and although he disagreed with Shavian socialist ideas, he could not help but admire Shaw's fusion of politics and art. Shaw had become an artist who was also a leader of men, and throughout his London years Pound continued to occasionally meet with and write approvingly of him.[58] In 1922 Pound asked Shaw to contribute to a subscription being raised to publish Joyce's *Ulysses*. Shaw declined despite pressure from Pound, finally writing that "I take care of the pence and let the Pounds take care of themselves." Pound turned on him, publicly calling him a "ninth-rate coward" and privately calling him "fundamentally trivial" and a "fake."[59]

Another literary leader in London was H. G. Wells. Approaching his fiftieth year, he had built his formidable reputation by mixing science fiction and political commentary in *The Invisible Man* and *The War of the Worlds*. Wells was a friend of Ford Madox Ford, who had published several chapters of Wells's new novel, *Tono-Bungay*, in the *Little Review* in 1909. The book, attacking irresponsible capitalists, could not have failed to attract Pound's attention, and at least by 1912 Pound had established a friendship. Wells is mentioned frequently in Pound's London correspondence, and Pound enlisted him in his fight to get James Joyce's work published. A luncheon Pound and Wells shared in 1918 was later memorialized in Canto 42, and the two continued corresponding until World War II.

Yeats was the third literary giant on the London scene. One year older than Wells, he had also successfully mixed political interests with his art. As a poet Yeats was pre-eminent, and Pound's propinquity to him was undoubtedly an asset in the young poet's striving for professional respectability. At Yeats's Monday evening soirées Pound "distributed Yeats's cigarettes and Chianti and laid down the law about poetry," and Yeats accepted Pound's criticism of his poetry as he would accept it from few others. In November 1913, Yeats took Pound on as his private secretary and the two spent three months together at a rural cottage in Sussex. Always underlying their friendship was their shared passion for the occult, a monomania which, Polyphemus-like, may have restricted their peripheral vision.[60]

Pound's interest in the establishment's literary leaders was matched by his enthusiasm for discovering talent among younger writers. London was at the time a mecca for aspiring illuminati, a city in which one might not only share a glass of wine with Shaw, Wells, or Yeats but also get work published in one of the myriad literary journals which were blossoming. An ability to write was valued, and everything claiming literary merit was debated except for the importance of literary merit itself.

Thus in 1912 Robert Frost, an unknown New England school-teacher, sold his farm and moved to London. He was eleven years older than Pound but had had no success whatever in getting his poetry published in America where, he said, "it were better that a millstone were hanged around your neck than that you should own yourself a minor poet." London was different; Frost was immediately recognized for his talent and by early 1913 his first volume of poems, *A Boy's Will*, had been accepted for publication. Frost was introduced to Pound, who was impressed by the page proofs of *A Boy's Will*. Pound wrote a review and sent it to Harriet Monroe for *Poetry*. Monroe demurred, but Pound insisted; it was the first review of Frost's work to appear in America.

Another expatriate arrival in London was a young Harvard graduate, Thomas Stearns Eliot, who came to Pound with a letter of introduction from Conrad Aiken. Eliot had also been unsuccessful in publishing his poetry in America, and he brought with him "The Love Song of J. Alfred Prufrock," which he had finished in 1911. "Do I dare / Disturb the universe?" Prufrock asked, and Pound responded with a vigorous affirmative. "The best poem I have yet had or seen from an American," Pound wrote to Harriet Monroe, urging her to publish it. She hesitated and asked for changes, but Pound browbeat and bulldogged her for eight months until she finally included it; Eliot's career was launched.[61]

Pound worked just as assiduously to promote the work of young writers who were not in London. In New Jersey William Carlos Williams was trying to establish himself as a poet as well as a physician, and Pound enthusiastically championed his work at every opportunity. It was a trait which endeared him to friends such as Williams, who in later years wrote: "Ezra has always been thoughtfulness itself in his efforts to bridge the gap between my academic lacks and his superior learning," and: "I've always loved that guy. He was and is one of the most sympathetic human beings."[62]

Williams's admiration of Pound as an artisan was typical of many of the young poets whom Pound helped. "His language represents his last naiveté," Williams wrote, "the childishness of complete sincerity discovered in the child and the true poet alike." Through linguistic legerdemain Williams saw Pound creating a product greater than the sum of the words and meter: "His excellence is that of the maker, not the measurer—I say he *is* a poet. This is in effect to have stepped beyond measure." It was true synergism, and Williams as physician and scientist could describe the whole but not the individual parts: "It is impossible to praise Pound's lines. The terms for such praise are lacking. There ain't none. You've got to read the line and feel first, then grasp through experience in its full significance, how the language makes the verse live." Pound was said to be building "a fundamental regeneration of thought in our language . . . He is striking . . . at the basis of thought, at the mechanism with which we make our adjustments to things and to each other." Out of this verbal alchemy emerges "a sudden clearing of the mind of rubbish and the re-establishment of the sense of proportion."[63]

Despite deep personal differences with Pound's political beliefs, Williams retained his admiration of Pound's skills to the end of his life. "Pound has enlarged the scope of poetic opportunity," he claimed. At one point Williams assessed Pound and Cummings as "beyond doubt, the two most distinguished American poets of today"; on another occasion he called Pound simply "our best poet."[64]

An unknown language instructor originally from Dublin but then living in Trieste was also to become deeply indebted to Pound for his help. This young man, James Joyce, had sent some poems to Yeats, who in December 1913 showed them to Pound. Recognizing genius, Pound wrote to Joyce immediately, asking permission to include one of them in the imagist anthology he was compiling. Joyce agreed, and also told Pound about his difficulties in getting publishers for his book of short stories, *Dubliners,* and his novel *A Portrait of the Artist as a Young Man.* Pound was equally impressed by them, labeled Joyce "by far the most significant writer of our decade," and launched a one-person campaign to get Joyce published and recognized. He enlisted friends such as Eliot and Wells in support, wrote to numerous journals praising Joyce, arranged for the serialization of *Portrait* in the *Egoist,* and later got *Ulysses* published in America. When Joyce needed financial support, Pound even arranged for that as well. Probably no other writer was as indebted to Pound for his career as was James Joyce.[65]

Much of Pound's energies during these years was spent in such projects of literary succor, usually with no direct benefit to himself. English literature was in motion once again, and the nascent writers who flocked to London provided the fuel. Pound crossed paths frequently with them, and exchanged ideas in places like the Vienna Café near the British Museum. One such writer was Cicily Fairfield, who in 1911, only eighteen years old, began writing feminist and literary pieces for the *Freewoman*. She had aspired to be an actress and had recently played the role of Rebecca West in Ibsen's *Rosmersholm;* fearing that her mother would disapprove of her writing, she adopted the character's name as her pseudonym.

Pound came to know Rebecca West during these years; she reviewed his translation of Cavalcanti's poems in the *Freewoman* and later contributed an article on Imagism. She was a rebel by inclination, and in 1912 began an affair with H. G. Wells, married and twenty-six years her senior. When Wells broke it off in June 1913, she became "distraught, angry and suicidal"; they reconciled and later that year she became pregnant with his child. By this time she had emerged as one of the most militant feminists, socialists, and advocates of the new literature on the London scene.[66]

Katherine M. Beauchamp was another young writer of interest to Pound. An accomplished cellist from New Zealand who in 1909 began contributing short stories to the *New Age,* her style had overtones of poetry, and by 1915 she was co-editing another literary journal with D. H. Lawrence. By that time she had decided to use her middle name as a pseudonym and was known as Katherine Mansfield.

Ezra Pound's literary influence in England reached its pinnacle in 1913 and early 1914. Imagism had become respectable as a new verse form and was being widely discussed. Pound's poetry was being published, and his close relationship with Yeats further enhanced his reputation. So too did his role as "social master of ceremonies" at South Lodge, the home of influential Ford Madox Ford and Violet Hunt, the woman with whom he was living openly and (in post-Victorian England) scandalously. Pound had even addressed the Essay Society of Oxford, an invitation arranged by W. G. Lawrence at the suggestion of his brother T. E. Lawrence, who, in a letter from Carchemish, had assessed Pound as "a good poet" though "a very curious person." Pound would finally meet T. E. Lawrence six years later, after he had become the mythical Lawrence of Arabia.[67]

Ezra Pound chose this time in his life to take a wife. He was twenty-eight years old and perhaps feared that youth was slipping away from him; one poem he had written was called "Middle-Aged":

So I, the fires that lit once dreams
Now over and spent,
Lie dead within four walls
And so now love
Rains down and so enriches some stiff case,
And strews a mind with precious metaphors,

And so the space
Of my still consciousness
Is full of gilded snow,

The which, no cat has eyes enough
To see the brightness of.[68]

His friends were surprised, for Pound had criticized marriage as unnecessary. In 1913 he had written: "Modern marriage is, apparently, derived from the laws of slave concubinage, not from the more honorable forms of primitive European marriage." When Sophie Brzeska asked him why he was bothering, Pound replied: "It doesn't matter. Wife or mistress—it's the same thing. It's just a question of a few procedures for the sake of convenience." Sophie persisted: "Ah, but what if one wishes to separate? Look what terrible chores you'll have to go through." Pound replied: "Why get a divorce? One lives in mutual tolerance."[69]

Dorothy Shakespear, Olivia's daughter, was Pound's choice as his wife. An aspiring painter, she shared Pound's devotion to the arts. She was a beautiful woman who carried herself "delicately with the air, always, of a young Victorian lady out skating." One friend described her as "just sitting there like a beautiful ornament, silent most of the time." Pound himself said that "Dorothy was the only woman he had ever met who could say *anything*, and it 'would be all right, she was such a lady.' " In later years Pound described her as "a beautiful picture that never came alive."[70]

Ezra had known Dorothy for five years and they shared an intense interest in the occult. Hugh Kenner wrote of Dorothy: "Psychic hauntings were a given of her world, like gravitation and digestion: her world had been Yeats' world." Ezra's marriage to Dorothy, therefore, brought him even closer to Yeats and Olivia, both of whom strongly encouraged the match. For the same reason the marriage, as described by Hilda Doolittle's biographer, "would fit perfectly into his [Pound's] plans for his own literary future."[71]

Ezra and Dorothy spent the winter of 1914–1915 with Yeats at his country cottage. At the time Yeats was doing preliminary work on *A Vision,* an elaborate prose work describing his mystical system which would, in a dedicatory epistle to Pound, proclaim "a new divinity." The occult interests of Yeats, Ezra, and Dorothy were expanded two years later when Yeats, then a fifty-two-year-old bachelor, married the step-daughter of Olivia's brother (Dorothy's "stepcousin" and close friend), Georgie Hyde-Lees. Georgie had the powers of a medium and assisted Yeats with his experiments on automatic writing.[72] The voices of the dead could now be heard quadriphonically.

Ezra and Dorothy's marriage lasted for fifty-eight years, until his death, although they often lived apart. One of their agreements was that Dorothy should never have to cook. She followed Ezra as a devoted and faithful wife, apparently without much influence on him. Pound had very traditional ideas about the place of women and once advised Ernest Hemingway's wife never to try to change him: "Most wives try to change their husbands. With him it would be a terrible mistake."[73]

Marriage to Dorothy did alleviate one of Pound's most pressing problems—money. He was still dependent on his parents for funds, although his writing was slowly becoming more financially rewarding. Dorothy had an income from her father of £150 per year, and after the marriage her income was used to help defray their joint living costs. Dorothy's father was not pleased with this arrangement and was contemptuous of the American poet who could not even support himself.[74]

Isabel and Homer Pound took the occasion of the coming marriage to remind Philadelphia of Ezra's success and fame. A story in the *Philadelphia Press* announcing the coming wedding described him as "the brilliant young Philadelphia poet" who "went from Wyncote to England and there wrote poems of so much merit that he gained a special place in the highest literary circles." In the *Philadelphia Evening Bulletin* readers were reminded that Kipling had called Pound "one of the world's great poets."[75] This was part of a continuing campaign by Pound and his parents to keep him in the public eye at home. In 1911 the *Philadelphia Evening Bulletin* had carried a story describing him as a formerly "obscure graduate of the University of Pennsylvania" who had been "caught up on the wings of recognition and hurried to a place of eminence. When the echoes of acclaim sounded here Philadelphians were startled to realize that they had the claim of citizenship upon Ezra Pound whose [poetry] brought forth unqualified praise from the English critics . . . The recognition which has come so unreservedly to the American poet abroad is now being gradually yielded to him by his own countrymen. Pound however, cares nothing for that, he declares. He is only twenty-five years old now, and in his own estimation 'has not yet begun to write.' He prefers to live abroad and make only intermittent visits to his parents."[76] In 1913 the *Philadelphia Record*, under the heading "Native Poet Stirs

London," had told readers that "in years to come Philadelphia may brag of having furnished the world a great poet" and compared his achievements in poetry to those of Whistler in painting.[77]

AN INSATIABLE EGO

One might have thought that, given his talents, Pound would have continued on a steady path toward greatness such as was trod by Frost, Eliot, and Joyce. He had the poetic gift, the energy, and the will. One would have guessed that he could have traded forever on "the bubbling exuberance, the magical language, the delightful arrogance which so enchanted his admirers in earlier days."[78]

This might have occurred if Pound himself had not continuously strewn boulders onto the path. Foremost among these was his ego which, it was later said, "Might more equitably have been distributed among three or four of his contemporaries." An "extraordinary ego" added James Laughlin, Pound's later publisher.[79] "He always felt himself superior to anyone about him," claimed William Carlos Williams. As evidence of this trait, Williams cited Pound's habit of always walking one step ahead of his friends when going somewhere with them. Once, Williams recalled, "I remember my brother in the same situation turned and walked off in the opposite direction."[80]

Pound's egotism was focused primarily on his intellectual ability and poetic powers: "He did not desire to prove to the people he had come amongst that he was superior in physical strength," said Wyndham Lewis, "but that he was superior to all other intellectuals in intellect, and all poets in prosodic prowess. They were to be the spectators merely—they were of very little account. The feelings of dislike were mutual and immediate, as I could observe, and he never sought to hide the fact that he looked upon them as of very little consequence."[81] Others noted that Pound sought "to be the Dalai Lama of all poets" and regarded himself as "the greatest poet since Dante."[82]

England had another attraction for Pound which resonated with his immense ego. It was an aristocracy, with kings and queens, lords and peers, and hereditary privileges to distinguish the élite from the common man. Pound counted himself solidly among the former; in 1911 he had written: "I have met with the 'Common Man,' / I admit that he usually bores me, / He is usually stupid or smug."[83] Years later he recalled never being able to mix with "the lower classes."[84] He revered members of the aristocracy, and "his genuflections before bloated members of that crowd, men and women with money and position, were generally well known."[85] William Carlos Williams recalled an incident while visiting Pound in London, when the two of them had eaten dinner at a high-class restaurant:

> Then, we having finished, he pushed back his chair and stood up. I immediately took his heavy coat from the rack near us preparatory to holding it for him that he might slip his arms comfortably into the sleeves.
>
> With that he turned on me, laying me out in no uncertain way for my presumption, jerked the coat out of my hands and, presenting it to the waiter, made him hold it, as he continued scolding me, saying that one didn't do things that way in London. Angry now, I waited, gave my coat to the waiter to hold for me and as the whole restaurant smiled, we made our way to the street.[86]

In his writings Pound referred to "the people" as "undependable, irrational, a quicksand upon which nothing can build . . . docile, apathetic, de-energized." "There is no misanthropy," he wrote in 1917, "in a thorough contempt for the mob." In later years he was to express it more simply: "There is no more equality between men than between animals."[87]

Closely allied with Pound's élitist beliefs was his racial bigotry. As early as 1906 he had written of blacks as "coons,"[88] an epithet which was not unusual in Main Line Philadelphia at the time. He retained this attitude in England and in 1920 wrote: "There are ninety different ways of saying 'Damn nigger'; it requires knowledge to use the right ones . . . The nigger, like any other fine animal, is very quick to perceive certain tones of personality, of voice, modes of moving, not by cerebral analysis but by 'feel.' Some men never get on with horses; some men are perfect fools in the way they approach any animal."[89]

But it was anti-Semitism which developed most fully in Pound during his London years. In 1912 he noted that "The Jew alone can retain his detestable qualities, despite climatic conditions."[90] The following year he wrote: "Come let us on with the new deal, / Let us be done with Jews and Jobbery, / Let us SPIT upon those who fawn on the JEWS for their money."[91] Douglas Goldring, one of Pound's London friends, has written that in the lavish parties being given nightly during this period in the Ritz ballroom by members of "the financial aristocracy . . . The richer Jews outstripped all the others in the variety and magnificence of their entertaining."[92] Pound certainly was aware of this phenomenon and, significantly for the future, of the fact that some of these wealthy Jews were "armament makers" according to Goldring. Pound's beliefs about Jews have been called jejune; one critic claimed that his "sheer ignorance on the subject of Jews and Judaism is extraordinary.

He seems to have made no effort to read about Jewish history, thought or language."[93]

In addition to blacks and Jews, Ezra Pound also urged discrimination against the immigrant groups that continued to flock to America's shores. In 1918 he wrote about "the turmoil of Letts, Finns, Estonians, Cravats, Niberians, Nubians, Algerians sweeping along Eighth Avenue. . . ."[94] Two years later he declared: "I don't give a fried fahrt about nationality. Race is probably real. It is real."[95] His views were occasionally included in his writings and became part of his identity. One magazine to which he was a frequent contributor received "countless letters" from "Jews, Letts, Greeks, Finns, Irish, etc. protesting against Mr. Pound's ignorance and discrimination"; one contributor observed that "there is something about Pound's vituperations that savors of not too remote gutters— and coal stalls and tongues akimbo and herrings obvious in the rising temperature."[96]

Many of Pound's closest associates during this period shared his strongly bigoted views. John Quinn, his friend and patron from New York, wrote to Pound that his city had been usurped by "a million Jews who are mere walking appetites, seven or eight hundred thousand dagos, a couple of hundred thousand Slovaks, fifty or sixty thousand Croats, and seven or eight hundred thousand Germans."[97] W. B. Yeats, A. R. Orage, and D. H. Lawrence were all known for their anti-Semitism,[98] as was T. S. Eliot, who later wrote that "reasons of race and religion combine to make any large number of free-thinking Jews undesirable."[99] Most importantly Dorothy Shakespear was known for being excessively bigoted, especially anti-Semitic: "Hers is just Anglo-Saxon fear and hate, the weak of the world who want . . . the liver of the Jew."[100]

Another characteristic of Pound during his London years was his cultivation of eccentricity. He made his debut in 1908 "wearing a large cowboy hat and flourishing in his hand a cowboy whip, which he would crack to emphasize his remarks,"[101] and from that point on his appearance became legend. By early 1910 he was described as wearing "trousers made of green billiard cloth, a pink coat, a blue shirt, a tie hand-painted by a Japanese friend, an immense sombrero, a flaming beard cut to a point, and a single large blue ear-ring."[102] Douglas Goldring remembered that Pound's dress was as if he had "seen Puccini's 'La Boheme' and innocently believed it was all true."[103] Pound believed that such affected eccentricity would mark him as a poet and a genius. He associated these traits, as in his 1914 wedding announcement, where it was noted that "with the true eccentricity of real genius the poet had not disclosed the name of the officiating clergyman, nor the number of guests, nor the names of the members of the bridal party."[104] Pound's dress was his personal billboard and he selected his clothes carefully; letters to his parents suggest that he spent a significant portion of his meager earnings on them. He was part poseur, part apparition.

Pound's social behavior was marked by the same eccentricity. Shortly after his arrival in London he was invited to a dinner party with some other poets at the home of Ernest Rhys. He arrived in "a silk shirt, flowing tie and velvet jacket . . . a young satyr in disguise." During dinner Pound was reciting a passage from one of his poems when "his voice suddenly and most effectively broke, and with an expressive sweep of his hand he reached out to the bowl of red roses in the center of the table, deliberately plucked off a petal, and put it into his mouth and, after a brief dramatic pause, continued his peroration. By the time we reached dessert, most of the roses had lost their petals and Mrs. Rhys, with a charming smile and a wicked twinkle in her bright blue eyes, turned to him and said: 'Would you like another rose, Mr. Pound?' "[105] On another occasion, "at a literary breakfast in one of London's great houses . . . Pound, after refusing all offers of food, methodically ate with fork and knife the petals of a rose."[106] His hortulan tastes were not confined to roses, however, for at another dinner party he consumed the red tulips on the table.[107]

When flowers were not on the menu he could still call attention to himself by his table manners. At one dinner, for example, "Ezra distinguished himself by alternately leaning forward to spear potatoes with his fork from a dish in the middle of the table, and then lolling back to munch his capture."[108] After dinner he would often entertain his hosts with recitations of his poetry. As Ford Madox Ford described such occasions: "When I first knew him, his Philadelphia accent was still comprehensible if disconcerting; his beard and flowing locks were auburn and luxuriant; he was astonishingly meagre and agile. He threw himself alarmingly into frail chairs, devoured enormous quantities of your pastry, fixed his pince nez firmly on his nose, drew a manuscript from his pocket, threw his head back, closed his eyes to the point of invisibility, and looking down his nose, would chuckle like Mephistopheles and read you a translation from Arnaut Daniel. The only part of that verse you would understand would be the refrain."[109]

Away from London's drawing rooms Pound's behavior was also noteworthy. A woman companion described his dancing as follows: "Ezra danced according to no rules I understood. New steps one may invent, but surely the music sets time and rhythm. But for Ezra, no; with extremely odd steps he moved, to unearthly beats. One couldn't face it.

Easier to waltz with a robot."[110] He was equally flamboyant on the tennis court, playing "like a demon or a trick pony, sitting down composedly in his square and jumping up in time to receive his adversary's ball, which he competently returned, the flaps of his polychrome shirt flying out like the petals of some flower and his red head like a flaming pistil in the middle of it."[111] Others described the experience of playing tennis against him as like playing against "a galvanized, agile gibbon."[112]

Pound took all of these activities very seriously, for they were part of his role. He had auditioned as a great poet and was determined to play it. Far from interfering with his professional career, Pound believed that eccentricity enhanced it. His longtime friend William Carlos Williams captured the paradoxical qualities of poet and showman many years later in his recollections: "Ezra Pound is one of the most competent poets in our language, possessed of the most acute ear for metrical sequences, to the point of genius, that we have ever known. He is also, it must be confessed, the biggest damn fool and faker in the business. You can't allow yourself to be too serious about a person like that— and yet he is important. He knows all this and plays on it to perfection."[113]

Ezra Pound as English troubadour was an initial success in staid London, as it recovered slowly from the moral stringency of Queen Victoria. "His dashing appearance and alluring manner helped make him the rage of cultivated gatherings."[114] It was an act which can be seen only so often, however, before the jongleur turns into a boor.

Pound had been back in London less than two years when it was said that "everyone was deploring Ezra and running him down."[115] Conrad Aiken wrote to Harriet Monroe at *Poetry* complaining of Pound as foreign correspondent: "Must we also have his opinions thrust down our throats? . . . Must we share all of Mr. Pound's growing pains with him, pang by pang?"[116] Later in 1913 Pound himself wrote to Miss Monroe, acknowledging that he was fighting with everybody and that this was interfering with both his social and his professional life: "It hits me in my dinner invitations, in my weekends, in reviews of my own work."[117] The following year Richard Aldington, by then Hilda Doolittle's husband, was writing of his friend: "Mr. Pound is one of the gentlest, most modest, bashful, kind creatures who ever walked the earth; so I cannot help thinking that all this enormous arrogance and petulance and fierceness are a pose. And it is a wearisome pose."[118] Ford Madox Ford simply called Pound "the kindest-hearted man who ever cut a throat."[119]

Pound's social and professional acceptance by his English colleagues was further hindered by his increasing reputation for exploiting people. T. E. Hulme, an early acquaintance in London, broke with Pound after accusing him of using his notes on French symbolists for Pound's own publications. John G. Fletcher had a similar experience: "I felt that he had simply exploited the knowledge I had gained before him to serve his own ends."[120] Some friends doubted whether Pound possessed any original thoughts at all and suggested that all his ideas were borrowed; Samuel Putnam recalls that "Aldington in a hilarious moment once remarked to me: 'Why Sam, don't you realize that Ezra could no more have a thought than you or I could have a child?' This last impression was quite a common one."[121]

Young writers whom Pound was promoting had similar complaints. T. S. Eliot, while lauding Pound's help, simultaneously observed that Pound "was so passionately concerned about the works of art which he expected his protégés to produce that he sometimes tended to regard them almost impersonally, as art or literature machines to be carefully tended and oiled, for the sake of their potential output." D. H. Lawrence, who had just eloped with the wife of his language tutor and therefore had his own problems, wrote to a friend: "The Hueffer [F. M. Ford]-Pound faction seems inclined to lead me round a little as one of their show dogs."[122] And Robert Frost's friendship with Pound lasted only a few weeks for similar reasons. Frost gave Pound a new poem to read, "Death of a Hired Man," which Pound promptly sent to a journal without Frost's permission. Frost believed that Pound was trying to use him for his own ends as another example of an American poet neglected in his own country, and in 1913 wrote Pound a declaration of independence which was never sent:

> When you said I could not read
> When you said I looked old
> When you said I was slow of wit
> I knew that you only meant
> That you could read
> That you looked young
> That you were nimble of wit
>
> . . . .
>
> I suspected though that in praising me
> You were not concerned so much with my desert
> As with your power
> That you praised me arbitrarily
> And took credit to yourself[123]

By 1915 Frost complained that Pound's championing of his work as an American expatriate was hurting him: "Another such review as the one in 'Poetry' and I shan't be admitted to Ellis Island . . . Pound is trying to drag me into his ridiculous row with everybody over there. I feel sorry for him for by this time he has nearly every man's hand against him on both continents and I wouldn't want to hurt him."[124]

The longer Pound stayed in London, the more enemies he made. He was increasingly attacked in the literary magazines that had been the source of his fame. In 1914 one of them referred to Pound as "Mr. Isaiah Ounce" and called him "deplorable and ridiculous." Meeting him during this period for the first time, one observer was impressed with Pound as "an electric eel flung into a mass of flaccid substances . . . Ezra was an intensely uncomfortable young man, even to himself."[125] As the attacks increased, so did the acerbity of his responses. In June 1914 he began a book review: "In a country in love with amateurs, in a country where the incompetent have such beautiful manners . . . "[126] and in the following year published this verse:

> *When I carefully consider the curious habits of dogs*
> *I am compelled to conclude*
> *That man is the superior animal.*
> *When I consider the curious habits of man*
> *I confess, my friend, I am puzzled.*[127]

GAUDIER AND LEWIS

In late 1913 and early 1914 Ezra Pound forged alliances with two controversial figures in the London art world. Both accelerated his already deteriorating professional reputation, and when he looked back a year later on his fall from English grace, the names of Henri Gaudier and Wyndham Lewis came readily to his mind.[128]

Henri Gaudier was a young French sculptor whom Pound met in 1913 at an art exhibit. He was virtually indigent, living in a dilapidated flat beneath a railroad bridge with Sophie Brzeska, a Polish woman twenty years his senior. He was so enamored of her that he appended her last name to his own and was called Henri Gaudier-Brzeska; she in turn treated him as a son.

Pound admired his art and, as they became friends, his ideas. Both Gaudier and Brzeska were violently anti-Semitic: "A reader of his notebooks will be shocked by his hatreds."[129] Gaudier also had a strong belief in the importance of sexual energy and its relationship to creativity. He claimed that such energy was channeled through a vortex and represented in art as a phallus: "The vertical, when cylindrical becomes . . . the African and Oceanic *vortex of fecundity.*"[130] Gaudier's biographer noted that "he had a queer and obscene idea of humor. He had often produced works quite pornographic, and others indecent, thinking them very amusing."[131] Charles Norman wrote of Gaudier that a reader of his letters would be "disgusted by infantile fantasies about the woman whose name he had attached to his own and who passed as his sister and behaved like one."[132]

In early 1914 Pound brought Gaudier a piece of marble three feet high with which to sculpt a bust of Pound. "Much over life-size and cut from a rectangular block of marble, its purpose and beginning were entirely pornographic. Both the sculptor and the sitter had decided upon that. Brzeska informed me of the fact that it was to be a phallus . . . At one time it looked like a champagne cork with its bulbous top. But it was gradually assuming, in silhouette, the phallic idea. It was an exaggeration of Pound's features so exaggerated as to lose all possible resemblance. It was becoming more and more phallic, which was the only intention from the start. As a portrait it was ridiculous. There was little that was human about it. I met Pound during the work and he proved surprisingly shy and nervous. I couldn't understand why he should be so upset. He did not talk and was not at ease. I am sure that I had caught the conspirators in the act of developing the phallic idea. It was the kind of thing Brzeska would gloat over."[133]

The completed bust was solemnly anointed as a hieratic (priestly) head by Pound, thereby connecting the phallus to its divine origins. While posing for the work Pound had been told by Gaudier: "You understand it will not look like you, it will . . . not . . . look . . . like you. It will be the expression of certain emotions I get from your character." In recalling this in his memoir on Gaudier two years later, Pound facetiously added: "Oh well, mon pauvre caractère, the good Gaudier has stiffened it up quite a lot . . . We joked of the time when I should sell it to the 'Metropolitan' for $5000. and when we should both live at ease for a year . . . some two or three decades hence."[134] Most Pound scholars have accepted the bust surprisingly seriously, given its overtly phallic appearance, as a genuine hieratic head. Hugh Kenner noted that Wyndham Lewis had called it "Ezra in the form of a marble phallus,"[135] and Timothy Materer viewed it as portraying Pound "as the seminal figure of modern poetry, a notion this sculpture takes literally,"[136] but otherwise its sexual significance seems to have been neglected.

Pound found Gaudier "the best company in the world" and added: "Some of my best days, the happiest and most interesting, were spent in his uncomfortable mud-floored studio."[137] He compared sitting with Gaudier to escaping from the present into the Italian Renaissance: "He was, of course indescribably like some one whom one had met in the pages of Castiglione or Valla, or perhaps in a painting forgotten."[138] Gaudier also did a drawing of an old wolf for Pound and inscribed it:

"A mon ami Ezra Pound en admiration de 'Piere Vidal Old.' " The poem of that name, about a wolf, had previously been said by Pound to symbolize sexual passion.[139]

Pound's relationship with Gaudier brought out personality characteristics in him which, given Pound's already tenuous attachment to respectability, would better have been left undisturbed. Pound had been interested in women for several years—"his susceptibility to women (and theirs to him) was lifelong" is the way Hugh Kenner politely phrased it[140]—but in 1914 Pound became more public in his beliefs and practices. "The biology of sex was to the young Ezra a joyous discovery; and he yodelled the necessity of thinking objectively and the fun of living dangerously from every house-top in London," recalled Phyllis Bottome.[141] Discretion gave way to advertisement, which in post-Victorian England was not acceptable. He published a poem called "Coitus" ("The gilded phaloi of the crocuses / are thrusting at the spring air")[142] and in June 1914 contributed "Fratres Minores" to the first issue of *Blast:*

> *With minds still hovering above their testicles*
> *Certain poets here and in France*
> *Still sigh over established and natural fact*
> *Long since fully discussed by Ovid.*
> *They howl. They complain in delicate and exhausted metres*
> *That the twitching of three abdominal nerves*
> *Is incapable of producing a lasting Nirvana.*[143]

The poem was considered to be so scandalous that the first and last two lines were crossed out in many copies before distribution. It implied that "certain poets here and in France" had been criticizing Pound's increasingly public views that coitus was the royal road to wisdom.

Pound's actual practices during this period must remain a matter of speculation. He is recorded as admiring strong women who could dominate men, even if the women used subterfuge to accomplish their ends. On the other hand he viewed women primarily as sexual objects to be used by men. In a 1915 poem he wrote:

> *Woman? Oh, woman is a consummate rage,*
> *but dead, or asleep, she pleases.*
>
> *Take her. She has two excellent seasons.*[144]

And in a letter to William Carlos Williams the following year, he wrote of women: "You know I prefer them Bacchic." Years later, in thinking back on London, he described the city as having a "great proportion of females above that of males makes it THE land for the male with phallus erectus. London THE cunt of the world."[145]

Wyndham Lewis was the other strong influence on Pound during

this period. Born in Canada but educated in England, Lewis shared
with Pound a background of being an only son in a family of "impover-
ished gentility" and having had problems with his peers in school. The
two were first introduced at the Vienna Café in 1909, but Lewis initially
did not like Pound. Lewis had been told that Pound was probably Jewish,
and described his demeanor as that of a panther, "tense and wary, without speaking or smiling: showing one is not afraid of it, inwardly awaiting
hostile action." At their second meeting, during a discussion of a kidnap-
ped prostitute, Pound turned to Lewis "with mischievous goodwill" and
suggested that Lewis might know where she was. Lewis recalled: "Ezra
was already attributing to those he likes proclivities which he was persuaded must accompany the revolutionary instinct."[146]

Slowly, over the next four years, the two became friends. Lewis
was considered to be one of the most promising avant-garde painters
and writers in London, and he shared with Pound an intense dedication
to the arts. He wrote admiringly that Pound "was a man of Letters, in
the marrow of his bones and down to the red follicles of his hair."
Lewis was also considered to be egocentric and apparently convinced
of his own genius; as one critic phrased it, "Lewis' vanity touches on
insanity." Lewis and Pound together made a formidable team, and they
made the rounds of London's salons entertaining the guests. As Douglas
Goldring recalled:

Both Ezra . . . and Wyndham Lewis, who introduced himself, made no
secret of their calling, in clothes, hairdressing and manner. Ezra, with his
mane of fair hair, his blond beard, his rimless pince-nez, his Philadelphia
accent and his startling costume, part of which was a single turquoise ear-
ring, contrived to look "every inch a poet," while I have never seen anyone
so obviously a "genius" as Wyndham Lewis . . . tall, swarthy and with
romantically disordered hair, wearing a long black coat buttoned up to
his chin.[147]

Lewis also shared Pound's fondness for sex. According to one of
his biographers, "he was interested in women mainly as a physical necessity, felt a faint disdain for them, kept them at a distance . . . and never
let them interfere with his emotions or his work . . . Lewis' sexual life
was closely related to his creative instinct, and he needed a stream of
women for distraction and inspiration." With his swarthy good looks
the stream seemed never-ending, and during the early years of his friendship with Pound, Lewis fathered the first two of at least five illegitimate
children; he also had chronic gonorrhea, which he believed was a sign
of potency. His principal mistress in 1913 and 1914 was Beatrice Hastings, a South African woman who was in transit between attachments

to A. R. Orage and Modigliani. Miss Hastings was later succeeded by poet Iris Barry, with whom Lewis had two more illegitimate children, ignoring them and even allowing one to be placed in an orphanage. In 1920, when Miss Barry returned from the hospital with their newborn daughter, "Lewis was having sex with Nancy Cunard in his studio, and she had to wait outside on the steps, holding the baby, until he was finished." Miss Cunard was the wealthy granddaughter of the shipping tycoon; her mother, Lady Maud Cunard, was a prominent patroness of the arts in London. Another Lewis consort during these years was musician Agnes Bedford. Misses Barry, Cunard, and Bedford were all close friends of Pound's as well, and Pound corresponded with them all for the following four decades. In 1953 Agnes Bedford wrote to Pound at St. Elizabeths, poignantly describing how she would read Pound's letters to Wyndham Lewis, who was slowly going blind.[148]

Perusing the Lewis-Pound correspondence which developed over the long course of their friendship, one is impressed with the strength of their shared commitment to art and to sex. They criticized each other's work, loaned each other money, and Pound persuaded John Quinn to buy many of Lewis's paintings. Their correspondence includes advice on how to recognize and treat gonorrhea, a discussion of impotence in England and America, and a description of a modern painter who was reputed to have used his penis rather than a brush. Pound closed one letter with the hope: "May your cock's shadow never grow less." Lewis's first portrait of Pound was markedly phallic in design, and was later used by Pound as one of the symbols for his letterhead.[149]

Lewis and Pound became fixtures in the nightlife of London, encouraging the city to discard its Victorian cloak. Many nights were spent at the Cave of the Golden Calf, which had been decorated by Lewis in 1912 "in violent colors." It was the meeting place for "every intelligent person in Edwardian London worth meeting" and "frequented by the intelligent wealthy, interested in letters and the arts." Among its patrons were Rebecca West and Katherine Mansfield. Its proprietress was Frieda Strindberg, the attractive and piquant second wife of the Swedish dramatist, known for "her sexual appetite and frequent attempts to commit suicide." She maintained her own table for particularly interesting artists who otherwise could not afford to come; on one occasion she was seen to "wave a customer away from her table saying as she did so that sleep with him she would but talk to him, never: 'One must draw the line *somewhere*.' "[150]

Lewis and Pound also shared many political beliefs. Lewis was strongly anti-Semitic, élitist, and disdainful of the public. He once wrote: "At the moments when the public's interest is aroused, the public is never well enough informed to have the right to an opinion."[151] In 1931 Lewis published *Hitler*, and he continued to staunchly defend the Führer long after most of his supporters in England had abandoned him.

By early 1914 Lewis and Pound had formally joined forces. Lewis had gotten financial backing from Kate Lechmere, one of his female admirers, to open the Rebel Art Center, from which he hoped to launch a revolution in the visual and verbal arts. He conscripted Pound, whom he called the "Trotsky of literature," and arranged a series of lectures on music, sculpture, and literature by such luminaries as Alexander Scriabin, Arnold Schönberg, Ford Madox Ford, and Henri Gaudier as well as Lewis and Pound. As the emblem of the Center, Lewis and Pound chose the vortex, which they believed to be "the point of maximum energy." The vortex was also an appropriate symbol for the fusion of artistic and sexual energy sought by Lewis and Pound, a cylindrical, irresistible, whirling mass of energy. In a letter to John Quinn, Pound took credit for originating the idea and described the vortex as "every kind of geyser from jism bursting up white as ivory, to hate or a storm at sea. Speratozoon, enough to repopulate the island with active and vigorous animals. Wit, satire, tragedy." The movement would be known as Vorticism and would, Pound wrote, "sweep out the past century as surely as Attila swept across Europe."[152] It was to be a renaissance. Pound hung a banner in front of the Rebel Art Center proclaiming the "End of Christian Era." Anglican England took startled notice.

Unfortunately the Rebel Art Center was never fully launched. Few of its advertised lectures took place and those that did were less than successful. On one occasion Ford Madox Ford, who in stature and mustache resembled a walrus, was giving a lecture when a large Lewis painting on the wall behind fell on his head. Kate Lechmere rapidly became disenchanted with the Center, and by June 1914 had turned her affections from Lewis to philosopher T. E. Hulme. Lewis, not accustomed to having women leave him, vowed revenge on his rival. Finding Hulme and seizing him by the throat, Lewis underestimated the philosopher's size and commitment to self-preservation. Hulme dragged Lewis into the street and deposited him upside-down on an iron railing, ignominiously and publicly displaying the Center's obituary.[153]

The official publication of Vorticism was to be a quarterly called *Blast* with Lewis as its editor. Its inauguration took place at a party at the Cave of the Golden Calf; invitations promised that "the Manifesto of Rebel Art will be read to the sound of carefully chosen trumpets." The first issue, swaddled in a shocking pink cover, contained essays and notes by Lewis and Pound which were "meant to scorn the public that saw fit to scorn the arts." Individuals disliked by Lewis and Pound were named and officially "blasted"; those they liked were included on another list to be "blessed." Rebecca West contributed a short story entitled "Indissoluble Matrimony"; she was at the time seven months pregnant with H. G. Wells's son, though he was apparently not ready to leave his wife. Distribution of the first issue was delayed because of having to cross out by hand (at the publisher's insistence) the references to "testicles" in Pound's "Fratres Minores." When it finally did appear in early July it caused a suitable scandal. "Irrespressible imbecility" intoned the *London Morning Post*, and the denizens of the city's finer salons crossed Lewis and Pound permanently off their guest lists.

DEATH IN THE BATHTUB

July 1914 not only brought *Blast* to London; Amy Lowell and World War I arrived as well. For Ezra Pound the signs were inauspicious.

Amy Lowell was a formidable foe. Scion of the influential and affluent Lowells of Massachusetts, she used her wealth and portly frame to intimidate those who stood in her way. Her trademark was a cigar, and she favored a Manila-made brand; with war threatening to close the shipping lanes, she ordered 10,000 of them to see her through. She was still unknown as a poet, but her ambition would change that rapidly.[154]

Lowell had visited London the previous year. After installing herself in a suite in the Berkeley Hotel in Piccadilly she had invited Pound to a private dinner. (She did not enjoy eating in public dining rooms.) Because of her interest in poetry, Pound saw her as a possible patron; he tried to interest her in purchasing a literary journal and making him its editor. She found him to be "a very thin-skinned and sensitive personality opening out like a flower in a sympathetic circle, and I should imagine shutting up like a clam in an alien atmosphere," and optimistically predicted that his "chip-on-the-shoulder attitude will disappear in time."[155] She demurred, however, at buying a journal.

In early 1914 Pound continued to pressure Amy Lowell by letter. He advocated that she buy the *Egoist* or start a new journal for the Imagists. By this time Pound's literary movement was well established and he was its acknowledged leader. In the spring of 1914 he edited an anthology of Imagist verse, called *Des Imagistes*, in which he included ten poems by Aldington, eight by himself, seven by H. D., five by Flint, and one each by Williams, Joyce, Ford, Cournos, Allen Upward, and Skipwith Cannell. He also included one by Lowell, which Pound undoubtedly believed was a great honor for her.

When Amy Lowell returned to London in July, Pound must have believed that she was ready to help. "He came to me at once as soon as I got to London, and it transpired that he expected to become editor of [an international literary review] with a salary. I was to guarantee all the money, and put in what [literary contributions] I pleased, and he was to run the magazine his way. We talked over the cost of expenses, and we both thought that $5,000 a year was the least that such a magazine could be run on. As I have not $5,000 a year that I can afford to put into it, I based my refusal upon that fact, and it was most unfortunate that Ezra apparently did not believe it."[156]

Given the wealth of the Lowells, Pound's skepticism was justifiable. Amy Lowell declined to set Ezra Pound up in business because she found his leadership of Imagism had become very tenuous. Everyone was criticizing him and, since the publication of *Blast,* trying to dissociate themselves from him. Shortly after arriving in London she wrote to a friend describing the situation: "I find our little group more or less disintegrated and broken up. Violent jealousy has broken out, whether because of the "Imagiste Anthology" and its reviews, I cannot say. Poor old Ezra has got himself into a most silly movement of which "Blast" is the organ . . . My feeling is that his slanging of the public, and his indecent poems, have flattened out his reputation, even Hueffer tells me that Ezra is very unhappy because he is so unsuccessful. The opinion of everyone is that he has nothing more to say."[157]

Lowell herself moved quickly into the vacuum. She proposed a successor to *Des Imagistes* in which the same group of poets would publish each year for the next five years. She guaranteed she could obtain the Macmillan Company as publisher for the annual anthology and—in contrast to Pound's autocratic editorship of *Des Imagistes*—she offered equal space for all contributors and the right of the contributors to select their own poems for inclusion. It was an offer the poets could not refuse, and Aldington, H. D., F. S. Flint, D. H. Lawrence, John G. Fletcher, and Ford Madox Ford quickly agreed to it. Pound was invited but, sensing that leadership in the movement was being taken from him, vigorously refused, as Lowell had expected. Pound had hoped to use Amy Lowell to set up a journal for himself and she, instead, was stealing the Imagist movement before his very eyes.

Pound, furious, went to H. D. and Aldington and told them they must choose between Lowell and himself. H. D., the Hilda of the tree house, and Aldington "told Ezra it was not a question of [Miss Lowell] at all, but a question of the principle, and they felt it only fair to let the poets choose their own contributions, and to give each poet an equal space."[158] Pound's declining reputation and his connection with

Blast almost certainly helped them make up their minds. The future of English poetry did not likely lie in the "End of Christian Era."

The battle was over almost before it began, but an official apodosis was still necessary. This was supplied at a dinner given by Amy Lowell on July 17 at the Dieu Donné restaurant. She purposefully followed by two days a similar dinner given by Pound, Lewis, Gaudier, and the Vorticists at the Tour Eiffel restaurant to celebrate the publication of *Blast.*

There were thirteen for dinner, including Ezra and Dorothy, H. D. and Aldington, Ford, Flint, Fletcher, Gaudier, and of course Miss Lowell. "The atmosphere from the start was one of embarrassed expectancy. The fact that Amy had definitely flung down a challenge to Ezra was known to most of us." Following dinner a series of speeches were made on the nature of Imagism; during them Ezra Pound slipped quietly out the back door. Fletcher recalls what happened next:

> . . . there was a sudden scuffle at the back, by the waiters' entrance, and in marched Ezra, flushed and disheveled, bearing upon his head a large tin bathtub, of the old-fashioned round-edged variety, to the amazement and consternation of all present . . . Several waiters followed him, crowding to the doors to see what next would happen. Ezra carefully deposited the unwieldy object on the floor, swept back the dank, disheveled locks from his forehead, and addressed the gathering.
>
> He wished, he said, to make an important announcement. Since, according to Mr. Hueffer and Mr. Upward, he was an authority on all schools of poetry, he wished to say that henceforward there would be a new school, no longer called the "imagiste," but the "nageiste," school. This bathtub might be taken as their symbol. Miss Lowell had herself inaugurated this new school with her poem "In a Garden," which had been included in the *Des Imagistes* anthology. Her poem had concluded with the lines "Night, and the water, and you in your whiteness, bathing." Hence this symbol was entirely appropriate to the new group.[159]

The relationship of Amy Lowell's large frame to the large tub was obvious and everybody laughed. It was a daring gambit by Pound to discredit her, one that "would have to completely succeed in laughing Miss Lowell out of contention or it would completely fail."[160] Amy Lowell was unruffled. She thanked Ezra for "his little joke" and everyone for coming to her dinner. She was certain that, either as "imagiste" or "nageiste," the new movement in poetry would go on. "The evening ended in a general display of high spirits, a good deal of it at Ezra's own expense, which he was forced to bear as he best might, his face twitching at every reference to his own wild West upbringing."[161]

Word quickly spread around London that Pound had been beaten, and by a woman at that. The players-on-words described it as yet another example of his being all washed up. Pound tried to negotiate a compromise with Lowell, but to no avail. She had correctly assessed his weakened position and on September 15, 1914, wrote to Harriet Monroe: "The truth is, Ezra has ducked and draked his reputation with his last work. His poetry is too indecent to be poetical, and even when it is not indecent it is too often merely vituperative . . . He looks very ill, and has a bad cough, and I am afraid that he is tuberculous. It has even been hinted that this may have attacked his brain."[162]

Pound made one last effort to regain his movement, and threatened to sue both the Macmillan Company and Amy Lowell to prevent publication of the Imagist anthology. Lowell, armed with considerable financial resources, told Pound to go ahead and sue. She took the book to Houghton Mifflin, who agreed to publish it, and by the end of 1914 Pound, resigned to his loss, told friends that Amy Lowell would turn Imagism "into a democratic beer-garden."[163] On the other side of the Atlantic Lowell was writing a preface for the book, in which she never mentioned Pound, and advertising herself as "the foremost member of the Imagists."[164] She had completely usurped Pound's literary movement.

As the battle with Amy Lowell occupied Pound's immediate attention, the war with the Central Powers became audible in the background. On July 28, 1914, Austria declared war on Serbia, and five days later Germany invaded France. England officially declared war on August 4, and within weeks all of Europe was involved.

For Vorticism the war brought hardships. Experimental art forms seemed frivolous when British and French troops were trying to halt the Germans at the Marne; the renaissance of art and literature which Pound so dearly desired would have to wait. In October, as England mobilized for a prolonged conflict and focused daily attention on the Battle of Flanders, the Rebel Art Center officially closed. Later the same month Pound received another insult to his aspirations. He wrote to G. W. Prothero, editor of the *Quarterly Review,* with a proposal to publish some work, but was informed by Prothero that "I do not think I can open the columns of the Q.R.—at any rate, at present—to any one associated publicly with such a publication as 'Blast.' It stamps a man too disadvantageously."[165] Humiliated, Pound described himself as a "banned writer." Hugh Kenner claims that the rejection was crucial: "The long-term psychic damage Pound underwent is beyond calculation."[166] The "End of Christian Era" was becoming the end of the Pound era.

During the autumn of 1914 Pound attempted to salvage something from the Vorticist movement. He rallied those among his friends who had not defected to Amy Lowell and proposed to set up a new college of the arts. The faculty was to consist of Gaudier, Lewis, and Pound plus a few others. Pound publicly announced the college on November 1 and sent notices to Harriet Monroe for *Poetry* and to his parents to forward to the press; he hoped to attract American students who wished to study in Europe but for whom the continent was closed because of the war. The college, he promised, would offer "contact with artists of established position, creative minds, men for the most part who have suffered in the cause of their art," and the level of teaching would be "no lower than that attained by the courts of the Italian Renaissance."[167] Nothing more was heard of the college and it apparently came to naught.

During the winter of 1914–1915, which Ezra and Dorothy spent with Yeats at his cottage, Pound vigorously promoted the work of Williams, Eliot, and Joyce and continued to write his own poetry. He was also at this time editing the notes of Ernest Fenollosa, an American Orientalist whose manuscripts had been given by his widow to Pound for possible publication. Pound was intrigued by the Japanese Noh plays, which he said "were made only for the few, for the nobles," and he also began reading Confucius.[168]

Excluded from the *Quarterly Review* and tainted by the lurid brush strokes of Wyndham Lewis and *Blast,* Pound's income fell off precipitously in 1915. Whereas he had realized £200 from his writings the previous year (approximately $1000 by the existing exchange rate), it declined in 1915 to only £42. His correspondence with Wyndham Lewis suggests an increasing preoccupation with pecuniary affairs, and in the following year he wrote to Lewis: "Can *you* suggest any bloody way to keep MY income wholly from disappearing, from innocuous desuetude, from what G. R. S. Mead calls the eternal mystery of non-being."[169]

Because of his financial straits, Pound cast his eyes back toward his homeland and, in an article for *Poetry,* revived the idea of governmental subsidization of artists:

> I need scarcely remind the reader that for some centuries Paris and London have been the centers of the world's literature. I believe I have pointed out as contributory causes to this effect the treatment accorded to writers in both cities. In England almost any writer of unusual talent who has not systematized and commercialized his production, can get support from the state: first, by pension for life; second, by temporary relief from a royal fund for that purpose. The pensions are announced publicly. The special donations from the royal fund are never published; they are known only to the recipient, to such people as he chooses to tell, and to the two literati of good standing who vouch for his desserts. Not only many of the best writers, but many of the writers who later in life have made very great commercial successes, have enjoyed this bounty in bad seasons and times of stress (late and early).[170]

America should do at least as much as part of its commitment to advancing civilization. When a civilization is vivid, Pound argued, it preserves its artists; when it is dull and anemic, it preserves only "a rabble of priests, sterile instructors, and repeaters of things second-hand."[171]

In the spring of 1915 Pound's ego received an additional insult. The May issue of the *Egoist* was devoted entirely to Imagism, including an article by F. S. Flint on the movement's history. Flint, who had joined forces with Amy Lowell, relegated Pound to a relatively minor role in the development of Imagism, claiming that when Pound joined the Poet's Club "he was very full of his troubadours; but I do not remember that he did more than attempt to illustrate (or refute) our theories occasionally with their example." The issue also contained an article by Richard Aldington assessing Pound's poetry: "In his books you will find nine poems out of every ten crude, trivial, perhaps pretentious . . ." but the tenth was said to be brilliant.[172] Aldington also criticized Pound for his association with *Blast*. Pound immediately told Flint what he thought of the reconstructed literary history and discarded the article as "bullshit"; Flint responded ad hominem by citing Pound's defects: "You had the energy, you had the talents . . . you might have been generalissimo in a compact onslaught [to promote the revival of poetry]: and you spoiled everything by some native incapacity for walking square with your fellows."[173] It was a logomachy which Pound could not win since his arguments were by definition self-serving.

During late 1914 and early 1915 Ezra Pound tried to ignore the war, but it refused to go away. In November 1914 he characterized it as "a conflict between two forces almost equally detestable," an indication of his disaffection for England at this time.[174] While living with Yeats at his cottage near the sea during the winter, Pound, as an American and thus an alien, was asked to report regularly to the nearest police station; the Germans were attempting to blockade England with submarines and therefore shore areas were considered restricted.[175] As Pound tried to rekindle interest in the subsidization of artists in early 1915, the British press trumpeted the heroics of English soldiers at Neuve Chapelle and the perfidy at Ypres when the Germans introduced chlorine gas warfare. On May 7, 1915, the *Lusitania* was sunk by German submarines, killing both English and American civilians, and the war became more difficult to ignore.

By 1915 the war was directly affecting many of Pound's closest acquaintances. Henri Gaudier had already joined the French forces and wrote Pound vivid descriptions of life in the trenches. Wyndham Lewis enlisted, as did Richard Aldington and Ford Madox Ford. Pound wrote to his friends: "I appear to be the only person of interest left in the world of art, London."[176]

Ezra Pound's interest in the war changed dramatically on June 5, 1915, when Henri Gaudier was killed in action. Pound was shocked, and thirty years later Charles Olson commented that he was still grieving for his young friend.[177] He immediately began organizing a book about Gaudier and by September had a publisher; the book came out in 1916 as *Gaudier-Brzeska: A Memoir*.[178] The world had lost one of its great artists, Pound said. Later in 1915 Pound himself volunteered for war service, according to a letter he wrote to a friend; for unknown reasons he was not accepted.[179]

To Pound Gaudier's death represented a tragic loss for society. Since artists were the natural leaders of civilization, and since Gaudier was in Pound's opinion one of the greatest contemporary artists, then to lose such a man was untenable:

> *There died a myriad,*
> > *And of the best, among them,*
> > *For an old bitch gone in the teeth,*
>
> *For a botched civilization*[180]

It was also a personal loss for Pound since Gaudier had been one of the pillars on which Pound hoped to build the renaissance. Now with Gaudier dead and Lewis fighting, the renewal of civilization must have seemed chimerical.

The voice of Ezra Pound, following Gaudier's death, became increasingly caustic and strident. It was as if something deeply within him had been touched, as if the death was a personal insult. The subsequent outpouring of vituperation served to isolate him still further from polite London society.

One month after Gaudier's death the second (and final) issue of *Blast* appeared. It contained work by most of the contributors to the first issue with the notable addition of T. S. Eliot, whose "Preludes" and "Rhapsody on a Windy Night" were his first poems published in England. Eliot had offered a third poem as well, entitled "Bullshit"; given the problems which Pound's "Fratres Minores" had caused in the first issue, it was decided to leave it out. The issue also included a memorial to Gaudier, whom Pound alluded to in one of his poems:

> *Cowardly editors threaten,*
> *Friends fall off at the pinch, the loveliest die.*
> *This is the path of my life, this is my forest.*[181]

In another poem Pound derided his critics as inconsequential:

> *You say that I take a good deal upon myself;*
> *That I strut in the robes of assumption.*

> *In a few years no one will remember the buffo,*
> *No one will remember the trivial parts of me,*
> *The comic detail will be absent.*
> *As for you, you will rot in the earth,*
> *And it is doubtful if even your manure will be rich enough*
>
> *To keep grass*
> *Over your grave.* [182]

In an article Pound superciliously responded to Prothero and other critics of the first issue: "The first number of 'Blast' which came to many as cooling water, as a pleasant light, was greeted by such a mincing jibber by the banderlog that one is fain examine the phenomenon. The jibber was for the most part inarticulate, but certain phrases are translatable into English. We note thereby certain symptoms of minds bordering on the human."[183]

In July 1915, the same month that the second issue of *Blast* appeared, the *Boston Evening Transcript* published a story about the poetic success that Robert Frost had achieved in London. Pound wrote to the paper immediately to announce that he too was a successful American poet in London and that he was partly responsible for Frost's success. Pound concluded his letter with intimations that American enemies were purposefully impeding his own success: "From the beginning, in my pushing Frost's work, I have known that he would ultimately be boomed in America by fifty energetic young men who would use any club to beat me."[184] At this same time Pound had been attempting to raise money to take over a literary magazine. Unsuccessful, he vented his spleen in a letter to John Quinn: "Je m'emmerde du public, they want shit and they get it, and they smack their dung smeared lips and hollar for more."[185]

CANTOS AND ECONOMICS

Bitter, stigmatized, and socially isolated by a war which had absorbed many of his friends, Ezra Pound approached his thirtieth birthday in October 1915 with misgivings. He was no longer a youth, and although he still had the dreams of his earlier years, they seemed no closer to fulfillment. He wrote of the approaching landmark: "Any man whose youth has been worth anything, any man who has lived his life at all in the sun, knows that he has seen the best of it when he finds thirty approaching; knows that he is entering a quieter realm, a place with a different psychology."[186]

It was at this time that Pound commenced work on two projects which were to occupy him for the rest of his life—his Cantos and the study of economic theory. The idea of the Cantos had been conceived during his college days. A great epic poem was the common heritage of Homer and Dante, and Pound apparently decided he would never achieve such stature without an epic. In September 1915, therefore, he began writing the first three Cantos and announced to a friend: "I am also at work on a cryselephantine poem of immeasurable length which will occupy me for the next four decades unless it becomes a bore."[187] His goal, he would later write, was "to cover the entire field of western culture and history in its multifarious manifestations in the form of epic poetry . . . On such a broad and variegated canvas, the mighty and the humble, landmarks and passing clouds, the great and the trifling have their own appointed places."[188]

Pound's interest in economic theory also dates to this period. He had taken a course on economics in college and had shown an awareness of such problems as trusts and monopolies as early as 1912. The death of Henri Gaudier, however, aroused Pound's concern about how war related to economic and political considerations; he later told Wyndham Lewis that his "serious curiosity" about economics and politics began at this time.[189] He continued thinking about such questions until 1918, when he was introduced to C. H. Douglas, a former major in the Royal Flying Corps who had worked as an engineer for British Westinghouse in India and Canada. Douglas espoused economic theories that placed responsibility for the world's economic ills, and for the war, squarely onto the shoulders of international financiers, most of whom were Jews. This provided Pound with a coherent framework with which to understand World War I and launched him on a course he would pursue for the next twenty-five years.

Throughout 1916 and 1917 Pound worked on his early Cantos and other projects. Across the Channel his colleagues tried to break through the German lines. Wyndham Lewis wrote Pound about being "shelled and gassed all night," and described in detail what a man looks like when his head gets blown off. At Verdun alone the Allies suffered 350,000 casualties. To the east the Russians attacked German positions around Lake Narocz in an attempt to alleviate the pressure at Verdun; over 100,000 Russians were killed in the process. Farther south T. E. Lawrence was organizing the Arab tribes against the Turks and becoming known as Lawrence of Arabia. In November 1916 the Germans began bombing London. Ezra and Dorothy lived directly across the road from a battery of antiaircraft guns and the noise was deafening; as the air raids increased, food rationing did likewise. Pound called it "the third year of the BBBBBBloody and Ensanguined WARRRR."[190]

Pound was having increasing difficulty getting his work published because of his reputation for acerbity and indecency. According to Yeats's sister, "after the Kaiser [Pound] seems quite the most hated man."[191] He was rescued from literary isolation in early 1917 by his friend and wealthy New York patron John Quinn, who agreed to help finance an American literary magazine, the *Little Review,* on the condition that Pound be allowed to publish in it. Quinn had provided increasing assistance for Pound during the war years—buying Gaudier sculptures and Lewis paintings, ordering twenty subscriptions to *Blast,* and eventually subsidizing eighty percent of a book on *Ezra Pound: His Metric and Poetry.* For his contributions to the *Little Review* Quinn paid Pound's salary of $750 a year, and he guaranteed to underwrite the magazine's deficits up to $5,000 a year.[192] Pound was allowed to control half of the magazine's contents.

In April 1917, the month in which the United States declared war on Germany and the first Allied offensive began, Pound officially accepted the foreign editorship of the *Little Review.* He did so, he said, because he wished to have "a place where the current prose writings of James Joyce, Wyndham Lewis, T. S. Eliot and myself might appear regularly, promptly, and together, rather than irregularly, sporadically, and after useless delays."[193] Over the next year and a half these authors did appear, as well as Pound's old friends William Butler Yeats and William Carlos Williams. Joyce's *Ulysses* was serialized, and the *Little Review* entered a period of vigorous literary communion.

The editors of the *Little Review,* Margaret Anderson and Jane Heap, were glad to have Quinn's backing and Pound's contributions. Pound's reputation made them wary of what he might bring, however, and in the June 1917 issue the editors assured its readers that "we have learned to be penny wise; we will not be Pound foolish."[194] By the September issue readers were already complaining about Pound: "An Ezraized 'Little Review' will have no appeal to a Young America . . . The Ezras know too much. Their minds are black, scarcely smouldering logs . . . Mr. Pound is digestible only in the early miniatures." The following month's issue was suppressed because one of its articles, "Cantleman's Spring Mate" by Wyndham Lewis, was ruled obscene. By January 1918 readers noted "Ezra's corrupting influence" and referred to him as "devil-begotten Ezra Pound."[195] At this time Pound encouraged Edgar Jepson to attack contemporary American poets, including Robert Frost, in an article that generated spirited controversy. Pound's frequent racial slurs over the months also offended readers, and by November 1918 the arranged marriage between Ezra Pound and the *Little Review* was on the verge of divorce. In the half of the magazine not controlled by Pound, Misses Anderson and Heap carried a note by Ben Hecht called

"Pounding Ezra": "There is about the writings of Ezra Pound the dubious charm of a graceful old maid. I find in him an elusive boredom. In fact my complaint against Ezra is that, having attracted me time and again with the promise of delightful cerebral embraces, he is forever bidding me adieu with no more than a languid handshake—a suave, a fastidious, an irreproachable, but still a handshake . . . he has always about him the air of a mimic . . . He does not present to me a style—but a series of portrayals . . . To me Pound remains the exquisite showman minus a show."[196] By early 1919 Quinn had withdrawn support for the magazine, and Pound exited with him.

The other literary magazine which provided Pound with a reliable outlet for his writings during his late London years was the *New Age*, edited by his friend A. R. Orage. In November 1917 Pound became its regular art critic, writing under the pseudonym "B. H. Dias," and one month later he took over the music column under the name "William Atheling." According to John Edwards, "readers of the paper were prepared for independent comment, but Pound's running attack on the piano as a musical instrument, for instance, or his non-academic position in regard to the art shows he commented on, frequently brought protest, and only occasionally sympathetic defense."[197]

Pound continued to write poetry during the war years, working on early versions of his Cantos and on "Homage to Sextus Propertius" and "Hugh Selwyn Mauberley." But he concentrated more assiduously on prose, as he increasingly perceived his role as a social critic and reformer rather than as a poet. In 1918 a collection of his essays was published in the United States as *Pavannes and Divisions*, and in 1920 a second collection called *Instigations* was published.

The reviews of the books were not encouraging. Conrad Aiken, who had once praised Pound's poetry and had sent Eliot to him with a letter of introduction, called *Pavannes and Divisions* the first entry for "a list of dull books by interesting authors . . . One may say at once that the book is without value . . . it is difficult to imagine anything much worse than the prose of Mr. Pound. It is ugliness and awkwardness incarnate. Did he always write so badly?" Aiken titled his review "A Pointless Pointillist" and speculated that the main reason for Pound's "decay" and the "strangling [of] his creative instinct" was his increasing "passion for the *decisive.*"[198] At the same time Louis Untermeyer, writing in the *New Republic*, called Pound's writings "criticism smothered in a mixture of snobbery and bad temper . . . It is a record of creative talent grown sterile, of a disorderly retreat into the mazes of technique and pedantry. No living American poet started with a more vigorous determination than Ezra Pound. He began by blazing his own path through a trampled poetic forest. Then he started wandering whenever he saw a by-road, followed every curious twist and turn, pursued the will-o'-the wisps of the bizarre, until finally he has lost himself in the backwoods and marshes of literature."[199] Even Pound's friend H. L. Mencken, in a letter to Untermeyer, opined that "Puritan pressure has converted [Pound] into a mere bellower. There is a lesson in this for all of us."[200]

EXIT LONDON

Given Ezra Pound's bitterness, professional isolation, and dislike of England by late 1915 it is surprising that he remained there for another five years. He did so partly because he had few alternatives; the war made a return to Italy or France impossible, and even travel to the United States carried some risk. But he also did so with the hope that the Vorticists would regroup after the war and resume the work of the renaissance.

On November 11, 1918, an armistice was declared: the war was over. Ford, Lewis, Aldington, and the others returned to London. The British Empire had lost over 900,000 young men, with another 2 million wounded. The scars of Verdun and Ypres and the penalties paid for crossing the Hindenburg Line were clearly visible on London's streets. People asked, "What did you do during the war?"

Aldington went to see Pound and found him "violently hostile to England . . . he kept tapping his Adam's apple and assuring me that the English stopped short there. I thought at first he meant that he had been menaced by the returning troops as a slacker, but it eventually came out that he was implying that the English had no brains. There can be no doubt that at this time appreciation of Ezra's works had diminished to a pin-point."[201] It was also apparently at this time that Lascelles Abercrombie, an influential London literary poet and critic, published a favorable review of traditional English poetry which so incensed Pound that he sent Abercrombie a challenge:

> Dear Mr. Abercrombie:
>   Stupidity carried beyond a certain point becomes a public menace. I hereby challenge you to a duel, to be fought at the earliest moment that is suited to your convenience. My seconds will wait upon you in due course.
>   Yours sincerely,
>   EZRA POUND[202]

Abercrombie apparently took the challenge seriously and, according to Ford Madox Ford, went to the police. Dueling was against the law, and a challenge to duel was considered as a conspiracy to commit murder.

The police in turn went to Pound. Ford implies that the incident took place late in Pound's London years and was a direct precipitating event to his departure. Other biographers of Pound say the incident happened earlier and treat it more lightly, reporting that Abercrombie, who had the choice of weapons, responded to Pound's challenge with the suggestion that they should bombard each other with unsold copies of their own books at twenty paces.[203]

Despite Wyndham Lewis's return, there was no revival of the Vorticists or *Blast*. The war had left the country economically and intellectually depressed, crushing out its "surplus vigor" according to Lewis. Pound found that "the minute the war was OVER England sank into black mud."[204] It was not fertile ground for growing a renaissance.

Pound's literary and financial position failed to improve following the war. In October 1919, he was appointed as a well-paid drama critic for the London *Outlook*. The job lasted just "two opulent weeks" at the end of which he was fired "in most caddish possible manner;" the reasons for the dismissal were not disclosed.[205] This scenario was repeated in 1920 when he was also fired as drama critic for the *Athenaeum*. The reason, according to Pound, was that he had intimated "that a certain British actress never changed her character to fit the roles, a criticism which involved my publisher in a libel suit." Pound's racial slurs apparently also contributed to the decision.[206] By 1920, then, Pound had by his own admission "been excluded from every review or weekly paper in England except the 'New Age.' "[207] He was in the same position as his autobiographical Mauberley:

> *Ultimate affronts to*
> *Human redundancies;*
>
> *Non-esteem of self-styled "his betters"*
> *Leading, as he well knew,*
> *To his final*
> *Exclusion from the world of letters.*[208]

Pound's published work met increasingly hostile reviews in literary circles following the war. *Poetry*, the journal of which he had previously been foreign correspondent, greeted his translation of French poetry as "a sequence of false steps made by its author in his effort to gain a recognition that he misses and longs for. And a sulking, aggressive, self-conscious man scowls at you from behind every sentence." Pound's efforts were merely evidence of "postmortem restlessness" and "a case of pain animating the dust of dead desire . . . His problems are unrealities that he has created out of his weariness and spleen, to throw sand

in the eyes of the ghost of insignificance and pettiness that haunts
him."[209] Pound's friends continued to try to defend him, but it was
becoming increasingly difficult. Ford Madox Ford observed that "Mr.
Pound's harsh aphorisms are like sharp splinters of granite struck off
by a careless but violent chisel," and Mary Sinclair acknowledged that
"people become unpopular through association with him."[210] John G.
Fletcher, who had sided with Amy Lowell in the Imagist struggles, accused Pound of having "put greater stress upon his own personal attitude
to life, to literature, to members of his own profession, and to society
generally than upon his poetry. He has said in effect that the thing
that matters is Ezra Pound and his opinions . . . The mere strong expression of one's likes and dislikes does not make any man a poet, and to
go about continually thumping the public on its head for its stupidity
leads merely to putting oneself on the level of the public, not above
it."[211] And Richard Aldington, viewing Pound's London years retrospectively, attributed his decline to "his own conceit, folly, and bad
manners."[212]

Pound read his obituaries and knew that it was time to go. He
had come "to have a month up the Thames somewhere and meet Bill
Yeats" and had stayed for twelve years. He considered returning to
New York but acknowledged that he was probably not wanted in his
homeland. In 1919 he described himself as "deliciously disliked in the
states" and in the following year told William Carlos Williams that "New
York wants me as little now as it did ten and fifteen years ago."[213] The
one thing which was certain was that the Pounds must leave London
because, as he later described it, "the water was creeping up and they
might wake up some morning to find they had web feet."[214]

Pound's response to his inglorious departure was pure rage. For
the second time in his life he had been unappreciated as the great man
that he believed himself to be. England, like the United States, had
failed to acknowledge its true artists; therefore in Pound's mind it was
another nation sliding down the scale of civilization toward its inevitable
demise. And the myopia of the English was even worse than that of
the Americans. When his colleagues in Philadelphia had thrown him
into the lily pond, they had not known that he was a great poet. But
in England he had shown them, and they had still ultimately rejected
him.

His invective rose to a crescendo. He was being denied his rightful
place by individuals like Amy Lowell whose "perfumed cat-piss wd.
[would] be putrid even if it had been done by a pueblo indian"[215] and
by nations like England which Pound described as "only a corpse kept
alive by maggots."[216] "A bloated usury, a cowardly and snivelling politics,

a disgusting financial system, the sadistic curse of Christianity work together . . . that the bright plumed and fine voiced species of the genus
anthropos, the favored of the gods, the only part of humanity worth
saving is attacked . . . in an age of pestilence like our own there is
little but the great art of the past to convince one that the human species
deserves to continue."[217]

As he did all his life, Pound put his strongest feelings into poetry.
The resulting Hell Cantos were, according to Pound, "the state of English mind in 1919 and 1920" and "a portrait of contemporary England
when I left her."[218] They are among the most vitriolic poems in the
English language, published only in a highly edited form, a pastiche
from the bathroom walls of London:

> *Io venni in luogo d'ogni luce muto* [*I came to a place utterly*
>   *without light*];
> *The stench of wet coal, politicians*
> *. . . . . . e and . . . . n, their wrists bound to their*
>   *ankles*
> *Standing bare bum,*
> *Faces smeared on their rumps,*
>   *wide eye on flat buttock,*
>
> *Bush hanging for beard,*
>   *Addressing crowds through their arse-holes,*
>
> *Addressing the multitudes in the ooze,*
>   *newts, water-slugs, water-maggots,*
>
> *And with them . . . . . . r,*
>   *a scrupulously clean table-napkin*
>
> *Tucked under his penis,*
>   *and . . . . m*
>
> *Who disliked colloquial language,*
> *Stiff-starched, but soiled, collars*
>   *circumscribing his legs,*
>
> *The pimply and hairy skin*
>   *pushing over the collar's edge,*
>
> *Profiteers drinking blood sweetened with sh-t,*
> *And behind them . . . . f and the financiers*
>   *lashing them with steel wires.*
>
>
> *And the betrayers of language*
>   *. . . . . . n and the press gang*

And those who had lied for hire;
the perverts, the perverters of language, the perverts, who have
    set money-lust
Before the pleasures of the senses;

howling, as of a hen-yard in a printing-house,
        the clatter of presses,

the blowing of dry dust and stray paper,
foetor, sweat, the stench of stale oranges,
dung, last cess-pool of the universe . . .

    . . . . .

        Above the hell-rot

the great arse-hole,
        broken with piles,

hanging stalactities,
        greasy as sky over Westminster,

the invisible, many English,
        The place lacking in interest,

last squalor, utter decrepitude . . . (Canto 14)

Ezra Pound was ready to depart from the Stygian region, the "last cess-pool of the universe," and find a place where he would be properly appreciated and honored.

CHAPTER 4

A POUND OF FLESH

[PARIS: 1921–1924]

THE CLOUD UNDER WHICH Pound left London followed him across the Channel to his new home. "There can have been few men whose deaths have so often been announced," commented Ford Madox Ford at the time.

Before settling down, the Pounds took a three-month holiday on the French Riviera, finally arriving in Paris in late March 1921. It was a magical city for artists and the logical place for Pound to settle. The creative spirit was unfettered from its past, and experimentation was everywhere—in prose, music, sculpture, painting, photography, theater, ballet. As Pound noted, Paris was "the meeting point for those who have cast off the sanctified stupidities and timidities and are in defiance of things as they are . . . The paradise of artists irrespective of their merit or demerit . . . in a state of pleasing and possibly pregnant fermentation."

The intellectual climate was agreeable. James Joyce had moved there, and Pound had met and liked Jean Cocteau during an earlier visit to the city. Pablo Picasso, Henri Matisse, André Gide, Paul Valéry, Marcel Proust, and Igor Stravinsky could all be found in the cafés or sitting by the Seine. Pound's youthful dream of a cultural renaissance had been disrupted by his London experience, but in Paris he could once again hope: "In 1910 we wanted to set up civilization in America. By 1920 one wanted to preserve the vestiges or start a new one anywhere one could."[1]

The end of the war had released an unprecedented creativity in the city. Dadaism, which was conceived in Zurich in 1916 by Tristan Tzara, Hans Arp, Hugo Ball, and Richard Huelsenbeck, had been born and moved to Paris. Francis Picabia, André Breton, Louis Aragon, Eric Satie, Paul Eluard, and Philippe Soupault provided nourishment, and by 1920 the new style had usurped the local artistic throne. Dadaism "aimed at the liberation of the individual from dogmas, formulas and laws" and represented "a permanent revolt of the individual against art, against morality, against society."[2] It would give birth to Surrealism, "Dada's sawed-off son" and to modern movements in music, literature, and art.

The soul of Dada was composed of one-third wisdom, one-third protest, and two-thirds nonsense. Tristan Tzara, in his "manifesto of Mr. Fire-extinguisher," explained its purpose:

> Dada is our intensity: it sets up inconsequential bayonets the sumatran head of the german baby; Dada is life without carpet-slippers or parallels; it is for and against unity and definitely against the future . . . Dada remains within the European frame of weaknesses it's shit after all but from now on we mean to shit in assorted colors and bedeck the artistic zoo with the flags of every consulate. We are circus directors whistling amid the winds of carnivals convents bawdy houses theatres realities sentiments restaurants Ho Hi Ho Ho Bang . . . Dada exists for no one and we want everybody to understand this because it is the balcony of Dada, I assure you. From which you can hear the military marches and descend slicing the air like a seraph in a public bath to piss and comprehend the parable

Dada was avant-garde in all the arts. It was a cup and saucer covered with fur, Da Vinci's *Mona Lisa* with a superb mustache, an ink spot on a canvas entitled *Blessed Virgin,* the *Vaseline symphony* for twenty persons, proverbs such as "elephants are contagious." The recommended way to make a Dadaist poem was to take a newspaper article, cut out each word, put them in a bag and shake it. "Then take out the scraps one after the other in the order in which they left the bag. / Copy conscientiously. / The poem will be like you. / And here you are a writer, infinitely original and endowed with a sensibility that is charming though beyond the understanding of the vulgar."[3]

Pound was aware of Dada's birth and followed its germination carefully. In January 1919 he had written excitedly to William Carlos Williams about the "Dadaique Manifestoes re the Nothingness of the All," and during 1920 he had contributed poems to at least two Dada publications. In October 1920, in a letter in *Dial,* Pound described Dadaists as possessing "a desire to live and to die, preferring death to a sort of moribund permanence," and also noted that "they talk about 'metallurgie' and international financiers whose names are never mentioned in the orderly English press."[4]

Dada educated the public by manifestos, articles, poems, painting, sculptures, and public exhibitions. One of the best known, the Dada Festival, occurred on May 26, 1920, at the Salle Gaveau; the Dadaists all wore long funnels on their heads and Andŕe Breton had two revolvers attached to his temples. Initially only tomatoes and eggs were hurled at the Dadaists, but the nature of the missiles escalated when "some young people in the audience went to a butcher shop and brought some veal cutlets which they later hurled at the actors . . . the two grand pianos on the right and left of the stage were splattered with eggs thrown by the audiences; the actors were also covered with eggs." It was considered an unprecedented success. At other exhibitions "the Dadaists hurled insults and obscenities, which proved to be excellent reagents, at the audience who still expecting art, tried in good faith to 'understand' what it was really being asked to undergo."

Ezra Pound was intrigued by the subversive and cuckolding nature of Dada; it was more sacrilegious, more outrageous than he was. Francis Picabia, a guiding spirit of the movement, became one of his closest friends in Paris. Picabia's manifestos were cornerstones of Dada: "Honor can be bought and sold like the arse. The arse, the arse, represents life like potato-chips, and all you who are serious-minded will smell worse than cow's shit. Dada alone does not smell: it is nothing, nothing, nothing. It is like your hopes: nothing." Louis Aragon and Tristan Tzara also were friends of Pound, and as co-editor of the revived *Little Review* Pound helped publish the work of Picabia, Tzara, Arp, Breton, Eluard, Satie and Soupault. Pound continued his own contributions to Dada publications, dedicating a poem in 1921 to Baroness Elsa von Freytay-Loringhoven, described as "one of the most bizarre characters in the whole mad pantheon of Dada—among other things she was addicted to wearing pots, pans, and bits of hardware in lieu of clothing."[5]

It is unclear whether Pound attended the more celebrated ceremonies of Dada during his visits to Paris in 1920, but he did attend the highly publicized Barrès trial on Friday, May 13, 1921, two months after he had settled in Paris for good. The occasion was a mock trial of Maurice Barrès, a French writer who had been highly esteemed by the Dadaists but who then started writing conservatively and was branded a traitor to their cause. Barrès, represented by a reclining department-store mannequin, was charged with "offence against the security of Mind." Prosecutors, lawyers, and judges were "dressed in white smocks and clerical caps (red for the defense and black for the prosecution)," and the proceedings were an odd mixture of philosophy and buffoonery. Tristan

Tzara ended his testimony by singing a song, but the testimony that caused the greatest scandal was that of "the Unknown Soldier" who appeared in a German uniform. Louis Aragon, as counsel for the defense, asked for the death penalty for his client and the trial broke up in predictable chaos.[6] It was a trial Pound would remember clearly twenty-five years later.

UNE GÉNÉRATION PERDUE

Pound was ready to forget his inglorious retreat from London and to get on with his work. He rationalized his failure by saying that the English hadn't been ready for him; his poetry and ideas had been too avant-garde. "With each successive book he lost old readers and, after a time, gained some new ones, who disappeared in their turn; he had always outdistanced his audience."[7] But now in Paris, the hub of the artists' universe, surely Pound could not outdistance his audience here.

He continued seeing many friends from his London days. Ford Madox Ford moved to Paris to edit the *Transatlantic Review*, a literary magazine subsidized by John Quinn with which Pound became closely connected. Wyndham Lewis and Richard Aldington visited from London, as did Quinn and William Carlos Williams from America. James Joyce's work continued to be of great interest to Pound, who assisted Joyce in a variety of ways.

In late 1921 T. S. Eliot stopped by Paris en route from Lausanne, where both he and his wife had been treated in a sanitarium. He had with him a long poem which he asked Pound to look over and edit. Pound did just that, reducing the poem to approximately half its length, and out of what Pound described as a "Caesarian operation" emerged *The Waste Land*. Eliot was very grateful for the help and subsequently dedicated the poem to Pound as "il miglior fabbro," the better craftsman. This contribution to Eliot's lucubration was one of Pound's major literary achievements during his Paris years.

Pound was also concerned about Eliot's mental health, and railed against the fact that a man of his poetic talents had to work in a bank. To free his friend from economic problems, Pound inaugurated a "Bel Esprit" project to solicit pledges of £10 per year ($50) from thirty persons to provide for Eliot's support. Pound called it "a sort of consumers' league to pay for quality rather than quantity in literature and the fine arts."[8] Eliot, finding the charity "slightly undignified," demurred and the project died.

Pound made new acquaintances in Paris as well. He met E. E. Cummings and Samuel Beckett for the first time and became good friends with Jean Cocteau. Cocteau, in addition to being a poet, novelist, and playwright, also sponsored new movements in painting, music, and the ballet; he represented the fusion of the arts that was occurring in Paris. It was a period when Picasso and Matisse might discuss music while Stravinsky and Ravel were discussing painting. Much of this artistic fermentation was centered in Sylvia Beach's bookstore, Shakespeare and Company, on rue de l'Odéon and at Gertrude Stein and Alice B. Toklas's flat on rue de Fleurus. Pound spent time at both places, although he and Miss Stein did not like each other. He probably found her domineering manner and Jewish heritage offensive, and "in conversation she put it all over Ezra." Gertrude Stein was angered when, during a visit, she offered Pound a treasured antique chair to sit in with a warning to be careful; Pound "sprawled in it in his usual fashion and broke one of the back legs."[9] She also tired of Pound's instant expertise on every subject discussed and characterized him as "a village explainer, excellent if you were a village, but if you were not, not."[10]

Pound's own literary activities in Paris included frequent contributions to Ford's *Transatlantic Review*, co-editing of the revised *Little Review*, and acting as foreign correspondent for the American literary journal *Dial*, the last position having been arranged by John Quinn and T. S. Eliot.[11] Another book of his poetry, *Poems 1918–21*, was published by Boni and Liveright in New York, and he continued work on his Cantos. He also collected his autobiographical notes which had been published in the *New Age* and brought them out as a book, *Indiscretions*, one of a series of titles published by the Three Mountains Press, which had been started by William Bird, another American expatriate.

One of Pound's most important literary contributions during his Paris years was the help he gave Ernest Hemingway. They met early in 1922 and immediately liked each other. Hemingway, an unknown newspaper correspondent at the time, was experimenting with new prose styles. They shared an interest in sports as well, and at Ezra's request Hemingway undertook to give him boxing lessons. Hemingway's letters of this period indicate a genuine fondness for Pound,[12] though he was less enthusiastic about some of his friends, describing Wyndham Lewis as "the nastiest man I've ever seen" with the eyes of "an unsuccessful rapist."[13]

Hemingway gave Pound one of his short stories, "Up From Michigan," and Pound strongly encouraged him to persist. Pound then got Hemingway hired as assistant editor of the *Transatlantic Review* and arranged for the publication of some of his poems, a short story, and *In Our Time*. Hemingway's career was successfully launched.

In later years Hemingway acknowledged his debt to Pound: he had learned more from Pound about how to write "than from any son of a bitch alive."[14] Pound was "the man I liked and trusted the most as a critic then, the man who believed in the 'mot juste'—the one and only correct word to use—the man who taught me to distrust adjectives."[15] Clearly Pound was partly responsible for the sparse style that became a Hemingway hallmark. Hemingway also described Pound retrospectively as "the most generous writer I have ever known and the most disinterested" and "so kind to people that I always thought of him as a sort of saint."[16] Since these recollections were penned during efforts to get Pound released from St. Elizabeths Hospital they may be selectively optimistic, but there is no question that Hemingway highly valued Pound both as a teacher and as a friend.

Like many members of the Paris literati, Pound did not confine his artistic endeavors to a single art form. He pursued his interest in sculpture begun by Henri Gaudier and tirelessly promoted the work of Constantin Brancusi, a Rumanian sculptor. For a brief period Pound even tried sculpting himself.[17]

Music became very important to Pound during the Paris years. He had always believed that poetry and music were closely allied, and for a few weeks he took up the bassoon.[18] This was unanimously agreed to be a failure, and next he tried his hand at composing an opera, *The Testament of François Villon,* based upon the life of the medieval troubadour. Villon's poetry was set to music for the arias and tied together by spoken passages from Villon and by Pound himself.[19] The opera was eventually performed in 1924 with T. S. Eliot and other friends in attendance, and was apparently well received. For Pound it was a success and, according to Robert McAlmon, "Ezra's delight in having held an audience as a composer was, for the time being, flawless."[20] Pound continued to produce musical compositions of various types for the next two decades, although none achieved much success.

As he had done with writers, Pound focused much energy on discovering unknown but promising musicians and then promoting them. The recipient of Pound's Paris enthusiasm was George Antheil, a young American expatriate pianist and composer who lived above Sylvia Beach's bookstore. Antheil's modernistic works were violently controversial, so much so that he carried to performances a .32-caliber automatic pistol which he wore under his tuxedo in a silken padded pistol holster. On one occasion when a concert audience in Budapest threatened to riot, he "placed it on the front desk of [the] Steinway and proceeded with [the] concert. Every note was heard."[21] Pound helped secure halls for Antheil's works, wrote favorable reviews of them, and in 1924 published a book, *Antheil and the Treatise on Harmony,* analyzing his compositions.

Antheil reciprocated Pound's friendship by helping him with the Villon opera. On one occasion, when Pound decided that he did not like the gentleman living in the apartment above his studio, he conscripted Antheil "to practice his latest symphony for piano and orchestra in Mr. Pound's studio. This lasted all day for several weeks. When Mr. Antheil was fatigued, his orchestra played unceasingly Mr. Antheil's own arrangement of the 'Wacht am Rhein.' In the meanwhile, turning sculptor, Mr. Pound fiercely struck blocks of granite with sledge hammers." Pound was arrested for disturbing the peace, but the gentleman upstairs moved.[22]

In October 1923, Antheil created his first sensation in Paris when his music was played at the Théâtre des Champs-Elysées. Antheil recalled that "rioting broke out almost immediately. I remember Man Ray punching somebody in the nose in the front row . . . A big burly poet got up in one of the boxes and yelled, 'You are all pigs.' " The police then came and arrested the surrealists "who, liking the music, were punching everybody who objected."[23]

The apogee of Antheil's career in Paris took place on June 19, 1926. It was the first performance of his *Ballet Mécanique,* and the Théâtre des Champs-Elysées was again the setting for the musical anarchy. The public had been primed for the event by a preview in the *Paris Tribune* which promised that "during the playing a film of machinery will be shown, which will also prove startling." The composition, the article said, would "wipe out big orchestras, and audiences too." Clearly this was an event not to be missed, and according to Lincoln Steffens it attracted "all the queer people in Paris . . . wild hair, flannel shirts, no hats and big hats for both men and women." James Joyce and his wife, T. S. Eliot escorting an Italian countess, Sylvia Beach, and Lincoln Steffens were all there; so was a "distinguished-looking lady in black, rumored to be royalty," but, alas, she merely "turned out to be Sylvia Beach's concierge." Pound was there of course, visiting from Rapallo (where he had settled in 1925) and occupying the top gallery with Antheil's close friends. It would be, according to Steffens' biographer, "one of the more notorious cultural events of the decade."

The evening opened with a Handel *Concerto Grosso.* The curtain then reopened to display the instruments for which the *Ballet Mécanique* had been scored: a player piano, eight other pianos, xylophones, several fans, electric bells, whistles, automobile horns, pieces of tin and steel, and an airplane propeller. Antheil had likened his music to "just as if you were to listen to the notes of circular saws biting their way through steel mixed with the crash of a steel die plant."

The ensuing cacophony produced immediate chaos. "Cries of 'Enough!' filled the theater, and the aisles were instantly thronged by people trying to get at the musicians or to get out, but impeded by Antheil partisans, while hisses rained on them. And suddenly the center-piece on the stage, which had appeared to be merely a modernistic decoration, unnoticed by most, began to whir. It was the airplane propeller. A blast, as from the Arctic, blew straight down the middle of the theater, and there was a gasp of surprise, followed by a groan of discomfort. More people got up, and as they could not get into the aisles, began to climb over seats. Fights broke out everywhere, and elegantly dressed men and women were seen striking strangers with their sticks and umbrellas, and were struck in return." Above the din could be heard the voice of Ezra Pound shouting: "Silence, imbeciles!" And later he was seen "hanging head downward from the top gallery."[24]

THE BARD OF THE LEFT BANK

The social life of Paris in the early 1920s was as vigorous as its intellectual life. Decorum had exited with traditional art forms, and experimental life-styles were in vogue. A large American expatriate community flourished, attracted by the inexpensive living, the intellectual élan, and the absence of the mores which still enfettered Dayton and Des Moines. John Calvin, it was rumored, had drowned in the Seine.

The salon of Gertrude Stein and Alice Toklas and the bookstore of Sylvia Beach were natural gathering places not only for Pound, Hemingway, MacLeish, Cummings, and Antheil. John Dos Passos, Hart Crane, Kay Boyle, Djuna Barnes, Stephen Vincent Benét, Allen Tate, Robert McAlmon, Caresse Crosby, Scott and Zelda Fitzgerald, Cole Porter, Aaron Copland, Walter Piston, and Virgil Thomson were all in residence at various times during these years. At Harry's New York Bar, birthplace of the Bloody Mary, one might also find such prewar celebrities as Pearl White, star of the *Perils of Pauline* film series. When a ten-year-old American violin prodigy named Yehudi Menuhin came to Paris to give a concert, "the hall shook with applause."

Alcohol and opium were abundant. Ernest Hemingway's legendary drinking bouts were matched by many of his colleagues; on one occasion Wyndham Lewis "could not be awakened for a full day" after three straight nights of revelry. Pound often attended such saturnalias despite the fact that he was not a heavy drinker. He is pictured with Tzara and Cocteau at the opening of a new Parisian nightclub, and he usually attended Ford Madox Ford's Thursday parties which "would begin at nine in the morning and last for twelve hours . . . They began again on Friday and lasted till Saturday."[25] Addiction to opium was not rare; Pound helped care for Cheever Dunning, a young poet addicted to the drug, even buying opium for him to ease his withdrawal and arranging for his hospitalization. Another opium user was composer Virgil Thomson.[26] For those with milder appetites Alice B. Toklas served her famous hashish brownies.

The avant-garde also foraged in new pastures of sexual preference, setting standards which were certain to be whispered about by Presbyterians and Methodists all over America. Robert McAlmon was one of the best-known homosexuals and a close friend of both Hemingway and Pound. Gertrude Stein, characterized by Lincoln Steffens as "a cubist writer," lived openly as woman and wife with Alice B. Toklas; as Hemingway phrased it, Paris was full of "lady writers of all sexes." James Joyce once kept Wyndham Lewis from a "lapse of decorum" with a prostitute by reminding him that he was the author of *The Ideal Giant.* And Nancy Cunard, recently arrived from London, mixed affairs with Dadaists Tristan Tzara and Louis Aragon with an intermittent attachment to Aldous Huxley; going to bed with Huxley, she said, "was like being crawled over by slugs."[27]

Pound's circle of friends during these years met the rigorous Parisian standards for scabrous and labyrinthine alliances. Following the breakup of her marriage to Richard Aldington, Hilda Doolittle spurned John Cournos, Pound's close friend, in favor of D. H. Lawrence. Following the affair with Lawrence she had a child by an unnamed father, then began a long lesbian relationship with Winifred Ellerman, known as Bryher and the daughter of one of England's wealthiest men. To keep up appearances Bryher contracted with Robert McAlmon for a marriage of convenience which took place in 1921 on Valentine's Day in New York City. Bryher's proud father reserved the bridal suite for the honeymoon couple on the ship back to Europe, and H. D. went with them. Bryher gave McAlmon an allowance and had him accompany her when she made visits to her parents; the rest of the time she lived with Hilda. When Bryher and McAlmon divorced in 1927 he received such a generous settlement from her father that he became known to his friends as "Robert McAlimony."

Richard Aldington, meanwhile, following the breakup of his marriage with Hilda, began an affair with Brigit Patmore, an Irish writer and close friend of Pound. Miss Patmore was achieving notoriety by helping D. H. Lawrence, Hilda's old paramour, distribute copies of his banned *Lady Chatterley's Lover.* The shifting alliances and complex couplings frequently made determination of paternity difficult, and in later years when one of the writers ran off with a young woman it was widely rumored that, although ostensibly not related in any way, the woman was in fact his own daughter-in-law.[28] Clearly Pound's circle of friends contributed their share of gossip morsels to the movable feast which was then Paris.

The energetic élan of the Latin Quarter had its risks as well. At a dinner in a sedate restaurant near Sylvia Beach's bookstore, a Surrealist who "was under the influence of drugs suddenly whipped out a long wicked-looking knife from somewhere under his clothes and, turning around, made as if to plunge it into the back of Pound who was seated immediately behind him." Pound was saved by Robert McAlmon, who seized the assailant and "tussled with him until someone from the rear came down with a well-aimed seltzer bottle and that ended the fray."[29] No motive for the attack was mentioned.

Perhaps the most colorful of all the Parisian salons was that kept by Natalie Barney. An American expatriate and heiress from Ohio, Miss Barney settled in Paris at the turn of the century and established regular parties for the crème de la intellectual crème. These were frequented not only by the American and British writers and artists in residence, but also by continentals such as Anatole France, André Gide, Marcel Proust, Rainer Maria Rilke, Auguste Rodin, and Paul Valéry. The very latest in ideas and fashions were served as hors d'oeuvres, and Barney herself was known for her wit and aphorisms. "Why attack God?" she asked; "He may be as unhappy as we are." "He who confuses reproduction and love spoils both of them; the result of this mess is marriage."

In addition to the writers and artists, Natalie Barney entertained large numbers of lesbians, whose leader she counted herself. François Maurice called her "the Pope of Lesbos," and among her friends she was widely known as "l'Amazone." Many of her parties were for women only and became legendary, such as the one at which an exotic Dutch dancer named Margarete Zelle appeared naked riding a white horse. Miss Zelle had wanted to make her entrance on an elephant, but Miss Barney was afraid the beast would upset the tea and cookies. Miss Zelle was also known by her stage name, Mata Hari, and it was under that name that she became a spy for Germany during World War I and was executed by a French firing squad in 1917.

Pound first met Natalie Barney during a trip to Paris in 1913, and they established a friendship which lasted for over half a century. Their initial attraction was a shared interest in poetry and mutual admiration for Rémy de Gourmont, a French writer and critic who was Barney's neighbor and close friend. When Pound moved to Paris, Barney became a regular tennis partner, and she generously provided backing for many of Pound's literary and musical causes, including the *Transatlantic Review,*

the Bel Esprit project, Antheil's *Ballet Mécanique,* and later Pound's concert series in Rapallo.

A visit to Natalie Barney's for tea was a regular stop for Pound's
visitors in Paris. When Pound took William Carlos Williams by to meet
her, Williams admired her wit, her garden, her Japanese servants, and
her laughing doves. And women—always there were clusters of women
around, talking, dancing, surreptitiously sneaking off together to the
bedrooms. Williams tells the story of a French member of the Chamber
of Deputies who, having accepted Miss Barney's invitation for what he
thought was a routine party, became enraged when all the women danced
only with each other. Taking his penis in his hand in the middle of
the floor he waved it in all directions and shouted: "Have you never
seen one of these?"[30]

Pound entered the Parisian social life with enthusiasm, assuming
the role of sartorial standard-bearer. He was described as wearing "pearl-
buttoned velvet coats, fawn or pearl-gray trousers, a loose-flowing dark
cape . . ." and sometimes a sombrero.[31] On other days "he was dressed
in the large velvet beret and flowing tie of the Latin Quarter artist of
the 1830's,"[32] which one observer described as "a queer combination
of an international Bohemian and of an American college professor
out of a job."[33] One woman who was not impressed by his attire speculated that Pound "had got himself up to look like Christ . . . It was
not a perfect likeness, but recognizable."[34]

As in London, Pound's clothing was carefully chosen to enhance
his role as a poet. His finery transformed him into an advertisement
for his profession and he clearly enjoyed it. One visitor recorded his
impressions of first meeting Pound playing this role:

> On the evening of my arrival in that city [Paris], sitting behind the private
> hedge of a small restaurant in the Latin Quarter, I became aware of some-
> thing slightly disturbing on the sidewalk. This was a tall individual in his
> late thirties who, while obviously an Englishman or an American, appeared
> to have stepped straight out of the opera La Bohème. A swarthy sombrero
> covered his head. The collar of his Wotan-blue shirt lay widely open on
> the lapels of his coat, which had a good English cut, setting off a ruddy,
> well-trimmed beard. He sported a cane. Resembling the 1830 artists in
> Puccini's opera, he also resembled a Norse pirate, but an ornamental Norse-
> man, who infrequently had been to sea. His glance, as momentarily he
> lingered, took in the diners: not, however, it seemed to me, so much in
> order to gather their identities as to gather the impression he was making."[35]

Another described Pound "walking up and down in the breeze of the
summer evenings, his head thrown back and windblown, reciting his
own verse aloud. He was seemingly heedless of passers-by."[36]

Friends such as Hemingway, Ford, and Lewis found Ezra charming. One young woman was looking for a laundry: "A male American voice spoke over my shoulder. It said, 'I know a very good one not far off. I can give you the address.' . . . It was Ezra at last. He smiled at me, turning on his considerable charm. There was in fact the charmer's note in his voice and manner; that note which says, 'The world thinks we speak of laundry, but you and I know what lovely secret lies beneath.' "[37]

Others found Pound's behavior pretentious and gauche. Margaret Anderson, the editor of the *Little Review*, described their first meeting in Paris: ". . . after an hour in his studio I felt that I had been sitting through a human experiment in a behaviorist laboratory . . . It gave me somehow the sensation of watching a large baby perform its repertoire of physical antics gravely, diffidently, without human responsibility for the performance . . . Ezra had become fairly patriarchal in his attitude to women. He kissed them upon the forehead or drew them upon his knee with perfect obliviousness to their distaste for these mannerisms . . . It will be more interesting to know him when he has grown up."[38] On another occasion, joining a party in progress, Pound jokingly accused Harriet Weaver, a very proper teetotaling Quaker lady, of being drunk. Harriet "sat back as though struck" and her companions gasped audibly. "The party was dumb with consternation. Ezra realized that his comedy had not gone over and he sat down, self-conscious and fidgety . . . hoping that someone would rescue the situation." Harriet left. "Ezra sat cowed and self-conscious, doubtless reflecting that once more he'd been awkward, and perhaps this time more awkward than usual."[39] Such episodes led others to describe Pound as "so awkward as unintentionally to knock over a waiter and then so self-conscious as to be unable to say he is sorry."[40]

Pound could also be insulting at times. When he was told on one occasion that a woman editor "had spoken of him with great admiration," he laughed. " 'That old creature?' (It was a stronger word). 'Every time I want her to do anything I write her an insulting letter. And the more insulting it is, the more eagerly she does what she's told. Doesn't she, John?' John Cournos, in a voice of enthusiastic discipleship, said, 'She does, she certainly does! And you can say more insulting things, Ezra, than anybody I know.' He spoke as if the capacity for insult was the most admirable thing in the world."[41] It was Cournos who had called Pound "one of the kindest men that ever lived."[42]

Pound's bigotry also continued to be in evidence during his years in Paris. In 1922 he objected to the prevalence of Jews among contributors to the *Dial*,[43] and he also wrote to Harriet Monroe: "Damn remnants in you of that Jew religion, that bitch Moses and the rest of the tribal barbarians."[44] The following year he characterized Russians as "the Caucasian with the top-layer of his head removed."[45]

Another characteristic which often alienated Ezra Pound's acquaintances was his assumption of omniscience. Take a subject—any subject—and Pound would invariably appear to know more than others present. In later years he was described as trying "to be a portable substitute for the British Museum," and having the mien of "a man who confidently assumes that his answers to the problems of the world will have a validity denied to mere experts. In an age of experts, his casual presumptions have the charm of rarity . . . the spectacle of a man speaking out his whole mind on every imaginable issue, with no regard for the enabling apparatus of formal learning."[46] For example, when poet Malcolm Cowley approached Pound in Paris with a question about Shakespeare, Pound produced a worm-eaten leather-bound folio. "I've found the lowdown on the Elizabethan drama," . . . "It's all in here," he said, tapping the volume. "The whole business is cribbed from these Italian state papers."[47] Shortly thereafter Pound gave an interview to the *Christian Science Monitor* in which he suggested orchestrating the sounds of a factory to produce a symphony: "The whole clamor of a great factory will be rhythmically regulated, and the workers work, not to a deafening din, but to a superb symphony. The factory manager would be a musical conductor on an immense scale, and each artisan would be an instrumentalist."[48] There is no evidence that Pound had ever been in a factory at this point in his life.

Occasionally his pretense of knowledge caused him embarrassment. In 1923, for example, he wrote in the *Dial:* "The trouble with 'all Russian literature' is that it contains no didacticism on any points that can be of interest (oh, well, omit some of Dostoyevsky, and Turgenev, et cetera)," and he went on to discuss Russian literature's lack of merit at length.[49] When J. W. N. Sullivan and Robert McAlmon visited him at this time, Pound berated Sullivan for overrating Dostoyevsky. Sullivan and McAlmon, suspecting that Pound did not know what he was talking about, "insisted that Ezra say which book of Dostoyevsky's and of what Russian writers he was speaking. Ezra backed down gracefully, for his knowledge of Russian literature from the actual reading of it was very slight."[50] The truth is that Pound had not read any Dostoyevsky or other Russian authors, an acknowledgment he made to Hemingway the same year he was confidently writing about them in literary journals.[51] Pound could speak and write about books he had not read because "years before he had made the statement in print that one need not have read a book or an author to have a fairly clear idea about a book's quality."[52] Again it was Pound's egocentricity, the same quality which led him to boast of a young English author who "had come over to Paris just to sit at my feet."[53]

SEMINAL THEORIES

The role of sexual passion and its relationship to creativity had been of interest to Pound since his university years and the evenings with Hilda in the tree house. His ideas evolved in London, but it was only after settling in Paris with its more tolerant milieu that he felt confident enough to write about them. The result was two important publications, his 1921 postscript to Rémy de Gourmont's *The Natural Philosophy of Love* and his 1922 book review of Louis Berman's *The Glands Regulating Personality*.

Pound had been influenced by de Gourmont since at least 1912, when he told William Carlos Williams about him.[54] Pound mentioned him in an article in 1913[55] and eulogized him as a great man when he died in 1915.[56] Like Pound de Gourmont had a strong interest in the troubadours, in sex, and in politics.

De Gourmont's book (which Pound translated into English), *The Natural Philosophy of Love,* is an exaltation of sex as a natural function. Sex is seen as not only good but inexorable. Adultery and homosexuality are perfectly natural, and the only true sexual perversion is chastity. De Gourmont compared the concept of virginity in various animal species and concluded that it was utterly without value: "The maidenhead is, therefore, not peculiar to human virgins, and there is no glory in a privilege which one shares with the Marmoset."[57] Sexual emancipation was viewed by de Gourmont as equally important as religious, political, and intellectual emancipation. "Every infringement on the freedom of love is a protection granted to vice," he wrote, and he ridiculed society's hypocritical condemnation of adultery and implicit condonation of prostitution. His book became popular in Europe and America and was invoked by Havelock Ellis, Aldous Huxley, and D. H. Lawrence.

De Gourmont viewed woman as primordial. "Her shape is purer and more primitive than the male's, whose sexual organs distinguish themselves from hers by their supplementary development . . . masculinity, in short, is an augmentation, an aggravation of the normal type represented by femininity; it is a progress, and in this sense it is a development." The function of the female is to be a repository for the traditions of the species, a transmitter of cultural heritage. "Man, on the other hand, functions as intelligence, for he has centralized in himself most of the activities independent of disinterested works, that is to say of aims unconnected with the physical conservation of the race."

In his postscript to the book, Ezra Pound not only indicated agreement with de Gourmont but carried his views further. De Gourmont had written: "There is, perhaps a certain correlation between complete and profound intercourse and cerebral development." Pound used this idea as the starting point:

Not only is this suggestion, made by our author at the end of his eighth chapter, both possible and probable, but it is more than likely that the brain itself, is, in origin and development, only a sort of great clot of genital fluid held in suspense or reserve; at first over the cervical ganglion, or, earlier or in other species, held in several clots over the scattered chief nerve centers; and augmenting in varying speeds and quantities into medulla oblongata, cerebellum and cerebrum. This hypothesis would perhaps explain a certain number of as yet uncorrelated phenomena both psychological and physiological . . . the brain is thus conceived not as a separate and desiccated organ, but as the very fluid of life itself . . . It remains that man has for centuries nibbled at this idea of connection between his sperm and his cerebration.[58]

In the remainder of the postscript, and in his review of Berman's *The Glands Regulating Personality,*[59] published the following year, Pound enlarged on this thesis. The two brain lobes, he said, are "two great seas of fecundative matter" which are "mutually magnetized." This view of the brain is reminiscent of his 1910 description of sex as a "tension" between electrical charges.[60] The pineal gland, sitting in the middle of the brain, secretes lime salts "not as a slow effusion, but ejected suddenly into sensitized AREA, analogy [sic] to the testes." Thus the pineal gland and the testes are closely connected and similar in function.

Woman was viewed by Pound as "the conservator, the inheritor of past gestures, clever, practical, as Gourmont says not inventive, always the best disciple of any inventor . . . always the enemy of . . . abstraction." Man on the other hand is "the phallus or spermatozoide charging, head-on, the female chaos," the inventor, the originator of everything new "merely because in him occurs the new up-jut, the new bathing of the cerebral tissues in the residuum."

The act of thinking was viewed by Pound in mechanistic terms as "a sort of shaking or shifting of a fluid in the viscous cells of the brain." Dreams occur when the head is tipped on its side, as in sleep, "like the pouring of a complicated honeycomb tilted from its perpendicular." "Thought is a chemical process, the most interesting of all transfusions in liquid solution. The mind is an upspurt of sperm."

Some men, gifted and endowed, have a capacity for more creative thinking. The upspurt of sperm and release of lime salts by the pineal "into static sensitized areas" of the brain "causes the *new* juxtaposition of images. The original thought, as distinct from the imitative thought." Pound acknowledged that women's pineal glands may also function but, because they lack the upspurt of sperm, "the ejection of lime salt particles in a female would tend to give her merely an even temperament . . . freeing her from the general confusion of her sex." "Creative thought," insisted Pound, "is an act like fecundation like the male cast of the human seed." He himself had felt the relationship of his sexual energy to his creativity: "Even oneself has felt it, driving any new idea into the great passive vulva of London, a sensation analogous to the male feeling in copulation."

Among creative men there are a few who are specially gifted, geniuses. As early as 1910 Pound had distinguished this élite group whose "consciousness is 'germinal.' Their thoughts are in them as the thought of the tree is in the seed, or in the grass, or the grain, or the blossom. And these minds are the more poetic, and they affect minds about them and transmute it as the seed the earth."[61] Three years later Pound claimed that "the secret of genius is sensitiveness . . . He was more quick than other men to feel the changes of the atmosphere; perhaps he had rendered his nervous system more sensitive still by fasting or mental abstraction; and he had learned to read his own symptoms as we read a barometer."[62]

In the postscript Pound enlarged on the characteristics of genius: "The thought of genius . . . is a sudden out-spurt of mind which takes the form demanded by the problem . . . the individual genius [is] the man in whom the new access, the new superfluity of spermatozoic pressure (quantitative and qualitative) up-shoots into the brain, alluvial Nile-flood, bringing new crops, new invention." The genius has certain inborn physiological characteristics, perhaps a special relationship between his testes and his pineal gland or a stronger upspurt of sperm which enables the brain to achieve insight and wisdom denied to most men. It is "the actual quality of the sieve or separator" which keeps "the due proportion of liquid to viscous particles" and thus makes genius possible. Pound had often numbered himself among the geniuses, telling William Carlos Williams as early as 1908 that "*I* happen to be a genius"; he had also characterized his brain as working in "flashes, not a steady beat."[63]

Two other ideas are contained in Pound's 1921 postscript which would recur repeatedly in his future work. He likens original thoughts, the product of fertile male brains, to seeds which develop a life of their own and may grow to fruition elsewhere. "The thought once born . . . does lead an independent life much like a member of the vegetable kingdom, blowing seeds, ideas from the paradisal garden at the summit of Dante's Mount Purgatory, capable of lodging and sprouting where they fall." Seeds and their dissemination are found frequently as images throughout the Cantos.

The image of light is also explained by Pound: "Let us say, quite simply, that light is a projection from the luminous fluid, from the energy that is in the brain." In his review of Berman's book he explained that the pineal gland contains pigment similar to the pigment in the eye's retina. "Light, or the sensation of light, may well be the combustion or encounter of this retina-pigment either . . . with exterior vibrations or in the pineal with the emanation of brain cells." Light is creativity and wisdom, the product of the seminal upshoot. And since the upshoot arises from sexual passion, which Pound had previously characterized as a flame, then "the body of light come[s] forth / from the body of fire" as he summarized it years later in Canto 91.

By 1921, then, Ezra Pound had found a biological theory that logically and coherently tied together his previous ideas about sex and creativity. The sexual passion he had felt for Hilda had brought forth his first poems, "As the flame crieth unto the sap . . . as the sun calleth to the seed."[64] Coitus was the royal road to wisdom and light, as described in his 1915 poem "Phanopoeia":

> *The swirl of light follows me through the square,*
> *The smoke of incense*
> *Mounts from the four horns of my bed-posts,*
> *The water-jet of gold light bears us up through the ceilings;*
> *Lapped in the gold-coloured flame I descend through the aether.*
> *The silver ball forms in my hand.*
> *It falls and rolls to your feet.*[65]

Pound's theory also enabled him to fully understand the troubadours, for it was they who had "discovered the joy of love under the ascetic, mystical tidal wave of the Middle Ages."[66] The sexual excesses of men like Sordello were not only excusable in Pound's mind, but necessary to the production of their poetry and music. Ten years earlier Pound had hinted at such a relationship among the troubadours in a poem significantly entitled "The Flame": "'Tis not a game that plays at mates and mating, / Provençe knew; . . . We of the Ever-living, in that light / Meet through our veils and whisper, and of love."[67] Passion is a means to an end, the attainment of wisdom and knowledge.

Pound apparently took his theory about the relationship between the testes and the pineal gland very seriously. His formal education had concentrated heavily on languages and literature and was devoid of basic sciences; thus he lacked the background to critically evaluate his ideas. A friend in Paris noted that Pound's "craze then was endocrine glands. He would talk about it a great deal—very learned discussion."[68] In 1922 when James Joyce was having back problems Pound persuaded him to consult Dr. Berman, who treated him with "endocrine treatment."[69] And Ernest Hemingway was also aware of Berman's theories; in writing to Pound in 1923 he noted that the high altitude in Switzerland had decreased his sexual drive and that he would like to discuss the matter with Dr. Berman: "I don't mean that it has removed the sexual superiority of the male but that it has checked the activity of the glands."[70] Perhaps most significantly, it was at this time, when Pound was intensively studying the works of de Gourmont and Berman, that he considered returning to the United States to study medicine.[71] One wonders what would have happened if he had decided to become a neurosurgeon.

According to Pound's theories, the role of woman was as a passive receptacle for man's sperm; it was a secondary role in the creative process but an essential one. Kevin Oderman noted that "Pound's ultimate interest is not in the lady herself but in the visionary reality she makes available."[72] Coitus, not onanism, was the path to knowledge. As Pound phrased it in poetry: "Yet you ask on what account I write so many love-lyrics . . . My genius is no more than a girl."[73]

It was not just any woman who could supply the receptacle for Pound's creative upspurts, however. In his postscript he cited as one condition for creativity "the balance of ejector and retentive media." The better the quality of the "retentive media," the greater the creativity. Thus it is not surprising that Pound selected artistic women exclusively with whom to have affairs.

What evidence exists about Ezra Pound's personal life during the Paris years suggests that he was having many such affairs. One was with Bride Scratton, a married writer whom he had known since 1910. In Canto 29 there is a reference to a trip with her to Verona which took place in 1920 or 1921. In 1923 she was divorced by her husband and Pound was named as corespondent.[74] When Pound had first arrived in Paris he had written to Picabia complaining that he had been there for three months "without finding a congenial mistress."[75]

Olga Rudge, another woman Pound knew well at this time, eventually became a lifelong friend and the mother of his daughter. An accomplished violinist, she was born in Youngstown, Ohio, but raised in Italy and England by her mother, a professional singer. Pound met her in London, and Hugh Kenner notes that Ezra and Olga were immediately attracted to each other.[76] By November 1920, Pound was writing favorable reviews of her violin concerts for the *New Age*.[77] In Paris they spent increasing amounts of time together, attended concerts, worked on his opera, and he wrote violin concertos for her.

There were other women as well. Kathleen Cannell, separated from her husband and living in Paris, recalled Pound dropping in "at all hours, even midnight," to take her to a dive in the Rue du Lappé, to the Bal Bullier, or to a party.[78] What Dorothy thought of Ezra's activities is not recorded. He undoubtedly rationalized them as necessary for his role as modern troubadour and as a biological stimulant to his creativity. In Paris at this time such nontraditional life-styles were de rigueur, especially among artistic types.

THE TRUE RELIGION

In addition to facilitating Ezra Pound's role as troubadour and poet, women served another important function for him. They were his means to transcendent experiences and were thus integral to his mystical beliefs. Sex, creativity, and mysticism had been interwoven in his thinking for many years, and by Paris his thoughts had fully matured.

Pound had been raised as a Presbyterian and was a regular attender at Sunday school, where his father taught a class. He later recalled that he "took the stuff for granted and at *one* time with great seriousness."[79] At Hamilton College he continued to be a believer, officially joining the College Church and receiving communion one month before his graduation in 1905.[80]

Between 1905 and 1907, during the period in which Pound began writing poetry and in all likelihood became sexually active, he apparently lost his faith. In a letter to Viola Baxter written from Crawfordsville on October 24, 1907, he defined religion as "another of those numerous failures resulting from an attempt to popularize art. By which I mean that it is only now and then that religion rises to the dignity of art." In this letter Pound also said: "I am interested in art and ecstasy, ecstasy which I would define as the sensation of the soul in ascent, art as the expression and sole means of transmuting, of passing on that ecstasy to others."[81] Art and creativity appear to have replaced religion as his summum bonum, and although he was still interested in transcendental experiences these were rooted in artistic creativity rather than in the Bible.

From 1907 onward Pound increasingly linked religion with art: "the only true religion is the revelation made in the arts." At the same time he became more critical of traditional western religion. In 1914, the same year he hung the "End of Christian Era" banner, he described Christianity as "a bastard faith devised for the purpose of making good

Roman citizens or slaves, and which is thoroughly different from that originally preached in Palestine. In this sense Christ is thoroughly dead."[82] Pound posed the possibility that Christianity had been corrupted from the original intent of its founder: "Christ can very well stand as an heroic figure . . . he is not wholly to blame for the religion that's been foisted on him."[83]

Pound thought he knew where Christianity had gone astray:

> I think all established churches an outrage, save in so far as they teach medicine and courage to the more obfuscated heathen, and they don't do such a lot of that.
>
> But on the whole they are nearly as great a pest as were the "fat bellies of the monks toward the end of the Middle Ages"; they sit in fat livings; they lead lives of intellectual sloth supported by subsidies originally intended, at least in part, for "clerks", for clerics who were supposed to need a certain shelter wherein to conduct the intellectual life of the race. One demands purely and simply that people oust the parson from his feathered eyrie, and put in it some constructive person, some thinker, or artist, or scientific experimenter, or some teacher of something or other.[84]

It was medieval monks who had corrupted Christianity; they also appropriated to themselves financial resources intended for the support of intellectuals. And it was, significantly, medieval monks who suppressed the troubadours and caused the extinction of their art following the bloody Albigensian Crusade.

Pound's loss of faith progressed during his London years and turned increasingly bitter. In 1916 he wrote that "perhaps 10 percent of the activities of the Christian churches are not wholly venal";[85] later the same year he advised H. L. Mencken that "Christianity has become a sort of Prussianism and will have to go . . . Religion is the root of all evil or damn near all."[86] Christianity was not just dead; it now dwelled in Hell.

In Paris Pound expanded on his religious beliefs. Monotheism he characterized as "a philosophic shallowness and frivolity . . . monotheism is unproven . . . monotheistic thought leads to all sorts of crusades, persecutions, and intolerance." In place of monotheism Pound offered: "I consider the Writings of Confucius and Ovid's *Metamorphoses* the only safe guides to religion."[87] The central theme of the *Metamorphoses* is passion and the transformation of individuals; it is explicitly erotic and directly followed Ovid's earlier love elegies.

One aspect of Christianity Pound especially disliked—its asceticism. B. A. Charlesworth, in a study of Pound's religious thought, concluded that the things Pound found most "hateful" in organized religions were "a narrow dogmatism, a concentration on sexual morality with disregard for other important values, particularly those applying to the use of money, and an asceticism which thinks of the body as evil."[88] Another Pound scholar, W. S. Flory, came to the same conclusion: "Pound objects to Protestantism mainly because it reduces morality to sexual morality. . . ."[89] Pound confirmed this in 1934 when he wrote that Christianity degenerated as religious ethics became exclusively a "question of where, and when, and subject to what documents people should copulate."[90]

In contrast to prevailing Christian asceticism, Pound believed that the human body is good and is a "perfected instrument of the increasing intelligence."[91] Rather than denying the senses, "one comes to the divine *through* the senses, by refining the emotions . . . one could receive revelations of divine truth."[92] There are innuendos of such thinking in Pound's earliest lyrics in homage to "Saint Hilda," when he described "A wondrous holiness hath touched me . . . As her fingers fluttered into mine," and "Holy, as beneath all-holy wings / Some sacred covenant had passed thereby / Wondrous as wind murmurings / That night thy fingers laid on mine their benediction."[93]

By the time Pound settled in Paris he had reconstructed church history to his satisfaction. The original Christianity had appreciated the human body as a divine instrument; thus "Christ follows Dionysus / Phallic and ambrosial."[94] The church had been corrupted, however, by medieval monks who denied the body and made sex inherently immoral; this led to the suppression of groups like the troubadours and an attenuation of artistic creativity. The contemporary Christian church, then, not only denied man pleasure by stressing asceticism but was responsible for poverty in the arts as well.

Ezra Pound's antidote for contemporary religion as he perceived it was a simple one—sexual liberation. Through the female form one could experience the divine and become transcendent. In 1918 he published his "Child's Guide to Knowledge," in which he began:

> *What is a god?*
> *A god is an eternal state of mind.*
>
>   . . . .
>
> *When is a god manifest?*
> *When the state of mind takes form.*
> *When does a man become a god?*
> *When he enters one of these states of mind.*
>
>   . . . .
>
> *By what characteristics may we know the divine forms?*
> *By beauty.* [95]

In poetry written at this time he repeats the theme that coitus is the way to experience the divine and, in fact, to become divine:

> Now with bared breasts she wrestled against me,
>   Tunic spread in delay;
>
> And she then opening my eyelids fallen in sleep,   .
> Her lips upon them; and it was her mouth saying:
>   Sluggard!
>
> In how many varied embraces, our changing arms,
> Her kisses, how many, lingering on my lips.
>
> . . . .
>
> Nor can I shift my pains to other,
>   Hers will I be dead,
>
> If she confer such nights upon me,
>   long is my life, long in years,
>
> If she give me many,
>   God am I for the time. [96]

Coitus is also the way to wisdom and creative inspiration: "And if she plays with me with her shirt off, / We shall construct many Iliads."[97]

Pound's personal life during the London and Paris years reflected these beliefs. His sexual activity could be rationalized as necessary not only for his creativity but also to reassert the principles of original Christianity. Those principles had been lost in the Middle Ages but were represented by the teachings of Eleusis and the Greeks. Coitus was sacred, the origin of creativity and wisdom. The light from Eleusis, passed down through the troubadours to Pound, was the light of sexual energy and inspiration. Eleusis, not Christianity, represented the true religion. Pound shared his dream with his consorts, and it is probably in this context that a biographer's description of Pound and Bride Scratton should be read: "Ever since their first meeting together in London they had shared the idea of building a temple to the true religion."[98] And it is also in this context that Pound's "hieratic" (priestly) head should be viewed: Pound's phallus and head were one, and together they pointed the way to heaven.

THE POWER OF THE DJINNS

Ezra Pound's religion also included an appreciable measure of mysticism and reincarnation. This was evident in early poems such as "Histrion,"[99] and also in "Comraderie":

Sometimes I feel thy cheek against my face
    Close-pressing, soft as is the South's first breath
    That all the subtle earth-things summoneth

To spring in wood-land and in meadow space.

Yea, sometimes in a bustling man-filled place
Me seemeth some-wise thy hair wandereth
Across my eyes, as mist that halloweth
The air a while and giveth all things grace.

Or on still evenings when the rain falls close
There comes a tremor in the drops, and fast
My pulses run, knowing thy thought hath passed
That beareth thee as doth the wind a rose. [100]

When Pound wrote in Paris of "external vibrations" affecting the pineal gland's retina-pigment, thereby producing light and wisdom, he may well have been alluding to mystical vibrations received from his Parnassian predecessors. Pound's belief in reincarnation was also consonant with his continuing interest in astrology throughout the Paris years. In 1922, for example, he contributed to the *Little Review* a complex astrological calendar tying personality and life events to the signs of the zodiac and to the Greek gods; Pound's birth date fell under Bacchus on the calendar. The idea of reincarnation is also consistent with Pound's belief in the universe as a vortex, "a system of energies that is unified at some mysterious point," and of the energies flowing on from soul to soul.[101]

A belief in reincarnation would also explain Pound's assumption about his predestined role in the affairs of men. In London he had written that the artist "knows he was born to rule but he has no intention of trying to rule by general franchise." Pound also noted that "artists are the antennae of the race but the bullet-headed many will never learn to trust their great artists." The artist "has had sense enough to know that humanity was unbearably stupid . . . But he has also tried to lead and persuade it, to save it from itself."[102] "The bourgeoisie are . . . the stomach and gross intestines of the body politic and social, as distinct from the artist who is the nostrils and the invisible antennae." "This rabble, this multitude does not create the artist. They are aimless and drifting without him. They dare not inspect their own souls."[103] In Paris Pound summarized it more succinctly: "Humanity is malleable mud, and the arts set the moulds it is later cast into."[104]

Pound believed that it was time for the "aristocracy of the arts" to take control of civilization. "We turn back, we artists, to the powers of the air, to the djinns who were our allies aforetime, to the spirits of our ancestors."[105] This aristocracy would "combine and form a new civilization in the midst of the unconscious and semi-conscious gehenna."[106] "My problem," Pound wrote, "is to keep alive a certain group of advancing poets, to set the arts in their rightful place as the acknowledged guide and lamp of civilization."[107] He was increasingly derisive of the common man, whom he characterized as "men who simply haven't the brains to do anything else without intolerable mental fatigue."[108] Civilization, Pound wrote from Paris, cannot be based "on an illiterate multitude. It has never come out of slaves, though every state has had slaves or 'the employed.' It, the vortex, has historically come from free groups, or from groups formed about men who had reached a condition of more than freedom."[109] Ezra Pound believed himself to be a leader of such a group, whatever the source of his special powers might be.

EXIT PARIS

Despite the libertine literary atmosphere of Paris, Pound was not content. In March 1922, just one year after arriving, he left for a four-month sojourn in Siena and Venice; when he returned he referred to Paris as "an enervated center" and contrasted it with "a reawakening Italy."[110] Italy at the time was being taken over by Fascist bands coordinated by Mussolini; in October 1922 the Fascists took control of public buildings in cities across northern Italy, and later that month Mussolini, il Duce, arrived in Rome to form a government. Pound was aware of these events, returning to Italy in late 1922 and remaining in Rapallo and Sicily until the spring of 1923.

Ernest Hemingway and his wife joined Ezra and Dorothy for a holiday, and it was at this time that the four of them made a walking tour of central Italy. Hemingway wrote to Pound in January 1923 asking: "Can I . . . preserve my incognito among your fascist pals?"[111] By July 1923, Hemingway had interviewed Mussolini[112] and later wrote that he had not found him very interesting.[113] By March 1924, Hemingway was addressing letters to friend Ezra as "Dear Duce."[114]

In Paris Ezra Pound was having problems. Foremost among them was money, for he still had no means of support except occasional small sums from his writing. He continued to rely on Dorothy's income and checks from his parents, and in October 1921 he borrowed $250 from John Quinn. Earlier he had written William Carlos Williams exploring the possibility of a lecture tour of the United States; if he could make enough to guarantee himself "leisure for a year," Pound said, he would be interested.[115] Nothing came of the plan.

Pound had means of making money if he had wanted to do so. On January 4, 1922, he signed an agreement with Boni and Liveright, a New York publishing house, to translate books from French to English with payments of up to one thousand dollars a year. Pound translated only one book, a mystery story, and received five hundred dollars.[116] At this time he was engaged in the Bel Esprit project to obtain financial backers who would free T. S. Eliot from his bank job. If successful Pound hoped it "will be much easier to get out the second, third and tenth prisoners," presumably including himself.[117] Great writers, Pound argued, should not have to "interrupt serious work doing the vendible trivial."[118] "Only certain men . . . can produce the grade of stuff we want. They must be in a position to do so."[119]

Pound's literary career also was not advancing in Paris. He had access to the revived *Little Review* under Margaret Anderson and to the *Transatlantic Review* under Ford Madox Ford for his writings, but in May 1923 he was fired as foreign editor of *Dial*. In a letter to a friend he suggested that "public laments over this [firing] might be useful. I don't expect there will be any unless they are engineer'd or faked by my friends."[120] Pound also expressed discouragement to one of his old professors about his inability to promote the troubadours: "I have failed almost without exception; I can't count six people whom I have succeeded in interesting in XIIth Century Provence."[121] By late 1924 Pound had become frankly bitter: "I shall never again take any steps whatever to arrange publication of any of my work in either England or America. Tant pis pour les indigenes [So much the worse for the natives]. They will have to cure their own sores and spew out their idols."[122]

Probably the most discouraging thing of all for Pound was the fact that he was being ignored in Paris. Eccentric dress and behavior always attracted attention in London, but failed to do so in a city that had patented the outrageous. Worse yet was the lack of interest among his literary colleagues. Dadaism had died and Surrealism risen from its ashes; André Breton was its leader and relied heavily on Freud's theories and a stream of consciousness for expression. Pound was not part of the Surrealist group, whom he referred to spitefully as "that little coterie."[123] He gradually withdrew, and according to Ford Madox Ford soon decided "that all Frenchmen were swine and all French art the product of scoundrels."[124]

Pound turned increasing attention to politics and economics. Not only was fascism and Italy of interest, but communism and the Soviet

Union were also worth a close look. In his last months in Paris, he spent more time with friends with similar interests. One of these was Lincoln Steffens, whom Pound had introduced to Joyce, Antheil, and Ford; by late 1923 their common bond was an admiration of both C. H. Douglas and Mussolini. On one occasion Mary Collum, a Pound acquaintance, recalled that "Ezra insisted on taking us to a lecture by Lincoln Steffens on Soviet Russia, the Russia of Lenin, in the apartment of one of his friends . . . Ezra listened to it with rapt attention, his eyes glued to the speaker's face, the very type of a young man in search of an ideology, except that he was not so very young. He seemed to have an intense interest in new political and economic ideas, and after Steffens had finished he rose to his feet and started talking about the Douglas plan, to which he had tried to convert Arthur Griffith and through him the new Irish state. He had begun the writing of those letters of his to every prime minister in Europe on this subject."[125]

Steffens liked Pound, but recognized in him a sore that was festering. In his autobiography, published in 1931, Steffens wrote of Pound: "He was a good revolutionary influence, but he had been hurt somehow at home, deeply wounded."[126]

Pound's personal life was increasingly occupying his energies. On the best of days it was complex, on the worst, chaotic. Dorothy hated Paris and much preferred Italy.[127] Olga had been raised in Italy and spoke fluent Italian. In October 1924, Ezra and Dorothy moved permanently to Rapallo. Nine months later Olga gave birth to Ezra Pound's daughter.

CHAPTER 5

FATHERHOOD
AND FASCISM

[RAPALLO: 1925–1939]

THE BIRTH OF Mary Rudge on July 9, 1925, brought permanent changes to Ezra Pound's personal life. He now had not only a wife to consider, but a daughter and her mother as well. Reaction to the news among Pound's acquaintances varied from genteel astonishment to avant-garde amusement; it was difficult for them to imagine Pound as a family man. The birth took place in Bressanone, located amidst the limestone serrations of the Dolomite Alps in northern Italy. It was a town richly shrouded in history, with a twelfth-century cloisters and thirteenth-century cathedral—the period of the troubadours. It was also part of the Tirol, a German-speaking province of Austria which, until it was ceded to Italy after World War I, extended south as far as Lake Garda.

Pound's approach to fatherhood was as idiosyncratic as his other interpersonal relationships. In the Bressanone hospital there was a local peasant woman who had miscarried. Ezra and Olga contracted with her to raise Mary for 200 lira a month. The little girl therefore grew up on a farm in the Tirol, visited occasionally by her mother and father. As she grew older she was taken on holidays to Venice, where Olga had settled. Mary's published recollections of her childhood suggest that surrogate parenting was not an ideal arrangement, and in letters she acknowledged its shortcomings more forcefully.[1]

As Mary grew older her father became more interested in her. He wanted her to be a writer and sent her to a Catholic boarding school in Florence when she was twelve. When she wrote an article about "The

Beauty of the Tirol" at age thirteen, Pound translated it into English and sent it to a friend in Japan who published it in a girls' magazine.[2]

The effect which Ezra's second family had on Dorothy can only be surmised. She was a member of the English gentry, who elected discretion in life; having children by one's mistress was considered both gauche and unnecessary. One of her responses was to become pregnant for the first time after eleven years of marriage. Thus a boy, Omar Shakespear Pound, was born at the American Hospital in Paris on September 10, 1926, fourteen months after Mary's birth.[3]

Like Mary, Omar was not raised by his parents; he was sent to England to be raised by his grandmother shortly after birth. Pound apparently next saw Omar when he was four years old, in 1930, and then not again until he was twelve. Dorothy visited her son in London each summer while Ezra went to Venice to be with Olga and, when she was visiting, Mary.[4]

Pound's correspondence during these years is virtually devoid of news of Mary or Omar; even when a close friend like William Carlos Williams wrote proudly about his growing sons, Pound ignored it in his replies and said nothing about his own children.[5] In accounts written about Pound at this time there is apparently only one mention of his relationship with children and that was by Brigit Patmore, one of Pound's close friends in London. She claimed that Pound "was movingly kind" to her son and that he "always loved looking after the young and advising them."[6] It appears that Pound became interested in younger people when he thought they might be creative but otherwise ignored them. Children also play no role in Pound's poetry or prose works.

In late 1938 Pound went to London to settle the estate of Dorothy's mother, who had died that October. While there he had time to entertain freely. He held dinner parties for Eliot, Lewis, Yeats, and other friends, arranged a private performance of a Noh play using his own translation, and sat for an oil portrait of himself by Lewis. He saw twelve-year-old Omar for only about four hours. Pound returned to Italy, leaving the youth to be raised in a strict English boys' boarding school.[7] He would not see him again until nine years later, when Omar visited him at St. Elizabeths Hospital.

Amidst these changes in his personal life, Pound settled into Rapallo, where he would live for the next twenty years. Set on the Italian Riviera west of Genoa, it was only a few hours' drive down the coast from Nice, Cannes, and Monte Carlo and had become a favorite of Englishmen "taking the sun." Yeats described Rapallo as "mountains that shelter the bay from all but the south wind . . . houses mirrored in an almost motionless sea . . . thin line of broken mother-of-pearl along the water's edge." Yeats also claimed that Rapallo was the little town described in "Ode on a Grecian Urn." In that poem John Keats had asked: "Who are these coming to the sacrifice? / To what green altar, O mysterious priest, / Leadest thou that heifer lowing at the skies."[8]

Rapallo's small size contrasted sharply with London and Paris, and Pound quickly became a town fixture as "il poeta." He involved himself in local affairs, urging the removal of billboards from the Via Aurelia leading to Genoa and contributing frequent articles to the local newspaper. He also introduced new models of bedizenment, dressing "in Byronic sport-shirts imported from London at twelve dollars each" and "a velvet jacket, à La Bohème."[9] In the evening he could often be found at the local cinema, "feet propped on the balcony rail, in a cowboy hat and a velvet coat, eating peanuts and roaring with laughter at bad indigenous comedies."[10] A chance encounter with Pound on the streets of Rapallo was described by Elizabeth Delehanty in the *New Yorker:* "I had been walking about five minutes on the boulevard toward the baths when I heard a slight commotion behind me. All around people stopped moving. It was as if a fire siren had sounded and nobody could hear anything or even move until it had stopped. I leaned up against a balustrade and waited. They were all looking at a man advancing with giant strides. He was tall and broad, with a pointed beard. He had on a white suit that, large though he was, literally flowed from him. The spotless trousers wrapped around his legs as he walked, the shining coat billowed in the breeze. There was a towel tied about his waist and the fringe from it bobbed rhythmically. His hat, which was white too, had been slapped on at a dashing angle. He marched by me, swinging a cane, ignoring the awed Italians, his eyes on an interesting point in space."[11] This adulation was apparently quite satisfactory to Pound, who in 1933 published an article entitled "The Master of Rapallo Speaks."[12]

Pound's personal life took its toll on his professional output during the early years in Rapallo. The period following Olga's delivery and during Dorothy's pregnancy is labeled as "his most unproductive period since 1908" by biographer Noel Stock.[13] Following Omar's birth and departure for London, Pound's activities resumed. He started a new literary magazine, *The Exile,* which survived for four issues during 1927 and 1928. Ernest Hemingway contributed a notable two-line poem to the first issue:

> The Lord is my Shepherd,
> I shall not want him for long.[14]

Pound also worked on the poems of Guido Cavalcanti and sent off numerous exhortations to literary magazines around the world. He continued work on the Cantos, publishing numbers 17 through 27 in 1928. They are a mélange of esthetics, history, economics, politics, and personal beliefs. There are flashes of brilliant poetry, but their quality as a whole was considered inferior to his earlier efforts, and they were "received with hostility or bemusement."[15] T. S. Eliot, in a 1928 review, character- ized these Cantos as containing "some medieval mysticism without belief . . . mixed up with Mr. Yeats' spooks (excellent creatures in their native bogs) and involved with Dr. Berman's hormones and a steam-roller of Confucian rationalism . . . has flattened over the whole."[16]

One flash of public recognition broke the quiet of Pound's early Rapallo years. In 1927 the *Dial*, which four years earlier had fired him as foreign editor, awarded him its annual poetry prize of two thousand dollars for his services to literature. Pound agreed to accept the award only if mention of his Cantos was specifically included in the citation.[17]

Within the American and European literary communities, however, Pound's sun had gone down. In 1925 an American reviewer commented: "Not long ago Mr. Pound galloped up and down the frontier of criticism like an early American general, cursing the enemy, firing his recruits, and embarrassing the fearless with decorations of praise. The gallant fighter appears to have withdrawn from the hubbub; precocious children now mature in black ignorance, the makers of plaster casts grow rich, uncursed. He devotes his retirement no less than his notoriety to music and verse; the music is composed in forgotten modes, for the flute, and the poems have all been cantos." Two years later, when asked about Pound's influence on the younger poets, another reviewer noted: "Miss Monroe has asked me to express what the younger poets now think of Mr. Pound. So far as I can tell they do not think of him. I find no curiosity about him among young people who read or write poetry. Only here and there one runs across some vague knowledge of him. But he is spoken of without enthusiasm."[18] In Europe, meanwhile, Pound was said to be "dead and buried in Rapallo" and was castigated as "an ignorant clown" for his thoughtlessness and narcissism. Pound was aware of such criticism, acknowledging in a letter to Harriet Monroe that he had seen the article "that says what a delightful writer I used to be, and what a shame I have probably petered out."[19]

Another indication that Pound was considered at this time to be through as an effective writer were invitations to write his memoirs. Although still in his early forties he received at least two such requests in 1927 and 1930. He rejected both out of hand, saying "rightly or wrongly, I don't yet regard myself as finished," and "I have no inclination to start dying before it is necessary."[20] Even the literary magazine of his alma mater, Hamilton College, was characterizing Pound as "a little-heard-of man" who was "no longer the high priest of the poetic hierarchy as he was ten or fifteen years ago."[21]

Friends stopped in Rapallo to visit, but it was nothing like London or Paris had been. G. K. Chesterton and Louis and Jean Untermeyer sought him out; Jean described Pound as socially rude but still able to offer helpful criticism of her poetry.[22] There were occasional efforts to resurrect the past. Richard Aldington arrived in 1928, fresh from an island off the coast of France he had shared with Brigit Patmore, D. H. Lawrence, and Frieda. At one of Pound's parties in Rome he encountered Nancy Cunard for the first time. The next morning Aldington entered Cunard's bedroom and announced, "I've come instead of Ezra." Then, covering his testicles with his hand for protection, he "pounced." "Oh no no! Not this!" Nancy protested, and persuaded him to come for "a nice talk and a drive in the country instead."[23] But despite such goings on, Pound's life in Rapallo and Rome was never as salacious as Paris had been.

As the years passed the public memory of Pound's literary work grew dimmer. Aldington reviewed his poetry in the *Times Literary Supplement* in 1928 in an effort to revive interest in him. Ford visited several times, as the two old friends were still looking for "a syringe through which a few drops of our wisdom can be inserted in the syphilitic public." Ford also made efforts to rekindle interest in Pound's work, collecting tributes for a 1932 American edition of the Cantos and acknowledging that "Ezra is not half as much recognized as he ought to be in his own country."[24]

W. B. Yeats also came to visit and liked the climate so much that he took a flat for the 1928 winter season. He continued to seek out Pound's advice but found it less and less helpful. When Yeats returned to Rapallo in 1934 with the manuscript of *The King of the Great Clock Tower* and asked Pound to read it, Pound returned it the following day with a single word—"putrid"—scrawled on it. The play became Yeats's best known, and this permanently discredited Pound in his esteem. Yeats characterized his old friend as a man "who produces the most distinguished work and yet in his behavior is the least distinguished of men." Samuel Putnam, another friend from his Paris days, also noted at this time that "as a literary advisor, Pound was not a great help. In fact he was practically no help at all. It was not that he was not willing enough to be; it was, rather, that his range of interests was too narrowly personal. Pound and the half-dozen writers whom he approved—that was present day literature."[25]

Ezra Pound needed friends at this stage of his life, yet he frequently antagonized them. In Yeats's case the reason may have been the Nobel

Prize for literature, which he received in 1923, and the increasing recognition that followed. Pound was envious of his friend's success. Max Beerbohm, an English writer living in Rapallo during these years, pictured Pound as always mixing denigration with praise of his friends: "The treacle of admiration, don't you know, was always strongly tinctured with the vinegar of envy."[26] It was a pattern that was to be repeated in later years with Robert Frost, Ernest Hemingway, and T. S. Eliot.

Other friends who did not come to Rapallo expressed concern about Pound's literary demise. Hemingway noted the fading interest in his work, claiming that "like all men who become famous very young, he suffers from not being read." In a letter to Archibald MacLeish, Hemingway called Pound an "ass" but argued that his poetic accomplishments more than balanced his darker side; Pound, he said, "makes a bloody fool of himself 99 times out of 100 when he writes anything but poetry." MacLeish had previously told Hemingway that he was "a bit fed up with the Ezraic assumption that he is a Great Man," and added: "Honest to God, Ernest, that guy is as full of fears as a maiden school teacher and as full of shit as a cesspool."[27] James Joyce, responding in 1927 to Pound's disinterest in *Finnegans Wake*, characterized him as making "brilliant discoveries and howling blunders."[28]

Probably the cruelest blow of all for Pound during these years was public criticism of him by his old comrade-in-arms Wyndham Lewis. In 1925 Pound had nominated Lewis to the Guggenheim Foundation as the artist most worthy of their support and had told Lewis he had done so. Despite Pound's generous act of friendship, when Lewis published *Time and Western Man* less than two years later, he called Pound "a man in love with the past" and "a revoluntionary simpleton." Lewis intoned a literary obituary, saying that "Pound is . . . only pretending to be alive for form's sake. His effective work seems finished . . . Ezra's effective life-work is over."[29] The source of Lewis's anger toward Pound has not been disclosed, but it was several years before the two friends resumed their normal correspondence.

On October 30, 1930, Ezra Pound celebrated his forty-fifth birthday. Two years earlier he had written: "Quite simply, I want a new civilization."[30] The problem was that Rapallo was far from where opinions were formed or important decisions were made; it was a backwater, while Pound yearned to sail grandly down the mainstream. Most serious was the fact that he was being forgotten. To be praised was desirable, to be criticized acceptable, but to be forgotten was death.

Leaving Rapallo was impractical. Not only did he have his wife there and Olga and Mary elsewhere in Italy, but by 1928 his father and mother had also come to Rapallo to live. Moreover he had tried London and

Paris, and he was not willing to return to America; where else could he move? Pound was committed to Rapallo, and to obtaining a foothold for his name on the sheer cliffs of history. With renewed efforts he turned his attention to music, sex, economics, and politics.

MUSICAL EVENINGS AND SEXUAL THEORIES

Pound's interest in music, which had begun in London and Paris, became increasingly serious during his Rapallo years. He worked closely with Olga Rudge promoting the work of Antheil, Satie, and other modern composers and turned up frequently with her at concerts in Rome and Paris. In 1927 Olga, an accomplished violinist, gave a private performance for Mussolini after which she "did what she cd. [could] to pave way for Antheil audition later, bringing talk round to modern music and machines."[31]

In the 1930s Pound's musical activities increased sharply. In 1933 he began organizing a concert series in Rapallo, using Olga as a frequent performer. Pound was omnipresent, selecting the program, recruiting the performers, raising funds, renting the hall, sending out reviews to English and American newspapers, and even selling tickets at the door when necessary. The music was a mixture of classical and modern works including Bach, Telemann, Pergolesi, Debussy, Stravinsky, Satie, and Antheil. Olga Rudge played all the Mozart violin sonatas, followed by those of Bach and Pergolesi. The concerts were very successful, and thirty years later the concert group begun by Pound still existed.[32]

Once the Rapallo concerts were underway, Ezra and Olga turned their attention to Antonio Vivaldi, the Red Priest of Venice, whose Baroque compositions were little known. In 1936 Olga went to Turin to catalogue the Vivaldi manuscripts in the National Library and then to Dresden where other Vivaldi compositions were microfilmed. She organized a full week of Vivaldi concerts at the Music Academy in Siena in 1939, contributing in a major way to the revival of interest in this composer. Years later, after he had been arrested for treason, Pound claimed that the microfilming of Vivaldi's music had resulted in the saving of compositions which would otherwise have been destroyed in the bombing of the Dresden cathedral.[33] The Vivaldi manuscripts in fact were not destroyed, but Pound's work on behalf of this composer still stands as a major contribution.[34]

Pound's musical efforts were linked to the founding of his "new civilization," and he "began to dream of Rapallo as a center of a new culture."[35] He proposed that the Italian government build in Rapallo an academic center for advanced studies, and that a new building scheduled to be built for the Fascists should have a library for non-Italians, to promote an understanding of the new Italy. Rapallo would become the artistic center of the new regime, which Pound believed was destined for greatness. And Pound, as "the Master of Rapallo," would be its cultural leader.

Sometime during the early 1930s the living arrangements of Pound's two families changed. Olga moved from Venice to Rapallo and took an apartment at Sant' Ambrogio, just up the hill from the main town. Ezra began regularly spending five nights a week with Dorothy at their rooftop apartment along the water in Rapallo proper and two nights a week with Olga in the apartment up the hill.[36]

Pound's theorizing about sexual function and creativity continued during his Rapallo years. His hieratic head was uprooted from Violet Hunt's garden in Kensington ("the worse only for a few lawn-mower scratches")[37] and shipped to Italy. Initially it graced the dining room of the Albergo Rapallo, where the Pounds usually ate; according to one visitor it "was the most prominent object in the room, something like an American Buddha to which in spirit all present bent the knee."[38] Later it was moved to the terrace of Pound's rooftop apartment and "placed in a commanding position at one end of the roof garden," priapically gazing seaward.[39]

Pound's prose and poetry written during the Rapallo years enlarged on the sexual theories he had previously explored. Woman is viewed as a primitive creature, a kind of primordial biological receptacle:

> Chiefest of these the second, the female
> Is an element, the female
> Is a chaos
> An Octopus
> A biological process
>   and we seek to fulfill . . .
>
> .   .   .   .
>
> She is a submarine, she is an octopus, she is
> A biological process
>
> (Canto 29)

Men on the other hand are possessors of a penis, "the organ governing stability and order and whose emissions, coming as the culmination of the poetic and sexual measure, invest the female, the reader, and the earth with knowledge, law and light."[40]

> So light is thy weight on Tellus
> Thy notch no deeper indented
> Thy weight less than the shadow

> *Yet hast thou gnawed through the mountain,*
> *Scylla's white teeth less sharp.*
>
> *Hast thou found a nest softer than cunnus*
> *Or hast thou found better rest*
> *Hast'ou a deeper planting, doth thy death year*
> *Bring swifter shoot?*
> *Hast thou entered more deeply the mountain?*
>
> *The light has entered the cave. Io! Io! [Greek exclamation]*
> *The light has gone down into the cave,*
> *Splendour on splendour!*
> *By prong have I entered these hills:*
> *That the grass grow from my body,*
> *That I hear the roots speaking together,*
> *The air is new on my leaf,*
> *The forked boughs shake with the wind.*
>
> (*Canto 47*)

The process by which men bring order out of chaos is coitus, which is an act of nature:

> *Air moving under the boughs,*
> *The cedars there in the sun,*
> *Hay new cut on hill slope,*
> *And the water there in the cut*
> *Between the two lower meadows; sound,*
> *The sound, as I have said, a nightingale*
> *Too far off to be heard.*
> *And the light falls, remir,*
> *from her breast to thighs.*
>
> (*Canto 20*)

In coitus an "upspurt of sperm" stimulates the brain to produce intelligence, wisdom, creativity. The heat of passion leads to the light of wisdom. Certain men, the geniuses, possess special powers of creativity; as Pound phrased it in 1932: "For certain people the pecten cteis [genitalia] is the gate of wisdom."[41] And on his stationery at this time he printed "J'ayme donc je suis" [I love therefore I am], a Pound variant of Descartes' "I think therefore I am."[42]

Coitus and its consequent creativity are also the road to ecstasy and transcendent experiences and, as such, are sacred. Thus in Canto 36 Pound wrote: "Sacrum, sacrum, iluminatio coitu [Sacred, sacred, the wisdom of coitus]." The cult of Eleusis, the pagan Greek religion that celebrated ritual coitus, was the true religion according to Pound: "Paganism included a certain attitude toward, a certain understanding of, coitus, which is the mysterium."[43] As Christianity evolved it absorbed other cults and religions, but according to Pound, "one cult that it failed to include was that of Eleusis."[44]

One of the more explicitly sexual of Pound's poems, Canto 39, was written during this period. It opens in Olga's apartment, which had an olive press in the shop beneath it:[45]

> In hill path: "thkk thgk"
>   of the loom
>
> "Thgk, thkk" and the sharp sound of a song under olives
> When I lay in the ingle of Circe
> I heard a song of that kind.
>   Fat panther lay by me
>
> Girls talked there of fucking, beasts talked there of eating,
> All heavy with sleep, fucked girls and fat leopards,
>
> . . . .
>
> First honey and cheese
>   Honey at first and then acorns
>
> Honey at the start and then acorns
> Honey and wine and then acorns
> Song sharp at the edge, her crotch like a young sapling
>
> . . . .
>
> With plum flowers above them
>   with almond on the black bough
>
> With jasmine and olive leaf,
> To the beat of the measure
> From star up to the half-dark
> From half-dark to half-dark
>   Unceasing the measure
>
> Flank by flank on the headland
>   with the Goddess' eyes to seaward
>
> By Circeo, by Terracina, with the stone eyes
>   white toward the sea
>
> With one measure, unceasing:
>   "Fac deum." "Est factus." [Make god! He is made!]
>
> . . . .
>
> Beaten from flesh into light
> Hath swallowed the fire-ball

> *A traverso le foglie* [*Through the leaves*]
> *His rod hath made god in my belly*
> > *Sic loquitur nupta* [*So the bride speaks*]
> > *Cantat sic nupta* [*So she sings*]
>
> *Dark shoulders have stirred the lightning*
> *A girl's arms have nested the fire,*
> *Not I but the handmaid kindled*
> > *Cantat sic nupta* [*So she sings*]
>
> *I have eaten the flame.*
>
> > > (*Canto 39*)

Coitus is pictured as both a natural and a sacred act, with the creation of god as the product. The "rod" assumes a divine quality, for it is capable of creating "god in my belly." It also brings "flesh into light" and so is the fountain from which comes wisdom.

It is also in his poetry of the Rapallo period that Pound more clearly delineated the true character of the Cantos. This was to be his epic, the work with which he hoped to establish a lasting literary reputation. Pound portrayed himself as a modern-day Odysseus, a role clearly described by Leon Surette: "Odysseus' conquest of a cunning and dangerous opponent leads to the acquisition of knowledge and escape from his wanderings. His adventure is a model or paradigm for the adventure of the Cantos as a whole, and for each of the several adventures contained within them."[46] In Canto 39, Circe stands at the gateway to the underworld and must be conquered sexually by Odysseus / Pound in order to achieve wisdom, a theme which recurs throughout the Cantos. Once she is conquered, the hero can move on toward paradise, which Pound described in a 1927 letter to his father as "the 'magic moment' or moment of metamorphosis, bust thru from quotidien [sic] into 'divine or permanent world.' Gods, etc."[47] Given Pound's punctiliousness about using the perfect word, his use of "bust" in this context is interesting. He may have had in mind the Gaudier bust, the hieratic head, as the means for achieving paradise. It silently looked out upon the sea where Odysseus once sailed.

THE BEAST WITH A HUNDRED LEGS

Pound's interest in economics, the hallmark of his Rapallo years, did not spring full-blown from the Ligurian soil. One finds throughout his writings references to his grandfather's fortunes made and lost and also to his father's job in the Philadelphia mint, which Ezra visited as a child. In 1912 he had published comments on economic theories in the *New Age* and in 1915, his professional reputation in decline, he began to study economics in earnest. By the time he was introduced to C. H. Douglas and the Social Credit theories in 1918, Pound was being disparaged by most of literary London. It was a personal bear market, then, that provided the milieu for Pound's economic theories.

It is important to understand Douglas's ideas, for they assumed a dominant position in Pound's thinking. The theories state that people should be paid for work done as long as a product is involved, for example a sewn garment, a manufactured good, harvested corn, or a work of art. People should not be allowed to make money by manipulating money, as do landlords (from rents), bankers (from interest), and stockholders (from dividends). Usury, the making of money by manipulating money (literally moneylending) was considered by Douglas to be the great abomination of contemporary civilization. It allowed a small group of people, the usurers, to control the supply of money and to thereby regulate the economy for their own gain.

The cure for these economic evils, according to Douglas, was to put the money supply under the control of the state and thereby effectively abolish usury. No longer would money languish in banks and be used to make more money, but rather it would be put into permanent circulation. People would have more to spend, more jobs would be created, and everyone except the usurers would thrive. Douglas even proposed a dividend which would be paid to all citizens depending on whether more or less money was to be put into circulation; hence the label Social Credit.[48]

By 1920 Pound had become a firm believer. He gave Douglas's new book, *Economic Democracy*, a warm reception in the *Little Review*. In another issue of the journal Pound attacked "a bloated usury, a cowardly and snivelling politics, a disgusting financial system." The following year, in an interview with the *New York Herald Tribune*, Pound praised Douglas's theories as "the one contribution to creative thought which has been made in five years" and went into detail regarding the evils that usury had wrought.[49] In Cantos written during the late London years Pound had also excoriated usurers:

> *Directors, dealers through holding companies,*
> *Deacons in churches, owning slum properties,*
> Alias *usurers in excelsis,*
> > *the quintessential essence of usurers*
>
> > > (*Canto 12*)

> *dead maggots begetting live maggots,*
> > *slum owners,*

> *usurers squeezing crab lice*
>
> (*Canto 14*)

> *The beast with a hundred legs, USURA*
>
> (*Canto 15*)

Ezra Pound's economic beliefs were from the beginning closely associated with his own financial situation, with his theories about war, and with his political inclinations. "Whatever economic passions I now have," he wrote in 1933, "began *ab initio* from having crimes against living art thrust under my perceptions." Douglas was the first economist, claimed Pound, "to postulate a place for the arts, literature and the amenities in a system of economics." And he was also the first economist "to include creative art and writing in an economic scheme, and the first to give the painter or sculptor or poet a definite reason for being interested in economics; namely that a better economic system would release more energy for invention and design."[50] Under Douglas's system an artist would be paid appropriate remuneration for the art produced and would not have to work at menial tasks. It would be a return to the medieval tradition, when great artists were supported by society. Pound thought he had found someone "who understood the difficulties of the artist in an industrial world, and who was ready to speak in his defense."[51]

Pound's economics were also closely allied with his beliefs about war. His initial introduction to Douglas and Social Credit coincided with the termination of World War I, a war which had taken the life of both Henri Gaudier and the nascent Vorticist movement. Pound was enraged at these losses and, according to his own account, "in 1918 began investigation of causes of war, to oppose same."[52] He quickly concluded that wars were economic phenomena caused by a conspiracy of armaments manufacturers and usurers: "I can still hear the pleasant voice of a hale, hearty chap who was selling torpedo-boats to Russia back in 1912 or '13. 'Peace? Nao, not while yew hav' two billions of money invested in the making of war machinery.' That is about the size of it; and there is also the problem of usury and mankind's incapacity to grasp the simple equation $6 \div 6 = 1$."[53]

During his Rapallo years Pound sounded this theme increasingly often. In 1928 he co-authored a letter urging the Carnegie Foundation to study the causes of war, including the "intense production and sale of munitions" and "the intrigues of interested cliques."[54] Two years later in an interview with the *Chicago Tribune,* he complained that everybody was studying the effects of war but nobody was studying its causes. Pound believed that he knew the causes: "Usurers provoke wars to impose monopolies in their own interests, so that they can get the world by the throat. Usurers provoke wars to create debts, so that they can extort the interest and rake in the profits resulting from changes in the values of monetary units."[55]

Pound's economic theories also blended easily with his political leanings. He had expressed a distrust of democracy as early as 1912 in "Patria Mia," arguing that it weakened humanity. The American democratic system had begun as a noble experiment under men like Jefferson and Adams, but, Pound believed, it had become corrupted and debased. He focused especially on the decision by the United States government in 1913 to issue no more money itself but rather to turn that function over to the independent Federal Reserve Bank.[56] This not only put the control of money squarely into the hands of usurers but was contrary to the Constitution and a betrayal of the American people. History was viewed by Pound purely in economic terms: "History without econ. [economics] is just gibberish . . . the black hand of the banker blots out the sun."[57]

The problem with democracy in Pound's estimation was that people are not intelligent enough to elect good leaders: "The great mass of mankind are [sic] mediocre, that is axiomatic."[58] Therefore they elect presidents like Wilson, Harding, Coolidge, and Hoover, characterized by Pound as "the predominent SHIT chosen by the electorate = 4 barrels of pisss."[59] This in turn leads to a further transfer of economic power by these leaders to the usurers and armaments manufacturers: "It is this human stupidity that elects the Wilsons and Ll [Lloyd] Georges and puts power into the hands of the gun-makers, demanding that they blot out the sunlight."[60]

There was also a personal side to Pound's economic criticism of democracy. In 1922 he wrote that "democracy has signally failed to provide for its best writers," and later added that "the whole drift of democratic kultur is toward devitalization of letters and scholarship."[61] In 1933 he published an essay called "Murder by Capital." In it he flayed democracies for failing to recognize and support their best artists and connected this failure to the capitalist system. Pound's own "unemployment problem that I have been faced with for a quarter of a century" was alluded to as a case in point.[62] In a letter to a friend he phrased his grievance more succinctly: "The problem whether a country that does not provide me with $50. a month in regards to my literary work shd. [should] be regarded as a country or a shit house is one that I cheerfully leave to posterity."[63]

In place of democracy Ezra Pound preferred governments run by an intellectual élite, and from the early 1920s on he was attracted by such regimes. Rule by a totalitarian party, he argued, involves more real responsibility than does constitutionalism.[64] At first he was attracted by communism. He read John Reed's *Ten Days That Shook The World*, praised Lenin, and contributed to a communist-inspired journal called *Front*. In 1927 he wrote that "both Fascio and the Russian revolution are interesting phenomena."[65] In 1930 he sent Michael Gold, editor of the communist *New Masses*, a personally insulting letter, and Gold responded with a scathing open letter to Pound which he signed, "hoping to see you in hell first."[66] Pound's enthusiasm for communism abated thereafter.

FASCISM, MUSSOLINI, AND HITLER

In 1922 Pound became interested in Fascism as an alternative form of government. Mussolini had crushed the trade unions by burning their offices. Shortly thereafter, Il Duce led his Black Shirts triumphantly into Rome. Landowners, industrialists, Army officers, and the police loved him. Democratic principles had no place in his government for he, and the Grand Council of Fascism, would decide what was best for the people. He promised to recapture the glory that once was Rome.

Thus it is not surprising to find Pound praising Mussolini shortly after he settled in Rapallo. In a letter to Harriet Monroe in 1926 he said: "I personally think extremely well of Mussolini. If one compares him to American presidents (the last three) or British premiers, etc., in fact one can NOT without insulting him."[67] Pound began a scrapbook of Mussolini's life and work and became enthralled with his dreams. Writing to Mussolini to offer suggestions on economic and political issues, Pound signed his letters "with devoted homage" and "with all my faith."[68] In 1931 he began dating his personal letters using the Fascist calendar, which commenced with Mussolini's 1922 arrival in Rome; on his letterhead he inserted a motto by Mussolini ("Liberty is a duty, not a right"). The following year he helped plan a film on the history of Fascism.[69]

Pound wanted very much to meet Mussolini and in 1932 requested an audience. According to information in the FBI files, Olga Rudge, through her prior acquaintance with Mussolini, may have helped arrange it. The interview took place in Rome on January 30, 1933. They talked briefly about poetry, and Mussolini complimented Pound. Pound, flattered, was confirmed in his belief of Mussolini's greatness. He next presented Mussolini with a list of questions about economics. "These are very difficult questions," exclaimed Mussolini. "I can't answer these off hand . . . It will take a little thought." He then told Pound that he would let him know the following day if he wanted to talk to him further. He did not, and Pound returned to Rapallo. In Pound's estimation the interview had been a major success, and he subsequently referred to Mussolini as "Boss" or "Muss." In later years Pound requested other interviews, but Mussolini was always "indisposed."[70]

As Mussolini's power and influence increased, Pound's admiration followed. In 1932 Pound completed a book manuscript favorably comparing Mussolini with Thomas Jefferson. After being rejected by forty publishers, the book was finally published as *Jefferson And / Or Mussolini* in 1935. In it Mussolini was extolled as a modern-day Jefferson who was getting the trains to run on time, reclaiming swampland on which to build cities, ridding the nation of its parasites, and rebuilding it to greatness: "Jefferson was one genius and Mussolini is another . . . The fundamental likenesses between these two men are probably greater than their differences." The Fascist Revolution begun by Mussolini was viewed by Pound as a direct extension of the American Revolution: "The heritage of Jefferson, Quincy Adams, old John Adams, Jackson, Van Buren is HERE, NOW *in the Italian Peninsula* at the beginning of Fascist second decennio, not in Massachusetts or Delaware."[71]

An interest in Mussolini and sympathy with Fascist beliefs were not unusual in the United States and Europe in the 1920s and early '30s. American businessmen praised Mussolini, and the Luce publishing empire (*Time, Life,* and *Fortune*) was favorable to him. In England both Winston Churchill and Neville Chamberlain expressed admiration. Many artists had Fascist leanings, including some of Ezra Pound's closest acquaintances: Eliot, Yeats, Lewis, Cocteau.[72]

What distinguished Pound from his fellow travelers was the fanaticism of his belief and his persistence in it long after his friends had given it up. The watershed occurred in 1935 when Mussolini invaded Ethiopia in a clear demonstration of expansionist policy. The western world was horrified and condemned Mussolini strongly. Pound responded by praising Mussolini and defending his Ethiopian "acquisition," writing more than twenty articles over the next year for an Italian newspaper published in London for the English. "No man living," Pound claimed, "has preserved the Peace of Europe as often as Benito Mussolini."[73] Pound was aboard the Fascist express and the next scheduled stop was glory.

Pound continued to defend Mussolini and Fascism throughout the 1930s. He believed that the movement would gain momentum and spread, and he watched incipient Fascist stirrings in England and other European countries closely. Oswald Mosley was becoming a small but noisy political force in London, leading his British Union of Fascist

Black Shirts in forays reminiscent of Mussolini's early activities. Mosley also began publishing the *Fascist Quarterly* (which later became the *British Union Quarterly*) with articles such as "Gold and Silver," "The History of Usury," and (from Joseph Goebbels) "What is Socialism?" Pound wrote to Mosley in 1934, met him two years later, and corresponded with him until 1959.[74] He became a regular contributor to Mosley's journal, which published eight of his articles between 1936 and 1940; most were mixtures of economic theory and praise for Mussolini.

It is not difficult to identify reasons why Pound was so strongly attracted to Fascism in general and to Mussolini in particular. Foremost among these was economics. Pound believed that only Fascism could solve the economic ills of the world. "Usury is the cancer of the world," he wrote, "which only the surgeon's knife of Fascism can cut out of the life of nations."[75] Mussolini in Italy and Hitler in Germany had made preliminary steps to free their national economies from the international bankers and usurers, and so from Pound's viewpoint were moving in the right direction. "The Rome-Berlin Axis," said Pound, "was the first serious attack on the usurocracy since the time of Abraham Lincoln."[76]

Those who knew Pound best in Rapallo during the thirties confirm that economic beliefs were a major attraction of Fascism for him. Father Desmond Chute, who lived in Rapallo at that time and who helped Pound with the concerts, said that Pound freely admitted viewing Fascism "as a platform for monetary reform" and that he believed he could convert Mussolini to the economic theories of C. H. Douglas and Silvio Gesell, a German economist who advocated a tax on money being held by individuals as a means of ensuring its constant circulation.[77] James Laughlin, an affluent young man from Pittsburgh, spent several weeks with Pound. When asked in 1939 why Pound was such a devoted Fascist, Laughlin replied: "Mussolini's financial program has a distinct affinity to Social Credit. Manifestly the Duce has 'cracked down' on private banking by nationalizing the central bank of issue, foreign exchange, and large scale credit, and it is Pound's conviction that these steps, and others like them, portend the establishment of a monetary system along Douglasite lines." Laughlin went on to note that for Pound, "discipline which insures social security to him seems preferable to 'liberty' which fosters exploitation of the mass by the few. A rationalization, perhaps, but something to think about too!"[78]

The association between Social Credit's economic theories and Fascism, it should be noted, was Pound's. Douglas himself was not a Fascist, and when the American Social Credit Movement was organized in 1936 they specifically disavowed Fascism. One year previously Pound had complained that "even Douglas seems unaware of the profound harmony between his economics and Fascism."[79]

Another important attraction of Fascism for Ezra Pound was its inherent élitism and belief in a governing aristocracy. This was compatible with Pound's previous inclinations, although since his London years his theories had become considerably more sophisticated. During the 1920s Pound became intrigued with the writings of Leo Frobenius, a German anthropologist, and in 1928 Pound visited him. When Pound published his *Guide to Kulchur* in 1938 Frobenius's work was cited as one of seven essential books in a class with *The Odyssey* and *The Divine Comedy;* without it "a man cannot place any book or work of art in relation to the rest."[80]

Frobenius believed that cultures are living organisms which arise out of races and which express the races as the leaves of a tree. As races degenerate and die, so do the cultures. But there is a central core to a culture which cannot die, its essence; this Frobenius called the soul-culture or "paideuma." Pound believed that artists are the torch-carriers of all cultures, and Frobenius provided him with a mystical framework for this belief. The poet, musician, and sculptor become the keepers of the "paideuma," the soul of the culture.

Frobenius has been described as "a pacesetter of fascism." He influenced Oswald Spengler (*The Decline of the West*) and Carl Jung as well as Pound. Characteristics which others have noted were "his lack of critical acumen, his contempt for analytical knowledge, his hatred of any kind of education, his irrationality, his pseudo-scientific speculations" and "his megalomania."[81]

Just as Pound's dislike of democracy had a personal aspect, so too did his affinity for Fascism. Pound believed that Mussolini shared his view of the importance of poetry: "Mussolini has told his people that poetry is a necessity *to the state,*" a fact which Pound said proved "a higher state of civilization in Rome than in London or Washington."[82] Moreover Pound advocated viewing Mussolini himself as an artist: "I don't believe any estimate of Mussolini will be valid unless it *starts* from his passion for construction. Treat him as *artifex* and all the details fall into place. Take him as anything save the artist and you will get muddled with contradictions."[83]

As Mussolini was an artist, so too was Fascism sympathetic to the arts. "The fascist revolution was FOR the preservation of certain liberties and FOR the maintenance of a certain level of culture," Pound wrote.[84] To Wyndham Lewis he wrote that "certainly HERE in Italy is more freedom to print than under the shitten arse of the Times in London / and more goddam chance for any man who wants to paint or carve anything of ANY merit."[85] In Pound's estimation Fascism appreciated and valued its artists. As proof of this he received a free pass on the Italian railroads because of his profession as a writer.[86]

In the later Rapallo years Ezra Pound became interested in Hitler and National Socialism as well. The attraction was at least partly economic in origin. Pound frequently praised Hitler's "struggle against international finance and loan capital," and he corresponded with Feder and Schacht, Hitler's two chief economic planners.[87] On at least two occasions Pound signed letters with the Nazi swastika, and on others he closed with "Heil Hitler, yrs. Ez."[88]

Pound's friend Wyndham Lewis was a devout supporter of Hitler. In 1931 he published a book of praise, *Hitler*, in which he advocated Aryanism as "the only sane and realistic policy in the midst of a disintegrating world," and he continued to support the Führer until the late 1930s. In 1939, however, Lewis retracted his support and published *The Hitler Cult*, which was highly critical. Pound wrote to Lewis, very unhappy with his friend's change of heart, even suggesting that Lewis had done it for money.[89] Just as Pound persisted in his support of Mussolini after most other Western intellectuals withdrew, so he also continued to praise and support Hitler.

One of the most striking aspects of Pound's writings on economics and Fascism was his absolute conviction that he was right. Nowhere do doubts intrude into his line of reasoning, nowhere does he question whether he might be mistaken. Economists or political scientists who disagreed with his theories were dismissed with denigration or hauteur. John Maynard Keynes was merely a "saphead,"[90] and other opponents of Fascist economics elicited in Pound "contempt at the sight of some bloater with great position either stalling, or avoiding the point or being just too god-damned stupid or too superficially silly to understand something that is put plumb-bang in front of him, and if he weren't just a low-down, common, yaller hound dog he would look at and having seen would act on his knowledge."[91]

The reason for this certainty in Ezra Pound's thinking probably lay in the way he attained his knowledge. As explained by an Italian friend: "One day he explained to me that Fascist doctrine had its origin in Confucius, passed by way of Cavalcanti, Flaubert, the German ethnologist Leo Frobenius and Enrico Pea directly to Mussolini, Hitler and Oswald Mosley."[92] Since Pound believed that he also was in this line of succession, then he too had been given the special knowledge. It was a continuation of his mystical beliefs. The unusual man, the great artist, inevitably aims straight for the truth without such obstructions as human reasoning. In *Guide to Kulchur,* written during the late Rapallo years, Pound summarized this concept: "By genius I mean an inevitable swiftness and rightness in a given field . . . 'Human Greatness' is an unusual energy coupled with straightness, the direct shooting mind."[93]

THE PROTOCOLS OF ZION

It is impossible to understand Ezra Pound's economic and political beliefs without also understanding how he was influenced by *The Protocols of The Learned Elders of Zion*, usually referred to simply as *The Protocols of Zion*. The book consists of notes from meetings of Jewish "elders" which took place in 1897. At the meetings the "elders" outlined a secret plan by which Jews would achieve world domination, a plan which was said to have originated with King Solomon in 929 B.C. and been in operation for three thousand years. There are twenty-four Protocols; the first nine outline how world domination was to be effected and the other fifteen describe what the new world order would be like under the Jews. Central to the plan for achieving domination was control of the world's economy, to be achieved primarily by manipulating gold and causing economic crises. Democracy was said by the "elders" to be the best form of government for promoting the Jewish plan and the easiest form to subvert. The press was also integral to the scheme, for by controlling the press Jews could control public opinion. *The Protocols* suggest all types of machination and manipulations to achieve the ultimate goal: Jews are encouraged to masquerade as Gentiles for generations in order to acquire power, Jewish men should seduce Gentile women to disseminate Jewish genes, and Jewish bankers and businessmen should surround themselves with Gentile front men to avoid suspicion.

The Protocols first appeared in Russia about 1905. From the beginning the book was suspected of being a fabrication of the Czar's police force, and in the 1930s an international investigatory commission came to the same conclusion. Its purpose was to promote both anti-Semitism and antidemocratic feeling among the people, and in the former it succeeded. Its circulation helped stimulate pogroms against Russian Jews in 1916 and 1917, and it played an important role in the decimation of another sixty thousand Russian Jews between 1919 and 1921. By that time copies of *The Protocols* had circulated to the rest of Europe and to America.[94]

Pound's introduction to *The Protocols* came during the period in London when he had become seriously interested in economics and the causes of war. C. H. Douglas accepted *The Protocols* as authentic and incorporated its ideas into his economic theories. The Jews, Douglas wrote, were behind the "great secret organizations bent on acquisition of world-empire." And Jews had specifically taken over the banking and moneylending professions so as to achieve world domination. Douglas's economic theories were thus constructed on solid pilings of anti-Semitism, and in his Social Credit newspaper he urged readers to study *The Protocols* carefully. Douglas's close followers shared his beliefs; "what kept them warm in the face of cold indifference was the hot lamp of anti-Semitism."[95]

From the early 1920s onward there are echos of *The Protocols* in Pound's writings. An obsession with gold, wars as planned economic crises, a distrust of democracy, a hatred of the press, a preoccupation with genetic heritage, and anti-Semitism all became prominent. For example, in July 1921, Pound published "Kongo Roux" in a Dadaist journal. In it he explicity says that Jews—"totem de tribu SHEENY, Yid, taboo"—had caused World War I. Pound's allusions to a Jewish conspiracy were usually elliptical, as when he spoke about "certain facts that are known," "the intrigues of interested cliques," or "maleficient activity," although in later years he was often more explicit. In 1935 he wrote: "The merchants of money, the makers and dealers in money had privilege above all other citizens. This privilege was enormous, secret, unacknowledged." In 1938 Pound said that the history of Jews had been inimical to rational values, and in the following year he wrote: "I begin to doubt that yidd / fluence has ever been anything but a stinking curse to Europe."[96] That same year, in a discussion about international bankers, he wrote: "Some facts are now known above parties, some perceptions are the common heritage of all men of good will, and only the Jewspaper and worse than Jewspaper, try now to obscure them."[97]

Although his anti-Semitism undoubtedly had roots in adolescence and his college years and was clearly expressed in his early London writings, Pound's antipathy toward Jews became much more sophisticated and focused after he had been exposed to the teachings of the "elders" of Zion. Pound liked individual Jews and even had a few Jewish friends such as poet Louis Zukofsky, but he disliked Jews as a group because of their supposed plot to take over the world. The control of gold was the field on which the battle was being fought, and that became Pound's great cause. "Usurers" in Pound's writings are virtually interchangeable with "Jews," and the problems of the world can all be linked to one grand design. It is anti-Semitism with an economic veneer, but it is still anti-Semitism.

From the perspective of the present it is difficult to understand how a man of Pound's intelligence and worldliness could accept *The*

Protocols of Zion as authentic, replete as it was with internal contradictions and thinly disguised prejudice. It should be remembered, however, that Pound's education was almost exclusively in languages and literature, not in history, economics, or the natural sciences. Moreover, he thought from preconceived truths revealed to him in mystical reveries, not deductively from observation. As John Gwyer points out in *Portraits of Mean Men*, there has always been a belief that certain groups were secretly conspiring to rule the world; in recent centuries these groups have included the Quakers, the Rosicrucians, the Papacy, and the Mafia as well as the Jews. As Gwyer notes: "After a while one sees how convenient it really is. It saves so much thinking to think like this, to survey the world and know that all its disorders are due to the malignity of a single group of mysterious plotters."[98] It has a fatal appeal to those who see the world as hostile and rejecting; it beckons as the Sirens once called to Odysseus.

Anti-Semitism was not officially condoned by Italian Fascism, but neither was it inimical. Although Mussolini himself was apparently not anti-Semitic, many leading Italian Fascists such as Ciano, Pardi, Pavolini, Polvarelli, Por, Ricciardi, Delcroix, and De Stefani were blatantly so.[99] Pound knew many of them well.

British Fascism, on the other hand, incorporated anti-Semitism as an inherent part of its belief system. Mosley's British Union of Fascists promoted *The Protocols* as an important book, and Mosley insisted that it was the Jews who were trying to get Britain into a war against Hitler's Germany.[100] Pound also corresponded with Arnold Leese, the Director-General of The Imperial Fascist League, and subscribed to its newspaper, *The Fascist*. Leese was virulently anti-Semitic and was, by his own description, the pre-eminent "racial fascist" in Britain. Leese took elaborate precautions to prevent secret Jews from infiltrating the Imperial Fascist League by measuring the shape of the head of each applicant; this was the only certain test, he believed, to ascertain true "Nordic" stock uncontaminated with Jewish genes. On one occasion Leese asked Pound whether he might have some Jewish blood in him; Pound replied with a lengthy genealogy to prove that he did not.[101] Pound shared Leese's interest in genes and heredity. As early as 1926 William Carlos Williams had told Pound: "You talk like a crow with a cleft palate when you repeat your old gag of heredity, where you come from or where I come from." Later Williams told his friend more explicitly what he thought of his ideas: "Why . . . try to tell me that your whole initiative hasn't been anti-Semitic of recent years? You know damned well it has been so. Tell somebody else such things but don't try it on me if you value the least vestige of what we used to treasure between us."[102]

German National Socialism also incorporated anti-Semitism as an integral part of its theories. Hitler was introduced to *The Protocols of Zion* in the 1920s and praised it in *Mein Kampf.* Heinrich Himmler read *The Protocols* in 1919 and called it "a book that explains everything and tells us whom we must fight against next time"; later as head of the Gestapo he would implement its teachings as the "final solution." Pound contributed several articles to Nazi publications. According to Noel Stock, who examined these writings, Pound "was in no sense a simple follower of Nazism but philosophically he was moving in the same direction and in some of his writings about paganism he began to call for a truly European religion unpolluted by Semitic influences."[103] In an article in Mosley's *British Union Quarterly* in 1938, Pound displayed reasoning that had ominous overtones of a "final solution" to the Jewish problem: "The Semitic poison is in the Semite tempered by Semitic instability, by the Semite's wobble from one excess to another . . . A race may possibly be held responsible for its worst members . . . If you believe that a whole race should be punished for the sin of some of its members, I admit that the expulsion of the two million Jews in New York would not be an excessive punishment for the harm done by Jewish finance to the English race in America."[104]

The existence of a Jewish conspiracy to take control of the world explained for Pound many facets of civilization that he did not like. In 1930 he wrote: "Are you aware that Christianity emerged from Judaism and that a number of damnable features of Xtianity still show their hebrew origins?"[105] Later he said that Christianity had been tainted by "semitic insanity" and "semitic immoderation,"[106] and in letters to an English cleric Pound wrote of nefarious doings: "I strongly suggest you make a study of ecclesiastical money in England . . . to know what the Church issued, under what regulations; ratio metal value to currency value . . . When, if ever, did usury cease to be a mortal sin?" "Can you find out from the Bishop of Durham *who* it was who stopped the Church inquiry into the nature of money monopoly, credit and economics? . . . You as an intending parson have a right to know whether you will be expected to obey yr. [your] bishop or something more centralized and mysterious."[107]

What had happened according to Pound was that Jewish influences had corrupted Christianity, leading to the Christian approval of usury. "Protestantism as factive and organized may have sprung from nothing but pro-usury politics," he wrote.[108] "Putting usury on a pedestal, in order to set avarice on high, the Protestant centuries twisted all morality out of shape."[109]

A Jewish conspiracy also explained the causes of war. Since wars profited the international financiers and armament manufacturers, and since most of these persons in Pound's mind were of Jewish extraction, then wars were ultimately caused by Jews. Such reasoning recalls Douglas Goldring's description of lavish parties thrown by nouveau-riche Jews during Pound's early days in London; according to Goldring some of these Jews were "armament makers."[110]

Pound also decided that Jews were responsible for the difficulties he was having getting his work published. In the early 1930s he told his friends that "Jewish publishers" were what was wrong with American literature. "I have been for two years in a boil of fury with the dominant usury that impedes every human act, that keeps good books out of print, and pejorates everything." American publishers, being dominated by Jewish interests and values, refused to publish Pound and his friends "because the filthy money won't flow, because the profits to Judas aren't sufficiently probable and tempting."[111] In the late thirties Pound became less circumspect in his analysis of the problem: "Why the hell dont it occur to you that the lousy jews who run yr / [your] fahrt of an empire steal 7 bob to the quid from a man's royalties / naturally loathing the idea that one shd / [should] produce literature in a language not yit-tisch /."[112]

Of all the areas in which Pound was prepared to castigate the Jews and their conspiracy, none was more important to him than the Jewish corruption of sex. "In fact," he wrote, "I object as much to semitism in matters of mind as in matters of commerce."[113] Pound reasoned that "jews having been circumcised for centuries / it must have had some effect on the character."[114] In a letter to William Carlos Williams (a physician as well as a poet) Pound elaborated on this thesis:

> What the hell / history is written and character is made by whether and HOW the male foreskin produces a effect of glorious sunrise or of annoyance in slippin backward. Someone diagnosed Shaw years ago by saying he had a tight foreskin / the whole of puritan idiocy is produced by badly built foreskins. Criminology / penology shd / be written around the cock. The dissecting room shd / lay off that chaotic bucket of sweet breads from the skull and start research from the prong UPward. The lay of the nerves / etc. This don't blot out endocrinology / but it is the fount of aesthetics / means microscopic attention / dissection and micro / photographic enlargements / killers etc / shd have their prongs photoed postmortem.[115]

Williams replied that "if cutting off the loose hide over a few thousand years has altered the Hebrew character—I doubt it. By all the laws of heredity it should have affected the women and they are as bad as the men today, or worse. It ain't the skin that makes the difference in the man, its the stick in it that does it."[116]

Pound apparently believed that circumcision decreased the pleasure of coitus for Jews and therefore led them to turn away from, and denigrate, sex. In place of sex Jews turned to finance and usury for satisfaction. Circumcision was one of the practices of Judaism which had carried over to Christianity, and this had corrupted Christianity as well. Usury had been a mortal sin in the early church and coitus had not been; Jewish influence had reversed these and "moral was narrowed down to application to carnal relations."[117] In the last analysis Ezra Pound saw the current evils of the world as a consequence of circumcision— the history of the world reduced to a foreskin. Since he himself had not been circumcised, he had escaped this pernicious Jewish influence.[118]

THE CRASH OF 1929

History conspired against Ezra Pound to bring out his worst qualities. By the late 1920s he was a semiforgotten poet living in Rapallo, pushing steadily through middle age, writing letters to his friends reviling the Jews and espousing obscure economic theories. Nobody paid much attention to him.

Then came the stock market crash of 1929 and the ensuing Great Depression. The failure of the American economy, which began as a local event in New York's Wall Street, spread inexorably across the country and then overseas. Small businesses and banks failed, and unemployment in the United States grew until almost one-third of the labor force was out of work. By 1932 several thousand veterans had marched on Washington, the farmers in the midwest were growing violent, and unemployed workers in Detroit were being killed by the police in riots. President Hoover tinkered with the status quo, while New York's Governor Franklin D. Roosevelt prepared his campaign for the presidency. Economic theories for recovery from the depression were being offered by everyone. There was consensus that something had to change economically but complete confusion about what it should be.

Pound, sitting in his apartment overlooking the Mediterranean, knew what it should be. Take over the banks, he urged. If the federal government would only do this and thereby control the money supply, then everything would be corrected. The depression would disappear. After all it was the banks, and the hated usurers who controlled them, that brought about the market crash and subsequent depression. What further proof did anyone need that his economic analysis was correct? The failure of the world economic system following the crash of 1929 had proven to him that Douglas's theories were correct.

As a further stimulus to Pound, Social Credit began to be discussed in the United States in 1931 when A. R. Orage, Pound's old friend from London, gave some lectures on it in New York. A congressman introduced a bill promoting Social Credit, and hearings were held before the House Committee on Banking. William Carlos Williams and Archibald MacLeish both spoke favorably of it publicly, probably at Pound's instigation. Father Charles Coughlin, a popular but demagogic Catholic priest, and Senator Huey Long from Louisiana both publicly expressed interest in Social Credit ideas; Pound immediately wrote to both of them.[119] In Canada and England some politicians even ran for office on Social Credit platforms. For a brief period, as America was thrashing about looking for a way out of the depression, it must have looked to some like an idea whose time had come.

To Pound it certainly looked that way and he set to work with a zeal unmatched in his career. He wrote to every public figure and every newspaper that he thought might listen, filling the mails with admonitions, advice, and analyses. In 1933 he published ten lectures he had given as the *ABC of Economics*, trying to simplify Social Credit theories for the masses. In 1934 alone he contributed over 100 letters and articles on economics and politics to newspapers and periodicals. In 1935 he added 150 more articles, as well as another book and two pamphlets.[120]

Nobody was exempted from Pound's cajoling and exhortations. He wrote directly to President Roosevelt, and had his friends do likewise. Albert Einstein was the recipient of a Pound epistle, requesting him to drop physics for the weightier problems of economics. He advised Robert McAlmon that "I think both you and Hem [Hemingway] have limited yr. [your] work by not recognizing the economic factor."[121] He argued that the development of fiction had been retarded by the failure of writers to pay attention to economics. Even detective writer Dorothy Sayers, whom Pound enjoyed reading, received an unsolicited letter from him urging her to devote some time to the larger crimes of economics and government. She replied that there was not enough mystery in it. Economics for Pound became the panacea for the world's ills: "I personally know of no social evil that cannot be cured, or very largely cured, economically."[122]

Ezra Pound's poetry of those years clearly reflects his preoccupations. During the 1930s he wrote most of Cantos 31 through 71. They are a pastiche of historical facts about Thomas Jefferson, John Quincy Adams, and Martin Van Buren, with Chinese history, C. H. Douglas, Mussolini, and economic theories mixed in. Large sections of the Adams Cantos (62 through 71) are taken directly from a history of the Adams family; the end of Canto 33 is a transcription of a speech in the U.S. Senate attacking one of the governors of the Federal Reserve Board;

and Canto 37 is a report of the federal budget under President Van Buren:

> *4 to 5 million balance in the national treasury*
> *Receipts 31 to 32 million*
> *Revenue 32 to 33 million*
> *The Bank 341 million, and in deposits*
> *6 million of government money*
> *(and a majority in the Senate)*
> *Public Money in control of the President*

Everywhere lurks the apparition of usury, destroying the economy, interfering with normal sexual relations, and corrupting the true religion:

> *WITH USURA*
> *wool comes not to market*
> *sheep bringeth no gain with usura*
> *Usura is a murrain, usura*
> *blunteth the needle in the maid's hand*
> *and stoppeth the spinner's cunning.*
>
> . . . .
>
> *Usura slayeth the child in the womb*
> *It stayeth the young man's courting*
> *It hath brought palsey to bed, lyeth*
> *between the young bride and her bridegroom*
>   *CONTRA NATURAM*
>
> *They have brought whores for Eleusis*
> *Corpses are set to banquet*
> *at behest of usura.*
>
>   (*Canto 45*)

    Pound believed that the inclusion of historical facts and economic theories in an epic poem was consistent with the Homeric and Dantean tradition: "An *epic* includes history and history ain't all slush and babies' pink toes. I admit that economics are *in themselves* uninteresting but heroism *is* poetic."[123] He was acting consistently with the advice he had given another poet many years earlier: "Sing of the things one cares about however unimportant or unpoetical they may seem."[124] Critics have been less charitable to these Cantos, calling them "exercises in historical rhetoric" and saying that "one does not so much read the Cantos as undergo them." One reviewer described the Cantos as "a somewhat disjointed series of staccato remarks which leave one with the misleading impression that Mr. Ezra Pound's shirtcuffs have been sent to the printer instead of to the laundry."[125]

There were tantalizing glimpses of the glory Pound thought was coming. In April 1934, C. H. Douglas visited Washington to promote Social Credit, met with members of Congress, and gave radio addresses. Pound wrote excitedly to Mussolini listing the senators who attended a dinner in Douglas's honor. Pound had initiated correspondence with several senators and congressmen (Borah, Cutting, Taft, Tinkham, Vandenberg) and myriad other public figures, offering page after page of economic advice. It is clear that he was avidly following the American economic and political scene.

At this point in his life Pound apparently believed he was on the verge of greatness. He clearly knew what needed to be done, and it appeared to him that the world was about to recognize his wisdom. Thus in December 1934, when asked to write a letter on Joyce, Pound refused because of the pressing responsibilities he had as a self-appointed world leader. "There is too much future, and nobody but me and Muss and half a dozen others to attend to it." Similarly he wrote to Hemingway asking him to arrange that he be called back to Washington to participate in President Roosevelt's Brain Trust; Pound claimed fifteen years' experience as an economist and professed that "he himself knew things which some of those on government boards did not." Moreover, it was Roosevelt's obligation to summon home the "best brains" from abroad.[126] When Roosevelt failed to respond, Pound urged Senator Borah to run for president with Pound as his unofficial brain trust.[127]

TOWARD THE BRINK

Pound's ego was then punctured by a series of events. First came Mussolini's invasion of Ethiopia in October 1935 and the dramatic appeal of Emperor Haile Selassie to the League of Nations. Pound defended the invasion, claiming that Italy had a responsibility to civilize an uncivilized country. Besides, he added, the Ethiopian people were merely "black Jews." The League of Nations was dismissed by Pound as "an assembly of bank pimps."[128] The tide of world opinion had shifted, however; Pound was no longer allied with a bright and promising leader in Rome but with a man the world viewed as a pariah.

In the United States things were also not going well for Pound's causes. Senator Cutting died in a plane crash in 1935, and Senator Borah responded to Pound's twenty-seven letters with only three terse replies.[129] Furthermore, Social Credit was making no further gains. After its brief flirtation with public recognition it was settling rapidly into respectable obscurity in the footnotes of economic history. The American Social Credit Movement was organized in 1936, but it never achieved any importance. It made a specific effort to exclude Fascist followers from its ranks, and so Pound was not invited to participate. Gorham B. Munson, American leader of the movement, was advised that Pound's contribution would be worthless, "like a series of explosions in a rock quarry."[130] Here, then, was Pound's economic system being introduced into his own country and he was not even being asked to assist.

Most devastating of all was the fact that President Roosevelt not only failed to summon Pound home to help, but embarked on economic policies which were anathema to him. Roosevelt restored the banking system relatively unchanged, and did not take it over. For Ezra Pound this was proof that the President was merely a tool of Jewish interests.

Roosevelt instituted other policies with which Pound also strongly disagreed, such as increasing the federal bureaucracy. Pound had always opposed big government, writing in 1928 that "the job of America for the next twenty years will be to drive back the government into its proper place, i.e., to force it to occupy itself solely with things which are the proper function of government;" this function Pound had defined as traffic, water supply, and sewage disposal.[131] He ridiculed bureaucrats and suggested that they be employed "in computing the number of sandflies to every mile of beach at Cape May, but under no circumstances allow them to do anything what bloody ever that brings them into contact with the citizen."[132] Yet Roosevelt was rapidly adding to their numbers. Another policy that Roosevelt implemented was increased deficit financing and thus increased government debt. This, in Pound's view, simply put the government more under the control of the usurers and international financiers.

Pound's reaction against Roosevelt was immediate. Whereas in 1934 he had been willing to withhold judgment and simply described Roosevelt as "a more or less nebulous figure," by 1935 Pound attacked him directly: "If Roosevelt thinks he can borrow the nation out of debt, he is a fool. And if he knows he can't and goes on as if he could, he is a traitor."[133]

Ezra Pound had again been spurned by those he believed should recognize his worth. As had happened in the past, his fury was boundless and venom uncontrollably poisoned his discourse. America, he wrote, was "a rabbit headed country probably mongrelized past redemption." "Three shits in succession in Washington, the whole of an actively and fahrting active and maleficent activity going on all over the place."[134] Pound's mind, once noteworthy for its lyricism, was now a compost heap of hate as he became increasingly harsh, strident, and caustic. The angrier he became, the more he sounded like ancient Ezra and the other Old Testament prophets.[135] It was an irony that Pound could not appreciate.

Especially galling to Pound was the continued disinterest by American publishers and universities in his work. He had had no offers of professorships, no honorary degrees, and no requests to lecture. In 1939 he complained "that at the present moment there is NO weekly in America to print me, and not even a monthly where I cd. [could] print TWO pages a month . . . It is inconceivable that in ANY other country a man in my position wouldn't have that convenience."[136] He called Harriet Monroe, editor of *Poetry*, "that old pisspot in Chicago . . . god dry up her pancreas," and Henry Canby, Secretary of the National Institute of Art and Letters, was "that fahrt Canby."[137] In a letter to Irita Van Doren, editor of the *New York Herald Tribune Book Review*, he called her "merely gelatinous affability."[138] Nobody was exempt from Pound's philippic; even St. Thomas Aquinas was described as simply "an empty noise in a bungless barrel."[139] The reluctance of the American literary community to accept Pound's work was not surprising in view of the fact that he had insulted them all. One publisher, when approached by Ford Madox Ford on Pound's behalf in 1936, cabled back that he would rather die than print anything that Pound had written, or even print his name in the magazine.[140]

Nor was England forgotten by Pound as he cast forth his choler. It was the "Shittish Empire," he said, and did not amount to "more than half a horse terd."[141] Englishmen were "vermin," "spirochetes," and "pimps" with "a talent for servility, sycophancy and bootlicking."[142] Pound wrote to Wyndham Lewis that "there's only one thing to do with an Englishman—kick him in the teeth."[143] The British mind was characterized by Pound as a "sodden mass of half-stewed oatmeal," distinguished only by its stupidity:[144]

> *Oh the Henglish wuz so stoopid*
> *They'd fergotten how to fook*
> *Till Mrs. Doktor Mary Stoops*
> *Com to show them wid her book.*

> *She sez: O Jhon do mind the moment*
> *When her oviduct is full*
> *And then go in*
> *An' play to win*
> *And show-ye-are . . . . . JOHNBULL!*[145]

Ezra Pound's old friends in America became increasingly concerned about him as the volume and velocity of his diatribes increased. Some, like H. L. Mencken, urged him to "come home to the Republic" and rebuked him for abandoning poetry for politics: "You made your great mistake when you abandoned the poetry business and set up shop as a wizard in general practice."[146] But at the same time as he was rebuking Pound, Mencken was telling him things that reinforced Pound's world-view: "All of the ideas you have labored for for so many years are now taken over by a gang of Communists (chiefly kikes) and reduced to complete absurdity . . . New York [has] now become al [almost] wholly Jewish."[147]

Felix Schelling, Pound's professor at the University of Pennsylvania, chided him for his increasing bitterness and suggested that he had lost touch with his homeland. Pound replied: "As for my being embittered, it won't wash; everybody who comes near me marvels at my good nature."[148] Robert Frost, also concerned, wrote to Louis Untermeyer: "I wonder if Ezra will appreciate your effort to be temperate with what he has become in memory of what he once promised to become."[149] And William Carlos Williams, the family doctor of Passaic River mill towns, let his old friend have it directly: "You belong in this country . . . I think that if anyone needs a change, a new viewpoint it's you. You can't even smell the stink you're in any more . . . This ain't the old Ez I used to know. You're in the wrong bin. Your arse is congealed. Your cock fell in the jello. Wake up!"[150]

Another concerned friend was Ford Madox Ford, who had taken a teaching job at Olivet College in Michigan. Ford wrote to Pound that "it is one of my normal worries thinking about your material prospects" and offered Pound a job at Olivet. Pound would have "complete leisure to write whilst earning a living wage," boat fare from Europe and return, no teaching responsibility except insofar as he wanted, and access to a good library, a printing press, and the college orchestra. It was a genuine and generous offer which Ford had spent considerable time arranging with President Brewer of the college.[151]

Pound responded by ignoring Ford and writing directly to President Brewer. Ford was irate and sarcastically called Pound to task for his poor manners: "Dear God, Father Divine . . . I know that Your awful face must be veiled to the lesser mackerel nuzzling between Your toes in the ooze. Indeed this lesser mackerel knows also how it turns Your divine stomach to have to communicate with lesser ones at all. But in this case, it would be a convenience if Your Divinity would communicate directly to this l.m. the nature of its exactions . . . But for all other purposes this l.m. here may be regarded as tops too and thus time will be saved and confusion avoided. And your petitioner shall ever pray . . ."[152]

Pound turned down the job, but not without giving it serious thought. It was his first offer from an American college, and probably his first offer of full-time work in over thirty years. The realities of shifting his domestic ménage from Rapallo to Michigan probably seemed over-whelming, however, and in addition Pound thought that Olivet College was beneath his dignity. Ford confirmed this in another letter in which he told Pound: "The only conspiracy I am in is to get you the Charles Eliot Norton professorship at Boston [Harvard] to which Olivet would be a stepping stone." Shortly after rejecting the job offer Pound wrote to President Brewer that "*all* you blighted American College Presidents ought to be boiled in all [oil] . . . all of you criminals obfuscating your students by *refusal* (black and unexcusable) to teach American history . . . in yr. [your] courses—you can be damned and deserve no consider-ation as a man whatsoever."[153]

1939 VISIT

The year 1939 began inauspiciously for Ezra Pound when his old friend William Butler Yeats died in the south of France. Yeats had seen the coming of chaos with Mussolini, Hitler, and Stalin on the rise, and the previous year had told a friend to read his "The Second Coming" as a description of the current scene: "Things fall apart; the centre cannot hold / Mere anarchy is loosed upon the world," Yeats wrote. "And what rough beast, its hour come round at last, / Slouches towards Bethlehem to be born?"[154]

Pound had not returned to his homeland since 1911, and he finally decided to go. Part of the impetus for the visit was probably the urging of his friends. Another part may have been the urging of the Fascist government for him to return to America and propagandize on their behalf. They apparently offered to pay Pound's round-trip fare and even insisted that he travel first class. Pound was initially wary of the offer and wrote to Wyndham Lewis asking advice: "I hav bin TOLD that it is 'necessary' to go FIRST CLAWSS to Amurika if anything is to be accomplished. Waaal wot have I got to SELL, that wd / [would] justify this eggspence? Do you advise it."[155]

In the end Pound accepted the offer and sailed on April 13 on an Italian liner in a luxury suite.[156] He landed in New York, where he was interviewed by the press. Despite the fact that Germany had just invaded Czechoslovakia and Italy was invading Albania, Pound assured reporters that there would be no war. "The bankers and the munitions interests, whoever and wherever they may be, are more responsible for the present talk of war than are the intentions of Mussolini or anyone else," Pound told them. Besides, Mussolini had a mind with the "quickest uptake" of any man he knew except Picabia.[157]

Pound proceeded directly to Washington, where he stayed in Georgetown with Ida and Adah Mapel, sisters whom he had first met in 1906. He described them to Wyndham Lewis: "Gawd and the angels wd [would] not impress Miss Ida and Adah Lee is perfectly cable [capable] of continuun' to sip her tea quietly in the midst of an Earthquake."[158] Pound's purpose in Washington was "to advise Roosevelt to stay out of Europe," and to that end he met with Secretary of Agriculture Henry Wallace, at least six senators (Bankhead, Borah, Byrd, Taft, Wheeler, and Vandenberg), several congressmen, and influential friends such as Archibald MacLeish.[159] He offered advice on economics and politics and seriously suggested that the United States give Guam to the Japanese in exchange for three hundred films of Noh plays. At one point he inquired whether an official position might be available in which he could spend a few months each year as an adviser to the government.[160] Pound later recounted in Canto 84 Senator Borah's reply: "Am sure I don't know what a man like you / would find to *do* here."

Nobody in the nation's capital was willing to do more than politely listen to Pound. The President was too busy to see him and no offer of a position was made. One friend later interviewed by the FBI said Pound had been "laughed at by the New Dealers he met in Washington."[161] William Carlos Williams met him there "wrapped in sweaters and shirts and coats until I thought him a man mountain, but after awhile he returned to normal measurements again—I think he was afraid of our damp spring weather!" Williams said that Pound had been "very mysterious about his comings and goings while in this country, keeping his whereabouts more or less secret and all that sort of thing," and described him as "very mild and depressed and fearful."[162]

From Washington Pound traveled to New York, New Haven, and Boston, using the Connecticut home of Viola Baxter Jordan, his friend from Hamilton days, as his headquarters. Jordan's son recalls Pound assuring his hosts that "Brother Benito" was listening to his economic theories. He took an interest in the singing aspirations of Viola's daughter, Susan, and would sit by the piano while Viola played.[163]

By the accounts of his hosts, Pound's manners had not improved during the three decades he had lived abroad. One complained that she felt like a chattel in her own home, for Pound "considered everyone he associated with as one of his servants, including his host and hostess."[164] He "rarely paid for anything as though it really wasn't expected of him, and he casually borrowed from people."[165] His discourse invariably included large doses of Fascism and Mussolini. William Carlos Williams wrote that Pound "is sunk, in my opinion, unless he can shake the fog of fascism out of his brain . . . You can't argue away wanton slaughter of innocent women and children by the neoscholasticism of a controlled economy program." And when asked how he personally could support the regimentation of Fascism, Pound replied: "Fascism only regiments those who can't do anything without it."[166] His anti-Semitism was also very much in evidence. When he went to Harvard to read his poems he noticed that the audience included many Jews, whereupon he changed his planned program to include more anti-Semitic poems.[167] And in New York City he "refused to enter the bookshop of Frances Steloff . . . for the simple reason that Miss Steloff happened to be Jewish. Yet she had probably contributed more than any other one person in America toward winning a reading public for him."[168]

While Pound was sailing to New York, a letter was sent to him in Rapallo by President Harold Cowley of Hamilton College inviting him to receive an honorary degree. Upon reaching Washington Pound apparently received word of the invitation and contacted Professor Ibbotson to confirm it. Pound was very pleased, but wrote to ensure that no special fee would be required.[169] In early June he returned to his alma mater for the ceremonies—thirty-four years after he had graduated. He played tennis ("the most individualistic player I ever played with," said his doubles partner)[170] and was interviewed by the local press; he took the occasion to castigate England and push George Tinkham, a wealthy and conservative congressman from Massachusetts, for president. When the reporter asked Pound what fraternity he had belonged to as an undergraduate, the recollection still rankled.[171]

Following the June 12 commencement and awarding of honorary degrees there was a luncheon at which H. W. Kaltenborn, a journalist who had also been awarded an honorary degree, was the main speaker. During his talk he mentioned a "doubtful" alliance between Italy and Germany, a remark which President Cowley later characterized as provocative. If Kaltenborn had been trying to goad Ezra Pound into action he succeeded, for Pound interrupted the speaker and quickly escalated their dialogue into an unseemly shouting match. With the two recepients of honorary degrees loudly arguing politics and Pound praising Mussolini, President Cowley stepped into the fray and restored order, but it was an odious ending to a commencement luncheon.[172]

Ezra Pound had again played the boor, and he hastily retreated to New York. He had talked with senators, lectured at Harvard, and received an honorary degree—things he had longed to do—yet his trip had not really been a success. As he boarded the Italian liner for his return, he must have wondered what he had to do to get the full attention of his countrymen.

CHAPTER 6

TREASON

[ROME AND SALO: 1939–1945]

WHEN EZRA POUND DISEMBARKED in Italy he was met with the news of Ford Madox Ford's death on June 29, 1939. Both Ford and Yeats had died in southern France, the home of the troubadours, within six months of each other. It was an ill omen.

Within three months the war was on. Hitler swept one million troops into Poland without provocation or warning. German expansionist moves could no longer be rationalized; the goal was a new German Empire, a new Europe. France and England did the only thing they could do and declared war.

On the ship returning to Italy Pound had heard the name of William Wiseman mentioned as a New York banker with important influence behind the political scenes. On further inquiry Pound learned that Wiseman had previously lived in London and had been a high-ranking official in British Intelligence.[1] Pound seized on this as further evidence of a Jewish conspiracy to control British and American policy and get America into the war. He wrote to Wyndham Lewis: "America is damn well to keep out of the war / BAD enough to have european aryans murdering each other fer the sake of Willie Wiseman and . . . a few buggarin' kikes."[2]

Pound wrote to everyone he knew, urging them to keep America out of the war.[3] Support for neutrality in the United States was substantial, and many people hoped that America would sit it out as an observer. H. L. Mencken wrote repeatedly to Pound telling him that Roosevelt was trying hard to get the United States into the war, reinforcing Pound's views that the President was a tool of Jewish financial interests.[4] Increasingly Pound saw events in his homeland as a struggle between Jewish interests and Roosevelt, who were pushing America into the war, and the majority of Americans, who wanted no part in it.

Pound's invective escalated as he became increasingly frustrated. In November 1939 he wrote that "our louse of a President stands for Jewry, all Jewry, and nothing but Jewry,"[5] and by 1940 he was referring to Roosevelt as "Jewsfeldt" and "stinkie Roosenstein."[6] "Democracy is now currently defined in Europe," Pound wrote in the *Japan Times,* "as 'a country governed by Jews.' " In opposition to democracy Pound spoke of "the essential fairness of Hitler's war aims."[7]

There was no question in Pound's mind who was promoting the war. In February 1940, he wrote to the American ambassador in Rome advising him that certain groups were using the war to achieve a monopoly on metals. In March he informed the ambassador that the wife of Cordell Hull, the American secretary of state, was Jewish. It was also at this time that Pound contributed an article on "The Jews and This War" to an Italian publication; in it he referred to *The Protocols of Zion* in detail and said that the Jewish conspiracy promoting the war had control of nickel production as its ultimate goal. The article was reprinted in the Nazi *News from Germany.*[8]

Pound also attacked the Jewish religion during this period. "I doubt if any single ethical idea now honored comes from Jewry," he wrote. The "O.T. [Old Testament] is probably an over-willing fountain of pus," and "all the Jew part of the Bible is black evil."[9] Pound wished to retrieve true Christianity from its contemporary Jewish-corrupted form, and suggested that the best way to do this was to "get rid of worst and rottenest phases first, ie. the old testy-munk, barbarous blood sac, etc., and gradually detach Dantescan light (peeling off the Middle Ages bit by bit . . .)."[10]

Meanwhile the war was going well for the Axis powers. In May 1940 Norway, Holland, and Belgium fell. By June the British had been pushed off the beaches of Dunkirk, and France fell to the German and Italian armies. The Battle of Britain began, and it looked like just a matter of time until she too would have to capitulate; the only question was whether she would be bombed or starved into submission. Italy invaded North Africa, British Somaliland, and then Greece; Mussolini was rebuilding the glories of the Roman Empire.

In the United States, however, the President was winning his battle with the isolationists. In April 1940, H. L. Mencken gave Pound the bad news and told him that Roosevelt was virtually assured of renomination—and growing stronger. "There is not much chance," Mencken wrote, "of monetary reform in the face of war."[11] Thus by the summer of 1940 an Axis victory in Europe seemed certain; intervention of the United States into the war appeared to be the only force that could interdict that outcome.

Since the presidential elections were coming up, Pound decided to return to America and try to influence them. He had written to Senator Robert A. Taft offering advice on a possible Republican strategy to counter Roosevelt, and he presumably thought he could help promote isolationism.[12] Given the uncertainties of international travel with a war going on, Ezra and Dorothy packed their most valuable possessions and turned them over to Italian friends in Genoa for safekeeping. The friends agreed to hold them "for as long as you are gone" and praised Pound for wishing to "influence your fellow citizens . . . by your pen and by your speech."[13] There is no evidence that the Pounds intended the trip to be a permanent repatriation, as some Pound supporters claimed in later years. In the end the plan was aborted because passage could be guaranteed only as far as Lisbon. In October 1940, Pound wrote to a friend: "Great excitements last month; thought of going to U.S. to annoy 'em . . . Thank God I didn't get as far as Portugal and get stuck there."[14]

DEVIL OF AN INVENTION

Meanwhile Pound was doing what he could to help the Italian war effort and had decided to make radio broadcasts on Italy's behalf. The idea of broadcasting had originally been suggested to him by C. H. Douglas in 1935. After Pound returned from his 1939 visit to the United States, a Nazi officer with whom he played tennis encouraged him to pursue it.[15] Pound then approached the Ministry of Popular Culture and made his offer. It is likely that this occurred shortly after his return, for Pound was seen at the office of the minister "on several occasions in late 1939 and in January 1940 . . . apparently doing some research work."[16]

In March 1940, Pound was visited by Natalie Barney, his old friend from Paris, who was traveling in Italy. She had corresponded with him regularly and shared both his enthusiasm for Mussolini and his beliefs about the economic causes of war. As a gift Barney brought a radio; in the view of her biographer, "Natalie may have started Ezra Pound on the road to treason when she gave him a radio and praised Lord Haw-Haw's anti-British propaganda." The following day Pound wrote his oft-quoted letter to Ronald Duncan calling the radio a "devil of an invention. But got to be faced."[17] It is clear that he was already strongly committed to doing broadcasts for Mussolini, and when they finally began in January 1941, Pound acknowledged that he had worked for almost two years to gain access to the microphone.[18]

One of the motivating factors in Pound's offer to broadcast for Italy was money. The outbreak of war in Europe had led to major financial problems for Pound, as neither Dorothy's checks nor his own residual royalties could be sent from England. In addition, "Homer Pound's pension checks were not arriving from the United States and Italian banks in Rapallo and Genoa were refusing to cash American checks."[19] Pound acknowledged the pecuniary aspect of his motivation in a later interview when he said, "A German near my home at Rapallo told me they were paying good money for broadcasts."[20]

Officials in the Ministry of Popular Culture were divided on whether or not to let Pound broadcast, some suspecting that he might be an American spy. Finally in late 1940 his request was approved for broadcasts "in the English language destined for North America."[21] In January 1941 Pound began a regular series, speaking on the *American Hour* for seven minutes ten times each month. For each broadcast he received seventeen dollars, making his annual income from the broadcasts approximately two thousand dollars. Pound came to Rome from Rapallo for one week each month and prerecorded the broadcasts for the month; he usually made three recordings at a time.[22] He wrote the broadcasts himself, but they had to be approved by officials in the Ministry.

From the beginning Pound's broadcasts were pro-Fascist, pro-Mussolini, anti-England, and anti-America. Usurers and Jews were unmercifully excoriated, Churchill and Roosevelt personally pilloried. The broadcasts were offensive to many Americans still in Italy, and in early 1941 Pound had a "long interview with the American ambassador in Rome."[23] Pound's relationship with officials at the American embassy and at the American consulate in Genoa had never been good, but apparently they deteriorated still further during this period. "On several occasions," FBI files indicate, "when he appeared at the Consulate office . . . he made very undignified remarks concerning the United States Government and when he entered and left the Consulate office he gave the Fascist salute."[24] On July 12, 1941, the U.S. State Department notified Pound that his passport was being extended for six more months at the maximum and that it could only be used to return to the States.[25] The restriction of his passport was an implicit warning to Pound to be a loyal American.

Pound's friends at home were also becoming increasingly disgusted with him during 1941. William Carlos Williams replied "with a furious blast" after Pound wrote him that Mussolini's assistance to Franco in Spain "was no more than a gesture toward cleaning out a mosquito swamp in darkest Africa." And in October, E. E. Cummings addressed Pound as "Ikey-Kikey, Wandering Jew, Quo Vadis, Oppressed Minority of one, Misunderstood Master, Mister Lonelyheart, and Man Without A Country."[26]

Pound continued to broadcast regularly throughout 1941, and as he did so he watched the Axis powers grind toward what looked like inevitable victory. The Luftwaffe continued to bomb Britain. One victim was Frances Gregg, found dead in the rubble that once was Plymouth; among her possessions was *Hilda's Book*, which Pound had given to H. D. in 1907.[27] The Italian army had been stalemated in Greece, but in April the Germans avenged this by occupying that country and Yugoslavia as well. In June a German blitzkreig pushed into the Soviet Union and rapidly advanced toward Moscow. By September Kiev had fallen, with 400,000 Soviet prisoners taken. Hitler made a speech promising imminent victory. By November the Germans were within thirty miles of Moscow, where they paused for the winter.

That was how the world looked on December 7, 1941. In Rome Pound's broadcast was aired shortly after 6 P.M. as scheduled, beamed to England and the United States:

> The rot of the British Empire is from inside, and if the whole of that syphilitic organization, headed by Montague Skinner Norman, makes war on Canada, or Alberta, I see no reason for Canada not making war on the Jews in London. Whether they are born Jews, or have taken to Jewry by predilection . . . God knows I have loathed Woodie Wilson, and I don't want to see more evil done to humanity than was done by Woodrow codface. And the sooner all America and ALL England wake up to what the Warburgs and Roosevelt are up to, the better for the next generation and this one.
>
> And as an American I do NOT want to see my country annihilatin' the population of Iceland, as the British annihilated the Maoris. And as far for the Australians, they deserve a Nippo-Chinese invasion. Criminals were their granddads, and their contribution to civilization is not such as to merit even a Jewish medal. Why the heck the Chinese and Japs don't combine and drive that dirt out of Australia, and set up a bit of civilization in those parts, is for me part of the mystery of the orient.
>
> And in any case I do NOT want my compatriots from the ages of 20 to 40 to go git slaughtered to keep up the Sassoon and other British Jew rackets in Singapore and in Shanghai. That is not my idea of American patriotism.[28]

As Pound was speaking, Japanese bombs were dropping on the United States Pacific Fleet at Pearl Harbor.

Word spread quickly through Rome that Sunday evening. Pound was stunned. He is reported to have said: "I'm cooked. This is my end. But I want you to bear witness that I am first of all an American. I stand with my country, right or wrong. I will never speak over the air again."[29] Pound quickly made his way through the deserted streets of Rome to the home of Reynolds Packard, an American correspondent, and told him he intended to remain in Italy. Packard told him that if he did so he would be a traitor and that now was the time to be quiet about his Fascist beliefs. " 'But I believe in Fascism,' Pound said, giving the Fascist salute. 'And I want to defend it. I don't see why Fascism is contrary to American philosophy. I have nothing against the United States, quite the contrary. I consider myself a hundred per cent American and a patriot. I am only against Roosevelt and the Jews who influence him.' "[30]

Contrary to claims made by Pound and his supporters in later years, there is no contemporaneous evidence that he considered leaving Italy following Pearl Harbor. The only question in his mind was whether he should continue broadcasting and, if so, whether in his own name or anonymously. On December 9 Pound wrote to an official of the Ministry of Popular Culture that "even if America declares war on the Axis, I see no reason (from my point of view) why I should not continue to speak in my own name, so long as I say nothing that can in any way prejudice the results of American military or naval (or navel) action, the armed forces of the U.S.A. or the welfare of my native country."[31] On December 11, the day the U.S. Congress officially declared war on Italy, Pound was back at work writing propaganda. He justified his actions saying, "Damn it all, nothing but propaganda can prevent its degenerating into a ten year war of inexhaustible exhaustion / at any rate the enemy oughtn't to have absolutely free play with 180 million ang sax in Eng / and U.S.A."[32]

Pound applied to the Italian Supreme Command for permission to remain in Italy and eventually received it on January 26, 1942. He returned to Rapallo to think: "I had Confucius and Mencius, both of whom had been up against similar problems. Both of whom had seen empires fallin'. Both of whom had seen deeper into the causes of human confusion than most men ever think of lookin' . . . I could have avoided a war with Japan if anybody had had the unlikely idea of sending me out there with any sort of official powers."[33] Pound also had abundant personal responsibilities in Rapallo. His elderly father was hospitalized with a broken hip, and he also had his mother, Dorothy, Olga (whom he described as "semi-dependent upon him for her livlihood"), and Mary (who did not have a passport) to think about.[34] Money was scarce and likely to become more so.

The question whether Pound should broadcast anonymously or in his own name was not immediately resolved. Ministry officials suggested that it be done anonymously but Pound protested: "It seems to me that my speeches on the radio must continue IN MY OWN NAME and with *my* voice, and NOT anonymously . . . Either one fights, or one does not fight." It was, Pound said, "a war between two principles, between two orders."[35]

Pound's friends in America hoped that Pearl Harbor would finish his broadcasting career. Thus they were relieved to read in *Time* magazine on January 26, 1942, that Pound had "retired to Rapallo to continue his study of Chinese philosophy."[36] A picture of Pound accompanied the article with the caption: "No Haw-Haw he," a reference to the British Lord Haw-Haw who was broadcasting for the Nazis from Berlin.

THE BROADCASTS RESUME

Three days later, after receiving permission from the Italian Supreme Command to remain in Italy, Pound was back on the airwaves:

The United States had been for months ILLEGALLY at war, through what I considered to be the criminal acts of a president whose mental condition was NOT, as far as I could see, all that could or should be desired of a man in so responsible a position or office.

He had, so far as evidence available to me showed, broken his promises to the electorate; he had to my mind violated his oath of office. He had to my mind violated the oath of allegiance to the United States Constitution which even the ordinary American citizen is expected to take every time he gets a new passport . . . The United States has been MISinformed. The United States has been led down the garden path, and may be down under the daisies. All thru shuttin' out news . . .

He closed this broadcast with another reference questioning Roosevelt's mental health. In retrospect, it must be one of history's most ironic remarks:

Does look like there was a weakness of mind in some quarters. Whom God would destroy, he first sends to the bughouse.[37]

Two or three times a week his chiding, caustic voice could be heard on shortwave radio in the United States:

That any Jew in the White House should send American kids to die for the private interests of the scum of the English earth . . . and the still lower dregs of the Levantine.

(February 19, 1942)

F. D. R. is below the biological level at which the concept of honor enters the mind.

(March 26, 1942)

I think Roosevelt belongs in an insane asylum now. His writers are lunatics. You have come down far when a Jew by the name of Finkelstein runs your country . . . I don't want the United States to use Hawaii in the interest of a kike . . . The United States has been invaded by vermin. Whether it has been absolutely successful and taken over the White House remains to be seen. Ezra Pound trying to tell you that you will be invaded because you have been invaded.

(April 9, 1942)

For the United States to be making war on Italy and on Europe is just plain damn nonsense, and every native-born American of American stock knows that it is plain downright damn nonsense. And for this state of things Franklin Roosevelt is more than any other man responsible.

(April 16, 1942)

Had you had the sense to eliminate Roosevelt and his Jews or the Jews and their Roosevelt at the last election, you would not now be at war.

(April 23, 1942)

Every hour that you go on with this war is an hour lost to you and your children. And every sane act you commit is committed in homage to Mussolini and Hitler. Every reform, every lurch toward the just price, toward the control of a market, is an act of homage to Mussolini and Hitler. They are your leaders, however much you think you are conducted by Roosevelt or told up by Churchill. You follow Mussolini and Hitler in every constructive act of your government.

(May 26, 1942)

I am not arguing. I am just telling you, one of these days you will have to start thinking about the problem of race, breed, preservation.

(July 2, 1942)

You ought not to be at war against Italy. You ought not to be giving the slightest or most picayune aid to any man or nation engaged in waging war against Italy. You are doing it for the sake of a false accounting system.

(July 20, 1942)

Well, you have been fed on lies, for 20 years you have been fed on lies, and I don't say maybe. And Mr. Squirmy and Mr. Slime are still feeding it to you right over the BBC radio, and every one of the Jew radios of Schenectady, New York and Boston.[38]

(July 22, 1942)

The responsibility of the Jews for the war was repeated endlessly, like a broken record. Attack after attack was made on Rothschild, Sassoon, Isaac, Sieffl, Streiker, Baruch, Morgenthau, Cohen, Lehman, Warburg, Kuhn, Kahn, Schiff, Solomon, and every other prominent banker or government official with a Jewish-sounding name. "And it is for this filth that you fight," Pound said.

Ezra Pound was warned that he was risking treason by broadcasting for a nation with whom America was at war. In February or March 1942, an Italian friend told him that if Italy lost the war he might face a death sentence. "Pound made his usual gesture of shooing an insect away from his face. 'The Americans are used to it,' he said. 'They've known for years what I think of them.' "[39] He was worried enough about it, however, to add an elaborate preamble to each broadcast after Pearl Harbor which he hoped would exonerate him if it should ever be necessary: "It is understood that [Pound] not be asked to say anything whatsoever that goes against his conscience, or anything incompatible with his duties as a citizen of the United States of America." When he was eventually arrested Pound pointed to the preamble as proof that he had never committed treason. Legally, of course, it was nonsense, and would have the same effect as if a bank robber announced before robbing a bank that he would not do anything which was against his conscience or contrary to the interest of the state.

The war had become a true world war, with fighting going on from the Aleutian Islands to New Guinea, from East Africa to the fjords of Norway. Rommel and Montgomery battled across North Africa, and the Soviet Union was somehow holding the powerful German army to a standstill. Italian troops fought Allied troops at several different points on the globe, and Pound did everything he could to help the Axis forces. He invested his meager financial resources in the equivalent of Italian war bonds, broadcast over three hundred speeches, and wrote many others that were broadcast by Italian commentators; some of these Pound wrote under the pseudonym Pietro Squarcio. Department of Justice records after the war spoke of "hundreds of original manuscripts . . . which were obtained from subject's home in Rapallo and from the Ministry of Popular Culture in Rome."[40] In addition to the speeches, he wrote slogans for use by the Axis and considered himself an expert on the use of propaganda; at one point he even proposed that a university position be established for him so that he could teach it.[41]

Pound was convinced that the Axis would prevail, telling a friend in 1942 that "the Axis is stronger than the Anglo-Americans in armaments and military skill. The only thing that might cause us to lose the war in the long run is the scarcity of butter." For this problem Pound had a solution: "Sow peanuts in the Alps. There are fields there perfectly suited to raising the crop. One of these days . . . I'll go to Rome to explain the problem to Mussolini."[42] Pound enjoyed his role as a broadcaster on Radio Rome, and "at all times Pound gave the Fascist salute when greeting people" in Rome.[43]

THE SILENT PERIOD

Suddenly, in mid-August 1942, Pound became silent. Broadcasts took place on August 3, 6, 10, 13, 17, and 20 but then stopped. Records of the FBI and the Department of Justice list a single broadcast on September 19 and another on December 9, but otherwise there were no more until February 4, 1943, when they resumed a regular schedule. And since Pound's broadcasts were prerecorded, these might have been made at an earlier date. Financial receipts for payments made to Pound also stopped abruptly on August 12 and did not resume until October 19.[44] There is, then, a period of at least two months in the middle of the war in which Ezra Pound dropped from view.

There are several possible explanations for this silent period. One is that he became aware of an investigation of his broadcast activities which had begun in the United States in April 1942. Agents from the Federal Bureau of Investigation had started to systematically question all of Pound's previous acquaintances, and it is possible that one or more of them got word of this to Pound. The line of questioning involved loyalty and actions against the United States, and those who were questioned would have seen clearly that Pound was in trouble. Contradicting this theory is the fact that virtually no mail or private communications were going from the United States to Italy at the height of the war.

Another possible explanation is that Pound simply took a holiday or that he became sick. The former seems remote, since he believed he was engaged in a battle for the survival of mankind, a struggle between the Fascist forces of good and the Jewish forces of evil; to walk away in the middle of such a battle would have been most unlike him. The possibility that he became sick is more real, although it is puzzling that there is no reference to it in his letters or writings. Dorothy Pound later referred to a rumor that Pound had made a suicide attempt during the war but emphatically labeled it as false.[45]

Another possible explanation for the silent period is that Pound went to Germany for several weeks to help with Nazi propaganda efforts. In a 1941 letter to William Joyce, who was broadcasting for the Nazis in Berlin, Pound indicated an interest in coming to Berlin if all his expenses were paid.[46] Pound was certainly sympathetic to Hitler's goals and became more so as the war progressed: in 1939 and 1940 he had signed occasional letters with "Heil Hitler" or a swastika; by 1942 he was praising *Mein Kampf* and calling it required reading. Following the war Pound described Hitler as "a saint" and "a martyr,"[47] and in his Cantos continued to indicate sympathy with Hitler's view of the world, as in this reference to Jewish interest in usury:

> *And who try to use the mind for the senses drive screws with a*
> *hammer*
> > *maalesh*
>
> *Adolf furious from perception.*

(Canto 104)

Pound received the Nazi *News from Germany* throughout the war, allowed some of his radio broadcasts to be replayed over Radio Berlin, and corresponded regularly with Nazi propaganda officials who were coordinating their efforts with the Fascist Ministry of Popular Culture in Rome.[48]

There is evidence that Pound had made a trip to Berlin in April 1942. He was invited by the German Press Association to give a lecture on "the principles of Italian Fascism," and got clearance for the talk from Fascist officials before he went. "The next day the Berlin press gave . . . courteous notices of the lecture and lecturer."[49] There is also reference to Pound's visits to Germany in a 1953 letter from Isaiah Berlin to Denis Goacher, one of Pound's protégés during the St. Elizabeths years.[50] When rumor of Pound's trips to Germany surfaced after the war, Dorothy Pound denied that her husband had been there since the late 1920s.[51]

If Pound was in Germany, how much did he know about Hitler's "final solution" to the Jewish problem and about the death camps? His supporters claim that he did not know, since he "only had access to German, Italian, and Japanese newspapers, which did not report the extermination of the Jews." Furthermore they argue that Italian Jews were transported to the death camps only after the middle of 1943, following Mussolini's downfall.[52]

On the other hand there is some evidence that Pound was aware of Nazi massacres of Jews. In early 1942 he was told by an Italian friend about a cultured young German Jew "who had escaped courageously to Italy after the SS massacred the rest of his family." Pound was sympathetic to the young man and told his friend that "the Jews taken individually, especially if they were poor, were human beings like ourselves. However, collectively, and controlled by the capitalists as they were, they had organized a relentless conspiracy against mankind. The conspiracy should be denounced, combatted, and destroyed by political action and not, surely, by murders and massacres."[53] One is reminded of Pound's remark to his friend Aldo Camerino, an Italian Jew, soon after the racial laws of 1938 went into effect in Italy. (They banned Jews from government jobs, industries employing more than one hundred persons, or large farms, and they made marriages between Jews and non-Jews illegal) "I'm sorry for you," said Pound, "but they have done the right thing."[54]

THE FALL OF MUSSOLINI

By January 1943, Pound was back at work in the Ministry of Popular Culture. He prepared a list of English books "available for the re-education of prisoners," presumably English and Americans who had been captured by the Axis.[55] On January 13 President Roosevelt announced that indictments were being considered against Pound and five other Americans who were broadcasting for the Germans.[56] William Carlos Williams read the news and wrote to Robert McAlmon: "And what do you think about Pound? . . . I suppose he's just a poor defeated son-of-a-bitch with certain virtues, to be sure, in his favor but not enough to save him. In some ways he's so marvelously stupid, just thick-headed, that I really pity him. Most people around here speak of him as poor Ezra."[57]

Pound also read the news in the Rome newspaper. To have Franklin D. Roosevelt threatening to indict him must have been more than he could bear. On February 4 he resumed his regular broadcasts. When he arrived at the studio the technicians were discussing Roosevelt's threat and asked Pound what he thought about it. "The bullet has yet to be made that will kill me," he is said to have replied.[58]

Pound resumed broadcasting with a vengeance:

Don't shoot him, don't shoot him, don't shoot the President. Assassins deserve worse, but don't shoot him . . . Don't shoot him, diagnose him, diagnose him. It is not only your affair, but it is your bound duty as American citizens.

(February 18, 1943)

Just which of you is free from Jewish influence? Just which political and business groups are free from Jew influence, from Jew control?

(March 19, 1943)

Don't start a pogrom. The problem, the Chewisch problem, is not insoluble. Don't start a pogrom; SELL 'em Australia . . . Don't GIVE 'em a national home; if they'll buy it. Of course at cut-rates; long term credit . . . My, your country is overpopulated. I mean, especially after the war with the loss of tonnage space and the loss of your markets, you will have to thin out your population. Sell 'em Australia.

(March 21, 1943)

What are you doing in the war at all? What are you doing in Africa? Who amongst you has the nerve or the sense to do something that would be conducive to getting you out of it before you are mortgaged up to the neck and over it? Every day of war is a dead day as well as a death day. More death, more future servitude, less and less of American liberty of any variety.

(May 4, 1943)

The Jew is a savage.[59]

(May 9, 1943)

Pound continued week after week, speaking of "kikes, sheenies and the oily people."[60] Nor did he completely forget other minority groups, broadcasting that German bombers could not find American troops because the "visibility of black troops is very low after dark."[61]

Stalingrad had been held by the Russians, and the tide of the war was subtly beginning to shift in the early months of 1943. In North Africa the Germans were in retreat, and by May they had been defeated there. Then on July 9 the British under generals Alexander and Montgomery and an American force led by General George Patton invaded Sicily; the Italian troops surrendered with little resistance and suddenly Italy looked vulnerable. A major political crisis ensued, with peace demonstrations springing up spontaneously in some cities. The Fascist Grand Council gave a vote of no confidence to Mussolini's government, and on July 25 King Victor Emmanuel ordered Mussolini to resign. He was imprisoned, and the new Italian government abolished the Fascist Party and all Fascist organizations and institutions. It was a bitter blow to Pound.

But the worst was yet to come for him. On July 26, 1943, one day after Mussolini resigned, a Grand Jury in the District of Columbia indicted for treason Ezra Pound and seven other Americans who had been broadcasting in Germany. Pound, the indictment read, "knowingly, intentionally, wilfully, unlawfully, feloniously, traitorously, and treasonably did adhere to the enemies of the United States . . . giving to the said enemies of the United States aid and comfort within the United States and elsewhere." Attorney General Francis Biddle held a press conference and noted that those indicted had "freely elected, at a time when their country is at war, to devote their services to the cause of the enemies of the United States."[62]

Pound heard the news on the BBC and must have experienced a variety of feelings. Francis Biddle was a descendant of Nicholas Biddle who, with Alexander Hamilton, had urged that the circulation of money be put into private hands; Nicholas Biddle had been criticized by Pound as having been an original betrayer of the American constitution.[63] Furthermore George Biddle, the brother of the attorney general, was one of Pound's friends. A lawyer, painter, and sculptor, he had visited Pound in Rapallo and corresponded with him intermittently since 1932. As the indictment was being read, George was with the American troops in Palermo, Sicily, preparing for the invasion of the Italian mainland.[64]

Indicted along with Pound was a collection of true believers, misfits, and soldiers of fortune who were all broadcasting for Hitler on Radio Berlin. Douglas Chandler, known on the air as Paul Revere, tried to incite his fellow Americans to throw out "Roosevelt and his Jews." Robert Best spoke of "the clique of Jewish reptiles which are today running America . . . Roosevelt and his Jewish bosses" and claimed "the most divine sanctity [for] my crusade for the overthrow of kike rule in America and Britain."[65] What contact, if any, Pound had had with these men is not known.

Conspicuously absent from the list of the indicted was George Nelson Page, a member of "a distinguished Virginia family" who had been raised in Italy. He was one of Pound's supervisors in the Ministry of Popular Culture and was in charge of English-language propaganda broadcasts on Radio Rome.[66] Page, however, had renounced his American citizenship and become an Italian citizen during the war; Pound had declined to do this.

Pound responded to the indictment immediately, forwarding a letter to Attorney General Biddle through the Swiss legation in Rome. The letter was carefully reasoned and remarkably temperate, especially when contrasted with his hysterical utterances of the preceding months over the airwaves:

> I understand that I am under indictment for treason. I have done my best to get an authentic report of your statement to this effect. And I wish to place the following facts before you.
>
> I do not believe that the simple fact of speaking over the radio, wherever placed, can in itself constitute treason. I think that must depend on what is said, and on the motives for speaking.

He then went on to develop a three-part defense of his broadcasts. The first of these was his preamble.

I obtained the concession to speak over Rome radio with the following proviso. Namely that nothing should be asked of me contrary to my conscience or contrary to my duties as an American citizen. I obtained a declaration on their part of a belief in "the free expression of opinion by those qualified to have an opinion."

The legal mind of the Attorney General will understand the interest inherent in this distinction, as from unqualified right of expression.

This declaration was made several times in the announcements of my speeches; with the declaration "He will not be asked to say anything contrary to his conscience, or contrary to his duties as an American citizen" (Citizen of the U.S.).

These conditions have been adhered to. The only time I had an opinion as to what might be interesting as subject matter, I was asked whether I would speak of religion. This seemed to me hardly my subject, though I did transmit on one occasion some passages from Confucius, under the title "The Organum of Confucius."

The second part of Pound's defense was a claim that he had just been speaking in general terms:

I have not spoken with regard to *this* war, but in protest against a system which creates one war after another, in series and in system. I have not spoken to the troops, and have not suggested that the troops should mutiny or revolt.

Just two months earlier, Pound's broadcast had been beamed to the 150,000 American troops fighting the German panzers in North Africa: "What are you doing in the war at all? What are you doing in Africa?" The third part of the defense was an invocation of the First Amendment, the freedom of speech:

The whole basis of democratic or majority government assumes that the citizen shall be informed of the facts. I have not claimed to know all the facts, but I have claimed to know some of the facts which are an essential part of the total that should be known to the people.

I have for years believed that the American people should be better informed as to Europe, and informed by men who are not tied to a special interest or under definite control.

The freedom of the press has become a farce, as everyone knows that the press is controlled, if not by its titular owners, at least by the advertisers.

Free speech under modern conditions becomes a mockery if it does not include the right of free speech over the radio . . .

At any rate a man's duties increase with his knowledge. A war between the U.S. and Italy is monstrous and should not have occurred. And a peace without justice is no peace but merely a prelude to future wars. Someone must take count of these things. And having taken count must act on his knowledge; admitting that his knowledge is partial and his judgment subject to error.[67]

It was, everything considered, a weak defense of his actions—but the best that Pound could do considering the facts. The letter is important in that it sheds light on Pound's mental state during the period when he was making his most extreme and virulent speeches on the radio. He understands that he has been indicted, he appears to understand the nature of the charges, and he has prepared his own defense of the charges.

Ezra Pound's world was beginning to crumble. Mussolini was in prison, the Axis powers in retreat, and Pound had been indicted for a crime in which conviction might mean death. The August sun must have seemed particularly oppressive in Rome and Rapallo that summer.

Pound, however, was never one to admit defeat. He resumed his broadcasts on Radio Rome and continued them into September. Marshal Badoglio, the new head of the Italian government, was negotiating secretly with the Allies, and on September 8 he announced an armistice. The German army immediately took over Rome. The following day an Allied armada so vast that its ships covered one thousand square miles of ocean approached the Italian coast, and General Mark Clark's Fifth Army established a beachhead at Salerno. The fight for Italy was on.

Fascist sympathizers streamed out of Rome in all directions, and on September 10 Pound joined them. Rather than return to Rapallo he made his way north by train and on foot. His destination was the home of his daughter, Mary, at Gais in the Tirol. He must have believed that his days were numbered, for he had something important that he wanted to tell her himself. He had another family, he said. A wife to whom he was legally married and a son. He had never told this to nineteen-year-old Mary before. Mary's reaction, as recorded in her biography, was to idolize him.[68]

On September 13, 1943, as Pound was arriving at Gais, a daring German raid liberated Mussolini from his Italian captors. He was being held in a ski lodge at the top of the Gran Sasso, the highest point in the Abruzzi Apennines, reached only by a funicular railway. Although his Italian guards were under orders to shoot him if a rescue attempt was made, most of them fled and the remainder stood at attention when German soldiers landed in gliders. Mussolini was flown to Germany to meet with Hitler, who had plans for his beneficiary.

The fall of Fascist Italy had been a severe blow for the Führer, who needed to rehabilitate Mussolini's government to give an appearance that all was not lost. Hitler therefore instructed Mussolini to set up a Fascist republic in northern Italy, which Mussolini proclaimed on September 15. From the beginning it was clear that the republic was merely a German puppet state taking orders directly from Berlin; German SS troops even guarded Mussolini. With the Allies in control of southern Italy, most prominent Italians, foreseeing their eventual victory, had gone over to the Allied side represented by the Badoglio government. As one historian noted, Mussolini's supporters in the new government consisted of "only the rogues and the dreamers."[69]

It was immediately apparent that the new Fascist republic was going to persecute the Jews as vigorously as Hitler's government was doing in Germany. Italian Jews had fared comparatively well heretofore; the racial laws Mussolini had enacted in 1938 had been only halfheartedly enforced, and no internment or deportation of Jews had taken place. With Berlin in charge, such moderation ceased. Joseph Goebbels talked increasingly about the conspiracy of Jews that sought world domination, and Mussolini was ordered to act.

On September 16, the day after the proclamation of the republic, the first 25 Jews were arrested in Merano, just a few miles from Gais. Ten days later the deportation of Jews began. Raids took place in Trieste on October 9 and in Rome on October 16; of the 1,007 Jews arrested in the capital only 12 survived the war. Genoa followed on November 3 and Milan on November 8. Large deportation camps were set up near Modena in central Italy and at Bolzano in the Tirol, and an extermination camp and crematorium were constructed at San Saba near Trieste. By the end of November almost 10,000 Jews had been arrested and prepared for deportation; most of them were murdered at Auschwitz.[70]

During the approximately two weeks when Pound remained at his daughter's, uncertain what to do next, he began Cantos 72 and 73, the only two he wrote during the war. They were also the only Cantos written in Italian, celebrating the achievements of Fascism and Mussolini as well as promising a rebirth of the Italian Empire. In one episode, Canadian soldiers with German prisoners ask directions of an Italian girl, who intentionally leads them across a mine field. Her legs are blown off, but the poem praises her for allowing two of the prisoners to escape.[71] The poems were published in Italy but have not been included in any edition of the collected Cantos.

Surveying the scene from Gais, Pound noted that the German lines south of Rome appeared to be holding against the Allies. And with Mussolini again in charge, anything was possible. Pound also could not have failed to notice that the Fascist republic, which had made its headquarters in villas around the village of Salo, was referred to as the Salo

Republic. Salo stood on the shore of Lake Garda, the mystical retreat where Pound had communed with souls of the dead; Sirmione lay just across the lake. Perhaps this would be the ideal republic Pound had so long sought, and he would be its poet laureate.

Pound journeyed to Salo and offered his help. In November his first writings in support of the Salo Republic appeared. As in the past, he saw education of the masses as a top priority, and proposed a national education program. Homer, Catullus (who had written many of his poems at Sirmione), Ovid, Dante, and Chaucer were all included; Mussolini, who was given the list, added the name of Plato.[72] Pound became a prolific contributor to periodicals being produced by the Republic, writing thirty-five articles for one journal alone. He castigated Italian journalists for their ignorance of economic affairs and proposed monetary reforms to everybody who would listen.

His writings in Salo were a continuation of his earlier efforts. He analyzed the economic history of the United States and portrayed the Civil War as a consequence of the discovery of gold in California in 1849; the war was a "Triumph of Finance," and "after Lincoln's death the real power in the United States passed from the hands of the official government into the hands of an evil combine. The democratic system perished." The American government was taken over by the usurers "who kept in touch with the arch-usurers in the mother-country [England]. Belmont used to represent the Rothschilds, etc. Today the Main Office is in New York, the Branch Office is in London. The ubicity of the victims does not matter, and the headquarters maintains a high degree of mobility."[73]

The problems of America, Pound claimed, were then exacerbated by the immigrants. Europeans "who wanted material gain emigrated to America. Those of a milder nature, the more contemplative, who were fond of beauty, who were more attached to their soil and home, remained in Europe. The strong, the restless, the malcontents, the misfits went." This led in turn to flaws in the electoral system which "expresses the imbecilities of a public that is ill-informed and which bases its opinions on the most incompetent strains available."[74]

What Pound wanted most was to return to the airwaves, and he was given the opportunity on December 10, 1943. In a program beamed from Milan to American troops in Europe and North Africa, Pound declared: "Every human being who is not a hopeless idiotic worm should realize that Fascism is superior in every way to Russian Jewocracy and that capitalism stinks."[75] Most of the broadcast discussed the upcoming trial of Galeazzo Ciano, Mussolini's son-in-law, and the other members of the Fascist Grand Council who had forced Mussolini's ouster the previous July. Ciano had been seized by the Nazis and turned over to Mussolini, who was trying to decide what to do with him. Pound advised showing no mercy. The following month, despite the pleadings of his daughter, Mussolini had Ciano shot. Pound then wrote that "Roosevelt is a dog and . . . deserves to be tried and given a sentence as harsh as the one meted out to Ciano."[76] Previously Pound had called for the execution of Churchill by hanging, and had indicated a willingness to assist in the shooting of Montague Norman, another British leader.[77]

There was at this time some discussion of sending Pound to Berlin or Paris to help with Nazi propaganda broadcasts, and on Christmas Day 1943, he wrote to Natalie Barney that he might be visiting Paris soon.[78] The trip apparently did not materialize. In February 1944, Pound was offered a position preparing propaganda for Radio Milan, the voice of the Salo Republic. The material was supposed to be "of a polemic nature suitable for insertion into news reports in foreign languages." Many of these were used in a program called *Jerry's Front Calling*, in which captured American soldiers were identified by name and messages were sent to their relatives in the States; the effect was supposed to produce sentiment in America for an end to the war. Pound contributed short news items and comments, many anti-Semitic in nature, for this program. He also created a character called "Mr. Dooley" who made humorous remarks about the Allied war effort. Throughout this period Pound was paid a regular monthly check by the Ministry of Popular Culture. His supervisor was Carl Goedel, a college-educated German who had been raised in Philadelphia and who received daily instructions from the Radio Bureau of the German Foreign Ministry in Berlin; Pound mentioned him in *The Pisan Cantos*.[79]

Throughout 1944 and into 1945 Pound persisted in these efforts, commuting regularly between Rapallo, Milan, and Salo. The specter of treason could never have been far from his mind. On one occasion in Salo when his treason indictment came up for discussion, Pound compared himself to Socrates, who had also opposed his own country while it was at war. He spoke of being guided by an interior light and claimed that his ideas were above warring factions.[80]

Meanwhile things were not going well for the Axis powers. On June 4, 1944, Rome fell. Two days later, D-day, the Allies landed at Normandy and began their relentless push to regain Europe. By August 25 they had entered Paris, and a month later they reached the German border. On the east the Soviets slowly regained their own territory and by late 1944 had pushed the Germans out of the Baltic States, Finland, Rumania, Bulgaria, and much of Poland, Hungary, Czechoslovakia, and Yugoslavia.

Pound carried on his mission. In November 1944, the Allies were closing in on Germany from both east and west and the Italian nation was in complete disarray. Pound suggested to the Ministry of Popular Culture that it might be a good time for the Salo Republic to produce a photomicrographic edition of the works of Vivaldi. Such a project, he argued, would demonstrate to the public that the Republic was "at peace with itself." Mussolini meanwhile continued to have virtually no responsibility; he busied himself with his mistress, astrological predictions, and playing solitaire on the shore of Lake Garda.[81]

In Rapallo life was anything but peaceful. Early in 1944, with the Allied army threatening to make a landing near Genoa, the German command expropriated all the seafront apartments in Rapallo to set up a coastal defense. Dorothy and Ezra, left without a home, moved in with Olga up the hill.[82] There, for the last year of the war, Ezra Pound lived with his wife and his mistress. His father had died, but his mother still lived elsewhere in Rapallo. Olga had a part-time job teaching school and brought home meat once or twice a month and occasionally fish. Coffee and butter were not available, wood and charcoal for heating and cooking were in short supply. Planes flew overhead almost every night, and Genoa, just down the coast, was bombed. Dorothy and Olga disliked each other intensely (after the war they were not on speaking terms). Ezra Pound, according to his daughter, was "pent up with two women who loved him, whom he loved, and who coldly hated each other . . . their hatred and tension had permeated the house."[83]

Back in the United States, Pound's name was becoming increasingly well known, often bracketed with Axis Sally, Tokyo Rose, and William (Lord Haw-Haw) Joyce. The *New York Times* speculated that he was "somewhere in northern Italy," and the U.S. Attorney General asked to be notified immediately when he was taken into custody.[84] Ezra Pound had longed for fame; he had achieved infamy.

Pound's old friends in America had become increasingly concerned about him since he had been indicted. Most of them were disgusted with his public utterances yet still willing to help and save his life if they could. "I wonder if he'll have the nerve to stand up and be shot if it comes to that," William Carlos Williams wrote.[85] "If Ezra has any sense he should shoot himself. Personally I think he should have shot himself somewhere along after the twelfth canto although maybe earlier," added Ernest Hemingway.[86] Both Williams and Hemingway were committed to sticking by Pound if and when he came to trial. "I have made up my mind to defend him if I am ever called as a witness in his trial," Williams stated.[87] Hemingway was more emphatic, writing to Allen Tate in an impressive display of fidelity that they should do everything possible to prevent Pound's death "even though we all should have to get up on the scaffold with a rope on our own necks."[88]

It was Hemingway who suggested a solution to Pound's problem. He asked Archibald MacLeish, who had become assistant secretary in the Department of State, to send him transcripts of those of Pound's broadcasts which had been monitored and recorded by the government. On July 27, 1943, the day following Pound's indictment, MacLeish did so. "Poor old Ezra," he wrote in an accompanying letter. "Treason is a little too serious and a little too dignified a crime for a man who has made such an incredible ass of himself, and accomplished so little in the process." Hemingway's reaction to the transcripts was immediate: "He deserves punishment and disgrace but what he really deserves most is ridicule." However Hemingway also saw in the transcripts a way to save his friend. The broadcasts, said Hemingway, could be used to prove that Ezra was "obviously crazy."[89]

Pound's insanity defense had thus been launched even as he was still broadcasting on Radio Rome. On August 31, 1943 Hemingway outlined the strategy in more detail, telling Allen Tate "how he [Pound] went nuts, how gradually and steadily he became irresponsible and idiotic, and what a great, sound and fine poet he was, and what a generous and really noble person he was." Hemingway urged the immediate implementation of the strategy, "not with publicity but to present the facts to those who should have them." One such person was MacLeish's old friend Harvey H. Bundy, who was serving as Assistant Secretary of War under Henry L. Stimson. On September 10, 1943 MacLeish explained to Bundy that Pound was "a half-cracked and extremely foolish individual" and the broadcasts a "product of a completely distracted mind" which "seems to have gone completely to pieces under the pressure of a swollen and dropsical ego." MacLeish urged Bundy to have Stimson issue an order to the military protecting Pound from "any summary disposition of the case by military authorities in Italy" so that Pound might avoid "the paraphernalia of martyrdom."[90]

Hemingway, MacLeish, and Pound's other friends had good cause for concern. Just five days after Hemingway's proposal, *PM,* a New York newspaper that would later play an active role in Pound's sanity hearings, printed a story severely critical of Pound; it called him "the man who despised people" and "the writer who hungered for knowledge," and said that for broadcasting for Mussolini "Ezra Pound may forfeit his life."[91] Sporadic attacks against Pound continued in the media as the Allies slowly pushed the Germans northward up the Italian peninsula. In 1944 a booklet was published noting that "Ezra Pound has certainly gotten himself into a tight fight with a short stick, and the fight is getting tighter and the stick is getting shorter." The author went on to speculate that if Pound came to trial he might be given "an unusually harsh court decree that he read his poems aloud twenty-four hours a day until he expires from nausea . . . It is better no doubt to let him pay the penalty which he must certainly have anticipated and which even now he must be contemplating . . . Only one question remains: Will he inflict the penalty upon himself, or will he allow the country of his birth to give him his death?"[92]

Pound continued to write material for *Jerry's Front Calling* into April 1945. As late as April 20, with Soviet troops approaching the suburbs of Berlin, Pound wrote to Fernando Mezzasoma, the Fascist Minister of Popular Culture, giving suggestions for new propaganda efforts.[93] By then Italy was in chaos, with Fascists being killed by groups of partisans, Communists, and Italian farmers who blamed them for the war; in Milan alone over one thousand Fascists were executed.

On April 28 Mussolini and his mistress Claretta Petacci were caught near Como as they tried to escape to the Italian Alps. He stood bravely, uttering his last words: "Shoot me in the chest." She threw her body in front of him at the last moment, trying to shield him, as the partisans machine-gunned them both to death.[94] They were taken to the Piazzale Loreto in Milan and displayed hanging by their heels. Two days later the Allies entered Berlin and Hitler killed himself in his bunker.

The following day American forces entered Rapallo. Ezra Pound went down the hill to town to surrender. An American soldier tried to sell him a bicycle, and nobody seemed to have any authority, so Pound returned home. On the next day, May 2, while both Olga and Dorothy were in town, there was a knock on the door. Pound opened it to find two partisans with tommy guns; they had heard that there was a reward on his head. He put his book of Confucius in his pocket and, leaving the house key with the girl downstairs, indicated to her that he expected to be hanged.[95] The partisans handcuffed him and took him away.

CHAPTER 7

THE NON-TRIAL

[WASHINGTON: 1945–1946]

NIGHT HAD FALLEN on the city of Washington when the Army C-54 carrying Ezra Pound approached Bolling Field for a landing. It was Sunday, November 18, 1945. Just off to the side as the plane approached could be seen the lights of sprawling St. Elizabeths Hospital, the federal mental hospital located up the hill from the airfield.

The flight from Rome had taken fifty hours with stops in Czechoslovakia, Belgium, England, the Azores, and Bermuda and two changes of planes; Pound was understandably exhausted. He had entertained the escorting officers with diatribes against Roosevelt and the Jews; "he knew approximately forty instances where the finances of the United States were used to improve the position of Jews in Europe or America . . . he had proof that four billion dollars . . . was diverted to the profit of individuals, most of them international Jews." Pound told the officers he had been trying to help America and denied that he was a Fascist. His defense, he said would be "based upon the fact that his mental capacity and studies placed him in a sphere above that of ordinary mortals . . . it would require a 'superman' to conduct his defense." Therefore he planned to conduct his own.[1]

Pound was taken immediately to the District of Columbia jail to await preliminary arraignment the next day. The weekend newspapers described the Nuremberg Trials, the war crimes trial for high-ranking Nazis, which were scheduled to begin in two days. The trials of death camp administrators were already underway. "Nazis Executed 8000 Russians, Czech Says." "Doctors' Testimony Describes Inhuman Tortures At Dachau," read the *Washington Post* of November 17, 1945. On Sunday, when Pound arrived, a front-page story was captioned "Belsen Beast, 10 Others Must Hang For Deeds." On Monday the front page of the *Washington Post* reported "Poet Ezra Pound Flown Here to Answer Treason Charges," and on the following page there was a story about atrocities described at the Japanese war crimes trials.

It was an unpropitious time to be coming to trial on treason charges. The American mood was not tolerant. Lives had been interrupted, people had been tortured, many had died. And it was all, people believed, because of a few fanatics, megalomaniacs, like Hitler and Mussolini. The American people wanted quick vengeance to ensure that justice was served. They felt strong and self-righteous; it had been a war in which the enemy really had been brutal and uncivilized. It was a war devoid of ambiguity. It was not a time to have compared Mussolini with Thomas Jefferson, or to have called Hitler a saint and a martyr.

At the same time as the American people wanted vengeance, they also wanted to put the war behind them and get on with their lives. Each day the newspaper headlined the number of American troops due to arrive home that day—20,600 on November 17; 20,000 on November 18; 24,100 on November 19; 35,800 on November 20. Grapefruits were 5 cents each and lamb chops 39 cents a pound; the people wanted to begin living again. Thus on November 18, the day of Pound's preliminary arraignment, the banner headline of the *Washington Post* read "Average New Car Prices Set at 1942 Level." And perhaps the most important news of the weekend for many people was the brutal drubbing the Army football team had given to the University of Pennsylvania, 61–0. It was as if the invincibility of Normandy had been carried back to West Point; the future rested upon Doc Blanchard and Glenn Davis, stars of what the sports page that day called "the greatest football team of the century." There was a sense that the war would indeed pass, and that in a few months the American people would probably be more tolerant, more forgiving of poets who had made mistakes.

Pound was interviewed by reporters shortly after his arrival and put on his best bravado. He joked that they had not been interested in him when he had returned to Washington in 1939; now he was news. Reporters described him as "somewhat decrepit but still debonair" and "in gay spirits." "There is an idea afloat here that I have betrayed this country," Pound sarcastically told reporters. "If that damned fool idea is still in anybody's head, I want to wipe it out . . . What I want to know is whether anybody heard my broadcasts and, if so, how they could have any earthly idea of what I was talking about."[2]

Bravado, however, would not be enough to help Ezra Pound escape the treason charges. He had been warned repeatedly to stop his broadcasts for Mussolini. The July 1941 restriction of his passport by the State Department was an implicit warning to return to the United States. At the time of Pearl Harbor his friends told him he would be guilty of treason if he stayed; he later admitted, "My mistake was to go on after Pearl Harbor."[3] After Roosevelt publicly warned in January 1943 that he might be indicted, and then after he was indicted that July, he still continued making broadcasts and doing everything within his power to help the Axis cause. Treason, as defined by the Constitution of the United States, consists of "adhering" to the nation's enemies and "giving them aid and comfort."

To be indicted for a crime is one thing. To be convicted of the crime, however, is often quite another, and the Department of Justice had a problem. All during the week of November 18, while Pound paced nervously in his jail cell, Department of Justice attorneys were preparing a second indictment and questioning the seven Italian radio technicians whom they had brought over to testify against him. The problem was that at that time all treasonous acts had to be proven by two separate witnesses. In the language of a 1944 Supreme Court decision:

> The very minimum function that an overt act must perform in a treason prosecution is that it show sufficient action by the accused, in its setting, to sustain a finding that the accused actually gave aid and comfort to the enemy. Every act, movement, deed, and word of the defendant charged to constitute treason must be supported by the testimony of two witnesses. The two-witness principle is to interdict imputation of incriminating acts to the accused by circumstantial evidence or by the testimony of a single witness. *The prosecution cannot rely on evidence which does not meet the constitutional test for overt acts to create any inference that the accused did other acts or did something more than was shown in the overt act, in order to make a giving of aid and comfort to the enemy.*[4]

The difficulty lay in the fact that the radio technicians spoke no English. It was therefore impossible for them to say that they had heard Pound make a particular remark—for example, "Every sane act you commit is committed in homage to Mussolini and Hitler,"—since they could not understand English. Furthermore, there was usually only a single technician in the studio at any one time when Pound was making the recording, thereby making the two-witness rule difficult to fulfill. Finally, the broadcasts were taped and stored for later use, so that the day it was made was not the same day it was eventually broadcast. The two-witness rule was modified in later court rulings to make it easier to get a conviction of treason, but in 1945 it was the law under which the Department of Justice had to operate.

As early as July 3, 1945, U.S. officials were aware that the prosecution's case would be difficult; one of them wrote to the army judge advocate of the Mediterranean region: "The long delay in holding Dr. Ezra Pound has been due to the necessity of securing two witnesses of the overt act of treason upon which to predicate the case." On October 29, 1945, Department of Justice officials acknowledged to reporters that they were still encountering problems. The *D.C. Times Herald* carried the story, proclaiming that "Justice officials said that they have been unsuccessful in locating witnesses who actually saw Pound make the disputed propaganda broadcasts praising Italy and Germany. Without such witnesses it is 'doubtful' conviction can be obtained, they admitted." An internal FBI memo to J. Edgar Hoover that same day confirmed that "there are no two witnesses at present who can testify that they both saw Pound broadcast at any one time," although it claimed to have available "two witnesses to overt acts of treason other than the act of broadcasting."[5]

The second indictment against Pound was much broader than the first and accused him of trying to create dissension and distrust between the United States and its allies, of trying to create racial prejudice in the United·States, of trying to create distrust of the American government among the American people, and of giving aid and comfort to the enemy, all done while in the pay and employment of the Italian government. The evidence for the indictment went to the grand jury on Friday, November 23, and was handed down by the court on Monday, November 26; it specified nineteen specific acts of treason. The purpose of the second indictment was to strengthen the legal case against Pound. According to a confidential departmental assessment, however, "with the exception of Overt Act 3, either the evidence available to prove the remaining eighteen overt acts alleged in the indictment was insufficient to meet the constitutional requirements of two witnesses to the same overt act or . . . the acts alleged could not properly be construed as giving aid and comfort to the enemy."[6]

Faced with the trial, the Department of Justice attempted to put on a brave front. When the second indictment was made public, departmental lawyers talked confidently of the trial which "may be set for early next month" and of the "20 or 25 witnesses" who would be called.[7] The mood of the nation was such that a conviction was likely despite the technical problems. At the same time it was recognized within the department that although "conviction of one overt act is all that is required under the law, it is felt that a case embodying a single overt act leaves no margin for error."[8]

THE HARVARD BARDS

For over two years Ezra Pound had been planning his defense, outlined in letters to Attorney General Biddle in 1943 and to his father-in-law's legal firm in October 1945. He would deny the charges, claim that his motivation was to save America, invoke the freedom of speech, and use the trial as a public forum to expose Roosevelt and the Jews: "The public has learned a great deal, but it still has the right to know MORE. If that be over my dead body, so much the worse both for me and for the public."[9] It would be a performance worthy of Laval, worthy of Demosthenes himself.

Pound's approach was evident when he was arraigned in court on November 19, 1945, the day after his arrival. According to reporters present he "made a scholarly 10 minute debate why he should be allowed to act as his own attorney."[10] The judge said that the charges were too serious and denied his request. Pound returned to his cell to contemplate the alternatives. Laval, he recalled, had used attorneys yet had still managed to turn his trial into an impressive display of elocution and public education.

Ezra Pound's friends, however, had other ideas for his defense. The chief planners among this group were Archibald MacLeish, Dudley Fitts, James Laughlin, and Merrill Moore. These men had three things in common—each was a Harvard graduate, each was committed to modern poetry, and each believed that Pound should be saved.[11]

Archibald MacLeish had had an illustrious career since his days at Harvard Law School. He was a well-known poet and playwright as well as being a statesman who had risen to be assistant secretary in the Department of State; in fact he spent much of the summer of 1945 helping plan the United Nations. He had known Pound since the early 1920s in Paris and had carried on a long and colorful correspondence with him over the years. MacLeish had known Fitts and Moore for at least twelve years, and also was good friends with Hemingway and T. S. Eliot, with whom he had corresponded about Pound's defense.

Dudley Fitts was a product of Boston and Harvard, where he had been editor of the *Harvard Advocate,* a position T. S. Eliot had previously held. He was an instructor at the Choate School in Connecticut and a published poet whose work was known for its erudition and use of Greek and Roman classics. He had favorably reviewed Pound's poetry as early as 1930 and had met him during his 1939 visit to the U.S. Fitts had also introduced one of his students, James Laughlin, to Pound's work and to MacLeish. Fitts had known Merrill Moore since 1931 and in 1939 had edited a book of his sonnets.

After James Laughlin left Choate he went to Harvard. An aspiring poet, he spent several weeks with Pound in Rapallo and then returned to the United States to set up his New Directions publishing house. In the late 1930s he became Pound's chief publisher and also the publisher and friend of William Carlos Williams. Laughlin met Merrill Moore in 1936 and asked him to contribute to an anthology of experimental prose and poetry; Pound and Fitts were among the other contributors. In 1939 Laughlin published a book of Moore's poems with a foreward by William Carlos Williams.

Merrill Moore would become the most important of the four in the planning of Pound's defense. He had been a member of the Nashville Fugitives, a group of poets who admired Pound and Eliot, and by 1938 had published five volumes of poetry in a style marked by experimentation and innovation. He was close friends with not only MacLeish, Fitts and Laughlin, but with Williams and Hilda Doolittle as well. Another close family friend was Louis Untermeyer, who had visited Pound in Rapallo in 1929. Moore was a psychiatrist as well as a poet and for six years had been a research fellow at the Harvard Medical School. In his capacity as physician and psychiatrist he was frequently consulted by his poet friends. One who did so was Robert Frost, who had become good friends with Moore when Frost's only son developed schizophrenia and subsequently committed suicide.[12] Frost and Untermeyer were very close friends as well.

This then was the "old boy" network that was in place in 1945— MacLeish, Fitts, Laughlin, and Moore with direct access to Eliot, Hemingway, Williams, Doolittle, Untermeyer, and Frost. From discussions among them there apparently emerged a consensus that Pound's best hope of avoiding execution or long imprisonment was to plead insanity, the idea put forward by Hemingway two years earlier. A major impetus to their thinking was probably a realization that any other defense was hopeless; as MacLeish put it in a letter to Eliot, "a calculated campaign of anti-Semitism . . . is hardly an expression of the right of the intellectual to tell the truth as he sees it."[13] At least MacLeish, and probably Eliot as well, had reservations about a plea of insanity, and this is reflected in their correspondence. MacLeish said in retrospect that "I never thought Ezra was insane unless a ludicrous egotism qualifies . . . Some of us thought Ezra's lawyer should have tried the case on the freedom of speech issue."[14]

There is no doubt, however, that there was an organized decision by some of this group to save Pound by claiming that he was insane. As Merrill Moore's widow recalls: "A group of poets who admired Pound seized upon the device of his being committed to a mental hospital as alternative to his being tried for treason . . . I don't know who originated the plan . . . I think that Merrill, like many others, felt that no good purpose would be served by punishing Pound, even if he were mentally competent, so long as he was rendered powerless to inflict harm."[15] Mrs. Moore remembers at least Fitts, Frost, and Louis Untermeyer as being included in the discussions.

James Laughlin may have been included as well, for he wrote to T. S. Eliot that Pound was of course sane but allowing him to go to trial would be dangerous; a plea of insanity was the safest means of avoiding it.[16] The day after Pound was found unfit for trial, Laughlin was asked "how much the unfit plea had been planned. And JL [Laughlin] allowed he had from the beginning thot [stet] the thing was to get P [Pound] out of trial the easiest way."[17] A strong suggestion of an organized effort is also reflected in the reports of FBI interviews with many of this group, among other friends of Pound's, during 1945; one of them told the FBI that "he, as well as any acquaintances of Pound's, should they be called to testify, probably all would state that they believed he has become mentally unbalanced."[18]

In September 1945 Laughlin approached his friend Julien Cornell and asked him to represent Pound. Cornell, a graduate of Swarthmore College and Yale Law School, was only thirty-five at the time. Laughlin then wrote to the London law firm of Pound's father-in-law and received their approval for his choice. Pound apparently knew nothing of these arrangements.

On the morning of November 20, the day after Pound had been told that he must get a lawyer, he had two visitors at the District of Columbia jail. The first was Ida Mapel, with whom he had stayed during his 1939 visit in Washington; she found him "nervous" but otherwise well. The second visitor was Julien Cornell. After they finished talking Cornell wrote to Laughlin: "I discussed with him the possibility of pleading insanity as a defense and he has no objection. In fact he told me that the idea had already occurred to him."[19] This was a remarkable turnabout for Pound, who just one day earlier seemed committed to defending himself and his actions. What led to his change of heart is not known. Possible factors include information given to him by Cornell, information given to him by other visitors, fatigue and fear exacerbated by that day's newspaper stories announcing the opening of the Nuremburg war crimes trials, and the recollection that he had used the psychia-

trists at Pisa to improve his living conditions. Whatever the cause of
the change, Ezra Pound became a full and voluntary partner in the
use of insanity to escape a trial for treason. Henceforth he made no
further attempts to defend himself in court but merely watched the
proceedings silently.

Insanity can be used as a defense in one of two ways, and it is
unclear which of the two Cornell or Pound had in mind initially. It
can be used to plead the person unfit for trial, in which case the trial
is not held, or it can be used at the trial itself to claim the person was
insane at the time of the crime and therefore not responsible for his
behavior—as was used, for example, in the John Hinckley trial. It is
clear that Cornell expected the psychiatrists who would testify to disagree
with one another, for he told Laughlin: "As you probably know, the
trial of such an issue is almost always a farce, since learned medicos
who testify for each side squarely contradict each other and completely
befuddle the jury. It then largely becomes a question of the sympathy
of the jury, assuming, of course, that there is no question of outright
faking."[20]

The first task for Cornell as defense attorney was to lay the ground-
work for a plea of insanity. On November 21 Cornell wrote to Laughlin,
regarding Pound's stay in the prison camp in Italy, that "even three
Army psychiatrists who examined him found that he was suffering from
claustrophobia."[21] That was an accurate description of what had happened. Five days later, however, in an affidavit in support of an application for bail, Cornell claimed that Pound had "suffered a complete mental
collapse and loss of memory . . . The period of violent insanity apparently began about mid-June, to endure for three months or more . . .
memory returned, but the great mind remained impaired, and fits of
shuddering terror balked his struggle to regain his senses . . . Although
he has partially recovered his health, I believe he is still insane and
that if he remains in prison he may never recover."[22]

Cornell's tactic succeeded. The *New York Herald Tribune* reported
Cornell as saying that Pound "had been kept 'incommunicado' in a
small iron cage for seven months." And the *Washington Post* quoted
Cornell as stating that Pound "may even lose his life if he is not sent
to a hospital."[23] Public sympathy had been elicited, which would be
necessary for the insanity defense to succeed.

The question arises whether Julien Cornell really believed the repre-
sentations he was making publicly about Pound's mental state. This
can be assessed, perhaps, by his reply to Dorothy Pound who, alarmed
by the newspaper accounts that described Pound's "violent insanity,"
wrote to Cornell on December 8, 1945. Cornell replied to her on January

25, 1946, apologizing for having "startled and alarmed" her by the 'reports of your husband's condition":

> You need not be alarmed about the report on your husband's mental condition. While, no doubt, his difficulties were aggravated by the ordeal of his imprisonment, he has been resting comfortably in a hospital for some time now, and I believe that his condition is just about normal. However, a state which would, no doubt, appear to you to be normal, is defined by the doctors as paranoid in character, to an extent which impairs your husband's judgment of his predicament and renders him unable to properly defend himself.
>
> While the doctors are agreed that he is to this extent mentally abnormal, I feel quite sure that you will find, when you see him again, that he is his usual self, and the mental aberrations which the doctors have found are not anything new or unusual, but are chronic and would pass entirely unnoticed by one like yourself who has lived close to him for a number of years. In fact I think it may be fairly said that any man of his genius would be regarded by a psychiatrist as abnormal.[24]

Cornell's conceptualization of Pound's "insanity" can also be surmised from his recommendations for "the treatment which I feel sure he needs, namely relaxation, recreation and a certain amount of physical freedom."[25]

Cornell's overall strategy for obtaining Pound's release was to use the insanity plea to counter the treason charges, then petition the court to gain release from the mental hospital on the grounds that he was incurably insane but not in need of hospitalization. Cornell expected that the case "would have to be carried on appeal to the Circuit Court of Appeals and probably to the United States Supreme Court" and said he was "confident that I could succeed if I could get the case before the Supreme Court." The issue, according to Cornell, was that a man cannot "be shut up indefinitely after being indicted when he cannot be tried because of illness."[26] For a young lawyer the case must have looked like the threshold to a brilliant legal career.

Whether other people shared Cornell's optimism about the intended course of events is not known, but he clearly believed in it. To Dorothy Pound he wrote, "You may rejoice that we have found a way to get around the difficulties presented by the indictment against him, and that these difficulties are all but surmounted . . . I expect, therefore, that after a few months the case will be dropped and he will be set free."[27] And Cornell apparently told Ezra Pound the same thing, for Pound later wrote from his room at St. Elizabeths: "What do you think they told Cornell ten years ago, when he thought I wd / [would] be back in Italy in six months a free man?"[28]

THE SECOND PSYCHIATRISTS

Friday, November 23, was the beginning of an unpleasant weekend for Ezra Pound. He spent the day confined to a cell in the District of Columbia courthouse, where the grand jury was hearing evidence for his second indictment. He had a lawyer and a plan for a defense, but he must have wondered whether it would succeed.

On Saturday there was a successful jailbreak at the District jail, resulting in the confinement of all prisoners to their cells without normal privileges or exercise. As he had done in Italy, Pound complained bitterly of claustrophobia and was allowed to spend the nights of November 25 and 26 in the jail infirmary.

But the worst news of the weekend came in the newspapers. On Sunday, November 25, the *Washington Post* featured him under the headline "Benito's Boy" and reprinted some of his broadcast remarks. More serious was a long and detailed account of his life and work in *PM*, a New York newspaper, in which eleven of his broadcasts were excerpted.[29] "You are at war for the duration of the Germans' pleasure." "You follow Mussolini and Hitler in every constructive act of your government." "And Mr. Squirmy and Mr. Slime are still feeding it to you right over the BBC radio, and every one of the Jew radios of Schenectady, New York and Boston . . ."

Appended to the *PM* article were interviews with five of Pound's colleagues and friends. Conrad Aiken contended that "Pound is less a traitor than fool." Louis Untermeyer said, "I do not believe he should be shot." William Carlos Williams attacked Pound's "vicious anti-Semitism," "callousness," and "infantile mental pattern." "He doesn't have a great mind and never did . . . It would be the greatest miscarriage of justice, human justice, to shoot him." Finally, at the end of the article, there was a comment from the editor-in-chief of Random House announcing that all Ezra Pound's poetry was being dropped from their *Anthology of Famous English and American Poetry.* "Random House is not going to publish any Fascist. As a matter of fact, we don't think Ezra Pound is good enough, or important enough, to include." To a man who believed himself to be the greatest poet since Dante, the news was not good.

The second indictment was handed down by the court, as expected, on Monday, November 26. On the following day Pound appeared for the scheduled hearing. Julien Cornell told the court that his client was mentally ill and could not enter a plea. Cornell then gave testimony and submitted his affidavit describing Pound's "period of violent insanity" and alleging that "he is still insane." He requested either that Pound be released on bail or that he be transferred immediately to a mental hospital for examination. Pound stood quietly by, and the Department of Justice lawyers did not object. The judge deferred action on the motion for bail but ordered Pound to be transferred to the psychiatric ward of Gallinger Hospital, a public hospital administered by the District of Columbia. After returning to New York, Cornell wrote to his client on November 29, reassuring him that he had nothing to worry about and promising to get him into a better hospital once the mental examination had been completed. As a postscript he told Pound he had ordered a subscription to *Newsweek* for him.[30]

Four psychiatrists were assigned to examine Pound and report their findings to the court by December 14. Three were appointed by the government and the fourth was to be appointed by Julien Cornell for the defense. The first government psychiatrist contacted was Dr. Marion R. King, then medical director of the Bureau of Prisons and the logical person to coordinate a psychiatric examination of a federal prisoner. On November 28, one day after the court hearing ordering an examination, Dr. King wrote to the Department of Justice requesting all information available on "the life-long history of Ezra Pound." He indicated that he already had in his possession the affidavit that Cornell had submitted at the hearing the previous day.

Marion King was fifty-six years old and had spent twenty-six years in the United States Public Health Service. He had had a single year of training in psychiatry, and had spent most of his career in general medical and administrative positions in prisons. His few professional publications were on infectious diseases and topics such as discipline in prisons. He was undoubtedly a competent general physician with some knowledge of psychiatry in a prison population, but by no stretch of the imagination could he be labeled an "eminent" psychiatrist as Julien Cornell subsequently called him.[31]

The second government psychiatrist was Dr. Joseph L. Gilbert, who was in charge of the psychiatric ward at Gallinger Hospital; thus he had to be included because that was where the examination was to take place. He was fifty-five years old, trained in psychiatry and psychoanalysis, and for the previous fifteen years had been at Gallinger Hospital and in private practice. Gallinger had only two psychiatrists on the staff at that time, and the quality of services was so poor that there had been an official investigation one year earlier.[32] Dr. Gilbert had no professional publications. According to psychiatrists who knew him he was a competent and decent man but not the kind who would have challenged Dr. Overholser.[33] He was hardly, as Cornell called him, "eminent."

Dr. Winfred Overholser, the third government psychiatrist, unquestionably was. He was fifty-one years old, secretary-treasurer of the American Psychiatric Association, and generally regarded as one of America's foremost authorities on the legal aspects of psychiatry.

Dr. Overholser's numerous publications prior to his examination of Pound help illuminate his subsequent psychiatric approach. Overholser was a psychoanalyst and, as such, believed that all human behavior is relative. "Between the fully normal," Overholser wrote, "and the grossly abnormal lies a vast no man's land of deviations from mental health, minor or major, slight or serious." Just as behavior is relative, so also responsibility for one's behavior is relative, and he said "there is no logic" in the assumption "that a person is either 'sane' and consequently fully responsible for all his acts, or else 'insane' and wholly irresponsible."[34]

The legal test for insanity in both the District of Columbia and a majority of states in 1945 was the M'Naghton test. A person was considered to be sane and therefore legally responsible for his actions if he understood the difference between right and wrong. Overholser was sharply critical of the M'Naghton test, saying that "it neglects entirely the emotional aspects of conduct" and that it had been "unmodified by one hundred years of psychiatric progress."[35] "While the jurist looks upon the actor as a free agent possessed of a free will, the psychiatrist realizes that conduct is actuated primarily by emotions, and that the sources of that conduct are more often than not unknown to the actor himself."[36]

Overholser had also written on the relationship of genius and insanity five years before he was called on to examine Pound. "Geniuses are peculiar people," he wrote. "The individual with special gifts is abnormal, but that is quite different from saying he is psychotic or mentally deranged." Overholser considered the thesis that genius is a form of insanity but specifically rejected it.[37]

Overholser had one other strongly held belief that had a direct bearing on his handling of the Pound case. He was extremely concerned about the professional image of psychiatry and deplored trials in which psychiatrists for the prosecution and for the defense contradicted each other. As early as 1938 he had urged psychiatrists for both sides to perform a joint examination and issue a joint report. "Above all," he wrote, the psychiatrist "should avoid as strongly as is possible to human beings partisanship or the appearance of partisanship."[38]

Winfred Overholser is remembered by all who knew him as a kind, honorable, and thoroughly professional man. Elderly patients and long-term staff members at St. Elizabeths still speak warmly of him, recalling that he treated the patients with respect and would spend Christmas

Day visiting each ward in the hospital. Colleagues also remember that Dr. Overholser was conscious of his place in history and of being compared with his eminent predecessor at St. Elizabeths, Dr. William A. White, probably the best-known American psychiatrist of his generation. Dr. White had had an unblemished professional career with the exception of one incident: he testified at the Leopold and Loeb murder case and was publicly accused of accepting a private fee while working for the government.

There is one other aspect of Overholser's background which is of interest. He had graduated from Harvard *cum laude* in economics and was well known as an erudite, widely read man. "Dr. Overholser had quite a literary turn of mind" is the way one of his contemporaries phrased it.[39] He was also very close personal friends with Merrill Moore. They lived nearby for many years in Boston and, according to Overholser's son, Dr. Moore spent much time with Overholser and looked up to him.[40] When Overholser's biography had to be written in the *American Journal of Psychiatry* in 1948 for his term as president of the American Psychiatric Association, it was Dr. Moore who was called upon to do it as the colleague who knew him best.[41] Moore and Overholser had a collegial and warm relationship, with Moore frequently sending "Win" sonnets that would not find their way into his published works:

> *A trollop who hustled at Yale*
> *Had her prices tattooed on her tail.*
> *And just to be kind*
> *To the boys who were blind*
> *She had a special edition in Braille!*[42]

Exactly when Dr. Overholser first met with Ezra Pound is not clear, for there is reason to believe that Overholser destroyed all records of these meetings. The destruction was deliberate, according to a psychiatrist who worked closely with him.[43] The most striking feature about the entire St. Elizabeths Hospital file on Pound is the virtual absence of clinical data by Overholser, despite the fact that he was intimately involved in the case for over twelve years. Overholser's records on everything else in his life were voluminous and meticulously kept, and can be examined in the National Archives and the Library of Congress; they even include a ticket from his first airplane ride, ticket stubs to a bullfight in Mexico, and the program from a talk he gave to the Meadville Theological School. But almost no mention of Ezra Pound is to be found.

If the ensuing cordial relationship between Overholser and Pound is any gauge, their first meeting must have gone well. Overholser's interest in economics and literature would have given them common ground for discussion. One of Pound's favorite books, *A Short Review and Analysis of the History of Money in the United States,* had been written by Willis A. Overholser, and Pound certainly would have wanted to know if Winfred Overholser was related.[44] Perhaps Overholser told Pound that he had recently publicly commented on the absence of structural defects found in the piece of Mussolini's brain examined at the Army Medical Museum in Washington.[45] Or perhaps he told Pound about his close friendship with Merrill Moore, and Moore's sodality with MacLeish, Fitts, Laughlin, Williams, Doolittle, and Frost. Dr. Overholser appreciated Pound's literary achievements; as he phrased it, "Pound was a person of eminent standing in the field of letters and having literary interests myself I visited him not infrequently and we discussed various persons and things of mutual interest."[46]

Pound reciprocated Overholser's regard. In later years Pound is recorded as saying, with a smile, that Overholser and he "had always seen eye-to-eye on things and that when he was first in the 'hellhole' [Howard Hall of St. Elizabeths] Mencken came to see him and told him that he was fortunate to be in a hospital where the superintendent knew who he was."[47] After he finally was released from St. Elizabeths, Pound and Overholser carried on a lively correspondence regarding literature, legal matters, and mutual friends.

King, Gilbert, and Overholser, then, were the three psychiatrists who were supposed to ensure that the interests of the United States government, the prosecution, were represented in the psychiatric examination of Pound. There was also a fourth psychiatrist, Dr. Wendell S. Muncie, who was retained by Julien Cornell as the psychiatrist for the defense. Cornell first had tried to get Dr. Adolf Meyer of Johns Hopkins, but he declined and suggested a list of alternates. Dr. Muncie was one of these.

Wendell Muncie was forty-eight years old, an associate professor of psychiatry at Johns Hopkins, and in private practice. He had authored a modest number of professional publications and, while not of the professional stature of Dr. Overholser, was a respected psychiatrist. When Muncie agreed to participate on December 6, 1945, Cornell wrote him a detailed letter similar to the affidavit in which Pound's experiences in the prison camp were apparently exaggerated: "It is conceded by the government that he became definitely insane during his imprisonment in Italy last summer . . . he was stricken with violent terror and hysteria, and also affected with amnesia." In closing, Cornell gave Dr. Muncie a strong suggestion about what he was expected to find in his examination:

In examining Mr. Pound I wish you would bear in mind that there is another question involved in addition to his sanity, namely, the question whether even if he is sane, he is sufficiently well to stand the ordeal of a lengthy trial. This would require several weeks of conferences with his attorneys in preparation for trial, and probably two weeks at least of proceedings in court. I have some reason to fear that even if he were sufficiently sane to understand the proceedings, the ordeal of the trial might bring on a relapse.[48]

By this point, then, Cornell clearly had decided to plead Pound unfit to stand trial.

THE PSYCHIATRIC EXAMINATION

Ezra Pound's treason trial never took place because the four psychiatrists claimed he was insane and unfit to stand trial. The unfit plea says that the person is unable to understand the nature and object of the proceedings against him, unable to comprehend his own condition in reference to these proceedings, and unable to assist in his own defense. It arose in English law out of a belief that people who are severely mentally disabled are unable to defend themselves in court and so it is inhumane to try them while they are in that condition.

Compared with the use of insanity as a defense during trial (the classic insanity defense), the unfit plea was used sparingly until the 1940s when its use increased sharply in both England and the United States. In some states it even was used more frequently than the insanity defense, and the state hospitals for the criminally insane became filled with persons unfit to stand trial but with the original criminal charges still pending against them. If the person recovered his sanity and became fit at any time, then he could still be brought to trial. The practical effect was that the unfit plea became an indeterminate sentence in a mental hospital. On the other hand, the unfit plea used a less stringent test of insanity than the M'Naghten test and so was more likely to succeed when evidence for insanity was weak.[49] The use of the unfit plea in the Pound case was regarded as important in legal circles and is used to illustrate the plea in at least one standard textbook of law and psychiatry.[50]

Given the facts of the case as were known to the Department of Justice in December 1945, one wonders how anybody thought an unfit plea could succeed. Pound's 1943 letter to the attorney general detailing his defense bespoke a sane mind that understood the charges and was able to rebut them. His October 1945 letter to the lawyers in England did likewise; this was probably in the hands of the Justice Department since it had had to pass the base censors to be sent from the prison camp. Even the Washington newspapers had commented on Pound's "scholarly 10 minute debate" in court at his initial arraignment. Most importantly, the Department of Justice had the psychiatric records from the three army psychiatrists who had examined Pound in Italy and who had found him to be perfectly sane.

Despite such obvious evidence that Pound was fit to stand trial, the unfit plea did succeed. The main reasons for this were that Dr. Overholser was determined that it should, and that it met the needs of both the defense and the prosecution. Overholser's role was crucial. He decided that Pound should be protected and then set about to ensure that protection. The first thing he did was to get an agreement from the other psychiatrists that they would reach a common conclusion and submit a single report. This was consistent with his preferred approach, and was described by Julien Cornell as follows:

> This turn of events was partly the result, I believe, of Dr. Overholser's insistence that four experienced psychiatrists should be able to reach an agreement about the condition of their patient and should not allow a sanity trial to develop into the usual farce where eminent psychiatrists on both sides of the case reach different results and leave to the jury a decision which should be made by the medical profession. Such a dispute between doctors, in Overholser's opinion, was unworthy of the profession, degrading to the doctors involved and a hindrance to the judicial process.
>
> When the four doctors first met, therefore, Dr. Overholser told them that he hoped they would reach common agreement on the condition of the prisoner, objectively, without partisan bias in favor of the government or the defense.[51]

Once a single report was agreed upon, Overholser persuaded his colleagues that their opinion should agree with his, and he was certain that Pound was insane and unfit to stand trial. An example of such persuasion is suggested by the fact that Dr. King revised his initial psychiatric report after discussion with Overholser and the others. The original report was destroyed, but the revised version still exists in the St. Elizabeths Hospital files. According to a letter from King to Overholser, the original report had been submitted to Overholser on December 10, but "subsequent examination and especially our joint examination on December 13, 1945, resulted in a revision of my report."[52] For seven pages King described Pound as querulous, egocentric, arrogant, and a gifted poet with obvious eccentricities. King included in his report the fact that "the reports of the Army psychiatrists do not suggest that he experienced a complete mental or physical collapse." Yet on the final page King concluded that "the symptoms are characteristic of a paranoid state of psychotic proportions and hospital care, with provisions for adequate treatment and control to prevent him from becoming a further menace to himself and others are indicated." Much in King's report does not support this non-sequitur conclusion, which has the appearance of being added after the original report had been finished.

Whether Overholser also had to persuade Gilbert is not known, but if so it should not have been difficult. When Dr. Gilbert's psychiatric unit had been publicly investigated in 1944 for alleged poor services, Dr. Overholser was one of the three psychiatrists appointed by the commissioners of the District of Columbia to conduct the investigation.[53] Thus Overholser was very familiar with Dr. Gilbert and, since Gilbert retained his job following the investigation, it is reasonable to assume that he may have felt obligated to Overholser. In addition Dr. Gilbert was not a man who was likely to have challenged a person of Dr. Overholser's stature.

That left only Dr. Muncie to be persuaded. He was the outsider in the group, not part of the Washington network, and the one psychiatrist appointed by the defense. He is also the only one of the four psychiatrists who is still alive and who can therefore comment on what took place.

Because of his other responsibilities, Dr. Muncie could not come to Washington to examine Pound until December 13, the day before the report was due in court. By that time Dr. King had examined Pound at least three times, Dr. Gilbert had examined him many times (since Pound was on his psychiatric ward), and Dr. Overholser had examined him at least once. The plan for December 13 was for all four psychiatrists to examine him together and then to agree upon their final report to the court; according to the ground rules laid down by Dr. Overholser, the report should express the unanimous opinion of all four psychiatrists.

Muncie later testified that he examined Pound for about three hours that day, partly alone and partly in the company of the other three psychiatrists. When he first went to Pound's room and examined him alone, Muncie later recalled for FBI investigators, "I had the impression that he was a plain psychopath."[54] In a recent interview he remembered it the same way: "I first thought he was just a damned psychopath."[55] A "psychopath," as the term was used at that time, was a person who disregarded social rules and laws, was immature, unable to accept responsibility, put his own needs before everything else, and rationalized his behavior to make it seem reasonable. They were "almost invariably held accountable" for their actions, and the clear implication of Muncie's initial diagnosis was that Pound was fit for trial.[56]

After interviewing Pound alone, Muncie went down the hall to consult with his three colleagues. "They called my attention to some things and so when I re-examined him I pursued these leads. When I went back in to examine him I found that he was all mixed up; I couldn't get an intelligible answer from him." Between the first and second interviews, within an hour, Pound had become "completely incoherent." When I asked Dr. Muncie whether Pound might have been faking some of the symptoms, he replied: "Yes, that's possible. I had never entertained it."[57]

That left the report to be agreed upon, and it was due in court the next day. Dr. Muncie does not remember exactly where it came from, but it appeared that day at the termination of the joint interview. He thinks that Dr. Overholser drafted it but he is not certain. When I asked Dr. Muncie whether the report might have already been prepared by Dr. Overholser prior to the joint examination of Pound on December 13, he replied: "I don't know but I wouldn't be surprised."[58] He recalls signing the report that day with the other psychiatrists.

In fairness to Dr. Muncie, he didn't have much choice except to find Pound unfit to stand trial. Most of his background information about Pound had been supplied by Julien Cornell, and Cornell had strongly suggested the desired outcome of the examination. The three psychiatrists who were supposed to be representing the government and who would have been expected to have found Pound fit to stand trial were telling Muncie that he was unfit. It would have looked absurd if the defense psychiatrist, the one who would have been expected to find him unfit, was the only one of the four psychiatrists who found him fit.

Also the persuasive abilities and power of Dr. Overholser cannot be underestimated. He was one of the foremost psychiatric authorities on legal matters in the country. How could Dr. Muncie, an academic and private psychiatrist with less experience in forensic matters, challenge such a man? Dr. Overholser was also about to become president-elect of the American Psychiatric Association, and as such was in a position to influence, either favorably or adversely, the professional careers of his colleagues. They deferred to his judgment. Following the sanity hearing Dr. Muncie wrote to Overholser: "I thought your testimony was very clear and must have had a telling effect with the jury. I hope we can join efforts in this or other directions again some day."[59]

Pound did his part to ensure that the examiners would find him unfit to stand trial. For someone who had been practicing eccentricities for many years it was not difficult to do. As early as 1916 Pound's speech had been described as "a wholly original accent, the base of American mingled with a dozen assorted 'English society' and Cockney accents inserted with mockery, French, Spanish and Greek exclamations, strange cries and catcalls, the whole very oddly inflected, with dramatic pauses and diminuendoes." Pound had made a career of experimenting and condensing communications, both written and oral, and was an expert at it. He enjoyed making up new words or adapting words from foreign languages, and often spoke with condensations and ellipses in the same way he wrote poetry.[60] For a psychiatrist who was not familiar with Pound's writings to be confronted with this for the first time, especially if Pound was purposefully trying to appear mentally disabled, would have been very confusing. Thus when Dr. Muncie said that Pound appeared to be "completely incoherent" when he examined him for the second time on December 13, it is easy to imagine that he did so.

Pound also facilitated the examiner's search for pathology by offering him his own version of what had gone wrong with his head. According to Dr. King's report, Pound "experienced a queer sensation in the head as though the upper third of the brain were missing and a fluid level existed at the top of what remained."[61] This exotic symptom and variations on it became a standard Pound offering to examining psychiatrists during his St. Elizabeths years. It corresponds to no known psychiatric or neurological condition, and its most noteworthy feature is its whimsicality. It should be remembered that Pound had already described his brain as being "a sort of great clot of genital fluid held in suspense or reserve . . . the very fluid of life itself."[62] One wonders what Pound thought had happened to it!

Pound also behaved during the examination in a manner in which he believed a mentally disturbed person should behave. According to Dr. Gilbert's testimony at the sanity hearing, Pound complained of extreme fatigue and exhaustion and "remained in bed practically all the time, with the possible exception of sitting up for his meals, or going to a bathroom nearby . . . He describes his feeling at the time as being unable to get flat enough in bed." The fatigue and exhaustion were of an unusual variety, however, for Pound could also "move quickly about from the bed to a table nearby to get some paper, book or manuscript, and then to as suddenly throw himself on the bed and again assume the reclining position."[63] This mix of rapid, energetic movements punctuated with assertions of extreme fatigue also became part of Pound's standard behavior for psychiatrists at St. Elizabeths.

As if to guarantee confusion among the examining psychiatrists, Pound mixed in a few prevarications. For example he told Dr. Muncie that he had not known that he had been indicted in 1943; "that came to him as a surprise later on." Dr. King said that Pound had not known he had been indicted until he arrived at the prison camp at Pisa. Finally, in case any of the psychiatrists missed the point of the examination, Pound told them what they were supposed to find. Dr. Muncie said that Pound "states categorically that he is not of sound mind and could not participate effectively in his own defense."[64]

THE DIAGNOSIS

The result of Pound's psychiatric examination was given to the court on December 14 in a letter signed by the four psychiatrists. It concluded as follows:

> The defendant, now 60 years of age and in generally good physical condition, was a precocious student, specializing in literature. He has been a voluntary expatriate for nearly 40 years, living in England and France, and for the past 21 years in Italy, making an uncertain living by writing poetry and criticism. His poetry and literary criticism have achieved considerable recognition, but of recent years his preoccupation with monetary theories and economics has apparently obstructed his literary productivity. He has long been recognized as eccentric, querulous, and egocentric.
>
> At the present time he exhibits extremely poor judgment as to his situation, its seriousness and the manner in which the charges are to be met. He insists that his broadcasts were not treasonable, but that all his radio activities have stemmed from his self-appointed mission to "save the Constitution." He is abnormally grandiose, is expansive and exuberant in manner, exhibiting pressure of speech, discursiveness, and distractibility.
>
> In our opinion, with advancing years his personality, for many years abnormal, has undergone further distortion to the extent that he is now suffering from a paranoid state which renders him mentally unfit to advise properly with counsel or to participate intelligently and reasonably in his own defense. He is, in other words, insane and mentally unfit for trial, and is in need of care in a mental hospital.[65]

Ezra Pound was thereby officially diagnosed as suffering from a paranoid state, as being insane, and as being mentally unfit for trial.

Psychiatric diagnostic criteria were not very scientifically developed in the United States in 1945. Four separate classifications of diseases were in use, and they were frequently further modified for a particular state or hospital.[66] It is therefore fortunate that Dr. Overholser was writing a textbook of psychiatry at the time of Pound's examination and in so doing provided a definition of what he meant by "paranoid state":

> These are more easily recognized as abnormal mental conditions. The delusions are not so well systematized or worked out and are likely to have a bizarre nature about them that strikes the layman as "crazy." However,

the fact that in many cases they can cover their delusions and give logical explanations for their conduct makes these people difficult to commit to an institution. They may go on for several years cherishing the most absurd delusions without anyone's finding it out.[67]

Overholser then went on to describe a patient as an example of a paranoid state. The patient had ideas of reference (i.e., he thought people were talking about him), delusions (he believed "people came into his room at night and misused him sexually"), a belief that people were inserting thoughts into his head, auditory hallucinations ("voices called him sexual epithets"), and he became assaultive in the hospital. He was suffering from what would now be called paranoid schizophrenia and was clearly insane. In later psychiatric classificatory systems, most paranoid states were subsumed under the paranoid schizophrenia diagnosis.

A comparison of the psychiatrists' letter to the court, in which they diagnosed a paranoid state, and the description of this disorder in Overholser's textbook shows little correlation. The letter described Pound as eccentric, querulous, egocentric, grandiose, expansive, and exuberant, demonstrating discursiveness, distractibility, pressure of speech, and extremely poor judgment. The textbook, on the other hand, describes frankly schizophrenic symptoms like bizarre delusions, auditory hallucinations, and thought insertion. Pound's symptoms did not fit into the category of paranoid state as Overholser (and other psychiatrists in 1945) defined the term.

Were Pound's beliefs about economics and Jews delusional? A delusion is usually defined as a false belief arising without stimulation or validation by others and which is impervious to reason. Pound's economic and racial beliefs had widespread external validation and are still shared by entire organizations such as the Liberty Lobby and the Ku Klux Klan; they cannot therefore be called delusions in the generally accepted sense of the word.

The probable reason that paranoid state was selected for Pound's diagnosis by Overholser and his colleagues is that they needed a diagnosis that would stand scrutiny in the courtroom. Egocentricity and eccentricity, even combined with grandiosity and extremely poor judgment, would not have been enough to make him unfit for trial. On the other hand if a label of schizophrenia were used, it might have been challenged because Pound's history and productivity were so clearly at variance with the diagnosis. Paranoid state provided an intermediate alternative and one which was sufficiently vague to be difficult to challenge.

The psychiatric report was made public on December 21, 1945.

The public reaction to the finding that Ezra Pound was unfit for trial was one of suspicion. Rudolf Hess, on trial in Nuremberg for war crimes, had also been examined by psychiatrists and was said to be suffering from amnesia; many people didn't believe it. The idea that war criminals might try to escape responsibility by using an insanity ploy was not a new one. In the *New Yorker* of August 14, 1943, there had been a cartoon showing Nazis sitting around a room and one of them saying, ". . . and as for those postwar trials, we can always plead insanity."[68] Ironically there was an article about Ezra Pound on the following page.

At the press conference when the report from the psychiatrists was released, attorneys for the Department of Justice reassured the public. They said "they believed Pound, like Rudolf Hess, might easily be feigning insanity to escape a trial that might cost his life." For that reason they would request a public hearing on the psychiatrists' report. The prosecutors also said that the army psychiatrists thought Pound might be suffering from claustrophobia, "but that it was a temporary condition, and that in other reports, except for his usual eccentricity, the prisoner was sane and able to stand trial for treason."[69]

The public hearing on the psychiatrists' report was a legal mechanism whereby the findings of the psychiatrists could be referred to a jury. It was a provision found in the laws of most states at that time, and the impaneling of a jury in such cases was not unusual.[70] The issue for the jury was solely the question of whether Pound was mentally fit to stand trial at that time; it was not a trial for treason.

Up to this point in the proceedings the Department of Justice appeared to be genuinely interested in bringing Ezra Pound to trial. The questioning of the Italian radio technicians and preparation of the case had continued. On December 3 a memo from the Department of Justice to the FBI asked them to interview the persons quoted in the November 25 *PM* newspaper account about Pound and to discreetly ascertain their assessment of Pound's mental status. On December 18 an internal Department of Justice memorandum to Attorney General Thomas Clark reminded him that three army psychiatrists had found Pound sane and could thus be used to rebut the findings of the four examining psychiatrists whose report the department had seen.[71]

TO ST. ELIZABETHS

At the court hearing on December 21 releasing the report of the psychiatrists, the judge also ruled on Pound's petition for bail. It was denied, and instead Pound was ordered transferred from Gallinger Hospital to St. Elizabeths Hospital, the federal asylum where Dr. Overholser was superintendent. The jury trial to review the psychiatrists' report was set for late January; it was not actually held until February 13.

Late in the afternoon of December 21, Ezra Pound entered St. Elizabeths. He was initially assigned to Howard Hall, the unit for the criminally insane, which had stricter supervision and less freedom than any other part of the hospital. It was also located in one of the oldest and most dilapidated buildings; Pound would henceforth refer to it as a hellhole.

The public was interested in Pound. On December 12 *Time* had run a story calling him "the ragbaggy old darling of the U.S.'s expatriate intelligentsia." It quoted Pound invoking his memory loss in a rueful plea for his life: "It's all very well to die for an idea, but to die for an idea that you can't remember . . ."[72] But Christmas was coming and people were anxious to enjoy themselves, ready to unwind after four long war years. For many the problem of Ezra Pound must have seemed a thing of the past.

But not for everybody. The daily news from Nuremberg was supplying vicarious vengeance and also reminding people of the atrocities perpetrated by the Axis powers. Four million persons had been killed at Auschwitz alone. On December 15 the *Saturday Review of Literature* served notice that Pound's case would not be forgotten: "Yet there is no alibi for a charge of treason . . . He preferred the Fascist way . . . he desired a world in which Mussolinis and Ezra Pounds could satisfy their egomanias . . . Such a man should not escape penalty for his misdeeds."[73]

England's William Joyce, Lord Haw-Haw of the airwaves, and John Amery, son of a former British Secretary of State for India, had both been convicted of treason and sentenced to hang; Amery was executed as Pound was transferred to St. Elizabeths, and Joyce a few days later. Newspapers compared Pound to Joyce. The *Washington Post* said Pound's crimes were less serious and doubted that he "was ever important or dangerous enough to make it really necessary to exact the price of his treason in his blood." The *Detroit Free Press* and the *Salt Lake City Tribune* said Pound was just as dangerous, and the latter suggested "petty-wise and Pound foolish" for his epitaph. A group of citizens from New York wrote to President Truman claiming that Pound "assisted the perpetrators of the slaughter chambers" and insisting that "he must suffer the same sentence meted out by the English people to traitors Amery and Lord Haw-Haw." A man from Little Rock, whose son had died on Bataan, advised Truman that Pound was faking insanity and urged the President to "hang him promptly."[74] Meanwhile Ernest Hemingway campaigned to separate the Pound and Joyce cases, saying that William Joyce had been a true traitor, whereas Pound was "a traitor but a silly, and a crazy and a harmless traitor," and that the two cases were really very different.[75]

The worst came as a Christmas present. The December 25 issue of *New Masses* featured a cover story asking, "Should Ezra Pound Be Shot?" in which five literary figures offered their opinions. Novelist Lion Feuchtwanger said: "He who regards the aim of justice to be not to avenge but to deter cannot draw a distinction between the talented or untalented wrecker." Playwright Arthur Miller claimed that "in his wildest moments of human vilification Hitler never approached our Ezra. For sheer obscenity Ezra took the cake. But more, he knew all America's weaknesses and he played on them as expertly as Goebbels ever did . . . His stuff was straight Fascism with all the anti-Semitism, anti-foreignism included."

Poet Norman Rosten noted: "We are not evaluating his poems. The case against Mr. Pound is a public and political one. Mr. Pound joined the war. He became a Fascist hireling. He contributed to the murder of the innocent . . . Because he was a traitor he should be shot. Or what else do we do with traitors these days? Send them on lecture tours? Have them write reviews for magazines? It was all a charming war, wasn't it? . . . It is unfortunate indeed that Mr. Pound considered his poisonous mouthings akin to the innocence of poetry. It was not. And Mr. Pound shall find death no clever metaphor."

Author Albert Maltz pointed out that Pound was accused of "the same crime" as William Joyce, John Amery, Tokyo Rose, and Benedict Arnold. "If Ezra Pound were a lawyer, doctor, businessman or factory worker, no voice would be raised in his defense. Yet it is *because* he is a poet that he should be hanged, not once but twice—for treason as a citizen, and for his poet's betrayal of all that is decent in human civilization . . . Do I sound savage? Yes—I remember the corpses of Buchenwald, Dachau, Maidanek. Who dares forget them?"[76]

In Italy also it was a depressing Christmas. Olga and Mary thought of going to America to see Pound but feared that it would only be to see him executed.[77]

Pound had no choice but to make the best of it, and he entered into the daily routine of the insane asylum. The ambiguity of his psychiatric situation was perfectly illustrated on the second day at St. Elizabeths when he told a psychiatrist: "If this is a hospital, you have got to cure me." "Cure you of what?" asked the psychiatrist. "Whatever the hell is the matter with me—you must decide whether I am to be cured or punished."[78]

During the next seven weeks Pound was examined by many psychiatrists at the hospital. He was a celebrity, and it was a popular pastime among the younger staff to exchange speculation about his mental status. Eight staff psychiatrists recorded impressions in the hospital chart between December 21 and February 13, and of these three are still living. All of them, of course, were aware that their boss had already publicly committed Pound to a diagnosis of paranoid state and had proclaimed him unfit for trial.

The irascible Ezra Pound is clearly in evidence in the psychiatric reports. One psychiatrist noted that "on several occasions he refers to 'niggers' with a look of disgust," and on the Rorschach test he found "a couple of degenerate blacks."[79] Pound's behavior during this period was noted to be completely normal: "During his stay in the hospital, the patient has cooperated with hospital procedures and in no way obstructed normal routines except by his persistent demands for extra attention. He spends most of his time lying upon his bed in his room, reading a Chinese text and a few slim volumes of poetry, making a few notes on random slips of paper."

His extraordinary egocentricity was noted by almost everyone who had contact with him. One psychiatrist said Pound "adopted a superior manner and spoke in a haughty, boastful and dogmatic fashion." Another noted his "traits of egotism, intellectual haughtiness, dogmatism, and a tendency toward the belief that he is infallible and practically omniscient along certain lines of philosophy, economics and political science." He compared himself with John Adams and Thomas Jefferson, and intimated to one psychiatrist "that there was no use to discuss his ideas about monetary theories and economics because most people, including the examiner, would not be able to understand and comprehend them."

In terms of Pound's mental functioning, he was noted by all examiners to be fully oriented and to have a superior intelligence. His speech and thought processes were said to be "clear, coherent and relevant" by several psychiatrists. A cogent summary of Pound's thinking pattern was provided by Dr. Harold Stevens, a young staff psychiatrist, who described Pound's speech as "fragmentary, although telegraphic in style, resembling the cryptic letters he writes. In fact, his present style of speech and writing resembles his poems and other artistic productions. He is apparently a true Symbolist, who compresses a large volume of words and concepts into a brief expression . . . His language is often esoteric, but does not represent condensation in a schizophrenic sense . . . This extreme economy of style still characterizes his speech and writing, and while he may be obscure he is never disconnected or irrelevant."[80]

Pound denied having auditory hallucinations, one of the hallmarks of insanity. When asked whether he had heard voices while in the prison camp in Italy, Pound "looked very intently at the wall for a long period of time, apparently unable to make up his mind whether to answer the question in the negative or affirmative. He finally dodged the question by saying that his memory was so full of gaps that he couldn't be sure just what had happened to him."

Only one psychiatrist who examined Pound during these seven weeks noted definite delusions of grandeur and persecution. As examples the psychiatrist cited Pound's beliefs that he could have prevented war if people had listened to him, that he claimed to "have connections in a half dozen countries and nerve centers of intellect," and that "he should have been brought to this country not as a prisoner but as an advisor to the State Department in dealing with Japan and, indeed, the rest of the world."[81] The psychiatrist who claimed these as delusions was Dr. Overholser; his brief note dated February 7, 1946, is his only clinical assessment of Pound in the record during Pound's twelve-and-one-half-year hospitalization.

The psychiatrists under Overholser discreetly hedged their phrases regarding Pound's delusions or denied them altogether. One psychiatrist said Pound "expressed what might be interpreted as delusions of persecution and grandeur." Another noted that Pound's "evaluation of his stature as a significant world figure appeared to border on the delusional." Most significant, however, was the psychiatric case conference of January 28, 1946, in which six hospital psychiatrists examined Pound and specifically denied that he was delusional. Pound made the usual claims regarding the correctness of his economic theories, but the summary of the conference noted that "nothing in the way of grandiosity or expansiveness beyond this was uncovered and he denied any idea that he was a world saviour."

The most striking aspect of Ezra Pound's hospital record, both during this period and in subsequent years, is the repeated suggestion that he was faking symptoms. For example he repeats his assertion that something happened to his head while incarcerated in Italy: "I broke—my head—I am all right when I am rested—but when I am not rested it goes beat, beat, beat in the back of my neck." When asked what goes beat, beat, beat, Pound replied: "Oh, you don't understand—no one seems to understand—fatigue—I told them in August that the main spring would bust." He also commented to the examiner giving him the Rorschach that "they won't believe me when I tell them the main spring is busted." At the case conference he told the psychiatrists that he "has a sensation in the vertex of his skull as if there were a vacuum there," and he "suddenly puts his hand over his forehead or on the frontal area of his scalp, bows his head and looks at the floor, ceasing his talk for a moment—these acts giving a rather dramatic appearance which on occasion appeared to be consciously exaggerated."

Pound's selective memory loss was also in evidence at this time. One psychiatrist noted that "he stresses that he has suffered 'memory gaps' as a result of his recent incarceration, but at no time during the examination does he falter for lack of memory on any subject." Another found Pound's memory for remote events "spotty," but "events forgotten during one interview, however, would often be recalled at another." Loss of remote memory in psychiatric conditions is almost never fluctuating, and Pound's selective "memory loss" is most compatible with fabrication.

Perhaps Pound's finest show for the psychiatrists, however, was his demonstration of his fatigue. And he was offered an opportunity for a grand performance at the time of the formal case conference on January 28 with an audience of six psychiatrists and many other mental health professionals in attendance. As recalled by Dr. Addison Duval, one of the senior psychiatrists at St. Elizabeths at the time and who later became vice president and treasurer of the American Psychiatric Association:

> There were 20 or 30 of us, all mental health professionals, at the conference. Dr. Overholser was not there. These conferences were quite formal in those days and the object was to interview the patient, discuss the case, and come to some diagnosis. We had all the records there including the results of the physical exam and laboratory tests. The whole thing took an hour or so.
>
> I interviewed Mr. Pound at some length. When he came into the room he begged our pardon but said he didn't feel strong enough to sit up and could he please lie on the floor. Well I had been interviewing people who were insane for many years but I had never had *this* happen before. So I said, "Well Mr. Pound, it's a bit unusual but I'll permit you to if you want to." So Mr. Pound lay on the floor during this whole conference while I interviewed him. I think he was surprised I let him.
>
> In interviewing him I tried to elicit some symptoms of insanity but I couldn't. Before the conference I had assumed that he was psychotic [insane] because our boss [Dr. Overholser] had already made a diagnosis and gone on public record. But I couldn't elicit any symptoms of psychosis at all. There were no delusions, no thought disorder, and no disturbances of orientation. He definitely did not seem to be insane.[82]

Dr. Carlos Dalmau, another psychiatrist who was present at the case conference, also remembers Pound's bizarre display of fatigue. Dr. Dalmau suggested that by lying on the floor Pound might have been imitating the Dadaist Barrès "trial" where the defendant had been represented by a recumbent mannequin.[83] Pound had attended and been impressed by the "trial," calling it "a definite intellectual act . . . It ought to have made people think *more.*"[84] Lying on the floor was also a hostile gesture toward the psychiatrists.

In terms of diagnostic impressions of the psychiatrists who examined Pound, none of them made a diagnosis of paranoid state or any other form of insanity. The Rorschach test was interpreted as suggesting "a marked personality disorder of long standing," but "there is no evidence of psychosis [insanity]." Most psychiatrists at the case conference believed that Pound had "a psychopathic personality," the same diagnosis arrived at initially by Dr. Muncie. Since this contradicted the diagnosis Dr. Overholser had made in his report to the court, however, it presented the psychiatrists with a problem. How could they contradict their chief? According to Dr. Duval's recollection:

> A very lively discussion ensued. After all our boss had already made a diagnosis and it produced quite a bit of anxiety because we didn't feel that we could differ from him. But Pound was not psychotic and he was not incompetent. We decided almost unanimously that he was neurotic, and that his lying on the floor was part of his neurotic acting out. Out of loyalty to Win [Dr. Overholser] we had to respect Win's diagnosis. And since we had come to such a different conclusion we finally decided not to make any formal diagnosis at all. Then it wouldn't embarrass him. So I went over to Win's office to tell him what we had found.
>
> He was very cordial when I told him. He said he respected our diagnosis and that we had had more time to examine Pound than he had. However he said that we didn't need to disturb the practicalities of the situation by making it public and that we should just keep it to ourselves. So that's what we did, so as to not embarrass our boss.[85]

The hospital clinical record of the case conference supports Dr. Duval's account. At the end of the record, after the diagnosis of psychopathic personality had been made, there is a line drawn and then the following notation: "After this case was discussed with the Superintendent and the above findings reported to him, he suggested a longer period of observation before a final decision is reached."[86]

It should also be noted that Ezra Pound himself came to a diagnostic conclusion regarding his own sanity, and it was duly recorded in the psychiatrist's notes. When asked whether he was insane, Pound responded: "No, I don't think I am insane, but I am so shot to pieces that it would take me years to write a sensible piece of prose. I think I am of unsound mind, and I don't think I have been shown good treatment here. I am absolutely unfit to transact any business." The "business" that Pound had in mind undoubtedly was assisting in his own defense. He was claiming that he was just insane enough to not be able to stand trial on his treason charges, but no more insane than he needed to be.

Beyond the question of sanity, the overriding psychiatric question about Pound's mental status during these initial seven weeks in St. Elizabeths Hospital was whether he was able to stand trial. The psychiatrists were supposed to assess such things as whether he could understand the charges against him and whether he could assist in his own defense. The psychiatric notes in his hospital record suggest that Pound was fully capable of standing trial.

For example, on December 21, the night he was transferred to St. Elizabeths, he gave the admitting psychiatrist an impassioned lecture on why he was not guilty of treason. "He boasts of his status as an American citizen and justifies everything he did in Italy on the basis that he found it impossible to find an outlet for the expression of his ideas in the United States whereas he found a ready outlet in Italy." Pound then went on to justify his broadcasts by saying that he had been saying the same things for years before the war, that he had really been performing a "patriotic duty" to the United States by educating them about the true causes of the war, that he was warning the American people that President Roosevelt had violated the Constitution, and that he was urging the United States to get out of the war because it was so costly. If the war were stopped, said Pound, the money being spent by the United States government would assure every average family "a decent income of approximately $2500 to $4000 per year."

On another occasion Pound was asked by a psychiatrist whether he realized the seriousness of the charges against him. "Get my notebook," said Pound, at which point he produced a notebook with several pages of notes outlining a defense of his actions, and he gave the examiner a long speech about how he was "not guilty as charged, but that he was in reality working in the interests of the United States and in the interests of mankind." To still another psychiatrist Pound expostulated at length about his actions as "a form of freedom of speech in a radio age." In summary, Pound's hospital record is replete with evidence that he was eminently capable of standing trial and in assisting in his own defense.

In addition to the St. Elizabeths Hospital records of Ezra Pound there is another set of notes that can be used to assess Pound's sanity and his ability to stand trial. These notes were compiled by Charles Olson, a poet and journalist who was one of Pound's first and most faithful visitors at St. Elizabeths. Olson recorded his interviews with Pound on January 4, 15, 24, 29, and February 7, 1946; the notes were subsequently edited and published by Catherine Seelye in 1975 after both Olson and Pound had died. Since Olson himself had no intention of ever publishing his notes, there is no reason to believe that he inaccurately portrayed Pound.

Olson's notes show that, during this period, Pound was unchanged; he was the same person who had been described by others for many years. His egotism, vulgarity, and anti-Semitism are much in evidence, and so are his charm, quick mind, and interest in everything going on around him. Olson notes that "his jumps in conversation are no more than I or any active mind would make." In terms of his mental state, Pound "said, quite quietly, he didn't think there was anything wrong with him."[87]

In their conversations Pound expressed anxiety about the approaching sanity hearing before a jury, anger toward the psychiatrists who examined him so frequently, and interest in Olson's work. With his usual epigrammatic style, he carried on completely rational discussions about the war (he believed that radar had been the key to the Allied victory), the Russian Revolution, economics, the drawings of Gaudier-Brzeska, English and American politics, his Cantos, and other work he hoped to complete. Pound referred to the January 28 case conference ("I was examined by 6 of them yesterday") and to re-examination by Drs. Overholser, King, Gilbert, and Muncie on February 7 ("4 medicos at me this morning"). The interview that Olson recorded on the afternoon of February 7 is of special interest since Dr. Overholser claimed to have found "numerous delusions of grandeur and of persecution" earlier in the same day. There is no evidence of them in Olson's account—just the same egotism that had always been there.

Another visitor to Pound during this period was Caresse Crosby, a publisher and old friend of his. According to Charles Olson she visited him between January 4 and January 15, 1946:

> She had gone to see him at the request of the hospital staff who wanted to get the impressions of someone who had known him many years ago. And to her Pound seemed no different. She marked, as a sign of his continued coherence, the way he corrected her as to dates in the past over when, for example, she had published at the Black Sun his "Imaginary Conversations." And others concerning people or events they had known in common.[88]

Mrs. Crosby also told Olson that Pound "spoke of his troubles to her, and she was impressed by one remark: 'My mistake was to go on after Pearl Harbor.'"

THE SANITY HEARING

As the psychiatrists observed and examined Pound in preparation for the formal sanity hearing before a jury, the world outside waited. America was slowly returning to normal, although the news from Nuremberg was a daily reminder of what the country had been through. On January 28, 1946, Albert Deutsch, a well-known journalist and mental health reformer, published an article in New York's *PM* entitled "Sanity Trial of Ezra Pound Stirs Up Psychiatric World," in which he discussed the legal and psychiatric issues of the forthcoming hearing. He reminded readers that Hitler and Mussolini had "brought the world to the brink of ruin" and asked: "Is it possible that psychiatry can be used as a cloak to protect an accused traitor from possible punishment?"[89] Overholser years earlier had called Deutsch "an experienced social historian."[90]

Drs. Overholser, King, Gilbert and Muncie saw very little of Pound during this period. Between December 14, when they submitted their report to the court, and February 13, when the sanity hearing finally took place, the four psychiatrists examined Pound only once together (on February 7), and Dr. King did once alone (on January 28). Dr. Gilbert made no further effort to examine him, and if Dr. Overholser did it is not recorded anywhere. Dr. Muncie appears to have had no intention of seeing Pound at all after December 14; a letter he wrote to Dr. Overholser indicated that he would join them on February 7 only because "I have been asked by Mr. Cornell to re-examine Mr. Ezra Pound before I go to court."[91]

Dr. King's visit to Pound on January 28 was noted by Charles Olson when he saw Pound the following day. "King came to see me yesterday and he sees I could be of use," Pound told Olson. Pound had expressed to many people the belief that he had a special understanding of European countries and of Japan, and that the United States government would be wise to use him as an advisor. Olson went on: "Pound was off like a runaway horse at the assumption that King seemed sympathetic and gave him the impression he might get out, be put to use."[92]

Dr. Overholser, meanwhile, had available to him an increasing amount of background material and psychiatric reports on Pound from his staff. James Laughlin sent Overholser four of Pound's books, and Overholser requested from the Department of Justice their complete file on Pound.[93] Yet when he testified on February 13, Overholser informed Albert Deutsch that "he hadn't even read the indictment against Pound because he didn't want to prejudice his psychiatric approach";

Deutsch also noted sarcastically that Overholser "had dipped into one or two Pound writings."[94] Dr. Overholser apparently felt assured that the outcome of the sanity hearing was a foregone conclusion. Evidence for this is suggested by Dr. Addison Duval, the psychiatrist in charge of the case conference. When Dr. Duval presented the diagnostic results of the conference to Dr. Overholser—results sharply at variance with Overholser's own—Dr. Duval recalls that "Dr. Overholser wasn't worried by the results of the conference because he thought the court had already committed Pound to St. Elizabeths and that the sanity hearing would just confirm it."[95]

But what about the psychiatrists at St. Elizabeths? Didn't Overholser have to worry about their going public with their opinions regarding Pound's sanity and fitness for trial? *Newsweek* reported on January 7, 1946, that some of the psychiatrists "who have looked into the [Pound] case believe the poet is sane enough to stand trial for treason." Shortly thereafter a *Newsweek* reporter gave the Department of Justice the names of three St. Elizabeths psychiatrists who "would testify that Pound was sane."[96]

In fact the junior psychiatrists at St. Elizabeths were almost unanimous in believing that Pound was fit for trial but were deeply divided about whether he should be protected. Dr. Jerome Kavka, the only one of the three named by the *Newsweek* reporter who is still alive, says he agreed with the course of action chosen by Overholser: "Ezra Pound was an exceptional poet and so he deserved exceptional treatment."[97] Dr. Harold Stevens, on the other hand, remembers: "Some of the St. Elizabeths staff took the position that a man of his literary accomplishments and contributions not only to literature but to the support of younger poets and writers, should be judged by a more charitable standard of conduct. I take the opposite view, namely that a man of his stature, learning and influence has an even greater responsibility to uphold ethical principles and serve as an exemplary role model."[98]

Disagreeing with Dr. Overholser in private was one thing, but to do so in public was quite another. Public disputes between psychiatrists were anathema to him. Overholser was a powerful figure in American psychiatry; a junior psychiatrist who trained at St. Elizabeths needed a letter from him to get a job elsewhere. He was also a team player and expected his team to heed the instructions of their captain. "Dr. Overholser told everybody not to talk publicly about the case," recalls Kavka.[99] In case any of them had doubts about what would happen if they did go public, they had only to remember the events of six months previous when Dr. Michael Miller, St. Elizabeths' chief of alcoholism treatment, had been publicly and summarily fired by Overholser for suggesting to the media that some members of Congress might have problems with alcohol. "Personally I think Congress is full of serious, hard-working men," Dr. Overholser had assured the nation.[100]

Julien Cornell, Pound's attorney, was also relatively inactive on the case during this period. Charles Olson noted that Cornell was absent for at least two weeks at a time, and Cornell's own book does not give an impression of activity or preparation for a possible treason trial. Rather Cornell, in his letter of January 26, 1946, to Dorothy Pound, conveyed the certainty that "the result [of the sanity hearing] is a foregone conclusion since all the doctors are in agreement that he is in no condition to be tried."[101]

Most significant of all was the fact that the Department of Justice was not actively preparing for a trial. At the December 21, 1945, press conference following the release of the psychiatrists' report to the court, attorneys for the department had assured reporters that they realized that Pound might be faking. They also reminded reporters that three army psychiatrists had found him perfectly sane. Clearly, if the Department of Justice wanted to bring Ezra Pound to trial for treason, they would need to refute the psychiatric testimony of Drs. Overholser, Gilbert, King, and Muncie with testimony from other psychiatrists. The three army psychiatrists, Drs. Finner, Baer and Weisdorf, were the obvious witnesses. Although they were younger as a group than Overholser et al., their credentials were respectable: Dr. Weisdorf had had six years' experience in psychiatry, and Dr. Baer, who later became deputy director of the Illinois Department of Public Welfare, had had twelve. Drs. Finner and Weisdorf are still alive, and when recently interviewed both said that the Department of Justice at no time contacted them regarding the possibility of their testifying. In fact in the thirty-six years since they examined Pound in Italy, nobody had ever contacted them to ask them anything about their findings.[102]

Not only was the Department of Justice failing to pursue these leads, but in fact the investigation of Ezra Pound came to a complete standstill. On December 27, immediately following the Christmas holiday, an urgent telegram signed by J. Edgar Hoover was sent to FBI field offices advising them: "Department has authorized discontinuance of investigation pending further court action as to Pound's sanity. You will be advised if investigation desired at later date."[103] It was a Christmas gift from the Department of Justice to Pound, but one wrapped in secrecy. At St. Elizabeths Dr. Overholser made his annual Christmas Day visit to each ward, and "O Come All Ye Faithful" echoed down the halls of the asylum.

One cannot help but wonder what was occurring behind the scenes.

Isaiah Matlack, in charge of the Pound case for the Department of Justice, was scheduled to meet "unofficially" with Dr. Overholser et al. on the afternoon of December 18, according to an internal departmental memo. Whether Matlack discussed the prosecution's problems with the two-witness rule is unknown, but certainly it was on his mind. Confinement of Pound to an insane asylum would effectively solve that problem. And sometime during this period Robert Frost was in touch with Dr. Overholser, according to Addison Duval's recollections, presumably through their mutual friend Merrill Moore. Brigit Patmore wrote that Ernest Hemingway "rushed to Washington, where he had considerable influence, and persuaded the Americans to drop the charge. But poor Ezra had to go into a mental hospital to avoid any further trouble."[104] However, Hemingway's biographer, Carlos Baker, denies that Hemingway came to Washington and says Patmore does not know what she is talking about.[105] Certainly former Attorney General Francis Biddle would also have been interested in the case, but he was in Nuremberg assisting with the war crimes trials.

On February 13, 1946, the sanity hearing to determine whether Ezra Pound was fit to stand trial for treason was finally held in the District of Columbia courthouse, three months after he had been brought from Italy and over eight months after he had been arrested. Isaiah Matlack and Donald Anderson handled the prosecution for the Department of Justice, while Julien Cornell represented the defense. The witnesses were Drs. Muncie, King, Overholser, and Gilbert. The transcripts of the hearing are reminiscent of another famous trial:

> "Herald, read the accusation!" said the King.
> On this the White Rabbit blew three blasts on the trumpet, and then unrolled the parchment-scroll and read as follows:
>
> > "The Queen of Hearts, she made some tarts,
> >   All on a summer day:
> > The Knave of Hearts, he stole those tarts
> >   And took them quite away!"
>
> "Consider your verdict," the King said to the jury.
> "Not yet, not yet!" the Rabbit hastily interrupted. There's a great deal to come before that!"
> "Call the first witness," said the King . . .[106]

After the jury was impaneled, the first witness called was Dr. Muncie, the psychiatrist hired by the defense. Muncie had spent less time examining Pound than the other three psychiatrists, had less experience with criminal cases, and also appears to have been less familiar with the records of the case.

For example, although it is certain that Drs. Overholser and King had copies of the psychiatric reports of the army psychiatrists, it appears that they may not have shared these records with Muncie. When recently asked about this, Dr. Muncie could not recall whether he had seen them or not.[107] In his testimony Muncie described Pound's prison camp experience as "a rather severe emotional crisis he went through at which time he was seen, I think, by some psychiatrists." The government attorneys failed to raise this apparent unfamiliarity with the Pisa records in their cross-examination. Muncie also testified that he had had access to the records of the St. Elizabeths staff psychiatrists, yet claimed that they added "nothing essential because they found the same things we did."

Muncie testified at length about Pound's "delusions":

> He has a number of rather fixed ideas which are either clearly delusional or verging on the delusional. One I might speak of, for instance, he believes he has been designated to save the Constitution of the United States for the people of the United States.
>
> I will come back to this item in a minute.
>
> Secondly, he has a feeling that he has the key to the peace of the world through the writings of Confucius, which he translated into Italian and into English, and that if this book had been given proper circulation the Axis would not have been formed, we would be at peace now, and a great deal of trouble could have been avoided in the past, and this becomes his blueprint for world order in the future.
>
> Third, he believes that with himself as a leader, a group of intellectuals could have gotten together in different countries, like Japan, for instance, where he is well thought of, to work for world order. He has a hatred of bureaucrats which goes back a long way, and one may conclude that his saving of the Constitution draws a clear distinction between the rights of the people and those who govern people.
>
> He feels he was double-crossed in being brought back to this country, thinking that he was being brought back to aid the country because of his special connections in Italy, and that his double-cross was at the hands of the British Commandos.
>
> So much for the rather fixed ideas he holds.
>
> In addition to that, he shows a remarkable grandiosity. He feels that he has no peer in the intellectual field, although conceding that one or two persons he has assisted might, on occasion, do as good work as he did.

On cross-examination Muncie conceded that each of these ideas by itself was not necessarily delusional or evidence of insanity. And when asked how Pound's schemes for saving the world differed from those of European leaders who wanted to conquer the world, Muncie replied that he had not examined the other European leaders. Cornell rescued the "delusions" on redirect examination by having Muncie agree that "it is the accumulation of delusions along different lines which leads you to suspect a deranged condition here."

Muncie was unclear about when Pound first knew he had been indicted for treason. He testified that Pound thought he was being brought back to the United States "to aid the country because of his special connections in Italy . . . He apparently did not realize that he was being brought back for treason." On cross-examination the government prosecutor asked: "Did he tell you that he had been indicted in 1943 as a result of his broadcasts?" to which Muncie replied: "No, that came to him as a surprise later on." Since the government prosecutor had in his possession absolute proof that Pound was aware of, and had responded to, the treason charges in 1943, it is inexplicable why he did not press the point. It would have established clearly for the jury either that Pound had lied to Dr. Muncie, or that Muncie was unfamiliar with the facts of the case, or perhaps both.

Dr. Muncie's testimony was also vulnerable when he described Pound's memory problems:

> The first time I saw him, December 13th, I referred in a social way to the fact that my brother had been a student at Wabash College, where he spent some six months in connection with his post-graduate career. He obviously did not remember my brother and the matter was passed off lightly. When I saw him on February 7th I was reintroduced to him by the other doctors, and his immediate comment was, "Yes, you have a brother," and "he was my best student, he had just come back from Europe, and he came from a family of the highest culture in Indiana."
>
> Now, irrespective of the merits of this latter issue, this is pure confabulation, I would say it is a confusion of facts in the face of real lack of memory about my brother. It is the only item I had that I could corroborate, although there may be other examples of confabulation. He complains of exhaustion as the cause of his breakdown in—
>
> Q. Before you go on, Doctor, will you explain the cause of confabulation.
>
> A. Confabulation may have a number of causes, with no ulterior motive, but ordinarily when we use the term, and I would think very strongly in that connection, it is occasioned by a definite loss of memory, and it usually appears in people with some kind of deteriorating process of the brain. I did not stress this point too much because it was just one item, and not necessary to my understanding of the case.
>
> He believes the exhaustion is the cause of the breakdown in his thinking processes. His memory definitely is not keen. It takes time for the answer to come.

Later Muncie testified that Pound's memory was "good except for the period last summer" (in the prison camp). The government prosecutors not only failed to point out the contradiction within Muncie's testimony, but failed to raise the issue again when the other psychiatrists testified that Pound's memory was unimpaired. Memory is one of the most quantifiable and testable parts of a mental status examination, and the prosecutors knew Pound had been extensively tested at St. Elizabeths. But they did not pursue the point or ask for such records. In fact the kind of confabulation described by Dr. Muncie is a psychiatric symptom found almost exclusively in a deteriorating brain condition caused by alcoholism; it is not found in paranoid state. Ezra Pound was indeed confabulating in his interviews with Dr. Muncie, but only in the generally accepted meaning of the term.

Dr. King was the next witness to take the stand. He had apparently developed a special relationship with Pound, as is evidenced by Pound's optimistic reaction to their meeting just two weeks earlier.[108] Now Dr. King opened his testimony by proclaiming, under oath, a more unequivocal diagnosis of insanity than any of the other psychiatrists.

> After rather careful consideration of his [Pound's] life-long history, and especially his progress during the last few years, it is my opinion that he has always been a sensitive, eccentric, cynical person, and these characteristics have been accentuated in the last few years to such an extent that he is afflicted with a paranoid state of psychotic proportions which renders him unfit for trial.

Thirteen years later, after leaving St. Elizabeths, Pound acknowledged his debt to King in a letter to Dr. Overholser: "At any rate my thanks. And some to King, whatever became of him. I thought he stuck his neck out possibly the furtherest."[109]

Dr. King did stick his neck out the furtherest, and consequently got himself caught in a semantic quagmire when he tried to support his diagnosis with clinical facts:

> PROSECUTOR: I presume a person can be psychotic, might even have paranoid tendencies, and be eccentric and cynical, and still be able to stand trial, is that true?
>
> DR. KING: Yes.
>
> PROSECUTOR: What other considerations are there in his case which make him unable to stand trial, in your opinion?
>
> DR. KING: He has deviated from his chosen profession in that he has become preoccupied with economic and governmental problems to such an extent that during discussion of those problems he manifests such a sudden and such a marked feeling and tone that he reaches the point of exhaustion, and this unusual propensity, intense feeling, is quite characteristic of paranoid conditions and is sufficient, in my opinion, to permit, at least create, considerable confusion; at least that was the situation when I

examined him, so that it is very difficult for him to explain his theories and proposals in a clear and concise logical manner.

And later in his testimony:

> PROSECUTOR: What classification would you state for Mr. Pound's mental condition according to your classifications pertaining to mental illness?
>
> DR. KING: I would say that he would fall in the category of paranoid states, sometimes called paranoid conditions. That is not a very satisfactory term because it is part way between so-called paranoid schizophrenia or dementia praecox, paranoid type, and true paranoia. There are all types of gradations between the extremes, and it is my opinion that he falls in between those two extremes.
>
> PROSECUTOR: Does he have a split personality?
>
> DR. KING: No.
>
> PROSECUTOR: Just what is it that makes you place him in that category?
>
> DR. KING: He does not have the clear, well-defined systematized delusions of the paranoiac type; neither does he have the dissociation, the personal hallucinations or delusions, the disordered delusions that go with the dementia praecox, paranoid type, at the other extreme, but he does have a rather diffuse paranoid reaction which falls somewhere between those two fields, and that is the reason I would not classify him as a dementia praecox patient, or a case of true paranoia.

King claimed knowledge of Pound's St. Elizabeths Hospital records, yet like Muncie displayed ignorance about when Pound knew he had been indicted:

> PROSECUTOR: Did he say when he first learned that he was charged with treason?
>
> DR. KING: I think it was while he was in Pisa.
>
> PROSECUTOR: And why did he give himself up? What did he think he was charged with? What was the purpose of giving himself up?
>
> DR. KING: I don't know for sure, but I suppose he knew that he was to be apprehended as soon as possible. I don't know for sure.
>
> PROSECUTOR: Do you know what he knew about that?
>
> DR. KING: No.
>
> PROSECUTOR: Or when he knew he was charged with treason?
>
> DR KING: No, I don't recall that.

Again, the government prosecutors failed to press the issue. Dr. King was equally vague about precisely why Pound was unable to assist in his own defense—despite an admission that Pound's IQ was over 120 and his intelligence not impaired. King simply said that Pound "was unable to give you a clear view at all of his defense or his motives, his actions, or his operations in connection with his past activities."

Throughout all this Pound sat quietly. "He held his head bowed, running nervous fingers through his hair; he slumped up in his chair with his knees raised against the edge of the lawyers' table facing the judge's bench, looking neither to left nor right."[110] He sat all day long listening to psychiatrists describe how his mind had deteriorated, how he was insane.

Dr. Overholser was the third witness. He opened his testimony inauspiciously by saying that Pound had been admitted to St. Elizabeths on January 1; the correct date was December 21. He emphasized Pound's grandiosity: "It was the fact that he felt he was so important and of such value to the United States that I put him down as suffering a mental disorder." Overholser claimed that Pound was unfit to assist in his defense because "you cannot keep him on a straight line of conversation," and "due to the episode he had in Pisa when he was under confinement I think there would be a much more violent reaction on top of this paranoid reaction if the trial were to proceed." Later in his testimony Overholser again invoked the episode in the prison camp as the reason Pound could not stand trial: "I think I have indicated that in a situation he might very readily have one of these, can I say 'blow-ups' again, during which he would be quite unable perhaps to concentrate enough to recognize the importance of his defense." The government prosecutor obtained an admission from Overholser that the army psychiatrists had found merely an "anxiety neurosis" and that they had concluded that Pound was "not insane," but the prosecutor failed to follow through on the obvious line of questioning as to why an anxiety state which only *might* recur should be an impediment to a man's standing trial. Surely most criminals undergo anxiety states when faced with trials.

Even more puzzling was the failure of the prosecutors to press Dr. Overholser for the specific opinions of his staff at St. Elizabeths and for a diagnosis:

> PROSECUTOR: Doctor, I understood you to say that you based your opinion partly on your own observation and partly on examination of records at the hospital.
>
> DR. OVERHOLSER: That is right.
>
> PROSECUTOR: Do you have with you the records of the hospital showing his present condition?
>
> DR. OVERHOLSER: Yes, sir.
>
> PROSECUTOR: Could you produce them?
>
> DR. OVERHOLSER: Surely, it is in my briefcase.
>
> PROSECUTOR: Have you, yourself, treated Mr. Pound, or has that been left to your associates out there?
>
> DR. OVERHOLSER: Partly to the associates.

PROSECUTOR: Are these records the records made by the staff?

DR. OVERHOLSER: That is right.

PROSECUTOR: And will you state by referring to them what the records show as to his present state of mental health?

DR. OVERHOLSER: It is a rather bulky record, as you see.

PROSECUTOR: Can you summarize it?

DR. OVERHOLSER: Essentially, it is that there has been very little change in his condition since he came in. A summary of the case from the time he came in is pretty much in line with what I said this morning, and the whole staff has seen him. There has been some discussion about him which has not been formal; in fact, no formal diagnosis has been made as yet.

PROSECUTOR: No formal diagnosis?

DR. OVERHOLSER: No.

It was an obvious opportunity to discredit Dr. Overholser, for after seven weeks of intensive examinations it was certainly reasonable to have expected the hospital psychiatrists to have arrived at a diagnosis. And if they had not, how could they be certain that Pound was unfit to stand trial?

The "records made by the staff" in Overholser's briefcase, which Overholser represented as "pretty much in line with what I said," were of great interest to Julien Cornell, Pound's attorney. The previous day Cornell had stopped to see Overholser "to pay my respects" while visiting his client at St. Elizabeths:

Dr. Overholser asked me to wait a moment, as he wanted to talk to me. When I was ushered into his private office he told me abruptly that he wished to disclose something to me which he had not told Matlack [the chief government prosecutor] and was not going to tell him. This was a great surprise to me, as Overholser was the government's "star witness" who would not ordinarily volunteer any information to the defense attorney, much less information which he had not disclosed to the prosecution. But Overholser, as I had already found out, was a most unusual man.

He told me that he remained firm in his opinion that Pound was mentally unfit to stand trial, but, he said, many of the young doctors on his staff disagreed. They thought Pound was merely eccentric, and wanted to see him tried and convicted. Overholser felt they were in error, perhaps their judgment was distorted by patriotism, but however that might be, Overholser was the responsible official, he had reviewed the opinions of his juniors, and remained unshaken in his own opinion. I asked him what he would say if the prosecution inquired about the views of the other doctors. He answered that he would take their reports with him to the courtroom in his briefcase, and if necessary would read them to the court and explain why he disagreed . . . Still, it was an odd situation, where the chief witness for the government was telling the defense attorney about evidence which was not going to be disclosed to the prosecution unless they asked for it.[111]

As a government psychiatrist, Overholser's handling of these records was, at the very least, unusual. When word of this incident leaked to the FBI in 1955, a full investigation was ordered and all parties concerned, including Dr. Overholser, were interviewed regarding the possibility that information damaging to Pound had been purposefully withheld at the trial. Dr. Overholser, interviewed February 23, 1956, denied any such possibility and the investigation was eventually dropped for lack of evidence.[112]

Dr. Gilbert was the final witness, but he added little to the testimony that had gone before. He focused on Pound's "delusions of grandeur" and testified that he was of "unsound mind and suffering from a paranoid state." Gilbert appeared to have been more impressed than the others with Pound's more whimsical symptoms, especially the "feeling of hollowness" in his skull, his complaints of being "unable to get flat enough in bed," and his severe "fatigue" which was periodically interrupted by "rather rapid movements about the bed, and suddenly sitting or rising to the upright position, or to move quickly about from the bed to a table nearby to get some paper, book or manuscript, and then to as suddenly throw himself on the bed and again assume the reclining position." Such bizarre symptoms should have invited a careful scrutiny from an alert prosecutor, but none was forthcoming.

Both sides rested their case; the outcome was a foregone conclusion. The judge then proceeded to dictate the jury's decision in his instruction to them:

> In a case of this type where the Government and the defense representatives have united in a clear and unequivocal view with regard to the situation, I presume you will have no difficulty in making up your mind.

The jury deliberated only three minutes before returning with the verdict: "Unsound mind."[113]

Ezra Pound had avoided being tried for treason and was pleased. "When the verdict of insanity was brought in, he jumped up with alacrity and engaged in affable conversation with his young lawyer," reported Albert Deutsch.[114] James Laughlin acknowledged this the next day in a letter to T. S. Eliot in which he described Pound as very pleased with the verdict and grateful to Julien Cornell for having saved his life.[115] The day following the verdict Charles Olson also visited him and recorded that Pound "came in with his bounce back, carrying the Pisa [sic] Cantos in his hand which Laughlin had delivered to him this morning . . . The sense, the whole sense of the meeting was Pound in power, anew. Flushed with his return to work. Full of plans to get on with new things, now that his fate was settled for awhile."[116] It was St. Valentine's Day.

A few people correctly assessed what had taken place. Albert Deutsch, in his account of the hearing, assailed the government prosecutors as having displayed "an impressive unfamiliarity with the psychiatric issues at stake and a lackadaisical interest in its political implications. They acted throughout as if they were going through the motions."[117] And Dr. Fredric Wertham wrote three years later: "Nobody can accuse the Department of Justice of persecuting Ezra Pound. It can hardly be urged that they even prosecuted him."[118]

The Department of Justice was probably pleased. Through passive indifference if not active collusion they had accomplished their major goal—the incarceration of Ezra Pound. The fact that he was incarcerated in a mental hospital rather than in a prison was incidental; some may even have believed that it was a more fitting punishment for him. And the department had brought it about without having gone to trial and being forced to test their evidence against the two-witness rule. Most importantly, this outcome did not foreclose the possibility of a future trial; it effectively incarcerated Pound for an indeterminate sentence. If in the future Pound was judged to be sane and fit for trial, the Department of Justice would still have the option of trying him on the treason charges.

Dr. Overholser must have also been pleased. He had saved Pound, a man whom he believed was a great poet, from trial. Perhaps he had saved him from death as well. As Pound had often seen himself as Odysseus, so Overholser had been his Aeolus, the keeper of the winds in Greek mythology, who saved Odysseus by giving him a favorable wind for his ship and hiding the unfavorable winds in a bag which could not be opened. Overholser had exaggerated Pound's symptoms and disabilities; when exaggeration under oath crosses an indefinable line it can be perjury. Some of Dr. Overholser's colleagues think he may have crossed the line but say such perjury was carried out with the best of intentions. As one of them succinctly summarized it: "Of course Dr. Overholser committed perjury. Pound was a great artist, a national treasure. If necessary I would have committed perjury too—gladly."[119]

CHAPTER 8

ASYLUM

[ST. ELIZABETHS HOSPITAL: 1946–1958]

THE PROCESSION OF LITERATI visiting inmate number 58,102 was unparalleled in asylum annals. Archibald MacLeish, T. S. Eliot, William Carlos Williams, and E. E. Cummings visited as close friends. Conrad Aiken, Robert Lowell, and Allen Tate came together one afternoon. H. L. Mencken, Stephen Spender, Thornton Wilder, Marianne Moore, Marshall McLuhan, Elizabeth Bishop, James Dickey, Alfred Alvarez, Katherine Anne Porter, even Alice Roosevelt Longworth came. Edith Hamilton arrived regularly in her black limousine with chauffeur. St. Elizabeths Hospital had become a sacrarium for savants.

Even before Ezra Pound took up residence there, St. Elizabeths had collected more than its share of men who had tempted the Fates. The seventh patient admitted after the hospital opened was Richard Lawrence, who, disgruntled and heeding the call of God, had opened fire on President Jackson from point-blank range. His guns misfired and he was subsequently found not guilty by reason of insanity.[1] During the Civil War the hospital had been used as a Union army hospital. Its commanding officer for part of this time was General Joseph Hooker, Commander of the Union Army of the Potomac. At Chancellorsville, Virginia, Hooker had engaged General Robert E. Lee's Confederate forces. "Even God almighty cannot deny us victory this day," Hooker proclaimed before the battle. Lee promptly routed the Union, whereupon President Lincoln relieved Hooker of his command. At St. Elizabeths Hooker distinguished himself by procuring from the streets of

Washington female companionship for his hospitalized troops. "Hooker's ladies" eventually became known simply as "hookers," and the general had achieved immortality.

Twelve and a half years, the period Ezra Pound stayed at St. Elizabeths, was precisely the length of time he had spent in London. St. Elizabeths rivaled London in being the most productive period of his life and also in being the period of greatest recognition. Incredibly, St. Elizabeths also rivaled London in being his happiest years as well.

For someone who had been indicted on nineteen counts of treason, Pound could have done much worse. The hospital sits on a hill overlooking the nation's capital, its spacious grounds covered with flowering trees planted by an early superintendent with arboreal interests. In 1946 there were over seven thousand inmates, and the hospital had its own laundry, bakery, fire department, library, auditorium, gymnasium, and tennis courts. It wasn't Harvard, but neither was it Leavenworth.

Pound spent his first year in Howard Hall, then moved to Center Building for the duration of his stay. His first room in Center Building overlooked the tennis court and front lawn; through hemlock trees the Capitol, the Library of Congress, and much of downtown Washington could clearly be seen. At night the lights of the city formed a broad panorama. His second room, to which he moved for more space, overlooked a small garden in the rear.

His room had one wall lined with bookshelves from floor to ceiling and served as both bedroom and study. It was described by all who saw it as a room of "phenomenal disarray." "All drawers were open and each with clothing and personal effects heaped within. The floor was littered with papers, boxes, and assorted bric-a-brac. The dresser top was covered several layers deep." Another visitor noted that "almost all the wall space was covered with paintings and pictures (which changed often) and schematic drawings and memos he made for himself concerning the structure and form of the developing cantos as well as designs for the work of others. Envelopes and pieces of paper containing lines and excerpts from books he was using dangled on strings tacked to the walls and even to the ceiling."[2] Pound worked at his typewriter in this room, often writing late into the night.

LITERARY OUTPUT

Ezra Pound settled into St. Elizabeths' routine and gratefully resumed his literary endeavors. Yet even as he did so his close friends let him know that the price he had paid for hiding behind the mask of insanity was exceedingly high. Wyndham Lewis wrote, "I am told you believe yourself to be Napoleon—or is it Mussolini? What a pity you did not choose Buddha." William Carlos Williams reminded Pound that both his sons had fought in the war against Italy and confronted his old friend with bitter candor: "That you're crazy I don't for one moment believe; you're not that good an American. And if you're shot as a traitor what the hell difference should it make to you? All it should mean is that you go down to the future, on which you seem to count so much, intact, your argument undamaged. Not many years left anyway for either of us." In a letter a few weeks later Williams added: "No one forgives you for what you did, everyone forgives you for what you are . . . You might as well realize that there is a point in all controversy beyond which a man's life (his last card) is necessarily forfeit. A man accepts that and goes on with his eyes open. But when the showdown comes he loses his life." Most devastating, perhaps, was a letter from his confidante of London and Paris years, Nancy Cunard: "Williams has called you 'misguided.' I do not agree. The correct word for a Fascist is 'scoundrel' . . . I cannot see what possible defense, excuse or mitigation exists for you . . . Nor do I believe anything concerning the 'advanced stage of schyzophrenia [sic] madness' etc. that was used as means to secure your non-execution. I do not believe you are insane or half-crazy. I think you are in full possession of your full faculties, as before." She had heard his radio broadcasts, she told him, and they were "idiotic"; but if his broadcasts represented insanity, then "Goering, Goebbels, Hitler, Streicher, the whole gang of criminals, were just 'merely' insane. Fascism uses the same hatreds and the same lies the world over. Fascism is not insanity, unless evil itself, all evil, be insanity."[3]

Pound tried to forget the past and immersed himself in work, composing two more books of poetry while at St. Elizabeths. *Section: Rock Drill* consisted of eleven cantos and was published in 1955; it was named after Jacob Epstein's sculpture *Rock Drill*, "the terrible Frankenstein monster which we have made ourselves into," which Pound had seen in progress when he visited Epstein's studio in 1913.[4] *Thrones* included fourteen more cantos and was published in 1959, although it was essentially finished before Pound left St. Elizabeths.

Some critics have praised Pound's St. Elizabeths poetry. James Dickey cites passages such as "the water-bug's mittens" (Canto 91) as "exactly, exactingly, observably and unforeseeably right! For that is what the water-bug's invisible tracks—his feet, his fingers—look like, transformed by the sun and water and rock into shadow. It is an amazing picture, and amazing image, and I for one would not want to do without it." And James Wilhelm calls Canto 90 "the most lyrical" of them all and says "surely this is one of the most charmed moments in world literature":

> *the viper stirs in the dust,*
>   *the blue serpent*
>
> *glides from the rock pool*
>   *And they take lights now down to the water*
>
> *the lamps float from the rowers*
>   *the sea's claw drawing them outward.*

Even William Carlos Williams put aside his criticism of Pound-the-politician ("A man does not have to agree with Pound to acknowledge the excellence of what he has written," Williams wrote) and praised Pound-the-poet in 1949: "Beauty may be difficult—as Ezra insists, but a sense of reality in the words is even more difficult. A sense that *connects* the past with the present so that the deepest past starts to life is (to say the least) astonishing."[5] Other critics find these cantos pretentious and obscure, especially with Pound's increasing use of Chinese in almost every poem. Pound defended himself against such criticism by including a caveat in the text of Canto 96:

> If we never write anything save what is already understood, the field of understanding will never be extended. One demands the right, now and again, to write for a few people with special interests and whose curiosity reaches into greater detail.

Many persons who have never read earlier poems by Ezra Pound assume his St. Elizabeths work is the product of an insane mind. In fact, although full of obscure and complex references, the later cantos are as highly structured and fully rational as any of Pound's other work. Irrationality is nowhere to be found, as James J. Wilhelm cogently illustrates in *The Later Cantos of Ezra Pound.* Pound may be charged with willful obfuscation in his poetry, but he cannot be accused of insanity. And it is, in fact, Pound's adoration of the abstruse that is probably one source of the popularity which he (and T. S. Eliot) have enjoyed. The admiration of obscurantism for its own sake has always been the Achilles heel of intellectuals.

Pound also published two books of Chinese translations during his years at the hospital. *The Unwobbling Pivot and the Great Digest* was a book of Confucian translations begun at Pisa and completed during his first two years at St. Elizabeths. *The Classic Anthology Defined by Confucius* was Pound's translation of three hundred traditional Chinese poems and was published, with good reviews, by the Harvard University Press in 1954. Pound himself regarded the anthology and two books of poetry as his major achievement of this period, as evidenced by his "thank you note" to Dr. Overholser written after he had left the hospital: "I don't know whether you will ever get credit for making possible the

Confucian anthology and two vols. of Cantos. At any rate my thanks."[6]

In addition to the poetry and Chinese translations, Pound also wrote and published a version of Sophocles' *Women of Trachis.* His output of journal and newspaper articles during these years was immense, including thirty contributions to the Australian literary journal *Edge,* sixty items to a political leaflet called *Strike,* and at least eighty to the *New Times,* a Social Credit paper.[7] The exact number of articles will never be known since many of his more vitriolic and political treatises were published anonymously. Pound also continued his prolific correspondence while at St. Elizabeths, writing by conservative estimate at least one thousand letters a year. So vast was his correspondence that his friends, when estimating his financial needs in preparation for leaving the hospital, only half facetiously predicted that his major expense might be postage.[8] One reason Pound was able to be so productive is that, in contrast to many other patients, he had no ward chores or job on the hospital grounds.

CHARM AND BIGOTRY

The personality characteristics manifested by Ezra Pound during his years at St. Elizabeths were identical to those that had made him famous and infamous in earlier years. A major attraction for visitors was his charm and intellectual vivacity, well described by Charles Olson, who was drawn irresistibly even after he had tired of Pound's bigotry:

I returned to see Pound yesterday. He has such charm. It is his charm which has betrayed him, for he assumes it can manage people. In itself, it is lovely, young, his maintaining of youth a rare thing . . . He remains, on the creative side of him, whole, and as charming and open and-warm a human being as I know. Despite all the corruption of his body politic.[9]

Pound remained ever the alchemist of words, describing poems shown to him as "lavender-scented cat-piss" and warning a friend to "lay off Martha-Ann, the pizoned [poisoned] gumdrop or the candy wumman's revenge."[10] To another he offered:

> There once was a brainy baboon
> Who always breathed down a bassoon,
>   For he said, "It appears
>   That in billions of years
>
> I shall certainly hit on a tune."[11]

It was a continuous infusion of apostasy and obscenity, but always with a good punch line:

Butt ji evver tell you about ole Abe Watrous and the Erie Canal? Naow
that is a consecutive story how as he wanted a ship's canal, and the other
buggars wanted a barge canal, an he sez: "Call the fahrty little ditch a
canal," he sez in the Noo Yok State Senate. "Wy, gentlemen, I cd. piss
half way across that little canal."

"Comecome, Mr. Watrous," sez th Speaker: "Yew air out of order."

"I know *damn* well I am out of order," yells Mr. Watrous: "Ef I wuzznt
out of order, I cd. piss *all* th way cross it."[12]

Closely connected with Pound's charm was his eccentricity. Achievement of this quality in an insane asylum, where it is the norm, is a
considerable feat, but Pound managed. As he had all his life, he used
dress to set himself apart from the masses. Since he had no access to
the tailors of London or Rapallo he reversed his strategy and affected
sloppiness of dress. According to one former hospital employee, Pound
"was famous for the scarf he wore, even in the summer. In warm weather
he wore shorts and sandals, and his shirt was *never* buttoned. He also
had a hat with a visor like the reporters wear. You could always tell it
was him coming from far off."[13] One psychiatrist described him as
"dressed in his usual attire consisting of brown shorts with undershorts
beneath (with the inner shorts descending below the outer) and bedroom
slippers. His hair was uncombed and his beard untrimmed." Another
psychiatrist noted that "he entered the room with his shirt tail out and
his fly open."[14] It was one way Pound could show contempt for his
surroundings and also provide a pleasing counterpoint to his earlier
years of playing the fop.

In his behavior he also periodically drew from his well of whimsy.
On one occasion a photographer was spotted behind a bush trying to
take a picture of Pound and one of his women friends. Pound pounced
toward the bush and let out a mighty ROAR "like a great white tiger.
It was terrifying. All he said was R R R R R R R R R R R R R R r r r
r r r r r R R R R R R R R but it took up the whole sentence and
roared all over the lawn."[15] It is not recorded what the other patients
thought of this display of ferocity.

Pound's behavior toward other patients was a mixture of friendship
and benign contempt. He told one visitor that the patients didn't bother
him because "he had never minded crazy people; it was only fools he
could not abide."[16] A staff member told Marianne Moore that "Mr. Pound
is a great help to us with the other inmates," and a visitor observed
Pound give fifteen cents to a black patient who was begging.[17] Other
reports on Pound's attitude, however, describe him as "rather disdainful
and contemptuous of his associates and fellow patients" and "showing
supreme contempt for the patients on the ward."[18] A patient who spent

four years in Center Building with Pound confirmed this attitude, and said that Pound was nice only to those patients who were aware of his importance.[19]

Pound's egotism and arrogance were, as always, just beneath the surface. He informed one visitor that "he is forty years ahead of his time and always has been"; another noted his "unwillingness to be told anything that he hadn't already found out for himself."[20] On one occasion Pound designated "twelve men, such as could be entrusted no doubt with important literary and educational work in the future." When asked why he had not included Marianne Moore on the list, Pound replied: "We couldn't have a woman among the twelve."[21]

It was Pound's arrogance that ultimately kept his closest friends at arm's length. The most articulate of these was William Carlos Williams, who intermittently assailed his friend with biting sarcasm:

You poor dumb cluck:
    Instead of sounding off on your pathetic little Ego-tooter why don't you use what is left of your head and try to think a little while? Or, since thinking is something that is probably not possible for you at the moment, why not just try for a few accurate statements. Start with simple things like saying, Did I brush my teeth this morning? Or something of the sort. From that you could build up until you felt strong enough to write a letter . . . Take my advice, Ez, and treat me with more intelligence or you will not even have *one* left in your audience." And later: "Go swallow a bottle of coke and let it fiz out of your ears."[22]

Psychiatrists who interviewed Pound also remarked on his arrogance. "His attitude toward the examiner was one of contempt and he [the examiner] was obviously included in the patient's reference to 'people who are children and have to have everything spelled out for them, C–A–T.'" Pound told another "that no psychiatrist could possibly understand him, and he gave the symbolism of a blacksmith trying to disassemble a jet plane." Still another psychiatrist, who had observed Pound closely over several years and who was familiar with both his work and his life history, wrote in 1953 that even "so skilled a wordsmith as Pound himself would have difficulty in finding superlatives by which he might describe the almost mythical and legendary figure 'Ezra Pound.'"[23]

Pound continued to express élitist and Fascist beliefs throughout his St. Elizabeths years. He praised Mussolini's humanistic traits and said that the only reason he had failed was because he had "tried to push Italy too fast."[24] Since Mussolini had decimated the labor unions in Italy, Pound's praise evoked a visceral reaction from visitor Charles Olson: "Here was a Fascist as evil as all of them . . . It is not enough to call him a Fascist. He is a Fascist, the worst kind, the intellectual

Fascist, this filthy apologist and mouther of slogans which serve men of power. It was a shame upon all writers when this man of words, this succubus, sold his voice to the enemies of the people."[25] Olson's father, an immigrant, had been killed fighting for the right of workers to organize into labor unions in America.

The Protocols of Zion also made its ugly entrance into St. Elizabeths. Like a gossamer veil covering a dungheap of hate, Pound invoked it frequently to rationalize his bigotry, and he urged his disciples to read the book. It was important, he wrote to one, "to recognize the design asserted in the Protocols allegedly of the Elders of Zion." Another follower prepared a summary of the Protocols for Pound in two or three pages.[26] Pound characterized the Ten Commandments as the "Chewlaw" composed of "9 points cribbed from Egyptian 'negative confession' plus Mose'z wangle to plug a leak. Plus a lot of regulations NOT based on any ethic whatsodam but merely aimed as imposing fines fer benefit of priests and levys."[27] The Old Testament continued to be pilloried: "The jew book is the poison / that, since A.D. it has bitched everything it got into . . . The jew book has been filling bughouses with nuts ever since they set up such institutions."[28] This was Pound's perspective from his perch in St. Elizabeths Hospital.

The conspiracy of Jews was responsible for everything wrong with the world, including the publishing business: "If the country weren't a sewer defiled with twenty years dog's pewk of the Spewsfeldian era the Odes wd / hv/ [would have] got printed 3 years ago."[29] Jews had caused World War II and had used people like Roosevelt as a front for their interests: "Wars are made to make debt, and the late one started by the ambulating dunghill FDR has been amply successful, and the stink that elevated him still emits a smell."[30] Hitler was aware of this and that is why he had been "furious from perception" (Cantos 90 and 104).

Pound's visitors, even his closest friends and admirers, were frequently embarrassed by his anti-Semitism. Michael Reck wrote that "the Jewish obsession was there all the time,"[31] and James Laughlin reported that Pound's anti-Semitism seemed to be growing stronger with the passing years.[32] Charles Olson's notes on his visits to St. Elizabeths describe the depth of Pound's anti-Semitism most vividly. Pound once claimed, "I was a Zionist in Italy, but now I'm for pogroms after what I've experienced in here [St. Elizabeths]." On another occasion Pound said: "There was a Jew in London . . . a doctor . . . and I used to ask him what is the effect of circumcision. That's the question that gets them sore . . . That sends them right up the pole. Try it, don't take my word, try it . . . It must do something, after all these years and years, where the most sensitive nerves in the body are, rubbing them off, over and over again." Olson wrote: "It was fantastic, again the Fascist bastard, the same god damned kind of medical nonsense Hitler and the gang used with the same seriousness, the same sick conviction."[33]

Pound also demonstrated crass anti-Semitism in interviews with psychiatrists at St. Elizabeths. He separated psychiatrists into two categories, Jewish and non-Jewish. Dr. Overholser was an example of the latter and thus a man who could be somewhat trusted. When faced with a new psychiatrist whose ethnic origin was not immediately apparent from his name, Pound "took out his close reading glasses and scrutinized the interviewer's face, asked questions about his name."[34] When faced with a psychiatrist with an obviously Jewish name, Pound was often rude and puerile, once even "kicking his foot in the direction of this writer" [a psychiatrist with a Jewish name].[35] Even Dr. Overholser acknowledged Pound's "definite anti-Semitic statements and feelings."[36]

Pound himself denied any anti-Semitism. On one occasion he told Charles Olson that people should not criticize him for anti-Semitism because "anti-Semitism is not in the indictment."[37] Later he advised Archibald MacLeish that "you may say to any shit you meet, quite truthfully, that Ez considers anti-Semitism un-Aristotelian and unscientific and that every man black yellow red or pink (as to cuticle) shd / [should] be judged on his own merits." In the next paragraph of the same letter Pound quoted Louis Zukovsky, a Jewish-American poet, as having said: "The only honest Jew I have ever met is my father and THAT is a pure coincidence."[38]

It was not his anti-Semitism that got Pound into trouble at St. Elizabeths, however, but rather his racism against blacks. Pound had made disparaging remarks against "coons" and "niggers" since his college days, but had spent most of his life in European cities where few blacks lived. Following the war Washington experienced a dramatic influx of blacks from the Carolinas and Georgia, and it slowly became a predominantly black city. As the number of black patients at St. Elizabeths increased, Pound complained vociferously about the "imbecilic mad niggers." With Jackie Robinson in the Brooklyn Dodgers' lineup and integration underway, pressure began to be felt at St. Elizabeths, a federal institution, to integrate the wards and provide equal care for blacks and whites. Equally disturbing to Pound must have been the daily reports he got from Dorothy. The neighborhood she lived in near the hospital was rapidly being integrated and, at the rate it was going, would soon be solidly black. Pound's friends from London also wrote him that dark-skinned people were taking over Kensington and occasionally marrying whites.[39] The blacks, it seemed, were going to degrade the Anglo-Saxon genetic stock just as the European immigrants had done half a century earlier.

On June 14, 1950, John Kasper wrote to Dr. Overholser requesting permission to visit Pound. Kasper indicated that he had already corresponded with the poet, and that Pound wished to see him on two consecutive afternoons.[40] (It was most unusual for Pound to agree to see somebody he had not met before for two visits.) Kasper had just graduated from Columbia University. In an undergraduate term paper he had praised Hitler and Stalin, and compared Pound favorably with Machiavelli and Nietzsche. "The weak have no justification for living except in service of the strong," Kasper wrote. "What is a little cruelty to the innocuous when it is expedient for the strong ones who have the right to alter the laws of life and death before their natural limits?"[41]

Kasper and Pound immediately became ideological kinsmen. At the end of their first meeting, according to Kasper, "Ezra shouted to me, 'Bravo for Kasp!'" Kasper's friends recall that he returned from Washington "almost as a person inspired . . . He seemed to think that he had met a very great man, a man who knew all the answers to life." From that point onward they corresponded at least weekly, and Kasper journeyed to Washington to see Pound frequently.

Kasper's devotion to Pound was complete. By 1951 he was proposing moving to Washington to be closer to Pound so that he could learn from him more quickly. Kasper's unpublished letters to Pound are extraordinary, indicating a complete master-student relationship and an apparent willingness to do whatever Pound asked. Kasper worshiped Pound and believed that he possessed a wisdom which was divine in origin.[42]

After meeting with Pound, Kasper opened a bookstore in Greenwich Village that stocked "venomous Nazi literature" and had a window display of anti-Semitic books. On one occasion Kasper proposed piling psychology books by Jewish authors in a fenced-in area on the floor, calling it a pigsty, and putting a sign over it, "Jewish Muck." That was too much even for Pound, who dissuaded him. Kasper and an associate, T. David Horton (a student at Hamilton College), began a publishing venture under Pound's guidance called the Square Dollar Series in which they published six books (including Pound's translations of Confucius's *Analects*) that Pound believed every student should read.

The 1954 Supreme Court decision mandating the integration of schools was of great interest to Pound. Referring to Frobenius's work in Africa, Pound told a visitor: "Ha! There're twenty-seven different types of nigger. Can you imagine that? Twenty-seven different types in Africa. You'd have to have a segregation law for each type!"[43] Immediately following the Supreme Court decision, integration of all wards at St. Elizabeths got under way, although Pound's ward, technically under the forensic division of the hospital, had in fact been integrated earlier.

Kasper continued to prove himself a willing pupil of Pound, and following the Supreme Court decision he moved to Washington. In June 1956, Kasper organized the Seaboard White Citizens Council with the avowed purpose of reversing the recent desegregation of the nation's capital; its motto was "Honor-Pride-Fight: Save The White." The following was used on a flyer for the Council:

> Now damn all race-mixers
> The stink: Roose, Harry and Ike
> God bless Jeff / Jax and John Adams
> Also Abe
> Loathe carpet-bag
> Despise scalawag
> Hate mongrelizer

As a later article in the *New York Herald Tribune* noted, "the language, references, manner of phraseology are patently derived from Pound; in some cases whole phrases have been lifted bodily from the poet's *Cantos.*" Pound's role in forming the Seaboard White Citizens Council was also confirmed by John Chatel, another Pound intimate, who noted that the economic ideas for the Council had been borrowed from a book on Nazi economics and that Pound's interest in "the Negro business" was "just a front" to propagandize for his economic theories.[44]

Pound's pupil was now officially launched on his new career. John Kasper billed himself as "Segregation Chief" and began speaking to anti-integration crowds in the South. In Louisville he told his audience that blacks "might have a soul, they might have a right to pray. I know some men who claim that they have seen niggers with tails." In Charlottesville the flyer advertising Kasper's talk promised that he would reveal "the red-led NAACP's plans to start full-scale marriage between Nigras and Whites by 1963." Some of his speeches in South Carolina were sponsored by the Ku Klux Klan, and in Alabama he was helped by George Lincoln Rockwell, later head of the American Nazi Party.[45] The Jews were behind integration, Kasper preached, and he plunged deeper into the territory where integration was a stick of dynamite with a short fuse. In September 1956, in Clinton, Tennessee, he finally lit the fuse—resulting in a riot, National Guardsmen, bayonets, tanks, and violence. He was arrested, released on bail, and resumed agitating. One year later in Nashville he was arrested as a suspect in the bombing of an elementary school undergoing integration; according to one historian, John Kasper "had a large hand in the violence that plagued Tennessee in 1956 and 1957." After a brief visit to Florida where he preached the necessity of denying Jews there the right to vote, Kasper returned to Tennessee where he was rearrested, convicted, and sentenced to federal prison. The book he carried into jail under his arm was *Mein Kampf.*[46]

Many people suspected that Pound had instigated the agitation in Tennessee and that Kasper was merely carrying out Pound's plan. An analysis of the correspondence between Pound and Kasper at this time reveals numerous requests by Kasper for material which could be used for slogans and short speeches on Jews, integration, miscegenation, eugenics, and related subjects, with acknowledgments to Pound for his help; on at least one occasion Kasper signed his letter with a Nazi swastika. Also of interest is a pamphlet published in Kasper's name after he had gone to prison in May 1958 by the Seaboard White Citizens Council. Called "Segregation or Death," it claimed that Jews were engaged "in a fanatic effort to subvert existing Gentile order everywhere;" a snake with a Jewish head was depicted winding around the White House, Capitol, Supreme Court, and United Nations. "Nigras" were said "to be a stooge of world-Jewry, blindly led into the vortex of Jewish power, dedicated to overthrowing all existing order." The racial theories of Leo Frobenius were given prominence, and phrases such as "race-mongrelization," "race-mixer," and "usurer" abounded. The pamphlet concluded with a two-page appeal to readers to write their Congressmen demanding Kasper's release from jail. Claiming he "is America's first political prisoner" his imprisonment was attributed to "the jargon of the juggling jewspapers" and "jewspaper lies."[47]

When Archibald MacLeish asked whether he was helping Kasper, Pound replied: "I doubt if Kasper hates anyone, his actions in keeping open shack for stray cats and humans seem to indicate a kind heart with no exclusion of nubians." A week later Pound added: "Why pick on Kasp who was NOT on the scene of the riot." The following month the *New York Hearld Tribune* published the entire story of the Kasper-Pound collaboration under the headline: "Segregationist Kasper is Ezra Pound Disciple."[48] Pound again declined to repudiate Kasper, telling a friend that "at least he's a man of action and don't sit around looking at his navel." To Wyndham Lewis he was more positive in assessing his pupil: "Kasp / has used expediency and may have done some good." And to Brigit Patmore he wrote: "Der Kasperl smiling in handcuffs and making the snooze [news] even in Ul / Brit / along with the LOOSEwypapers full page of fried nigger."[49]

John Kasper was only one of several disciples whom Pound educated during his years at St. Elizabeths. The common denominator of them all was devout reverence toward their teacher. Another was David Wang, a Chinese-American graduate of Dartmouth who had adopted the cause of white supremacy and attempted to organize segregationist groups on the campuses of Ivy League colleges. The bulletin of his "North American Citizens for the Constitution" accused Eisenhower and the Supreme Court Justices of treason and urged that they be tried.[50] Still another follower was Hayden Carruth, to whom Pound wrote: "Both Wang and I will probably have done our jobs on the Sacred Edict in time for you to use 'em."[51] On another occasion Pound offered advice on how to publish libelous statements with impunity: "You can also put difficult items (i.e. those you cd / [could] get jailed for) in the interrogative. Are we to believe that the foul Javitts was moved by order from kikes in s. america? Or merely followed their commie line?" And when poet James Dickey visited him after moving to Atlanta, Pound suggested that he join the Ku Klux Klan.[52] Ezra Pound was always the preceptor; as he had taught Richard Aldington and T. S. Eliot in London, so he taught John Kasper and David Wang in Washington.

THE MAN WHO CAME TO DINNER

When Pound made the decision to avoid treason charges by pleading unfit to stand trial, he hoped to be released from the hospital and be back in Italy within a few months.[53] It would be twelve and one-half years before that would actually occur. The reason why it took so long for Pound to get out of St. Elizabeths was a combination of legal miscalculations, historical accident, and personal preference.

Julien Cornell's initial strategy of using insanity to avoid the treason changes had succeeded. The next steps in his plan were to get the psychiatrists to confirm that Pound was never likely to improve, then have him released on the grounds that he was incurably insane but not in need of hospitalization. It was also hoped that the Department of Justice could be persuaded to drop the indictment, which would allow Pound to return to Italy.[54] Cornell and James Laughlin unquestionably believed this strategy would be successful, for in mid-1946 they asked author Charles Norman to delay release of his book about Pound (*The Case of Ezra Pound*) on the grounds that it might delay the poet's imminent release.[55] There is also a suggestion that Dr. Overholser was being consulted on strategy at this time, as he apparently advised against any further legal moves until after the November 1946 congressional elections.[56]

Problems with Julien Cornell's strategy quickly became apparent. One month after the sanity hearing at which Pound had been described as too insane to assist counsel in his own defense, Cornell attempted to have Pound assign him rights of power of attorney. Dr. Overholser protested that Pound was by definition not legally competent to make such an assignation but Cornell persisted, claiming that Pound had "an extraordinary clarity of mind, even shrewdness, in his approach to business problems . . . My view would be that Pound may be legally competent to carry on such business although he has been found insane to the extent that he is unfit for trial."[57]

On December 2, 1946, Cornell refiled a motion for bail for Ezra Pound, claiming that he was likely never to recover his sanity and that to continue his incarceration amounted to life imprisonment without trial.[58] A hearing was set for January 29, 1947. The day prior to the hearing Cornell gave an interview to Albert Deutsch, the journalist who had assiduously covered the sanity hearing one year previously. Cornell told Deutsch that "a number of doctors who have examined Mr. Pound since he was committed to St. Elizabeths have advised me that he is not insane enough to be further confined in a public institution. They told me that a long time ago. But I have been counseled that it would be best to wait at least a year after the insanity hearing to bring in this appeal for release, on the basis that public interest in the case might die down by then and there would be no public resistance to this move. If the government does not oppose this motion, we should be able to obtain his release within ten minutes." Julien Cornell then added, incredibly: "I am going to ask Judge Laws to bar the press from the hearing and to seal the papers on it. I don't see what concern the public should have in this case."[59]

Predictably, Deutsch went immediately to the Department of Justice to get their reaction for the public record. "Should Pound obtain a release, we intend to start proceedings immediately to have him brought to trial on the treason indictment," Deutsch was assured by Assistant U.S. Attorney General Theron Caudle. Caudle then reminded Deutsch that three Army psychiatrists had found Pound perfectly sane at Pisa. "Can you tell me why the official opinion of these psychiatrists was never produced at the insanity hearing last year?" Deutsch asked pointedly. "I haven't the slightest idea," Caudle answered.[60]

When the motion for bail was finally heard by Judge Laws it was dismissed. Both sides agreed, however, that Pound should be moved to more comfortable quarters, and so he was transferred from Howard Hall to Center Building. To some it must have been apparent that Ezra Pound was in for a long stay and he might as well be made comfortable. As long as reporters like Albert Deutsch were outside the St. Elizabeths walls, it was going to be difficult to quietly spirit Pound out the back gate.

Pound settled into a routine of writing and entertaining visitors as 1947 progressed. Nuremberg was past, but the war crimes trials of Japanese leaders continued in Tokyo. The peace treaties had been signed in Paris, and General George Marshall proposed a plan to rehabilitate Europe. In December 1947, Cornell met with Dorothy and Ezra and they agreed it was time to make another attempt at release. Cornell then prepared a writ of habeas corpus in the name of Dorothy Pound and presented it at court on February 11, 1948. It asked for Pound's release from St. Elizabeths on the grounds that he was "permanently insane and can never be brought to trial" and cited statements which Dr. Overholser had allegedly made to Cornell to the effect that Pound no longer required hospitalization. The Department of Justice immediately called Overholser, who replied that Cornell had been "guilty of making misrepresentations."[61] The writ was denied but Cornell, as planned, filed an immediate appeal. He was determined to take the case to the Supreme Court, where he thought he could win.

At this point the Pounds dismissed Julien Cornell as their attorney. In a letter dated March 13, 1948, Dorothy Pound told Cornell to "please withdraw the appeal at once. My husband is not fit to appear in court and must still be kept as quiet as possible; the least thing shakes up his nerves terribly." As might be surmised it was Ezra and not Dorothy who had initiated the firing. Cornell speculated that the reason was that the Pounds could not be certain of being able to return to Italy if he was released and quotes Pound as saying "that if he had to remain in the United States, St. Elizabeths was probably as good a place for him as any."[62] Given the active role that Dr. Overholser played behind the scenes and his embarrassment at being "misrepresented" by Cornell, it is possible that he also encouraged the Pounds to jettison their attorney.

Cornell's dismissal inaugurated a period of confusion among Pound's friends regarding the best strategy for obtaining his release. John Drummond and Ronald Duncan, English literati whom Pound had corresponded with for ten years, criticized Cornell and Laughlin for their inexperience, urging Pound to stand trial and take his chances: "It seems that they have got Ezra into an impossible fix . . . The 'insanity' is presumably a fake in that hundreds of people are just as 'crazy' as Ezra but don't have to be locked up for it. I now think the 'insanity' policy has been a tremendous mistake." Drummond even speculated that Pound suspected Cornell had been influenced by Jews. Wyndham Lewis, also in England, was equally perplexed; he believed that Pound had erred in not allowing Cornell to go forward with his legal attempts, but at the same time expressed grave apprehension about public statements Ezra might make if released. Pound's literary reputation, he reasoned, was being improved by his stay in St. Elizabeths, and he cited several other Pound friends who felt the same way. By November 1948, Lewis confessed to complete befuddlement in a letter to a friend, finally concluding facetiously that Pound's best strategy might be if "Thomas Eliot will pray for him."[63]

Pound himself was developing second thoughts about having gone the insanity route, and James Laughlin wrote him a long letter of encouragement. Laughlin argued that the public was unable to understand Pound's political and economic teachings, and that the insanity defense was still Pound's best strategy for eliciting public sympathy and avoiding responsibility for his broadcasts over Rome Radio. Laughlin claimed that he had discussed the strategy with several others, including Eliot, and that all agreed with it.[64] Laughlin's logic had assumed added weight on July 1, 1948, when Robert H. Best, another American radio traitor, had been sentenced to life imprisonment for his wartime activities.

In Italy Olga Rudge worked assiduously on Pound's behalf, organizing petitions to send to the American government. She claimed Ezra had written to her complaining about Cornell and Laughlin, and she wrote to Hemingway accusing him of doing nothing to help Pound.[65] Hemingway in turn wrote to Dorothy complaining about Olga and to another friend complaining about Laughlin.[66] Dorothy and Olga were not on speaking terms, which further complicated the coordination of initiatives, and mutual friends had to tread softly lest they be seen as taking sides with one woman or the other in their ongoing uxorial struggle.[67]

Meanwhile some of Pound's friends were developing a plan. In June 1948, a meeting took place which included Laughlin, Cornell, T. S. Eliot, E. E. Cummings, W. H. Auden, Allen Tate, and Dudley Fitts. It is likely that the strategy leading to the Bollingen Award was developed at this time. As described by Archibald MacLeish, who was not at the meeting but was intimately involved in the planning of strategy for Pound's release, friends "conceived the idea of a new national prize for poetry to be awarded by the Library of Congress through a jury of notables who would select Pound as the first recepient, thus dramatizing his situation and putting the government, and particularly the Department of Justice, in an awkward if not untenable position."[68] MacLeish had been the head of the Library of Congress before becoming assistant secretary of state, so was in a propitious position to oversee the affair. A one-thousand-dollar prize was then offered in 1948 by the Bollingen Foundation, subsidized by the Mellon family of Pittsburgh, for the best volume of verse published in America by an American each year. Pound's

Pisan Cantos, which had lain unpublished since their completion in late 1945, were published, and a fourteen-person awards committee was set up. Not coincidentally the committee included many Pound support- ers, among them T. S. Eliot, Robert Lowell, Allen Tate, Conrad Aiken Theodore Spencer, and Katherine Anne Porter. It also included Kather- ine Garrison Chapin, the wife of Francis Biddle, who as attorney general had indicted Pound; her inclusion was probably an attempt to further embarrass the Department of Justice by associating her with the award.

The vote for the initial prize was taken in 1949 by mail ballot, and the winner was Ezra Pound; only two votes (Katherine Garrison Chapin and Karl Shapiro) were cast in opposition.[69] The resulting public outcry was sustained and stentorian; how could a man indicted for trea- son, a man whose poems included crass anti-Semitism, be honored as a great American poet? Congressman Jacob K. Javits demanded a con- gressional investigation into the circumstances surrounding the award. The *Saturday Review of Literature* was most outspoken and implied that the award had been prearranged.[70] Virtually all literary magazines and many newspapers entered the debate. What were the limits of free speech? When does dissent end and treason begin? What is the obliga- tion of an artist to his society? Can an artist be judged purely on his skill without taking into consideration the content of his art? They were consequential questions and they sold literary journals, but they did not open the gates of St. Elizabeths Hospital.

Rather than helping Pound, the Bollingen controversy retarded his hopes for release by reminding the public of what he had said and done for Mussolini and Fascism. Most damaging was the response the award elicited from Dr. Fredric Wertham, a respected and nationally known psychiatrist who in late 1949 published a stinging critique in a psychiatric journal. There was no evidence whatsoever that Pound was mentally ill, Wertham wrote: "Not until Ezra Pound was in jail did the question of mental disease ever come up. And then in no time the public was informed that he was insane." The testimony of Dr. Overholser and his colleagues at the sanity hearing was closely scrutinized and found to be wanting: "Surely the psychiatrists know the difference between a political conviction and a delusion . . . Ezra Pound has no delusions in any strictly pathological sense. But we have let ourselves be deluded— into a belief that responsibility is not responsibility, guilt not guilt, and incitement to hate not incitement to violence."[71]

Wertham's article received wide coverage by the media. "Wertham Assails Pound Ruling," wrote the *New York Times.* "I Will Not Go Mad" was the heading on *Newsweek*'s story. And the *Washington Post* editorial- ized: "If Mr. Pound is not insane, the principle of legal impartiality and equal legal responsibility has been injured if, merely because of his putative literary gifts, he is to be placed in another category than, say Axis Sally or Tokyo Rose."[72] Rather than building public sympathy for Pound's release, then, the net effect of the Bollingen Award was to increase the public's suspicion that it had been cuckolded not once but twice—by the psychiatrists who initially saved Pound from trial and more recently by the poets who gave him an award to try to force his release. Pound, sitting on the hill overlooking the city, saw it differently: "My friends thought if they gave me that prize it would help pave the way for getting out. Ah, of course it raised a furor, and that so-called Republican Representative from New York, Jakie Javits, gathered all his noisy little forces and saw to it that that intention was blocked."[73]

As the reverberations from the Bollingen Award continued to be felt into 1950, the political world beyond the walls of St. Elizabeths was changing. A Committee on Un-American Activities of the House of Representatives had come into being, and zealous young congressmen such as Richard Nixon were digging for Communists. Alger Hiss was one of the first to be pilloried; Pound watched the case avidly, for Lloyd Stryker, who had been Pound's original choice as his own attorney, was defending Hiss. In 1949 the explosion of the first Soviet atomic bomb presaged more change to come, and the following year the new era emerged in shining splendor in the person of Senator Joseph McCarthy. Anti-Communist hysteria took grip. Pound in fact was supportive of the Senator's efforts to rout out nefarious Communist influence lurking behind the brows of civil servants, but he was in no position to be vocal in his support. Pound himself had contributed to *New Masses, Front,* and other Communist-inspired journals in the 1920s and 30s, and although he had become staunchly anti-Communist in the intervening years, he decided that silence was the wisest course. With McCarthyism rampant in the streets of Washington it was not a time to free poets who had been indicted for treason. Then when Julius and Ethel Rosenberg were convicted of spying in 1951, Pound's concern increased again. An official of the State Department told his daughter, Mary, when she inquired about getting her father released that she was lucky he had not ended up in the electric chair.[74]

ST. FRANCIS OF THE ASYLUM

Ezra Pound had no reason to tempt fate, for he was happy at St. Elizabeths. Many of his close friends were accessible, although Olga and Mary were back in Italy. Pound's mother had died in Italy in October

1948, giving him one more reason not to rush back there. Life in St. Elizabeths was at least tolerable and at times felicific, since he had the things he valued most—intellectual stimulation, attention, good food, and sex. And all of it was provided gratis, courtesy of the United States government. Pound had long argued that America had an obligation to support its artists; little did he realize that he would obtain this support in an insane asylum. What had been an ideal to be achieved by reason became a reality achieved by expediency.

Pound's access to books was an important reason for his productivity at St. Elizabeths. He devoured them at a rate of "up to 25 or more a week brought by different people from many a university library and store in the area as well as the Library of Congress."[75] Pound could obtain books from the last source by ordering them through the hospital library, or they would be brought by Robert Lowell and other literary friends. In addition to this the director of the Oriental Library in Washington brought material Pound was interested in.[76] For a bibliophile and a person with arcane intellectual interests, having such resources at one's disposal was bliss.

Even more important was the fact that intellectual minds often accompanied the books. To assist him in translating Confucius, a young Chinese woman would "sit opposite him with Chinese text while he read out his translations; her job was to warn him if he was straying too far from the original." Rudd Fleming, a professor at the University of Maryland, came once a week for nine years to discuss Greek translations; later he was joined by Greek scholar Edith Hamilton when Pound was translating the *Women of Trachis*. Professor José Vazquez-Amaral journeyed from New Jersey regularly for three years to help Pound translate the Cantos into Spanish, and Marianne Moore came to get Pound's help in translating Jean de la Fontaine's *Fables* from French into English. Huntington Cairns, secretary-treasurer of the National Gallery of Art, was a regular visitor, and his notes reflect discussions of Plato and Aristotle, Horace and Catullus. Poet friends like Williams, Lowell, Tate, Cummings, and Eliot occasionally stopped. "He taught me more than any other individual I've ever met," remembered literary critic Hugh Kenner, another regular visitor.[77]

The settings for these intellectual exercises were an alcove on Chestnut Ward and the lawn outside the building. It was Surrealism at St. Elizabeths, with the intelligentsia surrounded by "men in a kind of grey prison garb crawling on their knees, and some were standing on chairs shouting at the top of their lungs, but most of them sat with their hands clasped between their knees, sunk in dejection. 'I am Boris Gudonov,

master of all the Russians!' The shrieking voice went on and on, scream-
ing louder than gulls, a deep rhythmic and compulsive voice which endlessly repeated the same meaningless phrase."[78]

Pound had complete control over who could visit him at the hospital.
Letters requesting permission were routed through the administrative
offices to Pound, who would indicate either acceptance or rejection. A
secretary then prepared a reply, giving the person a date for the visit
if Pound's answer had been affirmative. Nobody was allowed to visit
Pound without his express permission, and he had the authority to cut
off visits from anyone he didn't wish to see.[79]

One visitor who was not encouraged to come was Omar Pound.
In May 1945, the same month that Ezra had been taken into custody,
Omar joined the United States Army. A few months earlier he had borrowed a copy of *Jefferson and/or Mussolini* "in order to determine if there
was something in it that could be used to his father's advantage in his
legal defense." In April 1946 he applied for emergency furlough from
the army and wrote to St. Elizabeths asking them to support his request
for compassionate leave. He had seen his father, he noted, for only
four hours in the past sixteen years. The letter was answered by Dr.
Samuel Silk, assistant superintendent, in a perfunctory fashion: "We
know of no reason why you should be alarmed about his condition,
and there seems to be no urgent need for you to receive an emergency
furlough."[80] Omar did visit St. Elizabeths later.

Visiting hours were 2 to 4 P.M. daily, and Pound "compartmentalized
his regular visitors into the days of the week. 'You' he will say with
good humor but finality 'will be a Wednesday' . . . His guests know
themselves and one another as Wednesdays or Mondays, and these
names are badges."[81] Each day was reserved for separate areas of interest
so that visitors with whom Pound was working on Greek translation
or Confucian odes would not be mixed with those with whom he was
planning to reverse desegregation. He kept his various interests strictly
separated, as evidenced by the fact that William Carlos Williams had
never heard of John Kasper until he saw television reports of Kasper's
arrest and link to Pound.[82]

Visitors clustered around Pound in large numbers in the screened-
off alcove or out on the lawn, depending upon the season and weather.
A nursing supervisor complained about the inside visits because Pound
left no room for other patients' visitors: "It is becoming a daily occurrence for six or more visitors to be with Mr. Pound simultaneously
. . . Mr. Pound's visitors bring books, briefcases etc. to these sessions.
Mr. Pound assumes the role of a professor lecturing to his pupils, rather
than an ill patient receiving comforting visits from loved ones."[83]

On nice days on the lawn there were always at least three or four visitors waiting, and sometimes as many as ten or fifteen. Pound would emerge from Center Building carrying his folding lawn chair, books, and food for his guests. It was the stage entrance of a rational man incarcerated among the insane, "as incongruous . . . as a Great Northern Pike in a guppy tank" according to a friend. Eustace Mullins, one of Pound's more devoted followers, described such afternoons in Elysian terms, with Pound benignly teaching his disciples while Dorothy passed out choice refreshments—"pet blue jays always set up a great screeching . . . The squirrels would come skipping down from nearby trees."[84] There was an air of expectant exhilaration as the great poet spoke. It was a portrait of a latter-day St. Francis of the Asylum.

Many of these visitors were young persons who had been attracted to Pound by his poetry or his politics. The son of Viola Baxter Jordan, Pound's old girlfriend, described them as "a string of budding bohemians, exhibitionist misfits, and college English majors," and said that in dress and manners many of them imitated Pound.[85] Other visitors included one of the guards from the DTC in Pisa and George Biddle; Pound, with at least a trace of sarcasm, told George that he would also be pleased to meet Francis.[86] A visit to the poet in the asylum became a status symbol among some circles in the mid-1950s, a sort of conservative chic.

A FINE RAPACIOUS BEASTIE

Pound had eaten at restaurants most of his life and enjoyed good food. He was able to continue exercising his gourmet tastes at St. Elizabeths despite the fact that the hospital was not rated as one of the world's great restaurants; this was accomplished mostly through food brought by Dorothy and his friends. His room was filled with boxes and jars of various cheeses, candies, and leftover food which he brought back from the tables of St. Elizabeths. According to one visitor, "he prepared tasty, simple, sometimes elaborate picnics for his friends, feasts that often delighted discerning palates. The only time in my life I ever had enough caviar was Xmas day at St. Elizabeths." The caviar was brought each Christmas by Huntington Cairns, and after leaving St. Elizabeths, Pound thanked him and said he would be rewarded by "a whatifficent deity." The food also brought the predictable problem of ants, described by Pound as "½ of one crumb equals 9 ants," but "the management against installin ice-boxes or other ant-proof apparatus."[87]

The food that Pound regularly confiscated from the St. Elizabeths tables was given to the young people who visited him regularly. This became public knowledge when David Rattray published an article on Pound's hospital life during his last years there. In the article Rattray quoted two of Pound's disciples who claimed that most of their food was supplied to them by Pound. Dr. Overholser was perturbed by this public acknowledgment of Pound's hospital life-style and asked the assistant superintendent to investigate. In his report to Overholser he noted that Pound "does admit quite frankly having taken food from the dining room but only after all the other patients had been served . . . He promised not to take any more."[88]

Wine was also available when Pound wanted it. One visitor recalled bringing a particularly fine bottle of wine which Pound uncorked with a resounding "pop" while sitting in the ward's screened-off alcove. "After several quaffs, Ezra became quite mellow. This was the first of many such bottles, always smuggled in and drunk without permission."[89]

Pound's fondness for women was also satisfied at St. Elizabeths. Sheri Martinelli, described by Noel Stock as "a strange, rather scatterbrained young woman," first wrote to Pound in 1951, eventually took an apartment near the hospital, and was a regular visitor until she was displaced by Marcella Spann in 1957. One person who knew her said she had been a model in New York.[90]

Sheri Martinelli's paintings adorned the walls of Pound's room; he also arranged for the publication of a small book of her work. She shared with Pound a propensity for referring to minority groups in unflattering terms, and also an interest in the mystical and occult. Pound occasionally burned olibanum, a kind of incense, on a special rock on the hospital lawn. According to one person who was present, "so far as I could tell the only visitor of those years who had any perception at all of what Pound was doing then was a young woman painter from one of those 'passionate religious traditions conscious of its roots in European paganism.'" The tradition was that of Eleusis, and Ezra described Sheri as possessing an element of "unstillness" which he himself possessed.[91] He nicknamed her Undine, for the Greek spirit of the water.

That Sheri Martinelli shared Pound's reverential enthusiasm for sex there is no doubt. In 1959 she wrote an article called "Duties of a Lady Female" in which she prescribed an "incense for love" composed of dried orange, tangerine, cloves, nutmeg, and olibanum. "Making love in a room kept perfumed is like being inside a flower . . . rub oranges and lemon oils into your skin . . . you'll smell like something good to eat . . . Love him as if his ancestors were watching." She also recommended focusing on the man, getting him to talk about himself, and treating him as if he were "wildly adventurous"; the result, she said, would be a man "used to being predatory, a fine rapacious beastie."[92]

By Martinelli's own admission she and Pound were lovers; she explicitly acknowledged this in a letter to Archibald MacLeish.[93] Descriptions of their relationship by other visitors corroborate this. For example David Rattray records her arrival while he was there: "Pound embraced her and ran his hands through her hair, and they talked excitedly, each interrupting the other. I turned and talked with Mrs. Pound." When she left, "Pound threw his arms around her, hugged her, and kissed her goodbye."[94] A nursing staff member who worked on Pound's ward during these years recalls that Pound was allowed to have certain visitors at any time of day or evening, that he entertained the visitors in his private room, and that the room was absolutely off limits to the staff. "None of the staff would have dared to interrupt him when he had visitors." Another visitor confirmed this: "A few of his closest disciples and helpers could come almost anytime, AM, PM or evening."[95]

In 1955 Pound asked Dr. Overholser if Sheri Martinelli could move onto the grounds of St. Elizabeths and rent "one of the attendant's rooms." Pound also wanted the hospital to employ her as an art therapist. Overholser replied in a note to another doctor: "Please tell Mr. Pound I am afraid the scheme is not practical. We have no paid position, and the present state of the case would really rule out employing Miss M."[96] Pound wrote back to Overholser that "there was no question of payment . . . it was to be voluntary, and with the rent for quarters paid to S. Eliz. Difficulties quite visible."[97]

Given the interests they shared, it is not surprising to find Martinelli in Pound's work. She is said to have inspired Canto 90, one of the most lyrical of his later poems:[98]

> *Trees die and the dream remains*
> > *Not love but that love flows from it*
> > *ex amino*
> > *and cannot ergo delight in itself*
> > *but only in the love flowing from it.*

It is in this canto that Pound wrote "UBI AMOR IBI OCULUS EST," or "where love is, there is the eye"; according to Timothy Materer this is a reflection on Richard of St. Victor's insight that love is the essential function of the human soul.[99] In Canto 91 Pound described sex as the origin of creativity: "that the body of light come forth / from the body of fire." And Wendy Flory believes that Martinelli was the inspiration for both Cantos 92 and 94, the latter as "the very idea of love as inspiration."[100]

Pound's behavior with his young female admirers was known to many members of the hospital staff. He was observed on several occasions openly fondling them while sitting on the lawn or in the alcove on the ward. One psychiatrist recalls that "he had many female visitors and was taking advantage of them."[101]

Ezra's love for Sheri eventually faded, and in 1957 Marcella Spann replaced her in the "position of Maestro's muse." Miss Spann was a young English teacher who had first written to Pound in 1956 requesting an interview to discuss his poetry. Martinelli was furious at being displaced and attacked her rival in letters to friends. As "Undine," Pound's water spirit, she appealed to Hilda Doolittle, who as "Dryad" fifty years earlier had been Pound's spirit of the trees. "The male just can't go about like that, ditching a spirit love," she wrote.[102] The attempted coalition of kindred spirits was not enough.

Dorothy, meanwhile, stood patiently by and played the role of hostess for the daily St. Elizabeths salon. One hospital staff member noted Pound's "arrogance and contemptuous treatment" of her.[103] On one occasion Dorothy wrote to Dr. Overholser requesting that Sheri Martinelli be allowed to take her place as his guardian while out on the lawn because she had to go away for a week; Dorothy reassured Dr. Overholser that Ezra thought of Sheri as his own daughter.[104] There has also been speculation that Pound's choice of the *Women of Trachis* to translate was partly due to the fact that Hercules, the hero, takes a mistress in the play and asks his wife to let the mistress live with them. "Let's figure out how we are to manage this cohabitation," Pound has Hercules' wife say.[105]

Olga Rudge waited patiently in Italy for Pound's release. She visited him in 1952 and again in 1955. She worked diligently to collect petitions and to influence Italian politicians to put pressure on the U.S. Department of State, and she was bewildered by Pound's lack of interest in getting out of the hospital. As early as 1948 she wrote to Dr. Overholser complaining that she could not get answers to her questions from Pound and asking for reassurance that Pound was in fact receiving her letters. Overholser assured her that he was. When Olga came to the U.S. to see him, Pound continued to see his regular visitors along with her. Dorothy, however, conveniently decided that it would be a good time to go away on vacation.[106] Although Dorothy Pound most certainly did not have her husband to herself during the St. Elizabeths years, at least she did not have to share him with Olga Rudge.

The fact that Ezra Pound was satisfied at St. Elizabeths is also reflected by the nursing notes. Such notes are kept on each patient and are intended to give an assessment of the patient's mental state so that doctors or other members of the staff can follow his progress. In Pound's case there is nothing in these notes in the twelve and one-half years that suggests a state of mind other than contentedness. For example:

July 7, 1949: Quiet and cooperative . . . Fully oriented. Receives morning paper. Stays in his room most of the time.

November 12, 1949: While in room constantly hums.

November 17, 1950: Receives a lot of visitors. At times thru the night will have a light in his room. Appears at times to be singing. Appears to be correctly oriented.

June 27, 1951: Stays in his room which is much cluttered up. At times he will put light on at night and read. Humming to himself.

February 23, 1951: If he has any resentment at being in confinement here he keeps it well concealed from attendants and has friendly attitude toward all employees.

April 4, 1951: At times have heard him humming some kind of tuneless chant at night. Appears to be correctly oriented in all spheres.

February 21, 1952: This patient continues the same, quiet and cooperative. He is correctly oriented in all spheres.

June 29, 1955: He is pleasant and responsive; enjoys a conversation, which is too often above the ordinary level. Mr. Pound never has any ward problems.

April 17, 1956: This patient continues to be very pleasant and cooperative. Has sustaining interests which occupy his time days and late into the night. Receives many visitors. Patient makes few complaints or requests.

November 27, 1956: Has very good appetite. Nearly every meal he carries some excess food to his room.

March 16, 1957: Mr. Pound plays chess each evening.[107]

The chess was played with another patient on his ward who had been an engineer. Pound also had access to the tennis courts next to his building and played regularly with visitors and members of the hospital staff. In his later years at the hospital he also had ground privileges until 9 P.M. so that he could take advantage of the long summer days.

Another reason Pound enjoyed St. Elizabeths is that for the first time in his life he had no financial worries. Hospital records show that his personal expenditures for the fiscal year from October 1954 through September 1955 were only $1,593.62; the main items were a typewriter and a radio. At the time he had saved over $13,000, a large amount of money for a man who had lived all his life close to the fiscal margin.

In view of Pound's comparatively pleasant life in St. Elizabeths it is not surprising that he made no effort to get out. He could have initiated legal action to come to trial at any time, simply by telling the court that he had recovered his sanity.[108] The case would then have been reviewed, and outside psychiatrists could have been brought in to examine him. Dr. Overholser could only keep Pound at St. Elizabeths as long as Pound himself wished to stay.

Many people commented on Pound's failure to take any steps to free himself. In a 1956 interview Overholser himself noted that Pound "has never made any attempt to be released from St. Elizabeths during the ten years that he has been there." The Department of Justice also duly noted Pound's indifference. His daughter, Mary, was perplexed by his attitude, noting that whenever she tried to raise the subject of his release with him he would not discuss it. Wyndham Lewis cited Pound's "obstreperous intractableness" as the main impediment to his release, and in 1952 confronted him directly: "It wearies me you remaining where you are. To take up a strategic position in a lunatic asylum is idiotic. If I don't see you make an effort to get out *soon*, I shall conclude either that your present residence has a snobbish appeal for you, or that you are timid with regard to Fate." John Drummond in England noted that Ezra "always seems to do his best to stall any initiatives . . . Ezra himself is by far the greatest obstacle." And T. S. Eliot observed how Pound would "find objections to make to any scheme which offers any reasonable possibility to success [for getting him released]." As one example of this, in 1951 Pound vetoed an eminent lawyer who would have worked for his release because the lawyer's office in New York was too close to Wall Street. Perhaps all these observations can be crystallized in a single description by Michael Reck as he, Dorothy Pound, and Greek-American Michael Lekakis took leave of Pound after a visit: "We left him and he went back to his room. Just as we were walking away from the little door at the foot of the stairs (Dorothy, Mike, and me), we heard a shout and saw Pound, up in his window, leaning out and singing Greek verse to us at the top of his lungs. Happy, full of happiness, and playing the part of Homer."[109]

Pound could not admit the fact that he was perfectly content in St. Elizabeths of course. If he had, his friends might have thought that he really *was* insane! He therefore told them that he wanted to get out and that he wanted to stand trial. "If they find me guilty, let them shoot me," he told one. To Archibald MacLeish he wrote: "It is damned nonsense to say that either I or DP [Dorothy] prefer me to stay in St. Eliz." To William Carlos Williams he gave the rather fanciful explanation that he might be shot by an agent of the "international crew" if he stepped outside the hospital gate.[110]

Despite Pound's contentedness, his continued acceptance of the façade of insanity must have rankled during these years. When he worked for Mussolini and the Fascist cause, he had believed in what he was doing, believed he was saving mankind from a Jewish conspiracy. Yet when he had had an opportunity to explain his actions to the world he had remained silent. Faced with possible prison or death, he had lost his nerve. Pound's friends did not let him forget this as the St. Elizabeths years rolled by, especially Wyndham Lewis who in 1954 published a story called "Doppelgänger." It was about Pound, thinly disguised as "Thaddeus Trunk."

Trunk was "a very majestic Word-Man, a great poet . . . known to his friends as Uncle Thad, . . . passing into his seventies [Pound was 69 at the time] . . . Stella, his wife, is an Englishwoman, possessed of considerable wealth. As he has no money himself this was for him a fortunate circumstance . . . he was in love with the Past, being an American . . . He had always the itch to offer advice, to tell others what to do with their lives, to teach them how to Write, to teach them how to Read . . . Trunk himself preferred to invite les jeunes—'discipular' youths (a favorite adjective of his), usually from one of the colleges, and usually versifying . . . Uncle Thad would never take very seriously any young poet who did not know a little Arabic, Tamil, Phoenician and Early German . . ." The trouble with Trunk, Lewis wrote, was "his childish mania for publicity . . . He wishes to live his publicity figure. There it is inside his house—in his bedroom, in his bed, a publicity figure, not a real man." At the end of the story Lewis's satire turns sharp, and Trunk suffers the fate of the Cheshire Cat: "But, bit by bit, this advertised figure evaporated, and there was nothing left at all of the one-time poet who had been devoured by that Moloch, the Public." Most devastating of all was Lewis's assessment of Trunk's courage: "He was a timid man, beneath his veneer of toughness, very averse to showdowns of any sort."[111]

THE HOST OF ST. ELIZABETHS

Dr. Overholser proved to be a good host who made life as comfortable for Pound as he dared. He respected Pound as a poet and told Archibald MacLeish that "he had never thought Ez's 'treason' amounted to much anyway." In a letter to Pound written after he had left the hospital, Overholser referred to him as having been a guest.[112] Overholser's living quarters were in the same building as Pound's ward, and in fact Pound's initial room on Chestnut ward was just thirty feet from Dr. Overholser's front door, the closest possible room. Pound was an occasional visitor in Overholser's apartment and the two became good friends over the years.

Most communication between Dr. Overholser and Pound was verbal, and so the full extent of their friendship may never be known. Fragments of that communication survive as memos back and forth and, like the shards of an ancient vase, can be reconstructed to suggest the outline of the original.

Some of the communications had to do with Pound's personal needs (e.g., getting a room for Sheri Martinelli) or were about the staff. In early 1946, for example, Pound complained to Overholser about the attendants in Howard Hall. On another occasion Pound urged Overholser to "do drift down without special urging, or for consideration of the bug-house as such, the fruits of ten years occasional observation in, and reflection on your REmarkable institution." But the vast majority had to do with literary matters and occurrences. "Is Cory arranging collection of S's letters?" Pound asked. "Have just been given G. S.'s [George Santayana] 'Poet's Testament' if you haven't seen it. Wd [would] you care to have it on loan," Pound offered in another. "Did you get the amusin' sequel to the Hammond Affair . . . He is no longer @ Univ. of Alabam," was the message in still another. "By chance Laughlin sends me this A.M. the Brancusi announcement 35 years after the introduction of Brancusi by the *Little Review* Brancusi issue," Pound informed Overholser. "Have just had letter from Senora Jimenez . . . It contains the germ of an idea which might not bore you. Too long to go into on paper . . ."[113]

The extent of Dr. Overholser's involvement in Pound's literary endeavors is illustrated by his behind-the-scenes attempt to promote Pound's work. In 1954 the Harvard University Press had published Pound's *Classic Anthology Defined by Confucius*, a translation of traditional Chinese poems, and they had promised to bring out a second edition. In order to bring pressure on them Overholser arranged with his friend Clarence B. Farrar, the editor of the *American Journal of Psychiatry*, to write a letter to the Harvard Press inquiring when they intended to bring out the second edition. A carbon copy of this letter was sent by Farrar to Overholser, and on the bottom of it Overholser wrote a note to Pound acknowledging that he had asked Farrar to write the letter.[114] Here was the Ezra Pound who had arranged for his own book reviews and written his own press releases when he was in London forty-five years earlier, only now he had a partner to help him.

Dr. Overholser did whatever he had to do to protect Pound, including stretching the truth. Whenever the Department of Justice inquired whether there had been any improvement in Pound's condition so that he might stand trial, Overholser dutifully replied in the negative. In response to a 1948 inquiry Overholser wrote that Pound was "highly disorganized in his train of thought . . . He is not mentally competent to stand trial at this time." In 1953 Overholser again told the Department of Justice that "he is still mentally incompetent to stand trial or to advise with counsel . . . There is no doubt that he is mentally unsound to a degree which renders him mentally incompetent." In 1955, 1956, and 1957 government officials made similar inquiries and each time Overholser repeated the same litany: "In our opinion he is still mentally incompetent to stand trial or to consult with counsel."[115]

At times Overholser had to become more imaginative. When the *Washington Daily News* ran an article in 1947 on Pound's numerous visitors and privileged life-style, headlined "Ezra Pound, Accused Traitor, Makes St. Elizabeth's Here a Mecca for the Literati," Overholser replied to reporters that "Ezra Pound has not had more than four or five visitors besides his wife since he was admitted to St. Elizabeths."[116] The truth was that he had had more than four or five visitors each week, and sometimes more.

Overholser's verbal legerdemain was also challenged when Harvard published Pound's *Classic Anthology Defined by Confucius* in 1954, as the book was widely and favorably reviewed. A letter from the U.S. assistant attorney general to Overholser followed immediately, inquiring about this poet "who seemingly is mentally capable of translating and publishing poetry but allegedly is not mentally capable of being brought to justice." Overholser replied that Pound's "mental processes are considerably disorganized"; furthermore, "the work of this translation was, so far as we can learn, substantially completed when he was admitted to the Hospital, and we have no evidence that he has done any productive literary work during his stay in the Hospital." Overholser had apparently forgotten that he had told reporters seven years previously that Pound "has been doing quite a bit of writing. I believe it has been mostly translations from the Chinese." In fact between 1946 and 1950 Pound had filled thirty spiral notebooks with Chinese translations and notes on the Chinese text; given Overholser's interest in Pound's literary endeavors he could not possibly have been unaware of this work.[117]

The façade of Pound's insanity could be maintained only as long as Pound was not seen as intellectually productive. For this reason Overholser and Pound agreed to keep a low profile for Pound's work. Reporters were absolutely forbidden to interview Pound by agreement of both the asylum host and his guest; memoranda between them regarding requests for press interviews reflect a mutual opinion that reporters are pariahs. When asked by government officials or members of the public, Overholser replied that Pound "does no writing and very little reading" or, on another occasion, that "as far as I am aware Mr. Ezra Pound has not done any recent writing of poetry." For his part Pound instructed his friends to say nothing about his literary endeavors. In

1953 Louis Dudek broke this rule and published an account of how Pound "has translated difficult prose and poetry into imperishable English, has edited and proofed his writings, has guided biographers and bibliographers of his life's work, [and] has carried on a voluminous, practical, benevolent correspondence with scores of editors and writers young and old." Pound's wrath rattled his typewriter: "God bloody DAMN it and save one from ones friends. SHUT UP. You are NOT supposed to receive ANY letters from E. P. They are UNSIGNED and if one cannot trust one's friends to keep quiet RE the supposed source whom can one trust . . . Who the HELL told YOU that E. P. has carried on correspondence?"[118] It could be said, then, that rather than locking Ezra Pound in St. Elizabeths, Dr. Overholser really was locking the press, the public, and the Department of Justice out.

PSYCHIATRIC DIAGNOSES

The most important role that Dr. Overholser played for Pound was to ensure that he never had to go to trial on the treason charges. The essential ingredient to accomplish this was Pound's psychiatric diagnosis. As long as there was no public contradiction to the diagnosis given by the four psychiatrists at the sanity hearing—"insane and mentally unfit for trial"—then Pound was protected. The insanity diagnosis was like a warm coat that protected him from a harsh indictment awaiting outside St. Elizabeths' gates. Overholser was his benefactor, the bestower of the diagnosis.

The diagnosis of "insane and mentally unfit for trial" stood as Pound's official diagnosis from the time of the sanity hearing until August 1953 for one simple reason: Overholser would not permit any other diagnosis to be put onto Pound's medical chart.[119] Overholser himself did not write a single note in Pound's hospital chart during the entire twelve-and-a-half-year stay except for his report of the interview by the four court-appointed psychiatrists on February 7, 1946, and a perfunctory statement that Pound had attended a court hearing for his lawyer's bail request in January 1947.

By 1953 the fact that Pound had never been officially diagnosed by St. Elizabeths Hospital psychiatrists had passed the point of absurdity—he had been there over seven years. In addition the American Psychiatric Association had published a *Diagnostic and Statistical Manual* in 1952, and all patients in the hospital were being rediagnosed using that nomenclature. Accordingly, in July 1953, one of the senior psychiatrists in the hospital entered a thoughtful four-page clinical note in Pound's hospital chart. The note indicates that the psychiatrist knew Pound well and was familiar with his writings. He concluded, with much supporting data, that Pound should be diagnosed as having a personality disorder of the narcissistic type: "What is unquestionably the most outstanding feature of his personality is his profound, incredible, over-weaning narcissism."[120] This indicated that Pound was not insane but just extremely egotistical. In psychiatry, personality disorders such as narcissistic personality are not considered to be disease entities but are rather descriptions of the predominant feature of the personality. Many people, including entertainers and politicians, have narcissistic personalities, and they are considered fit to stand trial.

The entry of narcissistic personality disorder on Pound's chart apparently made Dr. Overholser uneasy. One month later, in responding to the Department of Justice's annual inquiry about Pound, Overholser acknowledged that "the exact category in which he should be classified diagnostically is difficult to ascertain . . . Perhaps the nearest approach would be that of Personality Trait Disturbance, Narcissistic Personality. The implication of this diagnosis in the diagnostic category is that it is without psychosis, but there is no doubt in our minds that the disturbance of personality is of such an extensive degree that it may properly be said to constitute mental incompetence. In our opinion, one may be incompetent without being technically psychotic."[121] Thus Dr. Overholser was admitting to the Department of Justice that Pound was not psychotic, not insane. As an expert in forensic psychiatry, Overholser knew better than most that no jury in the United States at that time would rule a person unfit for trial or not guilty by reason of insanity on the basis of a narcissistic personality.

The Department of Justice failed to respond to this new information, suggesting that they had no intention of bringing Pound to trial. However, Overholser was aware that the diagnosis was a potential source of embarrassment to him and that if he had to return to court and use it as the justification for incompetence, it would require verbal artistry bordering on alchemy to be successful. To avoid such a problem, Overholser instructed another staff psychiatrist to change the official diagnosis to "psychotic disorder, undifferentiated," which was duly entered on May 31, 1955. Below it is written "Dr. O. gave instructions for this note to be filed as is."[122] "Psychotic disorder, undifferentiated" implies that the person is insane but the insanity does not fit any usual category such as schizophrenia or manic-depressive psychosis.

Because there was no clinical or other supporting data on Pound's record to support the changed diagnosis, Overholser called upon his old friend Merrill Moore to help him. Moore came to Washington, talked with Pound, and on July 10, 1955, sent Overholser a "Dear Dr. Overhol-

ser" letter in which he claimed "definitely that he is quite psychotic
. . . he is mentally ill and seriously enough so to warrant his remaining
in the hospital for an indefinite period . . . he is suffering from paranoid
schizophrenia with strong affective components."[123] Overholser anno-
tated the letter, instructing that it should be entered onto Pound's clinical
record.

The following day Pound wrote to William Carlos Williams about
the visit: "Have yu ever met your fellow medic and OUR leading sonne-
teer (unrhymed)? He was in yester, filled with appreciation . . . Well
now as he is wanting to DO something, but not to expose me to the
hired assassins of his political system." One week later Moore wrote
to Williams: "I did have a delightful visit with Cousin Ezra. He is a
most fascinating human being. There are many shade trees there which
will shade his head but best of all his friends will contain him and save
his neck. If he were out scotfree, the hounds would get him."[124]

Psychiatrists like Overholser and Moore were tolerated by Pound
because they were necessary to his survival as "not competent." In reality,
however, he disliked all psychiatrists, and it was a vengeful god who
placed his fate in the hands of that profession. Especially anathema to
Pound were psychoanalytic followers of Sigmund Freud, which Overholser, Moore, and virtually all the psychiatrists at St. Elizabeths Hospital
were at that time. During his years in the hospital Pound referred to
"Freud and his dirty insides" and said that America had "been up Freud's
asshole for 20 years." On one occasion he was asked whether he thought
Jung or Freud was better and he replied that he "couldn't distinguish
between contents of the sewer"; on another occasion he called Freud
"Viennese sewage."[125] Where Pound's intense dislike of Freud and his
theories came from is unclear; he appeared to dislike the emphasis on
sex inherent in psychoanalytic theory. It may be that Pound saw Freud
as yet another manifestation of the perversion of natural sexuality such
as he attributed to the Protestant Church. It may also be that Pound
was reacting to having been ignored, if not rejected, by the Surrealists
in Paris twenty years earlier; the Surrealists had been enchanted with
Freud at the time.

The fact that Freud was Jewish clearly contributed to Pound's dislike
of him. In Canto 91, written at St. Elizabeths, Pound wrote:

> And, in this, their kikery functioned, Marx, Freud
>   and the american beaneries
>
> Filth under filth

And on at least two occasions Dorothy Pound referred to psychiatrists
as if they all were Jewish. The traits of being preoccupied with sex

and being Jewish were agglutinated by Pound into the term "pussyKiKea-trists," which he used for psychiatrists.[126]

Despite Overholser's attempts to shield his illustrious inmate, hospital regulations required that all patients have a "chronic note" entered on their record each month. It was therefore necessary for Pound to be assessed by hospital psychiatrists, and over the years forty of them entered notes on his chart.

The notes vary from brief summaries to extended personality analyses. They included the usual Pound sprinkling of epithets and profanity (Woodrow Wilson was "that constipated jerk with prostatitis," FDR was "that fart," and the Capitol was "that shithouse"). They also included abundant examples of Pound's continuing fabrication of symptoms of an impaired head (e.g., "he complains again of the hollow sensation in his brain") and of a highly selective physical fatigue (e.g., "one striking feature was in evidence and that was that his weakness is certainly periodic and can be turned off and on at will"). Even Dr. Overholser commented on Pound's odd fatigue in a letter to Olga Rudge: "He constantly complains of great fatigue and weakness . . . fortunately this fatiguability is much less evidenced when he is working on his manuscripts in his room alone."[127]

The most striking feature of the psychiatrists' notes is that none of them support a diagnosis of insanity. Pound is seen as egocentric, eccentric, and clearly bigoted—but not insane. Examples culled from these notes are as follows:

March 31, 1946: No abnormal mental content is elicitable, and there has been no evidence of hallucinations, delusions, ideas of reference, or ideas of alien control.

May 9, 1946: He apparently appreciates his predicament fully.

June 27, 1947: Patient does not exhibit any delusional or other psychotic material.

March 12, 1948: He is obviously well-oriented and in good contact with his surroundings, his memory is good and no abnormal content was elicited.

September 30, 1948: His memory is apparently intact, he is precisely oriented, and his insight and judgment do not appear to be impaired.

July 29, 1949: No abnormal mental trends could be elicited.

April 12, 1951: No definite delusional trends were noted . . . He is correctly oriented, retains his intellectual capacities to a marked degree . . . His memory is intact for both remote and recent events.

January 21, 1952: The examiner was unable to elicit any psychotic content at this time.

October 16, 1952: He was precisely oriented and no abnormal mental content was elicited.

March 20, 1953: He spoke spontaneously, coherently, relevantly. He had a good range of affective reactivity. No psychotic ideation was manifested.

February 7, 1956: There was no abnormality of affect noted nor were there evidences of hallucinatory or delusional experiences.

The only psychiatric observations that even lean in the direction of insanity are occasional comments on Pound's ideas of economics and politics. For example:

October 8, 1946: There were some mild paranoid trends exhibited, especially in reference to international banking [and] his attempts to prevent the war in 1939 when he visited this country.

March 28, 1947: He seemed well oriented, and no abnormal content was elicited except that some of his ideas concerning government, politics and economics appear to the examiner to border on the delusional.

September 29, 1951: This patient continues to have some paranoid ideas.[128]

Even in these instances, however, it is doubtful whether Pound's thinking was truly "delusional" or "paranoid"; rather it appears to have been a product of his long-held political belief that an international conspiracy of Jews was trying to seize control of the world by controlling the money supply. An example of this was one interview when Pound obviously did not like the psychiatrist, who had a Jewish name. Pound declaimed at great length about people "whose basic aim was to overthrow the Government of the United States," and this was interpreted by the psychiatrist as "paranoid elements" in Pound's thinking. A moment later, in response to a simple question from the psychiatrist, Pound "referred to the question as an arch example of psychiatric horseshit and stormed angrily out of the room." Thus the "paranoid elements" were probably just bigoted beliefs which the examiner had provoked in Pound.

Of the forty psychiatrists who examined Pound and entered a note in his chart, thirteen are still alive and could be located. When asked whether, in retrospect, they believe that Pound was insane or unfit for trial at the time they examined him, six psychiatrists said they had no opinion or did not wish to say; some of these acknowledged that their silence was out of respect for Dr. Overholser. The other seven said they believe Pound was both sane and fit for trial. For example, Dr. Harold Stevens, a respected Washington psychiatrist and neurologist and professor at George Washington University Medical School, clearly stated, "In my opinion he was certainly fit to stand trial and further, in my opinion he was not of unsound mind [and] showed no evidence of mental disease or defect."[129]

It is also significant that there is not a single mention of "treatment" for Ezra Pound in his entire hospital record. At no time was he given drugs (which came into widespread use in the last years of his stay), individual psychotherapy, group psychotherapy, occupational therapy, psychodrama, or any other type of therapy; their possible use was apparently never considered, for the reason that he was generally acknowledged not to be sick.

Although it does not appear on his hospital record, many of the psychoanalytically oriented psychiatrists at St. Elizabeths enjoyed speculating on the psychodynamics of Pound's personality. They wondered, for example, whether he had symbolically raped his motherland or castrated his fatherland, whether his overt display of affection for women covered repressed homosexual urges, and whether his primary personality defect had originated in the oral, anal, or phallic stage of his development. Unbeknownst to them, Pound's case had been discussed in detail with Sigmund Freud in 1933 by Hilda Doolittle in the course of her own psychoanalysis. Freud had told her that Pound had "very difficult Oedipal problems" and said: "If I had known Ezra I would have made him all right."[130] Whether Hilda told Pound of Freud's opinion, and whether this contributed to Pound's dislike of Freud and psychiatrists, is not known.

Among Pound's close friends and visitors at St. Elizabeths there was absolutely no question about his psychiatric diagnosis. They all knew that he was in the asylum as an alternative to standing trial for treason, and among themselves they said so. William Carlos Williams, who had known him since student days, told Dr. Overholser that "Pound seems about as he has always been, not any worse or any better . . . the quality of his ideas has so far as I can tell undergone no change; he is interesting, amusing, and even profound in many of his observations." Viola Baxter Jordan, his girlfriend from college days, visited him and found "the same old Ez." Archibald MacLeish has admitted that "there is no use pretending, as some still do, that Pound was insane when all that happened." Katherine Anne Porter visited and doubted "that Ezra Pound was ever for a moment insane." Professor José Vazquez-Amaral, who worked with Pound over three years on a Spanish translation of the Cantos, claimed that "he was absolutely sane." Most articulate was German poet Rudolf Hagelstange, who visited St. Elizabeths and summarized his impression: "Pound was the first insane poet with whom I have ever held a conversation, and the only genuinely insane thing about that conversation was that Pound was not insane."[131]

ASYLUM EXIT

By the mid-1950s the political milieu in the United States was changing in Pound's favor. Joseph McCarthy was effectively defused in 1954, and paranoia among America's intellectuals receded. President

Eisenhower pursued a middle-of-the-road course, posing like old friends with Soviet chief Nikita Krushchev at the 1955 conference in Geneva. The world was finally at peace; "with the signing of the Indochinese Truce on July 20, 1954, no shooting war existed anywhere on the globe for the first time since the Japanese invaded Manchuria twenty-three years before."[132] America was in a forgiving mood, mellow after years of wars and witch-hunting.

Another development in Pound's favor was the introduction in the District of Columbia in 1954 of the Durham rule to replace the M'Naghten test as the legal test of insanity. The Durham rule stated that an accused person was not criminally responsible if his act was the product of a mental disease or defect. This was a massive liberalization of the old right-wrong test and meant that it would be much easier for juries to find a person not guilty by reason of insanity. Whereas if Pound had gone to trial for treason under the old rule he would almost certainly have been convicted, under the new rule he stood a reasonably good chance of exoneration.[133]

Pound's friends renewed their efforts to effect his release. An opportunity for a new prize strategy presented itself in 1954 when Ernest Hemingway was awarded the Nobel Prize in literature. The *New York Times* story on the award noted that "Ezra Pound, American poet whom the [Swedish] academy regards as one of the world's distinctive lyricists," had also been considered. Hemingway publicly announced that the prize should have gone to Pound and added: "This would be a good year to release poets." In July 1956, in a generous gesture, Hemingway sent Pound one thousand dollars of the prize money and told him he would send the medal later. It was Hemingway who had originally suggested insanity as the way to save Pound from treason, but he was uncertain how to get his old friend released. In 1951 he had written to a friend: "Remember that as soon as Ezra is declared sane he must stand trial for treason. You have to always remember that Pound the great poet who we respect and Pound the old friend who I care for greatly are legally not the Pound of the treasonable broadcasts. The Pound of the treasonable and anti-semitic broadcasts has been declared insane. That is his protection from the charges against him."[134]

Given the fiasco brought about by the Bollingen prize, one might have thought that Pound and his friends would have been wary of a Nobel Prize strategy. Such was not the case, and in 1955 Dag Hammarskjöld's aid was enlisted. An admirer of modern poetry including Pound's, Hammarskjöld was not only secretary-general of the United Nations but also a member of the Swedish Academy, so he could place names in nomination for the prize. In early 1956 Pound and Hammarskjöld began a correspondence, and the following year Hammarskjöld acknowledged privately that he was indeed working with Archibald MacLeish to secure Pound's release. MacLeish then wrote to Milton Eisenhower, brother of the President, and told him that "I have the very best reason to believe that Pound is shortly to be awarded the Nobel Prize in literature . . . the Nobel Prize situation should be treated as confidential except in so far as its repetition in confidence might help to bring about the desired action." Milton Eisenhower had previously told MacLeish that Pound's standing as a poet should not influence the legal charges against him, but MacLeish persisted: "In terms of logic this may be true but in terms of history and of civilization it is not. As you know better than I, nations are judged in the perspective of history by the way they treat their poets, philosophers, artists and teachers."[135]

The public became increasingly aware of Pound's predicament. A 1955 article in *Commonweal* was very influential in this regard, saying "it is only prudent that we Americans should from time to time remind ourselves that one room at St. Elizabeths is a closet which contains a national skeleton." *Life* magazine editorialized about the "national skeleton" in January 1956, under the heading "An Artist Confined."[136] The war had been over for ten years and even Tokyo Rose had been released from jail.

Given the atmosphere of forgiveness, the facts that Pound had turned seventy and that he had been incarcerated for over ten years, one wonders why it took so long to secure his final release. There were at least three impediments. One was Pound's involvement with John Kasper, which became public in January 1957. The Department of Justice had enough to worry about at the time, and Attorney General Rogers feared "Pound might join Kasper in the South and people would be killed." MacLeish gave Pound the news: "For the immediate future and so long as the Kasper mess is boiling and stewing the Department [of Justice] will not move. I have never understood—and neither, incidentally, has your daughter Mary—how you got mixed up with that character . . . We were left with the impression that once the Kasper stink has blown over they would be willing to consider proposals." Hemingway wrote to MacLeish that Pound's involvement with Kasper was an embarrassment for them all, and said it was Ezra's "megalomania" that "makes him receive dangerous fawning jerks such as Kasper." Furthermore, if Pound were released Hemingway feared he would continue to publicly praise Kasper, and would probably want to "go on the Mike Wallace show." Robert Frost, also involved with the negotiations for Pound's release, added a postscript: "Neither you nor I would want to take him [Pound] into our family or even into our neighborhood."[137]

A second impediment to Pound's release was Dr. Overholser, who had his own scenario for bringing it about and declined to compromise. MacLeish believed that the release could be obtained quickly if Overholser would be willing to declare Pound sane; the Department of Justice would quash the indictment and that would end the matter. Overholser, however, refused to cooperate, arguing that the Department of Justice should first quash the indictment and then Pound could be released. Later the Department of Justice offered to drop the indictment if Pound were moved to a private mental hospital, but Overholser vetoed this, arguing that "nothing much would be gained."[138]

Finally and perhaps most importantly, Ezra Pound was an impediment to his own release. Not only did he almost certainly prolong his incarceration for an extra year by his support of John Kasper, but he repeatedly hindered the plans of his friends. In 1955, for example, Pound vetoed one plan for his release by insisting that he wanted "complete exoneration and a conversion of official America to the views he expressed on Rome Radio." Previously he had suggested to one visitor that the government "should at once release him, send him by plane to Rome where he should be installed without cost to himself in the rooms maintained by the American Academy. He should be employed at a compensation by the American Government as a confidential advisor to the American Ambassador in Rome since he, Pound, has an exceptional grasp of European affairs." Even as late as December 1957 Pound was telling friends that all he really wanted was privileges to leave the hospital grounds, and telling Dr. Overholser that if the government released him but wouldn't let him return to Italy then "they shd / [should] house me in the stables at Monticello to stimulate local life." All of which led Eliot to complain that Pound "does not want to accept freedom on any terms that are possible." Even Mary, in a letter to Dr. Overholser, raised the possibility that her father really did not want to leave the hospital.[139]

Despite these impediments, the efforts of his friends went forward. MacLeish wrote to one friend that "whoever offers him [Pound] a hand will have his fingers broken," but continued to coordinate the plans. In August 1957, Senator Richard L. Neuberger of Oregon requested the Library of Congress to prepare an investigative report of the Pound case and Congressman Usher L. Burdick of North Dakota asked the House Committee on the Judiciary to hold hearings. Olga Rudge continued to bring pressure from officials in Italy, and Pound's friends in England sent the U.S. attorney general a petition for Pound's release signed by Jean Cocteau, Graham Greene, Benjamin Britten, Igor Stravinsky, and William Saroyan among others. The White House became involved, with Gabriel Hauge, Eisenhower's economic advisor (and James

Laughlin's brother-in-law) urging Sherman Adams, White House chief of staff, to put the matter before the President. In January 1958 Under Secretary of State Christian Herter sent a letter to Dr. Winfred Overholser, an old friend from Harvard, asking Overholser to "drop in some day at your convenience as I would very much like to be fully informed in respect to this difficult individual Ezra Pound." Herter had in fact previously met Pound during Pound's 1939 visit to keep America out of the war; Congressman George Tinkham of Massachusetts had directed Pound to Herter, then a member of the Massachusetts House of Representatives.[140] All that remained to effect Pound's release was to work out the details, and MacLeish induced Robert Frost to lend his considerable prestige to facilitate that goal. It had been a disjointed three-year minuet between the Department of Justice and the arts community, and finally they got their steps coordinated.

Even when the plan for Pound's release was agreed upon early in 1958, his supporters continued to tiptoe around him for fear that he would upset things once more. MacLeish wrote to Overholser: "I have been in touch with Pound! I put the general plan to him without telling him whom I had been in touch with in the government. I duly received the kind of reply you can imagine in which I was pretty roughly handled . . . I have asked him not to let his little apostles publicize these facts but there is always the risk that he or they will." Pound had his own sense of timing about his future, for on April 9, 1957, a reading of his horoscope had told him he would be released on approximately April 16, 1968.[141] Pound had become increasingly interested in astrology in his St. Elizabeth years and took such predictions very seriously.

On April 18, 1958, Ezra Pound sat in the United States District Court for the District of Columbia, flanked by Dorothy and Omar. His legal counsel was Thurman Arnold of the prestigious firm of Arnold and Porter; coincidentally Arnold had been a student at Wabash College in Pound's French class fifty years earlier. The judge, Bolitha J. Laws, was the same one who had originally sent Pound to St. Elizabeths. In a matter of minutes Judge Laws dismissed the indictment, thereby freeing Pound. Dr. Overholser submitted a sworn affidavit in which he claimed that Pound was still "suffering from a paranoid state which has rendered and now renders him unfit to advise properly with counsel or to participate intelligently and reasonably in his own defense, and that he is, and has continuously been, insane and mentally unfit for trial . . . he is permanently and incurably insane." In his order dismissing the indictment the judge further added that "there is available to the defense psychiatric testimony to the effect that there is a strong probability that the commission of the crimes charged was the result of insanity."[142]

Not only was Pound said to have been continuously insane since 1945, but he was now said to have been insane during the war when he was broadcasting as well. His fight for what he had believed in was permanently reduced to the babbling of a madman.

Pound didn't seem to notice. Dr. Overholser had warned him that he would have to make certain statements in court which Pound might find offensive but that this was a necessary part of getting the final release. Overholser played his role superbly to the very end and earned the accolades thrown at him by Pound's supporters as the poet's true guardian.[143]

Ezra Pound reacted to his new freedom by voluntarily living at St. Elizabeths for an additional three weeks. The ostensible reason was to complete some dental work, but in fact he could have been released on temporary leave status and returned to the hospital for dental appointments if he had wished. The truth was that Pound was ambivalent about leaving the hospital, perhaps sensing premonitorily that the outside world would be less interested in him once he was released. The insane asylum had served nicely as refuge and showcase; it had all been, in the words of a friend, "a tale told by an Eliot, full of Pound and fury, signifying nothing."[144]

On May 6, 1958, exactly thirteen years and four days after he had been arrested in Rapallo, Pound left the hospital. His final diagnosis, initialed "W. O.," was "psychotic disorder, undifferentiated." It had been an extraordinary setting for an extraordinary man, the greatest Dadaist show of all. No one captured the complex shades of both man and setting as well as did Elizabeth Bishop in her 1950 poetic portrait, "Visits to St. Elizabeths":

> This is the house of Bedlam.
>
> This is the man
> that lies in the house of Bedlam.
>
> This is the time
> of the tragic man
> that lies in the house of Bedlam.
>
> This is a wristwatch
> telling the time
> of the talkative man
> that lies in the house of Bedlam.
>
> This is a sailor
> wearing the watch

that tells the time
of the honored man
that lies in the house of Bedlam.

This is the roadstead all of board
reached by the sailor
wearing the watch
that tells the time
of the old, brave man
that lies in the house of Bedlam.

These are the years and the walls of the ward,
the winds and clouds of the sea of board
sailed by the sailor
wearing the watch
that tells the time
of the cranky man
that lies in the house of Bedlam.

This is a Jew in a newspaper hat
that dances weeping down the ward
over the creaking sea of board
beyond the sailor
winding his watch
that tells the time
of the cruel man
that lies in the house of Bedlam.

This is a world of books gone flat.
This is a Jew in a newspaper hat
that dances weeping down the ward
over the creaking sea of board
of the batty sailor
that winds his watch
that tells the time
of the busy man
that lies in the house of Bedlam.

This is a boy that pats the floor
to see if the world is there, is flat,
for the widowed Jew in the newspaper hat
that dances weeping down the ward
waltzing the length of a weaving board
by the silent sailor
that hears his watch

that ticks the time
of the tedious man
that lies in the house of Bedlam.

These are the years and the walls and the door
that shut on a boy that pats the floor
to feel if the world is there and flat.
This is a Jew in a newspaper hat
that dances joyfully down the ward
into the parting seas of board
past the staring sailor
that shakes his watch
that tells the time
of the poet, the man
that lies in the house of Bedlam.

This is the soldier home from the war.
These are the years and the walls and the door
that shut on a boy that pats the floor
to see if the world is round or flat.
This is a Jew in a newspaper hat
that dances carefully down the ward,
walking the plank of a coffin board
with the crazy sailor
that shows his watch
that tells the time
of the wretched man
that lies in the house of Bedlam. [145]

CHAPTER 9

AFTER THE FALL

[VENICE: 1958–1972]

EZRA POUND LEFT St. Elizabeths Hospital the same way he had entered—denying guilt and singing a personal Te Deum. In interviews with reporters his egotism and grandiosity showed no signs of having been obtunded by his incarceration, and he reconstructed history freely to meet the exigencies of The Pound Myth. Of his 1939 trip to England, when he was settling the estate of his mother-in-law, he said: "At that time I went to see Eden and Churchill, but I understood that their minds were made up, they had decided to have their war. Thereupon I was seized with disgust, and I returned to old Muss." There is no evidence that Pound made any attempt to see Eden or Churchill. Of his return to the United States to stand trial for treason he said, "I thought I was being flown home to give information to the State Department." Of his incarceration in St. Elizabeths: "They made me pass as a madman, in order that young people should not listen to me any more." When asked why he had broadcast for Mussolini, Pound said it was because he had become convinced "that Jeffersonian democracy was dead." The reporter likened this to the man who became so discouraged with the English weather that he jumped into the sea to avoid it. Another reporter, impressed by Pound's inaccuracies, asked him: "How is it that you who merited fame as a seer did not see?"[1]

Nor did Pound's friends, who had helped arrange his release, escape his roving tongue. T. S. Eliot was said to be "worthy of the toothless Megara [referring to England as one of the three Furies] of which he became a citizen." Hemingway, who had sent money and offered to turn his Nobel Prize over to Pound, was said to have "sold himself to the god dollar." And when asked about Robert Frost, who had played an important role in the final negotiations being orchestrated by Archibald MacLeish, Pound responded, "He ain't been in much of a hurry."[2]

For over two months after his release Pound visited friends and gave interviews, spreading the gospel according to Ezra. His eccentric dress style of earlier years reappeared; to a luncheon in his honor at the staid Rotunda Club in Richmond, Virginia, he wore "an open-necked shirt of a particularly god-awful magenta, tails out, and a pair of outsized slacks with the cuffs rolled up. A black coat, flung cloak-wise over his shoulders, completed the costume." Journalists who interviewed him found him to be egocentric and eccentric but perfectly sane. James J. Kilpatrick, a conservative columnist who had championed his release, concluded after two hours with him that "Ezra Pound surely is no lunatic; and if it is true, as Dr. Overholser says, that Pound's condition has not changed since he entered St. Elizabeths in 1946, then Pound was no lunatic then. Obscure, yes; eccentric, yes; full of apparent confusion, yes. But crazy, no."[3] From Richmond and Williamsburg Pound went on to Rutherford, New Jersey, to visit his old friend of a half-century, William Carlos Williams. Williams was not well, and "the two old men . . . had little to say to each other."[4] It was to be their last meeting.

Two days before leaving the United States Pound visited his boyhood home in Wyncote. It had been just fifty years since he had left, his academic career ignominiously curtailed. Now he returned, having been indicted for treason and having spent over a decade in an insane asylum. Late at night he left the house to walk the streets of Wyncote alone, pausing at the Presbyterian church, where he had planted a tree as a child. His life had been full of poetry and promise, but had not developed as it should. What started as an ode had turned into odium. As he walked Pound probably thought about Henry James's story "The Jolly Corner," a story which had fascinated him at St. Elizabeths. In it an expatriate American, who for thirty years had lived a "selfish frivolous scandalous life" in Europe, returns to his boyhood home and meets the ghostly spirit of the man he would have become had he remained in America. "You'd have had power" had you stayed, he is told.[5] It was a spirit which Pound probably wished not to meet; the what-ifs of his life were too painful to confront.

Finally, on June 30, 1958, Ezra Pound boarded a ship in New York for his return to Italy. He was accompanied by Dorothy and by Marcella Spann, who traveled as his secretary. A small bon voyage party was held in his stateroom. Omar guarded the door against the press, who wanted one last word from il poeta, the bard of St. Elizabeths. Hilda Doolittle, who had known Pound for almost sixty years, was there and remembered Ezra as "no different from ever."6 Like Odysseus, Pound was finally under way on the last stage of his journey.

RETURN TO ITALY

Pound arrived in Italy amidst considerable fanfare. He was celebrated by old friends as a native son, a man who had fought hard for his adopted country and who had paid a high price for it. Many changes had taken place since he had left; Italy was now a republic, a member of the United Nations, and elections for the third parliament had just been held. Standing on the ship's deck on arrival in the Naples harbor, Ezra Pound posed for reporters and gave the Fascist salute. "All America," Pound proclaimed, "is an insane asylum." When asked about World War II, Pound said that "the Fascist dictators made a mistake in the way they persecuted the Jews. The mistake was not in fighting the Jews, but the manner in which the Jews were fought. Rather than attack them as a bloc, each case should have been examined individually."7 Italy had changed, but Pound did not appear to notice. He was an anachronism.

His daughter, Mary, had married a Russian count following the war. They had restored an old castle at Brunnenburg in the Italian Tirol, near where she had been raised, and they had two children. She had collected her father's belongings, including the hieratic head, which stood proudly in the garden. Pound hugged his grandchildren (whom he had never seen), now ages eleven and eight, and moved in with Dorothy and Marcella to stay.

For several months at Brunnenburg Pound resumed the thread of his life and was his usual ebullient self. In December 1958 he wrote to Brigit Patmore that "there appears to be more chance of liveliness than at any time since 1919."8 He continued the Cantos and attempted to write a Paradiso to accompany the completed Inferno and Purgatorio sections of his epic. These "drafts and fragments," as they were eventually entitled, were mostly completed by 1960 and finally published in 1968.9 He also continued his lively and voluminous correspondence. With Dr. Overholser, for example, he exchanged ten letters between October 1958 and November 1959. They are typical Pound specimens with exchanges of literary information ("There is [an] amusing front page article by an adult in the *Figaro* for Feb. 8 which I have just seen"), personal problems ("British tax lice threatening to swipe 42½% brit [British] royalties if I DON'T maintain U.S. residence"), and political diatribes ("How ANY of you can stand the squalid imbecility of the tax SYSTEM squares only with Renan's view on relativity of human idiocy and the infinite"). These letters also demonstrated the mutual warmth in their relationship; Pound sent Overholser a copy of a book on ancient Egyptian religion written by the count, and Overholser responded effusively.[10]

Pound had not yet lost his vitriolic spirit, complaining to friends about the "Jew Pork Herald Tribune" and the "wops" in Italy. He also stayed in touch with John Kasper, who in October 1958 informed him that things were improving in the South since seven synagogues had been bombed in the previous ten days.[11] Pound continued to revile America and its institutions, appearing to have learned nothing from his indictment and incarceration. In September 1958, only two months after landing in Italy, a Pound interview about America in an Italian journal was noticed by officials at the American embassy and forwarded to Washington. Pound was either officially notified of this or told by friends, and he sent off the following letter to Under Secretary of State Christian Herter:

> I am informed that some subhuman ape in our embassy in Rome has stated that I have been making derogatory remarks about the U.S. . . . If some of the minor officials in your department consider the study of American history as aid and comfort to Moscow, that again displays a state of mind that might, or even should, arouse curiosity.[12]

Surrounded by the Dolomites and limitless vistas of Italian farmland, Pound busied himself with projects around the castle. He considered building a marble temple on the summit of an adjacent mountain but abandoned the plan. To complement the locally produced red wines he planted five hundred vines of white wine grapes in the castle vineyard. From Vermont he imported maple trees with the hope of beginning a maple syrup industry. Unfortunately, the only thing that survived was the poison ivy that accompanied them, and he thus introduced poison ivy into the region.[13]

Pound's personal life took a similar turn. Daughter Mary, wife Dorothy, and secretary Marcella (Mary referred to her as his "bodyguard")[14] could not get along. As one biographer discreetly phrased it, "there was also trouble about a female disciple."[15] According to Mary "the house no longer contained a family. We were turning into entities who should not have broken bread together."[16] Olga, Pound's longtime mistress and Mary's mother, was waiting in Rapallo. The question that Ezra had had to wrestle with for the past thirteen years—whether to live with Dorothy or Olga when he returned to Italy—had temporarily been decided in favor of Dorothy, although he was living in the house of Olga's daughter, accompanied by Marcella.

Throughout his life the women surrounding Ezra Pound had been devoted to him. Olga had been an apotheosis of amenability. Dorothy was equally resigned, telling a friend that "there was nothing for it but to give the creature his head." Mary followed their lead and wrote in her biography that whatever her father wanted to do was by definition acceptable—he came to live with her family as a "demigod."[17]

The relationship between Pound and the women in his life had been complicated, however, by his St. Elizabeths sojourn. Because he was legally insane, when he was in the hospital Dorothy had been appointed as a "Committee" to look after his legal affairs. She was in effect Pound's legal guardian. She had to report all of his financial transactions to the District of Columbia court on an annual basis. Thus she theoretically controlled all his expenditures, and he could not make legal contracts without her authorization.

This presented problems for Pound, for Dorothy's tolerance apparently had limits. As early as November 1958, Pound wrote to Dr. Overholser asking if he had "any bright brain waves as to how to relieve my patient and long-suffering committee of some of the pester."[18] Overholser in turn talked with William D. Rogers in the law firm of Arnold, Fortas and Porter. A letter from the firm to Pound advised him to merely have Dorothy cease filing financial statements with the court and eventually she would be removed by the judge. It was not possible to formally petition for her removal, Pound was told, for that would imply that he had returned to sanity and would therefore contradict Dr. Overholser's testimony in support of the motion to dismiss the indictment. That answer apparently did not satisfy Pound, however, for in late 1959 he wrote to Dr. Overholser again asking how he might get Dorothy removed as his "Committee."[19]

"Pride, jealousy and possessiveness / 3 pains of hell," Pound wrote in Canto 113. In March 1959, he took Dorothy and Marcella and moved to Rapallo. There the three took an apartment, with Olga living just up the hill. It was another attempt at a ménage-à-trois, with the theoretical option of including Olga to become à quatre. Since his wartime experiment in such living arrangements had been an unmitigated disaster, one wonders about his ability to learn from experience.

In May 1959 Ezra took Dorothy and Marcella on a short tour of Italy. One of their first stops was on the road north of Pisa where the army prison camp had stood. The spot was now a rose nursery. The wire fence was still there, along with two gray cans marked "Trash Only, U.S. Army."[20]

Ezra Pound, infatuated by Marcella, incorporated her into Canto 113:

> *And to this garden, Marcella, ever seeking by petal, by leaf-*
> *vein*
> > *out of dark, and toward half-light*
>
> . . . .
>
> *The long flank, the firm breast*
> > *and to know beauty and death and despair*
>
> *And to think that what has been shall be,*
> > *flowing, ever unstill.*

At Lake Garda he asked Marcella to marry him.[21] This may be the reference in Canto 113 to "sun and serenitas / (19th May '59)." Since Dorothy was along on the trip, still his legal wife and his legal guardian as well, the "serenitas" of that day was soon replaced by "agitatus." Dorothy would have no part of divorce, and Ezra was checkmated. He could not avail himself of the Italian courts because he was not an Italian citizen (and Italy did not allow divorce anyway). In the eyes of the American courts he was technically "insane" and unable to do anything without Dorothy's permission. He was caught in a legal and psychiatric web which he had helped spin. Dorothy decided that Marcella had seen enough of Italy and, with Olga's support, soon had Marcella on her way back to the United States.[22]

DEPRESSION AND SILENCE

The gatekeeper of Ezra Pound's personal life finally demanded to be paid. And for the years of interpersonal chaos which Pound had invited, the price was high. "When one's friends hate each other," he asked in Canto 115, "how can there be peace in the world?" In Canto 116, which he was also working on at this time, he added:

> *But the beauty is not the madness*
> *Tho' my errors and wrecks lie about me.*
> *And I am not a demigod,*
> *I cannot make it cohere.*
> *If love be not in the house there is nothing.*

There was no love in the house, and Pound surveyed its ruins. For the first time, now approaching his seventy-fifth birthday, he took stock. And he noticed that the sun was setting on Lake Garda.

Pound's new mental set was apparent almost immediately in his letters. On August 1 he wrote the previously quoted thank-you note to Dr. Overholser. The following month he wrote to Archibald MacLeish: "One thing to have Europe fall on one's head. Another to be set in the ruins of same." Still later he apologized to MacLeish: "Forgive me for about 80% of the violent things I have said about some of your friends. Some of 'em [the remarks] are deplorable, and it is probably too late to retract 'em."[23]

Regret had been a relative stranger to Ezra Pound up to that point in his life. When it finally did arrive, it brought remorse and depression as well. In September 1959, James Laughlin visited Pound and was alarmed to find his old friend melancholic, preoccupied with becoming mentally ill or dying.[24] Pound himself was concerned about what was happening to him, writing to an old friend that "I had a bad break down at start of July. Not able to finish a paragraph etc." There was a flurry of correspondence among Pound's family and friends regarding possible treatment. One suggestion was to take him to the clinic in Zurich where H. D., Pound's original spirit love, was under care; this was vetoed by H. D.'s doctor as not in her best interest.[25]

Dorothy and Ezra returned to Brunnenburg, this time without Marcella, to live with Mary and her family. In letters to friends he began to express doubts about the value of his work, a most un-Poundian sentiment. His friends attempted to reassure him; T. S. Eliot told him that "he was one of the immortals and that part at least of his work was sure to survive."[26] Pound was encouraged, and soon had everyone in the castle reading Eliot's plays. "Half the harm that is done in this world," Eliot wrote in *The Cocktail Party*, "is due to people who want to feel important."

In December 1959 Mary took her father to Germany to see a production of *Women of Trachis*, which Pound had translated while in St. Elizabeths Hospital. He was the guest of honor and took the stage to acknowledge the applause; this temporarily buoyed him. Once the lights dimmed, however, remorse and depression returned. In January 1960, he told a reporter for the *New York Herald Tribune:* "What mankind needs is an internal harmony which may balance the increase of brutality and desperation we are living through . . . In the past I used strong language. I also made a number of blunders in my life."[27]

Pound's family did not know what to do with him, and he did not know what to do with himself. He had been ebullient and optimistic all his life; now in his declining years he was sliding into despair. In desperation Mary arranged for him to go to Rome to stay with a friend who was a neo-Fascist sympathizer and bon vivant; perhaps that would get the blood running through his aging veins again.

It did not, and within weeks Pound was more depressed than ever. A young poet friend found him a spacious, top-floor apartment which was perfect for his writing. Pound declined to take it, telling his friend: "I won't take it. I might jump off." According to a medical report from an Italian clinic where Pound was later treated, he was obsessed with fears of disease and believed his body was covered with bacteria and other microbes. He also expressed feelings of guilt and failure.[28] Whereas a year earlier he had complained of difficulty in finishing a paragraph, he now had trouble finishing a sentence. When a visitor asked him in September 1960 what he thought about contemporary English writers, Pound replied:

> "I should think that English writers would—" he said. And that was all I could make out. The rest he mumbled, his head down over his plate, so it was impossible to make out the words. So I told him I was sorry but I hadn't understood him.
>
> "I should think that English writers would—" And he mumbled, head down, into his plate just the same way. This time I knew better than to ask him to repeat it. Everybody seemed a little embarrassed until we finally went on to something else and from then on E. P. only listened. But he did listen. I felt that he wasn't missing a thing.[29]

By February 1961, his despair had reached new depths. He had become almost totally silent, just "blinking and blinking at every question, such as 'What will you have to drink, Mr. Pound?' Blinking, staring, SILENCE . . . it's deep, *deepening* depression." The same visitor reported that when he complimented Pound on his poetic achievements, "he grabbed hold of my shoulders, stared straight in my eyes, and said, 'But don't you see? There was something *rotten* behind it all!' There were tears in his eyes and he looked utterly tortured; grief, it seemed to me, for something lost and irretrievable." His appetite decreased dramatically, and by April he had also stopped taking fluids: "It's been torture to watch him take a spoonful of something as far as his mouth and then put it down. Or lift a cup of tea—while we all watch hopefully—halfway up, then set it back on the saucer."[30]

Pound's depression was treated initially with reserpine (used as a tranquilizer at that time) and with testicular hormone; the use of the latter suggests that he may have also been experiencing impotence, a common symptom in severe depression. Neither treatment worked, and so he was taken to clinics and rest homes in search of a cure for his melancholia, a search which was to occupy much of the rest of his life. He was involuntarily put in a clinic in Merano in April 1961, and in the following years treated in Rome and in Montreux, Switzerland, where on three separate occasions he was given sheep cell injections. In 1966 he was hospitalized in Genoa, where he continued to have ideas of guilt, preoccupation with his body, extreme slowness of movements, and other signs and symptoms of severe depression. Treatment with tricyclic antidepressants produced some improvement.[31]

The development of depression in Ezra Pound's final years is not surprising when his life is examined in perspective. The causes of his melancholy were numerous and profound. Perhaps most importantly, his personal life was in shambles. He had neglected Omar, he felt Mary had let him down, he had rotated among wife and mistresses until they were all infuriated at him, and he had insulted virtually all his friends. "I have never made a person happy in my life," he confided with atrabilious insight.[32] It was a theme he returned to frequently in his last years.

He also felt acutely the loss of Marcella. "M'amour, m'amour/what do I love/and where are you?" he asks at the beginning of Canto 117. Having young and adoring disciples around him was one way Pound had convinced himself that he was still young. It had worked throughout his years at St. Elizabeths. Now suddenly the last of them was gone, and he felt old.

Related to this was the loss Pound felt at not having a constant stream of visitors. At St. Elizabeths there had been a line of them which lengthened as the years wore on. They had included such diverse persons as Archibald MacLeish and John Kasper, Edith Hamilton and Sheri Martinelli. For two hours every afternoon Pound could hold court as an important sage, with some of America's best-known scholars and most disreputable bigots sitting at his feet. Now all that was gone. When Michael Reck came to visit Brunnenburg in late 1959 he was told by Dorothy that there had been only two visitors in recent months.[33] For a person whose egocentricity was as pervasive as Pound's, this sudden withdrawal of attention was devastating. Pound used visitors like mirrors, holding them up and gazing at himself in their reflection. Now he was left like Narcissus, solitarily gazing at his reflection in a silent pool, gradually pining away.

Just as Pound missed his visitors after he returned to Italy, so he also missed the publicity to which he had become accustomed. He had been a cause célèbre during his years at St. Elizabeths, his work more widely read then than at any other time in his life. "Newspapers and magazines in England, the United States, Italy, Spain, Portugal, Germany, Mexico, Brazil and many other parts of the world carried reviews and articles."[34] When Pound finally left the gates of the hospital he was hounded by reporters and photographers until he was safely aboard ship. But after the initial welcome-home interviews in Italy, the newspaper and magazine articles about him rapidly slowed to a trickle. By early 1960 it was clear that Pound missed the public attention, and when Donald Hall came to interview him for a magazine article, Pound treated him with an eagerness and courtesy unknown in earlier years. Pound had learned the lesson Oscar Wilde had taught, that "there is only one thing in the world worse than being talked about, and that is not being talked about."[35]

Equally depressing for Pound was the realization, for the first time, that he was not going to achieve his life's ambition of writing a great epic, a goal he had set while a young man. Pound equated true greatness as a poet with the creation of such an epic. When he was once asked whether he thought Yeats was a major poet, he replied, "Is he a Homer, is he a Dante?"[36] Yeats had not written an epic. Pound's *Cantos* were going to be the literary sword with which he would fight for parity with Dante and Homer.

Now that dream was shattered, strewn amidst the rubble of his personal life. He had sailed back to Italy with the intention of writing a Paradiso section and thereby completing his epic. Paradise, however, had turned out to be "jagged / For a flash, for an hour. / Then agony, then an hour, then agony" (Canto 92). Pound had confused paradise with the satisfaction of his personal desires, and that was ultimately why he failed. The work which he hoped would return him to the mainstream of literary history instead ended up in the slough of despond. In January 1960 he told a reporter that he could not write a Paradiso section.[37] And in Canto 117 he equated his failure as a poet with his failure as a person:

> That I lost my center
> fighting the world
>
> The dreams clash
> and are shattered—
>
> And that I tried to make a paradiso
> terrestre.

During the last years of his life Pound came to doubt the value of his *Cantos* altogether. In 1966 he called his work "a botch . . . I picked out this and that thing that interested me, and then jumbled them into a bag. But that's not the way to make a work of art."[38] The following year Pound told Allen Ginsberg that his *Cantos* "don't make sense" because they "refer but they do not present . . . My writings. Stupidity and ignorance and the way through. Stupidity and ignorance."[39] Literary history will determine whether Pound's assessment of his work was accurate or not; current opinion ranges broadly from viewing the *Cantos* as a masterpiece of Western poetry to seeing them as "a weird junk shop and flea market of his random experiences."[40] The important fact is that Pound himself lived his last years believing he had failed in his life's great literary endeavor, and when he was asked to select his favorite poems from a lifetime of work, he often chose his earliest poems, written before the Cantos. Pound's sense of failure was reflected by Dorothy's remark to a friend at this time: "Ezra seems oppressed always by some sense of not having done what he should with his life."[41] Pound had written an Inferno, but he had also created one. And when a journalist appeared by his bedside and asked him where he was now living, Pound replied, "In hell." "Which hell?" asked the journalist. "Here, here," said Pound, pressing on his heart.[42]

Another source of depression, and a constant reminder of his professional failure, was the absence of major honors. In 1962 he received a $500 award from *Poetry,* and the following year a $5,000 prize from the Academy of American Poets.[43] But the important honors continued to pass him by. Robert Frost had collected four Pulitzer Prizes, and during Pound's years in St. Elizabeths many of his friends had received one as well. Karl Shapiro, Robert Lowell, W. H. Auden, Carl Sandburg, Marianne Moore, Wallace Stevens, Archibald MacLeish—all had been honored with a Pulitzer for their poetry. While in St. Elizabeths, Pound had been able to rationalize his failure to receive one as due to his more important political work:

> *Whose mind?*
>
> *Among all these twerps and Pulitzer sponges*
> *no voice for the Constitution,*
>
> *No objection to the historic blackout*
>
> (*Canto 95*)

Now, in the twilight of his life, the rationalizations no longer worked. Poets whose names were relatively unknown received Pulitzers—Stanley Kunitz in 1959, W. H. Snodgrass in 1960, Phyllis McGinley in 1961, Alan Dugan in 1962. In 1963 Pound's close friend, William Carlos Williams, was honored with one. By then Pound had ceased writing altogether, so there would be no Pulitzer for him.

Pound never gave up hope, however, of winning the most coveted honor of all, the Nobel Prize for literature. During his years in St. Elizabeths it went to friends and colleagues such as T. S. Eliot, William Faulkner, and Ernest Hemingway. In 1953 the literature prize had gone to his archenemy Winston Churchill. Pound was reported to have been

nominated for it while in St. Elizabeths, but this publicity may have
been initiated as a means of speeding his release.[44] Once Pound was
out of the hospital there were no more rumors of his nomination.

In 1959, shortly after Pound had returned to Italy, Italian poet
Salvatore Quasimodo received the Nobel Prize for literature. This must
have been especially galling to Pound, for Quasimodo had fought against
the Fascists during the war. It was not only that Pound was being passed
over, but that his enemies such as Churchill and Quasimodo were being
honored. In 1961 Pound attended a poetry reading by Quasimodo in
Milan and gave the Fascist salute to a group of supporters.[45]

As his depression stretched on through the 1960s, the Nobel Prize
continued to be given each year, but never to Pound. Steinbeck, Sartre,
Beckett, and Solzhenitsyn were honored. In 1963 Pound told a reporter
that he was being denied the prize "for political reasons."[46] In fact he
probably never was seriously considered because of his political liabilities, his name having been irrevocably tarred with the brush of Fascism.
This was demonstrated in the last year of his life when he was nominated
for a medal by the American Academy of Arts and Sciences "for outstanding contributions to the broad field of literature over the recipient's
entire lifetime." The nominating committee was overridden by the Academy's High Commission, however, and Pound did not get the award.
As summarized by sociologist Daniel Bell, who led the opposition to
Pound: "We have to distinguish between those who explore hate and
those who approve hate. In short, one may appreciate the painful work
of a man who has, at great personal cost, spent a season in hell; but it
does not follow that one honors a man who advocates a way of life
that makes the world hellish."[47] Pound was destined to wear the badge
of treason, rather than any medal of honor, to his grave, although he
never gave up hoping for the great honors even in his final months.

Of all the lost honors, however, there was one which certainly depressed Pound more than any other. He had yearned all his adult life
to return to his homeland in glory and to be acclaimed as *the* national
poet. Instead he had come home as a prisoner. Now, in January 1961,
at the inauguration of President John F. Kennedy, an American poet
laureate was effectively named when Robert Frost became the first poet
to ever read at an inauguration. For Pound it must have been a particularly painful reminder of things that might have been. On May 1 of
that year Pound revived from his depression long enough to be photo-
graphed at the head of a neo-Fascist parade in Rome, surrounded by
swastikas and anti-Semitic slogans.[48] It was Poundian rage, his usual
response to being rejected by his homeland. After this, his last hurrah,
the depression resettled over him and remained until the end of his
life.

Pound's depression was due not only to the fact that America was not going to honor him, a notion absurd to anyone but Pound himself, it was also due to the fact that his homeland did not even want him to visit anymore. Despite his bitter railings against America in 1958, by early 1960 he longed to return. In an interview with Donald Hall for *The Paris Review* in March 1960, Pound "talked mostly about the United States, how much he missed it, how much he wanted to visit the country." Hall assured him that he would have no difficulty securing invitations and "moving from campus to campus, as a great poet reading his poems," as T. S. Eliot and others had done.[49] When Hall wrote to the universities, however, he received "cautious or negative replies." Stephen Spender strongly advised against it, saying "they would crush him." Another friend predicted that "if he comes over, they'll picket him. They'll boo him off the stage."[50] Even Pound's publisher, James Laughlin, advised against his coming for fear of incidents.[51] Pound was told politely that he was not wanted.

Hall's interview with Pound revealed another source of the depression. For the first time in his life, Pound was actively questioning his own economic and political beliefs. He gave Hall letters which Basil Bunting had sent to him in the 1930s; in these Bunting had advised Pound "that Mussolini was no good, that Pound's thinking was cockeyed." Pound proffered the letters saying that Bunting had known more than he himself had. In addition to this Hall noted signs of guilt for the role Pound had played in the war:

> He told how the St. Elizabeths psychiatrists informed him about death camps, about which I doubt that he had known anything. He said that they tried to make him guilty. Hearing him excuse himself, I knew that they had succeeded. He let me know, gradually and reluctantly, that he doubted what he had done. Bunting knew more than Ezra Pound, he had told me. Now he said, "I guess I was off base all along." Now he was no longer defending his actions in themselves; he was defending the sincerity of his actions.[52]

Three years later Pound's doubts again surfaced. He was reading Canto 45, the canto which attacks usury most viciously, to a group of friends:

> *They have brought whores for Eleusis*
> *Corpses are set to banquet*
> *At behest of usura.*

"When he had finished this allegory on usury he slammed the book shut, snatched off his glasses and said, in a trembling, scarcely audible voice, 'It's not so, not strictly so, that's the trouble . . .' His prophet's head bowed and again he locked himself into silence."[53] History was not bringing the hoped-for vindication. Pound's prediction that the United States would be destroyed by international bankers had been wrong; America had become an even stronger world power. His errors had been egregious, for he had never understood the soul of changing America. Donald Hall describes this myopia:

> He spoke of the United States, that night at Crispi's with nostalgia and affection—but he did not speak of a United States I knew at first hand. He spoke of my grandparents' America. Leaving the country in 1908, he had returned briefly in 1910 and in 1939. His only lengthy visit had occurred within walls, and most of his St. Elizabeths callers were neo-Fascist toadies . . .
>
> Pound was a dinosaur, strangely preserved into a later millennium, stretching his long bones out of dinosaur valley into the chrome city— and not noticing that things had altered.[54]

Of all the causes of Pound's depression, one of the most important was his physical deterioration. He had exceeded his three-score-and-ten by several years, and time now was taking its toll. As he had once told a friend, he had begun with a swelled head and was ending with swelled feet.[55]

Pound's mind deteriorated perceptibly from early 1960 on. According to a December 1960 letter from Omar to Dr. Overholser, Pound was finding it increasingly difficult to concentrate or do any work, and his condition was worsening.[56] By early 1961 it was reported that Pound "can't concentrate at all apparently and it's even torture to get him to sign his name these days."[57] He was very aware of his mental deterioration, writing that "my head just doesn't work." Another observer spoke of his "aphasic losing of the thread of memory,"[58] and Donald Hall described the situation most poignantly:

> He spoke with a vigor that made anything seem possible. He settled his hat back on his head, flung his scarf around his neck, and took up his stick. Then he realized, with a short laugh, that he didn't know how to direct me to the Circus Maximus. He sat at the edge of his sofa bed, hat and scarf still on, and studied a map. Then suddenly it happened, horribly in front of my eyes: again I saw vigor and energy drain out of him, like air from a pricked balloon. The strong body visibly sagged into old age; he disintegrated in front of me, smashed into a thousand unconnected and disorderly pieces. He took off his hat slowly and let it drop, his scarf slid to the floor; his stick, which had rested in his lap, thudded to the carpet. His long body slid boneless down, until he lay prone, eyes closed, as if all the lights in a tall building went out in a few seconds, and the building itself disassembled, returning to the stone and water and sand from which it had come.

For a few minutes he said nothing, only breathing and sighing. If I had not seen similar catastrophes before, I would have thought he had suffered a stroke or a heart attack. After two or three minutes he opened his eyes and looked at me. I said nothing but looked back into the eyes that watched me.[59]

One friend who saw him like this in 1961 assumed that Pound had had a stroke,[60] but there is no medical evidence to support this.

In addition to the general deterioration of his mind, Pound also developed neurological symptoms suggesting brain dysfunction. He was noted to have some impairment in his orientation: "He needs careful watching since he may try to get up, as he has sometimes in the night, and is evidently not always sure where he is."[61] He also had slurred speech at times,[62] and an unusual kind of speech disorder. "When I put a question to him, he would not reply, or his lips would move as if he were trying to form an answer, but the answer would not come."[63] Such symptoms are usually accompanied by major paralysis, but Pound had no such symptoms. His inability to express himself clearly caused him much anguish, as was well described by a visitor in 1961:

He was trying to say something to me, and it was as if he couldn't get the words together in his mind. And he grabbed hold of the table where we were standing, gripped it hard and began to shake it. M. [Mary] and Mrs. P. [Dorothy] were near and we all stood there, unable to do anything to calm him, and he finally quit.[64]

In 1966 Pound showed some difficulty with voluntary movements. For example when washing himself he would suddenly stop and freeze in the middle of a motion; this was usually accompanied by general stiffening of his muscles.[65] He had no tremor or other signs of Parkinson's disease, but was treated with drugs used in Parkinson's, with partial improvement.

Other parts of his body showed the effects of age as well. Foremost among these was his prostate gland, which became enlarged and led to recurrent infections of the urinary tract. Prostate surgery is not unusual for men in their seventies, and many of Pound's friends had undergone the operation. Claudius A. Hand, his roommate from college years, had written to Pound six years previously announcing that he had just had his prostate removed and gleefully recalling President Clemenceau's farewell speech to the French Assembly: "My fellow countrymen: there are two things I shall not miss. One is my prostate and the other is the presidency of France."[66]

Pound eventually had his prostate removed in 1962, but there were complications. He had more surgery in 1963, this time a total prostatectomy. One of the consequences of this operation was the need to wear a urinary retention bag, an inconvenience on the best of days, a reminder of one's mortality on the worst. Of far greater seriousness was the fact that total prostatectomies result in impotence in a high percentage of cases. Pound had advised William Carlos Williams forty years earlier that "the phallus in many cases ceases to rise even before death comes for one,"[67] but the reality must have been profoundly depressing. Just as he began writing serious poetry when he became sexually active, so he ceased writing at this time. And he directed that the hieratic head in his daughter's garden be turned from facing east to facing west.[68]

Pound's vital axis had deteriorated simultaneously, as if proving to him one last time how closely linked his brain and genitalia had been. He was probably referring to himself in Canto 115 when he described "a blown husk that is finished." And when Donald Hall asked him, "What is it, now, that holds you to life," Pound replied, "Nothing holds me any longer to life. Simply, I am immersed in it."[69]

A final, and perhaps the most important, source of Pound's depression was the belated realization that he should have taken his chances and stood trial on the treason charges. He had intended to. In Canto 74, written in the army prison camp, Pound vowed to meet the charges facing him "with a bang, not with a whimper." He had told his captors a few weeks previously that "if a man isn't willing to take some risks for his opinions, either his opinions are no good or he is no good."[70] He had lived his entire life on that principle, insisting on intellectual honesty and denigrating those who sacrificed principles for earthly ambitions or out of cowardice. In 1913 he had written:

> If an artist falsifies his report as to the nature of man, as to his own nature, as to the nature of his ideal of the perfect . . . if the artist falsifies his reports on these matters or on any other matter in order that he may conform to the taste of his time, to the proprieties of a sovereign, to the conveniences of a preconceived code of ethics, then that artist lies. If he lies out of deliberate will to lie, if he lies out of carelessness, out of laziness, out of cowardice, out of any sort of negligence whatsoever, he nevertheless lies and he should be punished or despised in proportion to the seriousness of his offense.[71]

Ezra Pound had adhered to his principle of intellectual honesty throughout his life—until December 1945.

On the day of reckoning, however, he had lost his nerve. Faced with an uncertain outcome of his trial, and possibly even death, he had drawn back and sought refuge in feigned insanity. He had avoided the trial, but from the perspective of 1961 it must have seemed a hollow victory. Of the seven other Americans indicted with him in 1943 for broadcasting for the enemy, three had had their indictments dismissed, two had died before they could be brought to trial, and two had been convicted and sentenced to life imprisonment. Pound indicated an awareness of this in a 1958 letter.[72] Even Tokyo Rose, indicted separately, had been released from prison after only seven years. Ezra Pound, if convicted, probably would have served less time in prison than he spent at St. Elizabeths Hospital. And in the process his decision had sacrificed his most important principle. He had met the charges not with a bang, nor even with a whimper, but with complete silence. In this light, the silence Pound entered into in 1961 was not out of character. Consciously or unconsciously, it was a reminder of his biggest failure of all, the failure of will.

Much has been written of Pound's dramatic and often prolonged silences in his final years. Pound himself claimed, "I did not enter into silence; silence captured me."[73] The silences have been variously attributed to fatigue and old age, or to a symbolic commentary on the futility of life and words. "Others say Pound has discovered that words have more to do with lies and misunderstanding than with communications," wrote one interviewer, and another claimed the silences were Pound's means of atonement.[74]

An examination of interviews in his final years reveals that Pound's silences were voluntary and intermittent. On some occasions he would say nothing whatsoever, while on others he would comment very selectively.[75] As late as 1968 Pound was interviewed for an Italian television documentary, and he spoke logically and coherently with no silences. Young artistic women could still command his attention, and in Venice he spoke to "a tall blonde Austrian sculptress . . . long after he stopped speaking to his oldest friends."[76] The silences also ended in the evenings when he was alone with Olga and they read to each other; in late 1962 they were reading Dante's "Paradiso" section of the *Divine Comedy.*[77]

There was also a histrionic or playful quality to Pound's silences. Alan Levy describes an instance during an interview: "Then in the prolonged mutual silence, he [Pound] whistles! It is just one toot, but I laugh, he winks, and everything is going to be all right."[78] Despite his depression Pound retained a sense of humor that periodically bubbled out from beneath the silence. On one occasion a young man knocked on Pound's door in Venice, expecting it to be opened by Olga Rudge. "To his astonishment, the door opened to reveal Ezra Pound in bathrobe and slippers. In his confusion, the young man burbled, 'How are you, Mr. Pound?' Pound looked down at him for a moment, out of the hauteur of his silence, and then uttered a single word, in the melody which sometimes resembled W. C. Fields: 'Senile,' he said."[79] One is reminded of Pound playfully bounding from bed to desk in St. Elizabeths while complaining of severe fatigue, or sarcastically responding to young psychiatrists whose looks he did not like. In depression, in silence, and in old age Ezra Pound remained basically the same person he had always been.

ILLNESS, REGRET, DEATH

Ezra Pound's brain had always been a rare Mediterranean blend of chutzpah and hubris, a cerebral pastiche which was by definition unstable. His Odyssean voyages had really been journeys between the antipodes of his mind, and when his ship came to rest it did so with finality.

Depression in Pound's old age was predictable, for he had the personality type that is so predisposed. In current psychiatric nomenclature his would be called a narcissistic and cyclothymic personality disorder, which encompasses people who are highly productive, unusually creative, hypersexual, have inflated self-esteem, require constant admiration, lack empathy, often take advantage of others, and respond with rage when criticized.[80] Many politicians, corporate executives, and entertainers fall into this category.

Both the narcissistic and the cyclothymic personality types are prone to depression in late life. With the personal chaos surrounding Pound, the loss of disciples and attention, the failure to complete his work or win honors, rejection by his homeland, realization that he had made mistakes, and the physical deterioration of his mind and body, depression became inevitable. And when it came it did so in force, even bringing neurological symptoms with it in what is called pseudo-dementia. One of the greatest ironies of Pound's life is that he spent over twelve perfectly sane years in an insane asylum, and then when he left became seriously depressed.

Ezra Pound's last years were a dilatory descent toward death as his body slowly gave out. In early 1962 Olga retrieved him from a rest home and took him to live with her. As one observer noted, Olga was "a violinist who was never willing to play second fiddle."[81] By this time Dorothy was becoming frail herself and could no longer provide the care that Ezra required.

Ezra and Olga lived part of the year in Rapallo and part in Venice. He remained in bed until late in the morning, then took walks and ate out frequently. They lived on the increasing royalties from his works and on his Social Security; the last was ironic since he had railed against Franklin Roosevelt and the government's system of taxation for thirty years. Olga encouraged him to travel, as this seemed temporarily to alleviate his depression. In 1965, in his eightieth year, they went to Paris, where Natalie Barney, by then an aging "Amazone," gave one last party in his honor. One guest described Pound as "an addled ghost, lamenting a world that would not adjust to his ideas of it" and "as self-contained as a rotten egg in an unbroken shell."[82] From Paris Ezra and Olga proceeded to London for T. S. Eliot's funeral, then to Dublin to visit Georgie Yeats, W. B.'s widow and Dorothy Pound's childhood friend. Later in 1965 Olga persuaded Ezra to make his first visit to Greece, home of the sacred Eleusinian mysteries. Pound returned to Paris in 1966 and 1967, and in 1969 Ezra and Olga flew to New York for two weeks. They visited Wyncote for a final time, then went to Hamilton College, where he sat silently through the commencement. He was an aged, anaudic relic.

In Venice Pound played long games of chess with a friend, the game lending itself nicely to his silences. The hieratic head carved by Gaudier-Brzeska, brought from Brunnenburg, stood starkly in his study, a reminder of his past. Friends visited, but Pound would often say nothing at all. Occasionally Olga would fill the silence by playing the tape recorder or phonograph with recordings of Pound reading his own poems. He would appear not to even notice. It was, in the words of Donald Hall, a "disembodied voice floating out over a disenvoiced body."[83]

One of Pound's most memorable visitors during these last years was American poet Allen Ginsberg. He came in 1967 with a supply of marijuana and phonograph records to play for Pound, whose poetry he respected highly. After getting suitably stoned Ginsberg introduced Pound to the Beatles' "Yellow Submarine," Bob Dylan's "Sad-Eyed Lady of the Lowlands," and Donovan's "Sunshine Superman." Ginsberg "repeated the lyrics aloud, in fragments—for him to hear clearly." Pound declined the offer of marijuana—he had previously spoken out strongly against the use of drugs—but sat silently, "impassive, earnest, attentive, asmile." A few days later Ginsberg returned to honor Pound on his eighty-second birthday, chanting Hare Krishna and fifty verses of Gopala Gopala Devaka Nandina Gopala "high and sweet, and low solemn." "Happy Birthday Krishna" Ginsberg offered. Silence. Then a simple "goodnight" from il poetà.[84]

Pound's personal life remained anarchic until the very end. After fifty years of marriage he and Dorothy became completely estranged. Although they both lived part of each year in Rapallo, they rarely met. In 1965, when Dorothy was asked where Ezra was living, she replied that he was just up the hill with Olga. "She imparted this information as one imparts the location of a planet."[85] On another occasion, at a theater in Rapallo Pound sat in the same row as his wife, but "studiedly ignored her presence." In 1970 Dorothy wrote, "I do not know where E. P. is . . . I have not seen him in 18 months." In the last four years of his life Ezra saw Dorothy only twice.[86]

In 1971, in Pound's eighty-sixth year, Mary published a memoir of her mother and father called *Discretions.* (Pound's own biographical notes published fifty years earlier had been called *Indiscretions.*) Mary's recollections included suggestions that growing up had not been idyllic for the illegitimate child of Ezra and Olga. According to one account, "the publication shattered Olga, and shattered Ezra as well because of his double devotion to Mary and Olga."[87] When an interviewer later asked Olga about the book, it "unleashes a 90-minute confessional of love and anger and disappointment and grief, past and present, that is too private to print."[88] There would be no paradise to complete Ezra Pound's personal epic.

With each passing year Pound became more and more a lonely survivor of another era. Joyce and Lewis were long since dead. Then Hemingway and H. D. died in 1961, Cummings in 1962, Williams in 1963, and Eliot in 1965. Each death brought more memories and more depression. "It is sad . . . very sad to look back," he said.[89]

Ezra Pound spent his last twelve years regretting his life. Remorse and disappointment were the themes heard most often between the silences. In early 1960 he told interviewer Donald Hall, "The question is whether I give up now—or have another twenty years to write in . . . whether to live or die." Pound dwelled on the past, on choices made and not made. "After an hour of his excuses and my silence," Hall wrote, Pound finally asked: "Do *you* think they should have shot me?"[90]

By 1962 Pound was telling visitors that he had been "wrong, wrong, wrong. I've always been wrong. Eighty-seven per cent wrong . . . I've never recognized benevolence. You don't know what it's like to get off on the wrong path."[91] And to a reporter from an Italian magazine the following year he said:

> I have lived all my life believing that I knew something. And then a strange day came and I realized that I knew nothing, that I knew nothing at all . . . I have arrived too late to a state of total uncertainty, where I am conscious only of doubt . . . Everything that I touch, I spoil. I have blundered, always . . . Man exists only insofar as he becomes increasingly aware of errors . . . And the most foolish are those who believe they know something, that they possess a certainty . . . I was as stupid as if I had been a telescope used the wrong way. Knowledge came too late. Too late I arrived at the certainty that I knew nothing.[92]

It was an ironic echo of words he had written to his college professor forty years earlier: "If the poets don't make certain horrors appear horrible who will?"[93]

Despair was intermittent, and there were happier times; for example in 1965 he was described as going to plays and concerts, and able to joke about atheists in Hyde Park describing hell.[94] Yet depression was always close at hand, ready to abrogate whatever satisfaction he could find, an executioner doing the task in installments. "I regret my past errors, but I hope to have done a little something for some artists," he told a reporter in Paris. "He is in a state of profound remorse," said his French publisher.[95]

When Allen Ginsberg visited in 1967 Pound repeated his penitence: "At seventy I realized that instead of being a lunatic, I was a moron . . . Any good I've done has been spoiled by bad intentions—the preoccupation with irrelevant and stupid things." He then added, "But the worst mistake I made was that stupid, suburban prejudice of anti-Semitism." Ginsberg was pleased with the confession: "It's lovely to hear you say that. Well, no, because anyone with any sense can see it as a humour, in that sense a part of the drama, a model of your consciousness. Anti-Semitism is your fuck-up, like not liking Buddhists, but it's part of the model and the great accomplishment was to make a working model of your mind."[96] Pound could accept no absolution. Two months before he died he told David Heymann: "I hold no delusions . . . What's done cannot be undone . . . The error is all in the not done . . . I was wrong . . . Ninety-per-cent wrong . . . I lost my head in a storm."[97] It was a harsh punishment, but the crime of self-deception is a serious one. He had fooled many brilliant people in his time; too late he realized that he had fooled himself as well. He listened to the past:

> *Evening is like a curtain of cloud,*
> *a blurr above ripples; and through it*
> *sharp long spikes of the cinnamon,*
> *A cold tune amid reeds.*
> *Behind hill the monk's bell*
> *borne on the wind.*
>
> *Sail passed here in April; may return in October*
> *Boat fades in silver; slowly;*
> *Sun blaze alone on the river.*

> (*Canto 49*)

Ezra Pound was ready for his final stage exit. It had been a grand Greek tragedy, the kind he had urged others to read and used to discuss with scholar Edith Hamilton when she visited him at St. Elizabeths. She had written:

> Tragedy belongs to the poets. Only they have "trod the sunlit heights" and from life's dissonance struck one clear chord. None but a poet can write a tragedy. For tragedy is nothing less than pain transmuted into exaltation by the alchemy of poetry, and if poetry is true knowledge and the great poets guides safe to follow, this transmutation has arresting implications.
>
> Pain changed into, or, let us say, charged with, exaltation. It would seem that tragedy is a strange matter. There is indeed none stranger. A tragedy shows us pain and gives us pleasure thereby. The greater the suffering depicted, the more terrible the events, the more intense our pleasure. The most monstrous and appalling deeds life can show are those the tragedian chooses, and by the spectacle he thus offers us, we are moved to a very passion of enjoyment.[98]

It had been a story of Calliope, the muse of epic poetry, attracted by young Narcissus. The nymph Hubris jealously intervened, and was followed by Nemesis, the deity of those who allow themselves to be touched by Hubris. Ezra Pound had not written a great epic. He had lived it.

He died in his sleep on November 1, 1972, two days after his eighty-seventh birthday. A party had been scheduled with cookies, candy, and neighborhood children, but at the last moment it had to be canceled. Stomach pain, a trip to the hospital that evening, and a rapidly downhill course. The funeral was held two days later with relatively few mourners. Neither the Italian nor the American government sent a tribute. Olga and Mary were there, but Dorothy was too frail to make the journey. Omar "made desperate attempts to get to Venice in time for the funeral" or to have it delayed, but in vain; Olga refused to wait, and Omar arrived a few hours after it was over.[99] Ezra Pound's errors would live after him like the curse of Atreus.

He had foreseen his funeral with prophetic accuracy more than five decades earlier:

> *Nor at my funeral either will there be any long trail,*
>   *bearing ancestral lares and images;*
>
> *No trumpets filled with my emptiness,*
> *Nor shall it be on an Atalic bed;*
>   *The perfumed cloths shall be absent.*
>
> *A small plebeian procession.*
>   *Enough, enough and in plenty*
>
> *There will be three books at my obsequies*
> *Which I take, my not unworthy gift, to Persephone.*

You will follow the bare sacrified breast
Nor will you be weary of calling my name, nor too weary
    To place the last kiss on my lips

When the Syrian onyx is broken.

    "He who is now vacant dust
    "Was once the slave of one passion:"

Give that much inscription
    "Death why tardily come?"[100]

After the service his body was borne by a black gondola to the cemetery island of San Michele, where it was buried. He had wanted to return to Idaho with the hieratic head standing over his grave, but it was not possible, and in death, as in life, he remained on foreign soil.[101] Ezra Pound ended his life as he had ended his Cantos:

I have tried to write Paradise
Do not move
    Let the wind speak that is paradise.

Let the Gods forgive what I have made
Let those I love try to forgive what I have made.[102]

CODA

*The nymph still looks at herself and admires herself in
the water, as she has done since the beginning of time.
Long before Hubris entered Arcadia, the terrible intoxica-
tion was known. The gravest crimes, the most senseless
adventures have sprung from the self-regarding gaze,
and though we make poetry of pride in the West, and
pretend to ourselves that there are some forms of pride
which are legitimate and others which are not so, the
most deathly instrument placed in the hands of man
remains the mirror.*

Robert Payne,
Hubris: A Study of Pride

NOTES

EPIGRAPHS

1. "God damn it . . ." Pound letter to Lewis, December 3, 1936, unpublished, Department of Rare Books, Cornell University.
2. 'Whom God . . ." Pound, speaking on Rome Radio, January 29, 1942, in Leonard W. Doob, *Ezra Pound Speaking* (Westport, Connecticut: Greenwood Press, 1978), pp. 23–27.
3. "Time passes . . ." Williams letter to Pound, August 23, 1946, unpublished, The Lilly Library, Indiana University.

PREFACE

1. Alan Levy, "Ezra Pound's Voice of Silence," *The New York Times Magazine*, January 9, 1972, pp. 14–68.
2. Robert M. Adams, "A Hawk and a Handsaw for Ezra Pound," *Accent* 8 (1948):205–214.
3. Pound's published letters were edited by D. D. Paige and originally published as *The Letters of Ezra Pound, 1907–1941* in 1950. Comparison of Paige's selections with the original letters shows them to be heavily edited to put Pound in the best possible light; this is not surprising since the purpose of publishing them in 1950 was to increase pressure for Pound's release from St. Elizabeths Hospital. (See correspondence between Paige and Pound's family and friends in the Humanities Research Center, The University of Texas at Austin.) Pound's unpublished letters sold by his family to various libraries include many pages cut in half or missing altogether. An example of changes in his poetry as originally published is "Salutation the Third": "Let us be done with Jews and Jobbery" in *Blast* (June 1914) was changed to "Let us be done with pandars and jobbery" in *Personae* (New York: New Directions, 1971, p. 145). An example of changes in his prose as originally published is "Patria Mia": "The Jew alone can retain his detestable qualities despite climatic conditions" was in the original version published in the *New Age* 11 (1912):466, but not in the reprinted version in *Selected Prose 1909–1965* (New York: New Directions, 1973, p. 99).
4. Eustace Mullins, *This Difficult Individual, Ezra Pound* (New York: Fleet Publishing Company, 1961), p. 29.
5. Eveline Bates Doob, "Some Notes on E. P.," *Paideuma* 8 (1979):69–78.
6. Pound letter to Archibald MacLeish, December 16, no year, unpublished, Manuscript Division, Library of Congress.

CHAPTER 1: THE GORILLA CAGE

1. Pound, letter to *Poetry*, April 14, 1919. Quoted in Hugh Kenner, *The Pound Era* (Berkeley: University of California Press, 1971), p. 287.

2. Carl Sandburg, "The Work of Ezra Pound," *Poetry* 7(1915):249–257.
3. All information on the Disciplinary Training Center in this chapter was taken from the following sources unless otherwise indicated: Robert L. Allen, "The Cage," *Esquire* 49(1958):22–26; Michael King, "Ezra Pound at Pisa: an interview with John L. Steele," *Texas Quarterly* 49(1978):49–61; David Park Williams, "The Background of the Pisan Cantos," *Poetry* 73(1949):216–222.
4. Huntington Cairns notes on interview with Ezra Pound, January 17, 1949, Manuscript Division, Library of Congress.
5. Noel Stock, *The Life of Ezra Pound* (London: Penguin Books, 1974), p. 85. Quoting Mark Welkin in *Punch*. It should be noted that the page numbers in this English edition of Stock's biography differ from those of the American edition.
6. Stock, *Life of Ezra Pound*, p. 192.
7. Alfred Kazin, "The Writer as Political Crazy," *Playboy*, June 1973, pp. 107–209; and George F. Fraser, *Ezra Pound* (New York: Barnes and Noble, 1965), preface.
8. Sandburg, "Work of Ezra Pound," p. 249.
9. C. David Heymann, *Ezra Pound: The Last Rower* (New York: Viking, 1976), p. 160, quoting Department of Justice files.
10. King, "Ezra Pound at Pisa," p. 56.
11. Mary de Rachewiltz, *Discretions* (Boston: Atlantic Monthly Press, 1971), p. 243.
12. Indictment of Ezra Pound by Grand Jury of the District of Columbia, July 26, 1943, in Ezra Pound files of the Department of Justice. Reproduced in Heymann, *Ezra Pound*, p. 135.
13. The transcripts of the Pound broadcasts are available in the Library of Congress. Many of them were collected and edited in Doob, *Ezra Pound Speaking*. They are also widely quoted in Pound biographies, especially Heymann, *Ezra Pound*, pp. 116–121 and Charles Norman, *The Case of Ezra Pound* (New York: Funk and Wagnalls, 1968), pp. 51–53.
14. Edd Johnson, "Pound, Accused of Treason, Calls Hitler Saint, Martyr," *The Chicago Sun* May 9, 1945, p. 6.
15. See Wyndham Lewis, *Time and Western Man* (Boston: Beacon, 1957), p. 74. (Originally published in 1927.) Also John Cournos, *Autobiography* (New York: G. P. Putnam, 1935), p. 235.
16. Pound broadcast of April 30, 1942, is quoted in Heymann, *Ezra Pound*, pp. 116–120. For an account of the searching of Pound's apartment see de Rachewiltz, *Discretions*, p. 243.
17. Cable, T. S. Eliot to Archibald MacLeish, Manuscript Division, Library of Congress.
18. See Ernest Hemingway, *A Moveable Feast.* (New York: Charles Scribner's Sons, 1964), p. 134.
19. Heymann, *Ezra Pound*, p. 20, quoting Horace Gregory.
20. Allen, "The Cage," p. 22.
21. De Rachewiltz, *Discretions*, p. 255.
22. Psychiatric interview of Ezra Pound by Dr. William Weisdorf, MTOUSA Disciplinary Training Center, July 17, 1945, in the Ezra Pound files of the U.S. Army; also found in the Ezra Pound files of the Department of Justice.
23. Ezra Pound, "Indiscretions," in *Pavannes and Divagations* (New York: New Directions, 1958), p. 5. Originally published in *New Age*, 1920.
24. Carlos Baker, *Ernest Hemingway: A Life Story* (New York: Charles Scribner's Sons, 1969), p. 107.
25. Marcus Aurelius, *Meditations* (Baltimore: Penguin, 1964), No. 21, p. 96.
26. Ezra Pound, *Guide to Kulchur* (New York: New Directions, 1970), p. 40. Originally published in 1938.
27. Jack LaZebnik, "The Case of Ezra Pound," *New Republic* April 1, 1957, pp. 17–20.
28. Stock, *Life of Ezra Pound*, p. 390.

29. Canto 74 is from Ezra Pound, *The Cantos of Ezra Pound* (New York: New Directions, 1970), p. 425. Pound quote, "The world fell on me" is from David Gordon, "Meeting E. P. and Then . . . ," *Paideuma* 3(1974):343–360.
30. Johnson, "Pound, Accused of Treason," p. 6.
31. David Feldman, "Ezra Pound: A Poet in a Cage," *Paideuma* 10(1981):361–365.
32. De Rachewiltz, *Discretions*, p. 255.
33. Dr. Jerome Kavka, "Psychiatric Case History of Ezra Pound," January 24, 1946, Saint Elizabeths Hospital files No. 1381-k.
34. Psychiatric interview of Ezra Pound by Dr. Richard W. Finner, MTOUSA Disciplinary Training Center, June 14, 1945, in the Ezra Pound files of the U.S. Army; also found in the Ezra Pound files of the Department of Justice.
35. Psychiatric interview of Ezra Pound by Dr. Walter H. Baer, MTOUSA Disciplinary Training Center, June 15, 1945, in the Ezra Pound files of the U.S. Army; also found in the Ezra Pound files of the Department of Justice.
36. Affidavit in support of application for bail, *United States of America against Ezra Pound*, November 26, 1945, in the Ezra Pound files of the Department of Justice.
37. Pound letter to Laurence Binyon, August 30, 1934, in D. D. Paige, *Selected Letters of Ezra Pound: 1907–1941* (New York: New Directions, 1950), p. 260.
38. Pound letter to Wyndham Lewis, February 7 / 8, 1939, unpublished, Department of Rare Books, Cornell University Library.
39. Ezra Pound, *Jefferson and/or Mussolini* (New York: Liveright, 1935), p. 100.
40. Allen, "The cage."
41. Homer L. Somers, notes on Ezra Pound found in the Humanities Research Center, The University of Texas at Austin. A copy of these notes is also available in the Manuscript Division, Library of Congress. Mr. Somers was a guard at the Disciplinary Training Center during Pound's detention there.
42. Allen, "The Cage," p. 24.
43. King, "Ezra Pound at Pisa," p. 61.
44. Allen, "The Cage," p. 24.
45. Weisdorf interview (see n. 22).
46. Memo from Lt. Col. John L. Steele to Commanding General, MTOUSA, APO 49, U.S. Army, July 19, 1945, in the Ezra Pound files, U.S. Army.
47. King, "Ezra Pound at Pisa," p. 57.
48. John R. Harrison, *The Reactionaries: A Study of The Anti-Democratic Intelligentsia* (New York: Schocken, 1967), p. 111.
49. Louise Bogan, "A Poet's Alphabet," *The New Yorker*, October 30, 1948, p. 107.
50. Somers, Notes.
51. King, "Ezra Pound at Pisa," p. 58.
52. Homer L. Somers letter to his mother, November 10, 1945, unpublished, Humanities Research Center, The University of Texas at Austin.
53. Allen, "The Cage," p. 24.
54. Ibid.
55. Memo from J. Edgar Hoover to Assistant Attorney General T. L. Caudle, September 13, 1945, in the Pound file of the Federal Bureau of Investigation.
56. William French, letter to the editor, *Paideuma* 10(1981):185–186. See also William French, "Peacocks in Poundland," *Helix* 1983 (forthcoming).
57. French, "Peacocks in Poundland."
58. Stock, *Life of Ezra Pound*, p. 526.
59. Archibald MacLeish letter to T. S. Eliot, May 18, 1945, unpublished, Manuscript Division, Library of Congress.
60. T. S. Eliot letter to Archibald MacLeish, May 30, 1945, unpublished, Manuscript Division, Library of Congress.
61. T. S. Eliot telegram to Archibald MacLeish, August 7, 1945, Manuscript Division, The Library of Congress.

62. Archibald MacLeish letter to T. S. Eliot, August 13, 1945, unpublished, Manuscript Division, Library of Congress.

63. Doob, *"Ezra Pound Speaking."*

64. "Not a Traitor, Quisling Says," *Stars and Stripes,* Paris edition, August 21, 1945, pp. 1, 4. The accounts of the Quisling trial are taken from *Stars and Stripes,* Paris and Mediterranean editions, August 21–September 11, 1945.

65. Pound letter to Wyndham Lewis, n.d., 1950, unpublished, Department of Rare Books, Cornell University Library.

66. Pound letter to William Joyce, July 18, 1941, unpublished, Beinecke Rare Book and Manuscript Library, Yale University.

67. The information on William Joyce and his trial is taken from Margaret Boveri, *Treason in the Twentieth Century* (New York: G. P. Putnam, 1963); Rebecca West, *The Meaning of Treason* (New York: Viking, 1947); and Rebecca West, *The New Meaning of Treason* (New York: Viking, 1964), pp. 19, 122. It is of interest that West did not mention Pound's case in either book despite coverage of virtually every other contemporary case of treason.

68. Allen, "The Cage," p. 25.

69. Stock, *Life of Ezra Pound,* pp. 523–524.

70. The accounts of the Laval trial are taken from *Stars and Stripes,* Paris and Mediterranean editions, October 5–17, 1945.

71. Pound letter to Shakespear and Parkyn, October 5, 1945, reprinted in Julien Cornell, *The Trial of Ezra Pound* (New York: John Day, 1966), pp. 7–11.

72. William Cookson, quoting Pound in Introduction to Ezra Pound, *Selected Prose: 1909–1965* (New York: New Directions, 1972).

73. De Rachewiltz, *Discretions,* pp. 254–256.

74. " 'Right-O' Says First Haw-Haw, Told Treason Hearing is November 1," *Stars and Stripes,* Paris edition, October 23, 1945, p. 5.

75. Allen, "The Cage," p. 25.

76. Ibid.

CHAPTER 2: BAPTISM IN A LILY POND

1. Pound, "Indiscretions," p. 12.

2. The information on Thaddeus Pound is from Douglas MacPherson, "Ezra Pound of Wyncote," *Arts in Philadelphia* 2(1940):10–28; and Kavka, "Psychiatric Case History."

3. Pound, "Indiscretions," p. 14.

4. Pound's feelings about his grandfather's influence are found in Kavka, "Psychiatric Case History"; and in Mary McGrory, "Ezra Pound Still Sees Mad World out of Step," *Washington Evening Star* April 3, 1958.

5. Doobs, *Ezra Pound Speaking,* broadcast of May 5, 1942.

6. See Kavka, "Psychiatric Case History"; and Pound, "Indiscretions."

7. George W. Walter, *The Loomis Gang* (Prospect, New York: Prospect Books, 1953), p. 3. The book contains a good history of this colorful outlaw family.

8. Pound, "Indiscretions," p. 11.

9. Stock, *Life of Ezra Pound,* p. 21.

10. The 1944 description is in Ezra Pound, "An Introduction to the Economic Nature of the United States." Originally published in Italian in 1944, translated and reprinted in Pound, *Selected Prose,* p. 173. Pound's assessment of his grandmother is in Kavka, "Psychiatric Case History."

11. Kavka, "Psychiatric Case History."

12. The descriptions of Isabel Pound are from the following sources: Hilda Doolittle, *End to Torment* (New York: New Directions, 1979), p. 22; Stock, *Life of Ezra Pound,*

p. 3; Desmond Chute, "In Commemoration: Poet's Paradise," *The Pound Newsletter* 8(1955):12–14; Charles Norman, *Ezra Pound* (New York: Macmillan, 1960), p. 317.

13. Kavka, "Psychiatric Case History."
14. See Stock, *Life of Ezra Pound,* pp. 1–3.
15. Pound, "Indiscretions," p. 16.
16. Details of Homer Pound's life are found in Pound, "Indiscretions"; Kavka, "Psychiatric Case History"; and Stock, *Life of Ezra Pound,* p. 3.
17. The descriptions of Homer Pound are from Doolittle, *End to Torment,* p. 22; and Stock, *Life of Ezra Pound,* p. 4.
18. Pound, "Indiscretions"; and Kavka, "Psychiatric Case History."
19. Kavka, "Psychiatric Case History."
20. Ibid.
21. Ibid.
22. Stock, *Life of Ezra Pound,* p. 6; and Chute, "In Commemoration."
23. Kavka, "Psychiatric Case History."
24. Ezra Pound, "Plotinus" in *A Lume Spento.* Published in 1908, reprinted in *Collected Early Poems* (New York: New Directions, 1976), p. 36.
25. Stock, *Life of Ezra Pound,* p. 6; and Heymann, *Ezra Pound,* p. 132.
26. Phyllis Bottome, *From The Life* (London: Faber and Faber, 1944; republished in Folcroft Library Edition, 1974), p. 76.
27. Stock (*Life of Ezra Pound,* p. 131) refers to his father's continuing financial support in 1911. Norman (*Ezra Pound,* p. 313) noted the support to still be continuing in 1932 when Pound was 47 years old: "Homer Pound had deposited a sum on which his son could draw without explanation, provided each withdrawal was under one hundred dollars."
28. Stock, *Life of Ezra Pound,* p. 4. The same story is told by Max Beerbohm in S. N. Behrman, *Portrait of Max: An Intimate Memoir of Sir Max Beerbohm* (New York: Random House, 1960), p. 280, except that it purportedly took place at a Rapallo seaside café and went as follows: "His parents were staring at him, rapt, while he made these utterances. Ezra said, 'The greatest master of French literature was Louis the Eighteenth.' Ezra's father, who was sitting next to me, nudged me and beamed at me. 'That kid,' he said, 'knows everything!' "
29. Ezra Pound, "The Revolt of Intelligence," *New Age,* January 8, 1920. Quoted in Patricia Hutchins, *Ezra Pound's Kensington* (Chicago: Henry Regnery, 1965), p. 24.
30. Doob, *Ezra Pound Speaking,* broadcasts of July 22, 1942, and May 31, 1942.
31. William M. Chace, *The Political Identities of Ezra Pound and T. S. Eliot* (Stanford: Stanford University Press, 1973), p. 19.
32. Pound, *Pavannes and Divagations,* pp. 56, 30.
33. These details are from Kavka, "Psychiatric Case History"; and Dr. Marion R. King, Psychiatric examination of Ezra Pound, St. Elizabeths Hospital files no. 1371, 1945.
34. John H. Edwards, "A Critical Biography of Ezra Pound: 1885–1922." Ph.D. diss., University of California, 1952, p. 23.
35. Ibid., quoting conversations with Professors A. H. Quinn and C. Weygandt.
36. Stock, *Life of Ezra Pound,* p. 20.
37. Ibid., p. 17.
38. Ibid., pp. 23–24; and William Carlos Williams, *Autobiography* (New York: Random House, 1948), p. 58.
39. Reed Whittemore, *William Carlos Williams: Poet from Jersey* (Boston: Houghton Mifflin, 1975), pp. 235, 35.
40. Williams, *Autobiography,* p. 58.
41. Norman, *Ezra Pound,* p. 7.
42. George P. Elliott, *A Piece of Lettuce* (New York: Random House, 1957), pp. 128–129.
43. Samuel Putnam, *Paris Was Our Mistress* (New York: Viking, 1947), p. 150.
44. Emily Mitchell Wallace, "Penn's Poet Friends," *Pennsylvania Gazette* 71(1973):33–36.

45. Williams, *Autobiography*, pp. 57–58.

46. Kavka, "Psychiatric Case History."

47. Williams, *Autobiography*, pp. 58, 65.

48. MacPherson, "Ezra Pound of Wyncote," and Doolittle, *End to Torment*, p. 14. In some accounts of this incident the pond is referred to as a frog pond, in others as a lily pond. Like all good Pennsylvania ponds it presumably contained both.

49. Doolittle, *End to Torment*, p. 20.

50. William Carlos Williams letter to Babette Deutsch, January 18, 1943, in *The Pound Newsletter* 8(1955):22–23, and in John C. Thirlwall, ed., *The Selected Letters of William Carlos Williams* (New York: McDowell, Obolensky, 1957), p. 210. According to Wallace ("Penn's Poet Friends") the University of Pennsylvania yearbook says Pound transferred because "naughty boys" played too many tricks on him.

51. James E. Rader, "Ship in the Night," *Bachelor*, May 9, 1958, pp. 6–9.

52. "Weston" in "Talk of the Town," *The New Yorker* 19(1943):16–17.

53. Edwards, "Critical Biography of Ezra Pound," p. 27, quoting Robert U. Hayes, who was at that time the president of the fraternity. This story is also found in Norman, *Ezra Pound*, p. 13. By coincidence Mr. Hayes was a close friend of my family, but he died several years before I began work on Pound.

54. Frank K. Lorenz, *Ezra Pound at Hamilton College*. Pamphlet printed for the Hamilton College Library, Clinton, New York, n.d. See also Edwards, "Critical Biography of Ezra Pound," p. 27.

55. Norman, *Ezra Pound*, p. 13.

56. John L. Brown, "A Troubadour at Hamilton," *The Hamilton Literary Magazine* 62(1932):53–63.

57. The furniture moving episode is described in "Weston." This account of the story suggests that it occured at the University of Pennsylvania, but this is most unlikely since Pound's parents lived nearby. See also Mullins, *This Difficult Individual*, p. 34. Williams's description is found in Williams's letter to Babette Deutsch (see n. 50).

58. The poetry-reading occasions are described in "Weston" and in Norman, *Ezra Pound*, p. 13. The bathroom incident is described in Brown, "Troubadour at Hamilton." The story is reported by Michael Reck, *Ezra Pound: A Close-Up* (New York: McGraw-Hill 1967), p. 8, except that the time interval is reduced to a "a half-hour or more."

59. See Edwards, "Critical Biography of Ezra Pound," p. 31; and Lorenz, *Ezra Pound at Hamilton College*.

60. Brown, "Troubadour at Hamilton."

61. Ezra Pound letter to Isabel Pound, February 1905, unpublished, Beinecke Rare Book and Manuscript Library, Yale University. The letter is quoted in Edwards, "Critical Biography of Ezra Pound," p. 31. The dating of Pound's idea of writing cantos is found in Edwards, p. 32, in which Edwards is quoting a conversation with Pound.

62. Pound letter to Isabel Pound, February 1905, Beinecke Library.

63. See Edwards, "Critical Biography of Ezra Pound," pp. 27 and 30.

64. Ibid., p. 34. The fellow student and roommate was Oswald Backus. See letter from Backus to Pound describing this incident in the Beinecke Rare Book and Manuscript Library, Yale University.

65. Leon Surette, *A Light from Eleusis* (Oxford: Clarendon Press, 1979), pp. 40, 57.

66. Pound letter to Carlo Izzo, January 8, 1938, in Paige, *Selected Letters*, p. 303. See also Surette, *Light from Eleusis*, p. 63.

67. Ezra Pound, "Credo," in *Selected Prose*, p. 53. Originally published in *Front*, 1930.

68. Surette, *Light from Eleusis*, p. 63.

69. Williams, *Autobiography*, p. 57.

70. Williams letter to Babette Deutsch (see n. 50).

71. Ezra Pound letter to William Carlos Williams, February 6, 1907, unpublished, Poetry/Rare Books Collection, State University of New York at Buffalo. Viola Baxter's married name was Jordan, and they corresponded for over 40 years. See also Conrad B.

Jordan, "The Last Troubadour," *Yankee*, November 1981, pp. 124–282, for an account of Pound by Viola Baxter Jordan's son.

72. Faubion Bowers, "Memoir within Memoirs," *Paideuma* 2(1973):53–66. Bowers says that Katherine Heyman was born in 1874 which would make her 11 years older than Pound, not 15 years as some biographers have claimed. Miss Heyman's mother came from Herkimer, New York, which is near Hamilton College, and it is likely that the two met at a concert in nearby Utica.

73. Williams, *Autobiography*, pp. 67–68.

74. Doolittle, *End to Torment*, pp. 3, 12, 54; Janice S. Robinson, *H. D.: The Life and Work of an American Poet* (Boston: Houghton Mifflin, 1982), p. 31. Robinson claims that Pound's relationship with H. D. was not sexually consummated at this time, although no source is cited for this information.

75. Ezra Pound, "The Wings," in Doolittle, *End to Torment*, pp. 70–71. Ezra and Hilda's interest in the occult is also alluded to in Robinson, *H. D.*, pp. 8, 341.

76. Ezra Pound, "Ver Novem," in Doolittle, *End to Torment*, p. 72.

77. Ezra Pound, "The Arches," in Doolittle, *End to Torment*, p. 80.

78. Ezra Pound, "Rendez-vous," in Doolittle, *End to Torment*, p. 84.

79. A lucid analysis of Hilda Doolittle's role in Pound's later poetry is found in William French, " 'Saint Hilda,' Mr. Pound, and Rilke's Parisian Panther at Pisa," *Paideuma* 11(1982):79–87.

80. See French, " 'Saint Hilda' " and Doolittle, *End to Torment*, p. 68.

81. Ezra Pound, "Praise of Ysolt," in *Personae* (New York: New Directions, 1971).

82. Surette, *Light from Eleusis*, p. 69.

83. Hilda Doolittle letter to William Carlos Williams, 1907, quoted in Whittemore, *William Carlos Williams*, p. 43. The original engagement occurred in 1905 according to Hilda Doolittle's biographer (Robinson, *H. D.*, p. 11).

84. Perdita Schaffner, "Merano 1962," *Paideuma* 4(1975):513–518. See also Doolittle, *End to Torment*; Michael King, "Go, Little Book: Ezra Pound, Hilda Doolittle, and 'Hilda's Book,' " *Paideuma* 10(1981):347–360.

85. Michael J. King, "*HERmione* by H. D.," *Paideuma* 11(1982):339–344. For information on Frances Gregg see also Doolittle, *End to Torment*, p. 15; Robinson, *H. D.*, pp. 19–24.

86. Margaret Widdemer, *Golden Friends I Had* (Garden City, New York: Doubleday, 1964), pp. 126–127.

87. Hilda's withdrawal from college is described in Robinson, *H. D.*, p. 11. See also King, "*HERmione* by H. D."

88. Felix E. Schelling letter to Wharton Barker, March 30, 1920, in the University of Pennsylvania Library. Quoted by Edwards, "Critical Biography of Ezra Pound," p. 37; John Shea and Timothy Romano, "The Pound-Williams Conference," *Paideuma* 10(1981):411–418; and Wallace, "Penn's Poet Friends."

89. Wallace, "Penn's poet friends." The poetry distribution episode is alluded to in Marion R. King, Psychiatric examination of Ezra Pound.

90. Stock, *Life of Ezra Pound*, p. 44.

91. Widdemer, *Golden Friends*, pp. 123–124.

92. Pound's multiple attempts to get readmitted to the University of Pennsylvania and to get his degree are described in Edwards, "Critical Biography of Ezra Pound," p. 37; Stock, *Life of Ezra Pound*, pp. 102, 124, 380–381; Shea and Romano, "The Pound-Williams Conference"; and Pound's letter to Simon Guggenheim, February 24, 1925, in Paige, *Selected Letters*, p. 197.

93. Pound letter to Alumni Secretary, University of Pennsylvania, April 20, 1929, in Paige, *Selected Letters*, p. 225.

94. Stock, *Life of Ezra Pound*, pp. 22, 46.

95. Edwards, "Critical Biography of Ezra Pound," p. 38.

96. The information on Pound at Wabash is taken in large part from James E. Rader

who, as a student at Wabash in 1958, mailed a questionnaire to students who had been at Wabash with Pound. Copies of the 60 replies are found in the Beinecke Rare Book and Manuscript Library, Yale University. Some of the information has been published in Rader, "Ship in the Night," *Bachelor* 6–9 (May 9, 1958); and in Rader, Viola Wildman and Fred H. Rhodes, "A Pound of flesh," *The Wabash Review* 6(1959):5–10. Also useful are R. E. Banta, "Ezra Pound among the Hoosiers," *Wabash Bulletin* 11–13 (December) 1953; and Edwards, "Critical Biography of Ezra Pound."

97. Norman, *Ezra Pound*, p. 23, quoting an unsigned letter in the University of Kansas City *Review*.

98. Rader, Wildman and Rhodes, "A pound of flesh."

99. Ibid.

100. Pound letter to Viola Baxter Jordan, *Paideuma* 1(1972):109.

101. The Pound letters to Mary Moore are in the Van Pelt Library, The University of Pennsylvania. See especially the letter of October 3, 1907, for a discussion of love and marriage.

102. See Edwards, "Critical biography of Ezra Pound," p. 41, and Pound, "Pierre Vidal Old," in *Personae*, pp. 30–32.

103. Rader, Wildman, and Rhodes, "A pound of flesh."

104. Stock, *Life of Ezra Pound*, p. 51, quoting a letter by Pound to L. Burton Hessler. This letter is in the Humanities Research Center, The University of Texas at Austin.

105. Rader, Wildman and Rhodes, "A pound of flesh."

106. Ibid.

107. Acknowledgment of the affair is in King, Psychiatric examination of Ezra Pound. Hilda Doolittle, in *End to Torment*, p. 15, also recounts Pound's version of this episode but then adds: "There is more to it than that. Cousin Edd knows people in Wyncote who told him———." The possibility that this incident was just one of many was raised in Robert A. Corrigan, "Literature and Politics: The Case of Ezra Pound Reconsidered," *Prospects: An Annual of American Cultural Studies* 2(1976):463–482, 1976, n. 11.

108. Pound letter to L. Burton Hessler, November 20, 1907, unpublished, Humanities Research Center, The University of Texas at Austin.

109. L. R. Hesler letter to James Rader, November 26, 1958, Beinecke Rare Book and Manuscript Library, Yale University. For a fictionalized account of Pound's confrontation with the mores of Crawfordsville, see G. Thomas Tanselle, "Ezra Pound and a Story of Floyd Dell's," *Notes and Queries* 8(1961):350–352.

110. Pound, *Guide to Kulchur*, pp. 61, 245.

111. Doolittle, *End to Torment*, p. 20.

112. Ibid., p. 15.

113. This information is contained in interviews of Pound's friends by FBI agents in 1945, in the Pound files of the FBI.

CHAPTER 3: MIXED REVIEWS

1. See Pound, "Indiscretions"; Stock, *Life of Ezra Pound*, pp. 13–14; and MacPherson, "Ezra Pound of Wyncote."

2. Kavka, "Psychiatric Case History."

3. Pound, "Indiscretions," p. 5.

4. Bowers, "Memoir within Memoirs." See also Stock, *Life of Ezra Pound*, p. 58; and Edwards, "Critical Biography of Ezra Pound," p. 42.

5. Edwards, "Critical Biography of Ezra Pound," p. 43.

6. Stock, *Life of Ezra Pound*, p. 60, quoting Pound's letter to his mother of June, 1908.

7. Edwards, "Critical Biography of Ezra Pound," p. 44. Stock (*Life of Ezra Pound*, p. 70) says that this review appeared in London's *Evening Standard* newspaper.

8. Stock, *Life of Ezra Pound*, p. 60, quoting Pound's letter to his mother of June, 1908.

9. Ibid., pp. 68–69. Alan Levy claims that Pound got the lecture job on his own by simply going to the Institute and offering to give the course. "Who are you?" asked the person in charge of the course. "Let me give the course and you'll find out," Pound is said to have replied. See Levy, "Ezra Pound's Voice of Silence." The rejection of his poems is mentioned in Edwards, "Critical Biography of Ezra Pound," p. 49.

10. Edwards, "Critical Biography of Ezra Pound," p. 1, citing a Pound letter of October 24, 1908.

11. Ezra Pound, "Anima Sola," in *A Lume Spento.*

12. Pound letter to William Carlos Williams, October 21, 1908, in Paige, *Selected Letters,* p. 4.

13. Pound letter to "Centrobus," almost certainly Barney Antrobus, n.d., 1909, unpublished, The George Arents Research Library, Syracuse University.

14. Ezra Pound, "The White Stag," in *Personae*, p. 25.

15. Pound letter to James G. Fairfax, February 16, 1909, unpublished, The George Arents Research Library, Syracuse University.

16. Stock, *Life of Ezra Pound*, p. 76, quoting Pound's letter to his mother.

17. Ibid., pp. 77–78; and Edwards, "Critical Biography of Ezra Pound," p. 63.

18. D. H. Lawrence letter to Louise Burrows, November 20, 1909, in James T. Boulton, ed. *The Letters of D. H. Lawrence* Vol. 1 (Cambridge: Cambridge University Press, 1979), p. 145. See also pp. 147–148.

19. Edwards, "Critical Biography of Ezra Pound," pp. 80, 82.

20. Stock, *Life of Ezra Pound*, pp. 98, 85.

21. Ezra Pound, "Cino," in *Personae*, p. 7.

22. Donald Hall, *Remembering Poets* (New York: Harper and Row, 1978), p. 117. Also Paul Rosenfeld, "The Case of Ezra Pound," *American Mercury* 78(1944):98–102.

23. Ezra Pound, "Erat Hora," in *Personae*, p. 40.

24. Ezra Pound, *The Spirit of Romance* (New York: New Directions, 1968). First published in 1910. See also Edwards, "Critical Biography of Ezra Pound," pp. 72–73.

25. Mary Catherine Flannery. *Yeats and Magic: The Earlier Works* (Gerrands Cross, England: Colin Smyth, 1977), p. 13.

26. The letter is from Yeats to John O'Leary, July 1892, in Allen Wade, *The Letters of W. B. Yeats* (London: Rupert Hart-Davis, 1954), p. 211. The account of raising the ghost of the flower is in Flannery, *Yeats and Magic*, p. 25. For good accounts of Yeats's beliefs in this area see also the articles by John L. Allen, George M. Harper, James Olney, and Weldon Thornton in *Studies in the Literary Imagination* 14(1981):1–76.

27. The Yeats quote is in Flannery, *Yeats and Magic* p. 18. The quote by the Yeats scholar is Weldon Thornton, "Between Circle and Straight Line: A Pragmatic View of W. B. Yeats and the Occult," *Studies in the Literary Imagination* 14(1981):61–76.

28. Flannery, *Yeats and Magic*, pp. 113, 133.

29. Ibid., pp. 138–139, 101, 45. Flannery clearly indicates that Yeats was referring to himself as the "man of genius."

30. Ezra Pound, "Histrion," originally published in October 1908 and reprinted in *A Quinzaine for this Yule* (London: Pollock & Co., 1908). See also Stock, *Life of Ezra Pound,* p. 92; and William French and Timothy Materer, "Far Flung Vortices and Ezra's 'Hindoo' Yogi," *Paideuma* 11(1982):39–53.

31. Flannery, *Yeats and Magic*, pp. 15, 47. Also Yeats letter to Olivia Shakespear, October 2 or 4, 1927, in Wade, *The Letters of W. B. Yeats*, p. 730. See also James Olney, "Sex and the Dead: 'Daimones' of Yeats and Jung," *Studies in the Literary Imagination* 14(1981):43–60.

32. Stock, *Life of Ezra Pound*, pp. 95–96, 100; Edwards, "Critical Biography of Ezra Pound;" p. 70.

33. The Lewis quote is from Wyndham Lewis, "Ezra, the Portrait of a Personality,"

Quarterly Review of Literature 5(1949):136–144. The Lawrence quote is from his letter to Grace Crawford, June 24, 1910, in Boulton, *Letters of D. H. Lawrence*, p. 165.

34. Edwards, "Critical Biography of Ezra Pound," p. 69, quoting Pound letter to his father, February 11, 1910.

35. Ibid., p. 70.

36. Stock, *Life of Ezra Pound*, pp. 109–110.

37. Ibid., p. 103, quoting Pound's letter to his mother.

38. Ezra Pound, "Blandula, Tenella, Vagula," originally published in 1911 in *Canzoni* and probably written while Pound was in Sirmione. In *Personae*, p. 39.

39. Ezra Pound, "The Flame," published in 1911 in *Canzoni*. In *Personae*, p. 50.

40. Stock, *Life of Ezra Pound*, pp. 83, 99.

41. Ibid., pp. 91, 103, 107, 109.

42. Ibid., pp. 102–104. For Lawrence quotes see his letter to Grace Crawford, June 24, 1910, in Boulton, *Letters of D. H. Lawrence*, p. 165.

43. William Carlos Williams (*Autobiography*, p. 90) says that Pound returned to the United States because he got jaundice. This seems very unlikely, given his leisurely trip home via Italy, and also because D. H. Lawrence in a letter of June 24, 1910 (Ibid.) explicitly noted that Pound's health was good.

44. Edwards, "Critical Biography of Ezra Pound," p. 83, quoting a *Book Review Digest* review. See also Stock, *Life of Ezra Pound*, pp. 113, 117.

45. Williams, *Autobiography*, p. 92. See also Robinson, *H. D.*, p. 24; and Stock, *Life of Ezra Pound*, p. 114.

46. The descriptions of Greenwich Village are from Robert A. Rosenstone, *Romantic Revolutionary: A Biography of John Reed* (New York: Vintage, 1975), pp. 100, 104; and from Justin Kaplan, *Lincoln Steffens: A Biography* (New York: Simon and Schuster, 1974), p. 199.

47. Bynner's description of Pound is in Witter Bynner, *Journey with Genius* (New York: John Day, 1951), p. 144. The account of the trip to Coney Island is in Ezra Pound, *Patria Mia* (London: Peter Owen, 1962), originally written and published in 1913 in *New Age*. The evening at the Poetry Society is described in Jessie Rittenhouse, *My House of Life* (Boston: Houghton Mifflin, 1934), p. 229.

48. The Wyndham Lewis quote is in Ford Madox Ford, *It Was the Nightingale* (New York: Octagon, 1975), p. 296. Originally published in 1933. The Williams descriptions are in Williams, *Autobiography*, pp. 91, 129; and in Whittemore, *William Carlos Williams*, p. 58.

49. Stock, *Life of Ezra Pound*, pp. 103, 121. Pound letter to William Carlos Williams, September 11, 1920, in Paige, *Selected Letters*, p. 158.

50. The Pound quotations are all taken from the original series of articles entitled "Patria Mia" and "America: Chances and Remedies," published in *New Age* September 5 to November 14, 1912, and May 1 to June 5, 1913. The edited version of these were later published as *Patria Mia* and included in Pound's *Selected Prose 1909–1965*, pp. 99–141.

51. See Hugh Kenner, *A Homemade World* (New York: Alfred A. Knopf, 1975), p. 4.

52. W. B. Yeats letter to J. B. Yeats, August 5, 1913, in Wade, *Letters of W. B. Yeats*, pp. 583–584. Also Flannery, *Yeats and Magic*, p. 128; and Edwards, "Critical Biography of Ezra Pound," p. 98.

53. Stock, *Life of Ezra Pound*, pp. 136–137, 133.

54. Ibid., p. 133.

55. Edwards, "Critical Biography of Ezra Pound," p. 122.

56. The details of Hilda Doolittle's arrival in London are in Robinson, *H. D.*, pp. 24–28. Pound's letter to Harriet Monroe, August 18, 1912, is in Paige, *Selected Letters*, pp. 9–10. See also Edwards, "Critical Biography of Ezra Pound," p. 123.

57. "His immense will power . . ." is from Heymann, *Ezra Pound*, p. 15. "Everybody's schoolmaster . . ." is from Norman, *Ezra Pound*, p. 199, quoting Iris Barry. The

Eliot quote is from Walter Sutton, ed., *Ezra Pound: A Collection of Critical Essays* (Englewood Cliffs, New Jersey: Prentice-Hall, 1963), p. 18. Phyllis Bottome's quote is from her *From the Life,* pp. 72, 74. John Quinn's quote is from Benjamin L. Reid, *The Man from New York* (New York: Oxford, 1968), p. 272; see also p. 491. John Cournos's quote is from his *Autobiography* (New York: G. P. Putnam, 1935), p. 235.

58. A reference to a meeting between Shaw and Pound in 1918 is found in Shaw's letter to Pound of March 14, 1918, Beinecke Rare Book and Manuscript Library, Yale University.

59. For the details on the Pound-Shaw dispute, see Stock, *Life of Ezra Pound,* pp. 78, 253, 300. Also Pound's letters to Michael Roberts, July 1937, and to Felix E. Schelling, July 8, 1922, in Paige, *Selected Letters,* pp. 296, 181.

60. For information on Wells, see Stock, *Life of Ezra Pound,* pp. 86, 273; and Pound's letter to Wells, February 3, 1940, in Paige, *Selected Letters,* p. 337. The descriptions of Yeats's soirées is in Douglas Goldring, *South Lodge* (London: Constable and Company, 1943), p. 49. For a good study of Yeats's beliefs, see Brenda S. Webster, *Yeats: A Psychoanalytic Study* (Stanford: Stanford University Press, 1973).

61. Information on Frost is in Stock, *Life of Ezra Pound,* pp. 208, 225. T. S. Eliot's "The Love Song of J. Alfred Prufrock" is in *The Complete Poems and Plays, 1909–1950* (New York: Harcourt, Brace and Company, 1952). Pound's letter to Harriet Monroe, September 30, 1914, is in Paige, *Selected Letters,* p. 40.

62. Williams, *Autobiography,* p. 228; Linda W. Wagner, ed., *Interviews with William Carlos Williams* (New York: New Directions, 1976), p. 80.

63. Williams's praise of Pound is in the following sources: James Laughlin, "Gists and Piths: From the Letters of Pound and Williams," *Poetry* 89(1982):229–243; William Carlos Williams, "Excerpts from a critical sketch: *A Draft of XXX Cantos* by Ezra Pound," in *Selected Essays of William Carlos Williams* (New York: New Directions, 1969), p. 108; Williams, "A-1 Pound Stein" in *Selected Essays,* pp. 162, 165; and William Carlos Williams, "Penny wise, Pound Foolish," *New Republic* 49(1939):229–30.

64. Williams, "Pound's Eleven New Cantos," in *Selected Essays,* p. 167; Laughlin, "Gists and Piths"; and William Carlos Williams, "Ezra Pound: His Exile as Another Poet Sees It," *New York Evening Post Literary Review* 7(1927):10.

65. Pound's assistance to Joyce is well described in Stock, *Life of Ezra Pound,* pp. 184, 228–229. Also see Edwards, "Critical Biography of Ezra Pound," p. 142.

66. Information on Rebecca West is found in Motley F. Deakin, *Rebecca West* (Boston: Twayne, 1980); and in Leslie Garis, "Rebecca West," *The New York Times Magazine,* April 4, 1982, pp. 30–99.

67. See Goldring, *South Lodge,* p. 47; and Stock, *Life of Ezra Pound,* pp. 164–165. The Pound–T. E. Lawrence meeting is referred to in Lawrence's letter, December 20, 1918, Beinecke Rare Book and Manuscript Library, Yale University.

68. Ezra Pound, "Middle-Aged," published in 1912 and in *Personae,* p. 236.

69. "Modern marriage . . ." is found in Pound's review of Allen Upward's *The Divine Mystery,* first published in *The New Freewoman,* November 15, 1913, reprinted in *Selected Prose,* p. 404. The recollections of Sophie Brzeska are from her diaries quoted by Timothy Materer, *Vortex: Pound, Eliot and Lewis* (Ithaca: Cornell University Press, 1979), pp. 74–75.

70. The descriptions of Dorothy Pound are found in Stock, *Life of Ezra Pound,* pp. 243, 304; Norman, *Ezra Pound,* p. 317; and Peter Ackroyd, *Ezra Pound and His World* (New York: Charles Scribner's Sons, 1980), p. 317.

71. Hugh Kenner, "D. P. Remembered," *Paideuma* 2(1973):485–493. Robinson, *H. D.,* pp. 24–25.

72. William B. Yeats, *A Vision* (New York: Macmillan, 1956), p. 27, first published in 1925; George M. Harper, "Unbelievers in the House: Yeats's Automatic Script," *Studies in the Literary Imagination* 14(1981):1–16. See also Stock, *Life of Ezra Pound,* pp. 220, 265; and Heymann, *Ezra Pound,* p. 16.

73. The cooking arrangement is described in Kenner, *The Pound Era*, p. 468. Pound's remark to Hemingway's wife is in Baker, *Ernest Hemingway*, p. 114.

74. Pound's income is mentioned in Catherine Seelye, ed., *Charles Olson and Ezra Pound* (New York: Grossman, 1975), p. 75. The use of Dorothy's income for joint expenses is confirmed by a conversation with Dorothy Pound in Edwards, "Critical biography of Ezra Pound," p. 147. The unhappiness of Mr. Shakespear is mentioned by Widdemer, *Golden Friends*, pp. 129–130.

75. Noel Stock, *Ezra Pound's Pennsylvania* (Toledo, Ohio: The Friends of the University of Toledo Libraries, 1976), quoting *The Philadelphia Press* March 26, 1914. Also Stock, *Life of Ezra Pound*, p. 192.

76. Stock, *Life of Ezra Pound*, pp. 127–128, quoting *The Philadelphia Evening Bulletin*, June 29, 1911.

77. Ibid., pp. 163–164, quoting *The Philadelphia Record*, January 5, 1913.

78. Seelye, *Charles Olson and Ezra Pound*, p. xxv.

79. William V. O'Connor, "What Does Mr. Pound Believe? *Saturday Review of Literature* 31 (September 4, 1948). The Laughlin quote is from an interview with Laughlin by FBI agents and is cited in Heymann, *Ezra Pound*, p. 133.

80. Norman, *Ezra Pound*, p. 413.

81. Lewis, "Ezra, the portrait of a personality," p. 137.

82. Nathaniel Weyl, "Treason," in William V. O'Connor and Edward Stone, *A Casebook of Ezra Pound* (New York: Thomas Y. Crowell, 1959); and an interview with James Laughlin by FBI agents cited in Heymann, *Ezra Pound*, p. 133.

83. Ezra Pound, "Redondillas," written in 1911 but not published until 1966. Quoted in Irvin Ehrenpreis, "Love, Hate and Ezra Pound" (review of *Ezra Pound* by Donald Davie), *New York Review of Books*, May 27, 1976, pp. 6–12.

84. Kavka, "Psychiatric Case History."

85. C. David Heymann, *American Aristocracy: The Lives and Times of James Russell, Amy, and Robert Lowell* (New York: Dodd Mead, 1980), p. 192.

86. Williams, *Autobiography*, p. 116.

87. Pound quotes are from "Studies in Contemporary Mentality," *New Age* 21(1917):465; Editorial, *Little Review* 4(1917):6; and "National Culture—A Manifesto 1938," in *Selected Prose*, p. 165.

88. Stock, *Life of Ezra Pound*, p. 36.

89. Pound, *Pavannes and Divagations*, p. 31.

90. Ezra Pound, "Patria Mia," *New Age* 11(1912):466. This sentence was deleted when "Patria Mia" was reprinted in later collections of Pound's work.

91. Ezra Pound, "Salutation the Third," *Blast* 1 (June 1914). In reprinted version of this poem the word "Jew" has been deleted and "pandars" and "big-bellies" inserted. See the poem in *Personae*, p. 145.

92. Goldring, *South Lodge*, pp. 71–72.

93. Hyam Maccoby, "The Jew as Anti-Artist: The Anti-Semitism of Ezra Pound," *Midstream* 22(1976):59–71.

94. Pound, *Pavannes and Divagations*, p. 56.

95. Pound letter to William Carlos Williams, September 11, 1920, in Paige, *Selected Letters*, pp. 157–159. The first quotation and the word "fahrt" in the second quotation were edited out of the published version. The letter is in the Poetry/Rare Book Collection, State University of New York at Buffalo.

96. See Mullins, *This Difficult Individual*, p. 113, quoting Lola Ridge in *The Little Review*, January 1919.

97. Reid, *Man from New York*, p. 438. See also Corrigan, "Literature and Politics."

98. See Heymann, *Ezra Pound*, p. 76; and Norman, *Case of Ezra Pound*, p. 24.

99. T. S. Eliot, *After Strange Gods* (London: Faber and Faber, 1934), p. 20. See also Chace, *Political Identities*, pp. xiii, 160.

100. Seelye, *Charles Olson and Ezra Pound*, p. 93.

101. Corrigan, "Literature and Politics." The source of the story was Elkin Mathews, Pound's first publisher in London.

102. Norman, *Ezra Pound*, p. 53, quoting Ford Madox Ford.

103. Douglas Goldring, *Odd Man Out* (London: Chapman and Hall, 1935), p. 118.

104. Stock, *Life of Ezra Pound*, p. 193.

105. Eric Homberger, "A Glimpse of Pound in 1912 by Arundel del Re," *Paideuma* 3(1974):85–88. This incident is also described by Brown ("Troubadour at Hamilton"), who wondered whether the food in the Hamilton College Commons might have given Pound his taste for rose petals.

106. Heymann, *Ezra Pound*, p. 17.

107. Ernest Rhys, *Everyman Remembers* (New York: Cosmopolitan Books, 1931), p. 244.

108. Norman, *Ezra Pound*, p. 174, quoting Richard Aldington.

109. Ford Madox Ford, *Return to Yesterday* (New York: Liveright, 1972), p. 373. Originally published in 1932.

110. Brigit Patmore, *My Friends When Young* (London: Heinemann, 1968), p. 110.

111. Violet Hunt, *I Have This to Say* (New York: Boni and Liveright, 1926), p. 114.

112. MacPherson, "Ezra Pound of Wyncote." See also Mullins, *This Difficult Individual*, p. 49.

113. Norman, *Case of Ezra Pound*, p. 84, quoting William Carlos Williams.

114. Heymann, *Ezra Pound*, p. 17.

115. Norman, *Ezra Pound*, p. 90.

116. Conrad Aiken letter to Harriet Monroe, January 1913, in Joseph Killorin, ed., *Selected Letters of Conrad Aiken* (New Haven: Yale University Press, 1978), p. 22.

117. Pound letter to Harriet Monroe, October 22, 1913, in Paige, *Selected Letters*, p. 13.

118. Stock, *Life of Ezra Pound*, p. 204, quoting Richard Aldington.

119. Ford Madox Ford, *Thus to Revisit* (New York: Octagon, 1966), p. 167. Originally published in 1921.

120. John G. Fletcher, *Life Is My Song* (New York: Farrar and Rinehart, 1937), pp. 74, 76.

121. Putnam, *Paris Was Our Mistress*, p. 141.

122. T. S. Eliot, "Ezra Pound," in Sutton, *Ezra Pound: A Collection of Critical Essays*, p. 18; D. H. Lawrence letter to Edward Garnett, December 30, 1913, in Harry T. Moore, ed., *The Collected Letters of D. H. Lawrence* (New York: Viking, 1962), p. 259.

123. Robert Frost letter to Ezra Pound, July 17, 1913, in Lawrance Thompson, ed., *Selected Letters of Robert Frost* (New York: Holt, Rinehart and Winston, 1964), pp. 85–86.

124. Frost letter to Sidney Cox, January 2, 1915, in Thompson, *Selected Letters of Robert Frost*, pp. 147–148.

125. Stock, *Life of Ezra Pound*, pp. 215–216, quoting *The Traid*, a New Zealand literary magazine; Bottome, *From the Life*, p. 71.

126. Ezra Pound, "Mr. Hueffer and the Prose Tradition in Verse," *Poetry* 4(1914):111.

127. Ezra Pound, "Meditatio." Originally published in *Lustra* in 1916, reprinted in *Personae*, p. 102.

128. Stock, *Life of Ezra Pound*, p. 234. Pound was making this assessment in November 1915.

129. Norman, *Ezra Pound*, p. 176. See also Materer, *Vortex*, p. 69.

130. Kenner, *Pound Era*, p. 255. See also Materer, *Vortex*, pp. 97, 103, 105.

131. Horace Brodsky, *Henri Gaudier-Brzeska, 1891–1915* (London: Faber and Faber, 1933), p. 81.

132. Norman, *Ezra Pound*, p. 176.

133. Brodsky, *Henri Gaudier-Brzeska*, pp. 58–60. Jacob Epstein in his *Autobiography* (London: Hulton Press, 1955, p. 45) also says that Pound asked that the head be made "virile."

134. Ezra Pound, *Gaudier-Brzeska: A Memoir* (Hessle, England: Marvell Press, 1960), p. 50. First published in 1916.

135. Kenner, *Pound Era*, p. 256.

136. Materer, *Vortex*, p. 94.
137. Norman, *Ezra Pound*, p. 176.
138. Pound, *Gaudier-Brzeska*, p. 48.
139. Edwards, "Critical Biography of Ezra Pound," p. 41. See also Stock, *Life of Ezra Pound*, pp. 183–184.
140. Kenner, *Pound Era*, p. 266.
141. Bottome, *From the Life*, p. 74.
142. Ezra Pound, "Coitus," in *Personae*, p. 110.
143. Ezra Pound, "Fratres Minores." Published in *Blast*, June 1914, reprinted in *Personae* p. 148.
144. Materer (*Vortex*, pp. 72–73) relates the conversation between Pound and Sophie Brezska in which Pound describes the kind of women he admires. The poem is "Homage to Quintus Septimius Florens Christianus," first published in 1915 and reprinted in *Personae*, p. 165.
145. Pound letters to William Carlos Williams, October 6, 1916, and March 5, 1926, both unpublished. The first is in the Poetry/Rare Books Collection, State University of New York at Buffalo; the second is in the Beinecke Rare Book and Manuscript Library, Yale University.
146. The background information on Wyndham Lewis is in Jeffrey Meyers, *The Enemy: A Biography of Wyndham Lewis* (London: Routledge and Kegan Paul, 1980), p. 55. Lewis's description and second meetings with Pound are in his *Blasting and Bombardiering* (London: Calder and Boyars, 1967). Originally published in 1937.
147. Lewis's complimentary description of Pound is in *Blasting and Bombardiering*, p. 288. Descriptions of Lewis's vanity are in Meyers, *The Enemy*, pp. 28, 44. The Goldring description is in *South Lodge*, pp. 39–40.
148. Lewis's description of women is in Meyers, *The Enemy*, pp. 57, 88; his beliefs about veneral disease on pp. 70, 91; and the description of the Lewis-Cunard meeting on pp. 91–92. Agnes Bedford letter to Pound is in the Beinecke Rare Book and Manuscript Library, Yale University.
149. See the Pound-Lewis correspondence in the Department of Rare Books, Cornell University, especially the letters of December 3, 1924, and January 13, 1918. The phallic quality of Lewis's portrait of Pound is also cited in Materer, *Vortex*, p. 94.
150. The description of Frieda Strindberg is in Meyers, *The Enemy*, p. 36. The episode when she turned the customer away is in Stock, *Life of Ezra Pound*, p. 181. See also Goldring, *South Lodge*, p. 70.
151. The Lewis quote is from Materer, *Vortex*, pp. 47–48, quoting Geoffrey Wagner, *Wyndham Lewis* (New Haven: Yale University Press, 1957), p. 35. See also Wendy S. Flory, *Ezra Pound and the Cantos: A Record of Struggle* (New Haven: Yale University Press, 1980), p. 65.
152. The Pound letter to Quinn is quoted in Reid, *Man From New York*, p. 252. The other information on Vorticism is from Materer, *Vortex*, pp. 20–22; this book is also an excellent source of information about the Rebel Art Center and *Blast*. Other good sources are Meyers, *The Enemy*, pp. 52, 67; Goldring, *South Lodge*, p. 70; and French and Materer, "Far Flung Vortices."
153. The Ford episode is described in Meyers, *The Enemy*, p. 30. The Lewis-Hulme confrontation is also in this book, p. 54.
154. Descriptions of Amy Lowell can be found in Heymann, *American Aristocracy*, and in Jean Gould, *Amy: The World of Amy Lowell and the Imagist Movement*, (New York: Dodd Mead and Company, 1975). The account of the cigars is on p. 119.
155. Heymann, p. 192 gives Lowell's description of Pound in a letter to Harriet Monroe. See also Norman, *Ezra Pound*, p. 101.
156. Amy Lowell letter to Harriet Monroe, September 15, 1914, in Harley F. MacNair, ed., *Florence Ayscough and Amy Lowell: Correspondence of a Friendship* (Chicago: University of Chicago Press, 1945) p. 253.
157. Edwards, "Critical Biography of Ezra Pound," p. 148.

158. Amy Lowell letter to Harriet Monroe, September 15, 1914, in MacNair, *Florence Ayscough and Amy Lowell.* p. 253. Miss Lowell's account of these events in corroborated by John Fletcher (*Life Is My Song,* pp. 147–151) and also by Jessie Rittenhouse (*My House of Life,* pp. 267–269).

159. Fletcher, *Life Is My Song,* pp. 147–151.

160. Edwards, "Critical Biography of Ezra Pound," p. 151.

161. Fletcher, *Life Is My Song,* p. 151.

162. Amy Lowell letter to Harriet Monroe, September 15, 1914, in MacNair, *Florence Ayscough and Amy Lowell.* p. 255.

163. Pound letter to Harriet Monroe, January 1915, in Paige, *Selected Letters,* p. 48. See also Louis Untermeyer, *From Another World* (New York: Harcourt, Brace, 1939), p. 108.

164. Rittenhouse, *My House of Life,* p. 269; and Stock, *Life of Ezra Pound,* p. 206.

165. Stock, *Life of Ezra Pound,* p. 203, quoting the Prothero letter of October 22, 1914.

166. Kenner, *Pound Era,* p. 244. Also Materer, *Vortex,* p. 218.

167. Stock, *Life of Ezra Pound,* pp. 212–213. See also Edwards, "Critical Biography of Ezra Pound," p. 157.

168. Edwards, "Critical Biography of Ezra Pound," p. 213, quoting Pound's article in *The Drama* 18(1915):210.

169. Pound letter to Wyndham Lewis, July 18, 1916, unpublished, Department of Rare Books, Cornell University Library. See also Stock, *Life of Ezra Pound,* p. 234.

170. Ezra Pound, "Literary prizes," *Poetry* 7(1915):304–305.

171. Stock, *Life of Ezra Pound,* p. 221, quoting Pound article on the Renaissance in *Poetry,* 1915.

172. F. S. Flint, "The History of Imagism," *Egoist,* May 1, 1915. The Aldington quote is from "The Poetry of Ezra Pound" in the same issue.

173. Stock, *Life of Ezra Pound,* p. 216, quoting F. S. Flint's letter to Pound of July 1915.

174. Ibid., quoting Pound letter of November 1914.

175. Ibid., p. 238. Stock says that this occurred either during the winter of 1914–15 or that of 1915–16; given the war climate in England it could have been either.

176. Pound letter to Wyndham Lewis, June 24, 1916, unpublished, Department of Rare Books, Cornell University Library.

177. Seelye, *Charles Olson and Ezra Pound,* p. 45.

178. Pound, *Gaudier-Brzeska.*

179. Pound letter to Milton Bronner, September 21, 1915, unpublished, Humanities Research Center, The University of Texas at Austin. See also Stock, *Life of Ezra Pound,* p. 230.

180. Ezra Pound, "Hugh Selwyn Mauberley." Published in 1917, reprinted in *Personae,* p. 191.

181. Ezra Pound, "Et Faim Sallir Le Loup des Boys," *Blast,* July 1915. For the citation of T. S. Eliot's poem titled "Bullshit" see Meyers, *The Enemy,* p. 76.

182. Ezra Pound, "Monumentum Aere, Etc." *Blast,* July 1915, reprinted in *Personae,* p. 146.

183. Ezra Pound, "Chronicles," *Blast,* July 1915, p. 85.

184. Pound letter to the Editor, *Boston Evening Transcript,* August 1915, in Paige, *Selected Letters,* p. 63.

185. Pound letter to John Quinn, July 13, 1915, in Reid, *Man From New York,* p. 223.

186. Pound, *Gaudier-Brezska,* pp. 45–46.

187. Pound letter to Milton Bronner, September 21, 1915, (see n. 179). See also Flory, *Ezra Pound and the Cantos,* p. 89.

188. Moni Moulik, "The 'Insane' Poet," *The Visva-Bharati Quarterly* 16(1950):31–38.

189. Pound letter to Wyndham Lewis, January 25, 1949, quoted by Materer, *Vortex,* p. 63. See also Stock, *Life of Ezra Pound,* p. 178; and Mullins, *This Difficult Individual,* p. 114.

190. Lewis letters to Pound, August and September 1917, in W. K. Rose, ed., *The Letters*

of Wyndham Lewis (New York: New Directions, 1963), pp. 90, 94; Stock, *Life of Ezra Pound*, p. 207; Pound letter to Wyndham Lewis, July 18, 1916, unpublished, Department of Rare Books, Cornell University Library.

191. Reid, *Man From New York*, p. 272, quoting a 1917 letter from Yeats's sister.

192. Edwards, "Critical Biography of Ezra Pound," p. 223. See also Stock, *Life of Ezra Pound*, pp. 254–256.

193. Ezra Pound in *The Little Review* 4 (May 1917):3.

194. Edwards, "Critical Biography of Ezra Pound," pp. 223–224, quoting *The Little Review* 4(1917):27.

195. Letters, *The Little Review* 5(1917):32 and 9(1918):56. See also Stock, *Life of Ezra Pound*, p. 256.

196. Ben Hecht, "Pounding Ezra," *The Little Review* (November 1918), pp. 37–41.

197. Edwards, "Critical Biography of Ezra Pound," pp. 229–230.

198. Conrad Aiken, "A Pointless Pointillist," *Dial* (1918), p. 306.

199. Louis Untermeyer, "Ezra Pound—Poseur," *New Republic* 16(1918):83–84.

200. H. L. Mencken letter to Louis Untermeyer, August 21, 1918, in Guy J. Forgue, ed., *Letters of H. L. Mencken* (New York: Alfred A. Knopf, 1961), p. 127.

201. Richard Aldington, *Life for Life's Sake* (New York: Viking, 1941), p. 216.

202. Fletcher, *Life Is My Song*, p. 72.

203. See Ford, *It Was The Nightingale*, p. 204: Stock, *Life of Ezra Pound*, p. 200; and Norman, *Ezra Pound*, p. 122.

204. Materer, *Vortex*, p. 199, quoting Pound letter to Wyndham Lewis, no date.

205. Stock, *Life of Ezra Pound*, p. 283. See also Reid, *Man From New York*, p. 406.

206. Stock, *Life of Ezra Pound*, p. 293; Kavka, "Psychiatric Case History," refers to the libel suit.

207. Stock, *Life of Ezra Pound*, p. 364, quoting Pound.

208. Ezra Pound, "The Age Demanded" in "Hugh Selwyn Mauberley." Published in 1920, reprinted in *Personae*, p. 202.

209. Emanuel Carnevali, "Invitation," *Poetry* 16(1920):211–221.

210. Ford, *Thus to Revisit*, p. 167, and Mary Sinclair, "The reputation of Ezra Pound," *North American Review* 211(1920):658–668.

211. John G. Fletcher, "Some Contemporary Poets," *Casebook: A Monthly Miscellany* 11(1920):23–25.

212. Aldington, *Life for Life's Sake*, p. 255.

213. W. K. Rose, "Ezra Pound and Wyndham Lewis: The Crucial Years," *Southern Review* 4(1968)72–89, describing a conversation Pound had with Wyndham Lewis in 1919. Pound's comment about being disliked is from his letter to William Carlos Williams, September 11, 1920, in Paige, *Selected Letters*, p. 158.

214. Ackroyd, *Ezra Pound and His World*, p. 55.

215. Pound letter to William Carlos Williams, September 11, 1920, in Paige, *Selected Letters*, p. 157.

216. Fletcher, *Life Is My Song*, p. 284.

217. Ezra Pound, "Hudson: Poet Strayed into Science," *The Little Review*, May-June 1920. Reprinted in *Selected Prose*, p. 429.

218. Pound letter to John Drummond, February 18, 1932, in Paige, *Selected Letters*, p. 239; Peter Brooker, *A Student's Guide to the Selected Poems of Ezra Pound* (London: Faber and Faber, 1979), p. 259. Pound also verifies this in an unpublished letter to Ford Madox Ford, November 16, 1934, Department of Rare Books, Cornell University Library.

CHAPTER 4: A POUND OF FLESH

1. Ford's comment is in his *Thus to Revisit*, p. 168. Pound's appraisal of Paris is found in his Paris letters in *Dial*, 69(1920):406–411, 515–518, 635–639, and 72(1922):188.

His quote about civilization is from the *English Journal* 19(1930):698–699, found in Edwards, "Critical Biography of Ezra Pound," pp. 277–278.

2. Robert Motherwell, ed., *The Dada Painters and Poets: An Anthology* (New York: Wittenborn, Schultz, 1951), p. 102. Most of my information on Dadaism is from this source.

3. Ibid., pp. 75, 92.

4. Alan Young, *Dada and After: Extremist Modernism and English Literature* (Manchester: Manchester University Press, 1981), pp. 82–87; Ezra Pound, "The Island of Paris: A Letter," *Dial* 69(1920):406.

5. The descriptions of the Dada Festival are in Motherwell, *Dada Painters and Poets*, pp. 184–185; and Hans Richter, *Dada: Art and Anti-Art* (New York, Oxford University Press, 1975), pp. 180–182. Additional information on Pound's relationship to Dada, including the description of the Baroness, is found in Andrew Clearfield, "Pound, Paris and Dada," *Paideuma* 7(1978):112–140.

6. Information on the Barrès trial is from Motherwell, *Dada Painters and Poets*, pp. 116, 184–185; and Richter, *Dada*, p. 184. Pound mentioned the trial in his "Paris Letter," *Dial* 71(1921):456–463 and confirmed that he attended in his article, "For a New Paideuma," *Criterion*, January 1938, reprinted in *Selected Prose*, p. 287.

7. Malcolm Cowley, "Fox in Flight," *Furioso* 6(1951):7–10.

8. Pound, "Paris Letter," *Dial* 72(1922):337. For accounts of the famous editing of *The Waste Land*, see Heymann, *Ezra Pound*, pp. 52–53; and Stock, *Life of Ezra Pound*, p. 306.

9. Norman, *Ezra Pound*, p. 246, quoting Scofield Thayer; Williams, *Autobiography*, pp. 253–254.

10. Gertrude Stein, *The Autobiography of Alice B. Toklas* (New York: Harcourt, Brace, 1933), p. 246.

11. Stock, *Life of Ezra Pound*, p. 287.

12. Ernest Hemingway letter to Sherwood Anderson, March 9, 1922, in Carlos Baker, ed., *Ernest Hemingway: Selected Letters* (New York: Charles Scribner's Sons, 1981), p. 62.

13. Hemingway, *Moveable Feast*, p. 109.

14. Stock, *Life of Ezra Pound*, p. 396.

15. Hemingway, *Moveable Feast*, p. 134. See also H. M. Hurwitz, "Hemingway's Tutor, Ezra Pound," *Modern Fiction Studies* 17(1971–72):469–482.

16. Hemingway, *Moveable Feast*, pp. 107–108.

17. Ford, *It Was the Nightingale*, pp. 107–108.

18. Hemingway, *Moveable Feast*, p. 93.

19. Stock, *Life of Ezra Pound*, p. 299.

20. Robert McAlmon, *Being Geniuses Together: 1920–1930* (New York: Doubleday, 1968) p. 219. For a favorable review of Pound's opera in the *Paris Tribune*, see George Antheil, "Why a Poet Quit the Muses," in Hugh Ford, ed., *The Left Bank Revisited: Selections from the Paris Tribune 1917–1934* (University Park, Pa: State University Press, 1972), pp. 210–212.

21. Materer, *Vortex*, p. 64, quoting George Antheil, *Bad Boy of Music* (London: Hurst and Blackett, 1947), p. 11.

22. See Ford, *It Was the Nightingale*, p. 283 for a description of this. Pound said that he was arrested in a statement he made to psychiatrists at Saint Elizabeths; see Kavka, "Psychiatric Case Study."

23. George Wickes, *American in Paris* (New York: Doubleday, 1969), p. 207.

24. The description of the performance is a composite of information found in the following sources: Roger Fuller in the *Paris Tribune*, January 21, 1925, quoted in Ford, *Left Bank Revisited*, pp. 212–213, 220–221; Kaplan, *Lincoln Steffens*, p. 290; Norman, *Ezra Pound*, pp. 279–280; and Materer, *Vortex*, p. 65.

25. Lewis, *Blasting and Bombardiering*, p. 238; Norman, *Ezra Pound*, pp. 254, 266. For a good overview of Paris at this time see Hugh Ford, *Published in Paris* (London: Garnstone Press, 1975), and Ford, *Left Bank Revisited*.

26. Hemingway, *Moveable Feast*, pp. 143–146; and Ford, *Published in Paris*, p. 63.

27. The information on Robert McAlmon is in Waverley Root, "Montparnasse Memories: Robert McAlmon," *International Herald Tribune*, July 17–18, 1982, p. 5-W. Lincoln Steffens's characterization of Gertrude Stein is in Kaplan, *Lincoln Steffens*, p. 263. Hemingway's remark is in *Moveable Feast*, pp. 18–20. The Wyndham Lewis incident is mentioned in Richard Ellmann, *James Joyce* (New York: Oxford, 1959), p. 530. Nancy Cunard's attachments are catalogued in Meyers, *The Enemy*, p. 95. Miss Cunard is said to have been Huxley's model for Lady Tantamount in *Point Counter Point.*

28. The details of these various alliances can be found in Robinson, *H. D.;* and Ford, *Published in Paris*, pp. 37ff. The allusion to the writer who was suspected of running off with his own daughter-in-law is in a letter from John Cournos to Pound, January 18, 1938, Beinecke Rare Book and Manuscript Library, Yale University.

29. Putnam, *Paris Was Our Mistress*, pp. 89–90.

30. For accounts of Natalie Barney and Pound see George Wickes, *The Amazon of Letters: The Life and Loves of Natalie Barney* (New York, G. P. Putnam, 1976), and Richard Sieburth, "Ezra Pound Letters to Natalie Barney," *Paideuma* 5(1976):279–299. See also Stock, *Life of Ezra Pound*, pp. 308, 402; Stephen Longstreet, *We All Went to Paris* (New York: Macmillan, 1972), pp. 338–339; and Williams, *Autobiography*, pp. 228–229.

31. Fletcher, *Life Is My Song*, p. 71. See also Mullins, *This Difficult Individual*, p. 46.

32. Margaret Anderson, *My Thirty Years' War* (New York: Horizon, 1969), p. 243.

33. Fletcher, *Life Is My Song*, p. 71.

34. Widdemer, *Golden Friends*, p. 71.

35. Rosenfeld, "Case of Ezra Pound."

36. Widdemer, *Golden Friends*, p. 131.

37. Ibid., p. 130.

38. Anderson, *My Thirty Years' War*, pp. 243–244.

39. McAlmon, *Being Geniuses Together*, p. 100. Another description of this incident is in Jane Lidderdale and Mary Nicholson, *Dear Miss Weaver* (London: Faber and Faber, 1970), pp. 246–247.

40. Norman, *Ezra Pound*, p. 247.

41. Widdemer, *Golden Friends*, p. 131.

42. Cournos, *Autobiography*, p. 235.

43. Corrigan, "Literature and Politics," p. 466, quoting a 1922 letter by Pound.

44. Pound letter to Harriet Monroe, July 16, 1922, in Paige, *Selected Letters*, p. 182.

45. Pound, "Paris Letter," *Dial* 74(1923):275.

46. Meyers, *The Enemy*, p. 32; Chace, *Political Identities*, p. 75. See also Janet Flanner, *Paris Was Yesterday, 1925–1939* (New York: Viking, 1972), p. xvii.

47. Cowley, "Fox in Flight." p. 7.

48. Lewis, *Time and Western Man*, pp. 41–42.

49. Ezra Pound, "Paris Letter," *Dial* 74(1923):276.

50. McAlmon, *Being Geniuses Together*, p. 258.

51. Hemingway, *Moveable Feast*, p. 134.

52. McAlmon, *Being Geniuses Together*, p. 258.

53. Rosenfeld, "Case of Ezra Pound," p. 356.

54. Pound letter to William Carlos Williams, October 26, 1912, unpublished, Poetry/ Rare Book Collection, State University of New York at Buffalo.

55. Stock, *Life of Ezra Pound*, p. 171.

56. In the *Fortnightly Review*, December 1915. See William V. O'Connor, *Ezra Pound* (Minneapolis: University of Minnesota Press, 1963), p. 28.

57. Richard Sieburth, *Instigations: Ezra Pound and Rémy De Gourmont* (Cambridge: Harvard University Press, 1978), p. 136, quoting de Gourmont. For the discussion of de Gourmont I am heavily indebted to this book.

58. Ezra Pound, postscript to *The Natural Philosophy of Love* by Rémy De Gourmont, dated

June 21, 1921, and originally published in 1932. Reprinted in *Pavannes and Divagations*, pp. 203–213.

59. Ezra Pound, "The New Therapy," *New Age* 30(1922):259–260.
60. Pound, *Spirit of Romance*, p. 94.
61. Ibid., p. 92. See also Alan Durant, *Ezra Pound: Identity in Crisis* (Brighton, Sussex: Harvester Press, 1981), pp. 146–147.
62. Ezra Pound, "The Divine Mystery," *The New Freewoman*, November 15, 1913, reprinted in *Selected Prose*, p. 403.
63. Pound, Postscript to *Natural Philosophy;* Pound letter to William Carlos Williams, October 21, 1908, (see Chapter 3, n. 12); Pound letter to "Centrobus," (see Chapter 3, n. 13).
64. Pound, "Praise of Ysolt."
65. Ezra Pound, "Phanopoeia." Originally published in *Lustra* in 1915, reprinted in *Personae*, p. 169.
66. James J. Wilhelm, *The Later Cantos of Ezra Pound* (New York: Walker, 1977), p. 36.
67. Pound, "The Flame." See also Kevin M. Oderman, "The Servant of Amor in Pound's Early Poems," *Paideuma* 8(1979):389–403.
68. Norman, *Ezra Pound*, p. 233, quoting Mina Loy.
69. Stock, *Life of Ezra Pound*, p. 317 n.
70. Baker, *Ernest Hemingway: Selected Letters*, p. 79.
71. Stock, *Life of Ezra Pound*, p. 293.
72. Oderman, "The Servant of Amor."
73. Ezra Pound, "Homage To Sextus Propertius." Originally published in 1917, reprinted in *Personae*, p. 217.
74. Ford, *Published in Paris*, p. 103; Stock, *Life of Ezra Pound*, pp. 306–307, 360. See also Flory, *Ezra Pound and the Cantos*, p. 136.
75. The information on Olga Rudge comes from Levy, "Ezra Pound's Voice of Silence," and Ford, *Left Bank Revisited.* Wyndham Lewis letter to John Quinn, September 3, 1919, in Rose, *Letters of Wyndham Lewis*, p. 111.
76. Kenner, *Pound Era*, p. 388.
77. Stock, *Life of Ezra Pound*, p. 319.
78. Norman, *Ezra Pound*, p. 249.
79. Pound, *Guide to Kulchur*, p. 300.
80. Lorenz, "Ezra Pound at Hamilton College."
81. Pound letter to Viola Baxter Jordan, (see Chapter 2, n. 100).
82. Ezra Pound, writing under the pseudonym Bastien von Helmholtz, "On the Imbecility of the Rich," *Egoist* 1(1914):389. Pound letter to Harriet Monroe, January 20, 1914, in Paige, *Selected Letters*, p. 30.
83. Ezra Pound letter to Harriet Monroe, July 16, 1922, in Paige, *Selected Letters*, p. 183.
84. Pound, "Allen Upward Serious," *New Age*, April 23, 1914. Reprinted in *Selected Prose*, p. 407.
85. Ezra Pound, "Meditatio," *Egoist* 3(1916):37.
86. Pound letter to H. L. Mencken, September 27, 1916, in Paige, *Selected Letters*, p. 97.
87. Pound, "Paris Letter," *Dial* 72(1922):71–78. Pound letter to Harriet Monroe September 16, 1922, in Paige, *Selected Letters*, p. 183.
88. Barbara Anne Charlesworth, "The Tensile Light: A Study of Ezra Pound's Religion." Master's thesis, University of Miami, 1957, p. 6.
89. Flory, *Ezra Pound and the Cantos*, p. 33.
90. Ezra Pound, "Ecclesiastical History," *The New English Weekly*, July 5, 1934. Reprinted in *Selected Prose*, p. 61.
91. Charlesworth, "The Tensile Light," p. 6. Quoting Pound.
92. Flory, *Ezra Pound and the Cantos*, p. 18.

93. Pound, "The Wings" and "Ver Novum."
94. Pound, "Hugh Selwyn Mauberley."
95. Ezra Pound, "Religio or, The Child's Guide to Knowledge." Originally published in 1918, reprinted in *Selected Prose*, p. 47.
96. Pound, "Homage to Sextus Propertius," pp. 220–221.
97. Ibid., p. 217. For a cogent analysis of Pound's views of the female body see Kevin Oderman, " 'Cavalcanti': That the Body Is Not Evil," *Paideuma* 11(1982):257–279.
98. Stock, *Life of Ezra Pound,* p. 307.
99. Pound, "Histrion."
100. Pound, "Comraderie," in *A Lume Spento.*
101. The astrological calendar is in *The Little Review* (Spring 1922); Materer, *Vortex,* p. 138.
102. Pound, "The New Sculpture," *Egoist* 1(1914):67–68; Chace, *Political Identities,* p. 14, quoting Pound.
103. Pound writing under the pseudonym Bastien von Helmholtz, "The Bourgeoisie," *Egoist* 1(1914):53. Also Alan Holder, *Three Voyagers in Search of Europe* (Philadelphia: University of Pennsylvania Press, 1966), p. 50, quoting Pound.
104. Pound letter to Felix E. Schelling, July 8, 1922, in Paige, *Selected Letters,* p. 181.
105. Pound, "The New Sculpture."
106. Pound, "Paris Letter," *Dial* 74(1923):279.
107. Harrison, *The Reactionaries,* p. 119, quoting a Pound letter of December 19, 1913.
108. Pound, "Indiscretions." In reviewing this book Carnevali called it "The statute of the American-English elite." See Carnevali, "Irritation."
109. Pound, "Paris Letter," *Dial* 73(1922):550.
110. Ibid., p. 549.
111. Hemingway letter to Pound, January 23, 1923, in Baker, *Ernest Hemingway: Selected Letters,* p. 76.
112. See Baker, *Ernest Hemingway: Selected Letters,* p. 86.
113. Hemingway letter to Bernard Berenson, March 20–22, 1953, in Baker, *Ernest Hemingway: Selected Letters,* p. 815.
114. Hemingway letter to Pound, March 17, 1924, in Baker, *Ernest Hemingway: Selected Letters,* p. 112.
115. Pound letter to William Carlos Williams, February 2, 1921, in Paige, *Selected Letters,* p. 165.
116. Stock, *Life of Ezra Pound,* pp. 309–310.
117. Pound letter to William Carlos Williams, March 18, 1922, in Paige, *Selected Letters,* p. 173.
118. Pound, "Paris Letter," *Dial* 73(1922):551.
119. Pound letter to William Carlos Williams, March 18, 1922, (see n. 117).
120. Pound letter to Kate Buss, May 12, 1923, in Paige, *Selected Letters,* p. 186. Pound also discusses the firing in his letter to Ford Madox Ford, May (n.d.) 1923, unpublished, Department of Rare Books, Cornell University Library.
121. Pound letter to Felix E. Schelling, July 8, 1922, (see n. 104), p. 179.
122. Pound letter to R. P. Blackmur, November 30, 1924, in Paige, *Selected Letters,* p. 190.
123. Andrew Clearfield, "Pound, Paris and Dada," *Paideuma* 7(1978):113–140. See also Ackroyd, *Ezra Pound and His World,* p. 69.
124. Ford, *It Was The Nightingale,* p. 333.
125. Information on the Pound-Steffens friendship is in Kaplan, *Lincoln Steffens,* p. 263; Mary Collum, *Life and the Dream* (Garden City, N.Y.: Doubleday, 1947), p. 307.
126. Lincoln Steffens, *Autobiography* (New York: The Literary Guild, 1931), p. 834.
127. Williams, *Autobiography,* p. 226.

CHAPTER 5: FATHERHOOD AND FASCISM

1. Ackroyd, *Ezra Pound and His World,* p. 73; de Rachewiltz, *Discretions;* and Olga Rudge letter to Ronald Duncan, May 20, 1948, unpublished, Humanities Research Center, The University of Texas at Austin.

2. Stock, *Life of Ezra Pound,* p. 448.

3. Ibid., p. 334.

4. Heymann, *Ezra Pound,* p. 349. It may have been 1929 when Pound saw Omar again if Stock is correct; see his *Life of Ezra Pound,* pp. 361, 367.

5. The Pound-Williams correspondence demonstrates this. Most of the letters between them are in the Poetry/Rare Book Collection, State University of New York at Buffalo, and in the Beinecke Rare Book and Manuscript Library, Yale University.

6. Patmore, *My Friends When Young,* p. 99.

7. Stock, *Life of Ezra Pound,* p. 454; Omar Pound letter to St. Elizabeths Hospital, April 18, 1946, St. Elizabeths Hospital Pound file number 54; and Heymann, *Ezra Pound,* p. 57.

8. William B. Yeats, *A Vision* (New York: Macmillian, 1938), p. 3. "Ode on a Grecian Urn" is in *The Complete Poetry and Selected Prose of John Keats* (New York: Modern Library, 1951), pp. 294–295.

9. See Stephen Shorter, "Pound in Exile," *Intro* 1(1951):165–168; Stock, *Life of Ezra Pound,* p. 383; Putnam, *Paris Was Our Mistress,* p. 148; and Jean Untermeyer, *Private Collection* (New York: Alfred A. Knopf, 1965), p. 212.

10. Donald Hall, "Ezra Pound Said to Be a Publisher," *New York Times Book Review,* August 23, 1981, pp. 13–23. Quoting James Laughlin.

11. Elizabeth Delehanty, "A Day with Ezra Pound," *The New Yorker* 16(1940):92–95.

12. Stock, *Life of Ezra Pound,* p. 398.

13. Ibid., p. 332.

14. Ibid., p. 339.

15. Ackroyd, *Ezra Pound and His World,* p. 82.

16. T. S. Eliot, "Isolated Superiority," *Dial* 84(1928):7.

17. Norman, *Ezra Pound,* p. 290; and Stock, *Life of Ezra Pound,* p. 345.

18. K. L. Goodwin, *The Influence of Ezra Pound* (London: Oxford, 1966), p. 50, quoting G. Westcott, "A Courtly Poet," *Dial* 74(1925):501. Also Maurice Lesemann, "Mr. Pound and the Younger Generation," *Poetry* 30(1927):216–227.

19. Ethel Moorhead, "Ezra Pound and *The Exile,*" *This Quarter* 3(1927):282–285. Pound letter to Harriet Monroe, November 30, 1926, in Paige. *Selected Letters,* p. 205.

20. Leonard Greenbaum, *The Hound and Horn* (London: Mouton, 1966), p. 113, quoting Pound letter of June 29, 1930. Pound letter to Glenn Hughes, September 26, 1927, in Paige, *Selected Letters,* p. 212.

21. Brown, "A Troubadour at Hamilton," p. 53.

22. Untermeyer, *Private Collection,* p. 213.

23. Ann Chisholm, *Nancy Cunard: A Biography* (New York: Alfred A. Knopf, 1979), p. 127.

24. Stock, *Life of Ezra Pound,* p. 386; and Pound letter to Ford Madox Ford, n.d., 1925, unpublished, Department of Rare Books, Cornell University Library.

25. The Yeats incident is described in Norman, *Ezra Pound,* p. 299. See also Richard Ellmann, *Eminent Domain* (New York: Oxford, 1967), p. 81; and Alexander N. Jefferes, *W. B. Yeats: Man and Poet* (New Haven: Yale University Press, 1949), pp. 254, 285. Putnam's assessment is found in *Paris Was Our Mistress,* p. 151.

26. Behrman, *Portrait of Max,* p. 280.

27. Hemingway's comments are in Norman, *Ezra Pound,* p. 278 and in a letter to Archibald MacLeish, November 22, 1930 in Baker, *Ernest Hemingway: Selected Letters,* p. 331. MacLeish's assessments are in letters to Hemingway of February 14, 1927 and Febru-

ary 20, 1927 in R. H. Winnick, *Letters of Archibald MacLeish* (Boston: Houghton Mifflin, 1983), pp. 196, 200.

28. Stock, *Life of Ezra Pound*, p. 336. Quoting James Joyce's letter to Harriet Weaver, February 1, 1927.

29. Pound's letter of nomination is quoted in Stock, *Life of Ezra Pound*, pp. 326–327. His letter informing Lewis is November 23, 1925, in the Department of Rare Books, Cornell University Library. Lewis's attack is in his *Time and Western Man*, pp. 41, 69. See also Stock, *Life of Ezra Pound*, pp. 343–344.

30. Ezra Pound, Editorial, *The Exile*, number 3, 1928.

31. Pound letter to William Bird, March 4, 1927, in Paige, *Selected Letters*, p. 208. See also Putnam, *Paris Was Our Mistress*, p. 149.

32. Chute, "In Commemeration"; Stock, *Life of Ezra Pound*, p. 404; Louis Dudek, *DK/Some Letters of Ezra Pound* (Montreal: DC Books, 1974), p. 32.

33. See Pound's letters to Wyndham Lewis, n.d., 1952, and another with no date, Department of Rare Books, Cornell University Library.

34. Stephen Adams, "Pound, Olga Rudge, and The 'Risveglio Vivaldiano,'" *Paideuma* 4(1975):111–118. Pound's claim to have saved the Vivaldi manuscripts has been repeated by many of Pound's biographers.

35. Stock, *Life of Ezra Pound*, p. 430.

36. Hall, *Remembering Poets*, p. 124.

37. Pound letter to Joseph G. MacLeod, March 28, 1936, in Paige, *Selected Letters*, p. 279.

38. Putnam, *Paris Was Our Mistress*, p. 146.

39. Norman, *Ezra Pound*, p. 279.

40. Durant, *Ezra Pound: Identity in Crisis*, p. 100.

41. Ezra Pound, "Terra Italica." Published in *New Review*, Winter 1931–1932, reprinted in *Selected Prose*, p. 56. "Pecten" means pubic bone in Latin and "cteis" is a Greek word for genitalia. See also Oderman, "Servant of Amor."

42. This stationery was used on many Pound letters of this period. See also French and Materer, "Far Flung Vortices."

43. Pound, "Religio." Published in *The Townsman*, November 1939, reprinted in *Selected Prose*, p. 70.

44. Pound, "Terra Italica," p. 58.

45. Flory, *Ezra Pound and the Cantos*, p. 140.

46. Surette, *Light from Eleusis*, p. 65, gives an excellent analysis of this.

47. Pound letter to Homer Pound, April 11, 1927, in Paige, *Selected Letters*, p. 210.

48. For an extensive discussion of Douglas's theories see Earle Davis, *Vision Fugitive: Ezra Pound and Economics* (Lawrence, Kansas: University of Kansas Press, 1968).

49. Norman, *Ezra Pound*, p. 226, discussing Pound's review. Pound, "Hudson," *Little Review*, May/June 1920, reprinted in *Selected Prose*, p. 430. Stock, *Life of Ezra Pound*, p. 296.

50. Pound quotes are from "Murder by Capital," *Criterion* 12(1933):49, 590, reprinted in *Selected Prose*, p. 227. See also Heymann, *Ezra Pound*, p. 33, quoting Pound.

51. Edwards, "Critical Biography of Ezra Pound," p. 231.

52. This was included in the biographical data supplied by Pound for *Ezra Pound: Selected Poems* (New York: New Directions, 1957).

53. Ezra Pound, "Paris letter," *Dial* 72(1921):188.

54. Stock, *Life of Ezra Pound*, p. 350, quoting Pound's letter to Nicholas M. Butler, June 18, 1928.

55. Ibid., pp. 365–366; Norman, *Ezra Pound*, p. 377. See also Pound, "History and Ignorance," in *Selected Prose*, p. 267.

56. Pound's focus on 1913 as a turning point in American history recurs throughout his later writings. See for example his letter to Forrest Read, July 23, 1950, in the Hamilton College Library.

57. Pound letter to W. H. D. Rouse, December 30, 1934, in Paige, *Selected Letters*, p. 263.
58. Pound, *Jefferson and/or Mussolini*, p. 70.
59. Pound letter to Archibald MacLeish, October 24, no year, unpublished. Manuscript Division, The Library of Congress.
60. Pound, "Paris Letter," *Dial* 73(1922):333.
61. Ezra Pound, "Credit and the Fine Arts," *New Age* 30(1922):284; Putnam, *Paris Was Our Mistress*, p. 154, quoting Pound.
62. Pound, "Murder by Capital."
63. Pound letter to Edward A. Filene, April 21, 1931, unpublished. The George Arents Research Library, Syracuse University.
64. Victor Ferkiss, "Ezra Pound and American Fascism," *Journal of Politics* 17(1955):173–197.
65. Stock, *Life of Ezra Pound*, pp. 335, 352, 374. Pound, "The State," published in *Exile*, Spring 1927, reprinted in *Selected Prose*, p. 214. See also Pound, "Bureaucracy the Flail of Jehovah," in *Exile*, Autumn 1928, reprinted in *Selected Prose*, p. 217.
66. Pound letter to Michael Gold, August 27, 1930, in the Humanities Research Center, The University of Texas at Austin. Michael Gold letter to Pound in *New Masses*, September 1931.
67. Pound letter to Harriet Monroe, November 30, 1976, in Paige, *Selected Letters*, p. 205.
68. See Stock, *Life of Ezra Pound*, p. 390; and Heymann, *Ezra Pound*, pp. 317–327.
69. Stock, *Life of Ezra Pound*, pp. 379, 388.
70. Ibid., pp. 389–391; Dudek, *DK/Some Letters of Ezra Pound*, p. 33; and Heymann, *Ezra Pound*, p. 147.
71. Pound, *Jefferson and/or Mussolini*, pp. 11–12, 19.
72. See Davis, *Vision Fugitive*, p. 168; and Alastair Hamilton, *The Appeal of Fascism* (New York: Macmillan, 1971), p. 257. See also Norman, *Ezra Pound*, p. 178.
73. Stock, *Life of Ezra Pound*, p. 426; and Heymann, *Ezra Pound*, p. 76, quoting Pound 1935 writings.
74. Some of the Mosley-Pound correspondence is in the Beinecke Rare Book and Manuscript Library, Yale University. The reference to the meeting between Mosley and Pound is in Oswald Mosley, *My Life* (New Rochelle, New York: Arlington House, 1968), p. 226. Mosley says he was 40 when he met Pound; since he was born in 1896 that would place the meeting in about 1936.
75. Ezra Pound, "What Is Money For?" published as a pamphlet in 1939, reprinted in *Selected Prose*, p. 300. See also Ferkiss, "Ezra Pound and American Fascism."
76. Ferkiss, "Ezra Pound and American Fascism," p. 190.
77. Chute, "In Commemoration," p. 12.
78. James Laughlin, "A Portrait of Ezra Pound," *The University Review* 6(1939):111–119.
79. Hamilton, *The Appeal of Fascism*, p. 287, quoting Pound.
80. See Norman, *Ezra Pound*, p. 294; and Pound, *Guide to Kulchur*, p. 352.
81. The information on Frobenius is from Janheinz Jahn, *Leo Frobenius: The Demonic Child* (Austin, Texas: University of Texas African and Afro-American Studies and Research Center, 1974), pp. 13–17. See also Norman, *Ezra Pound*, p. 301.
82. Harrison, *The Reactionaries*, p. 125, quoting Pound.
83. Pound, *Jefferson and/or Mussolini*, p. 34.
84. Ibid., p. 127.
85. Pound letter to Wyndham Lewis, February 7/8, 1939, unpublished. In The Department of Rare Books, Cornell University Library.
86. The FBI Pound files claim that Pound received free passes for the railroads. Most Pound biographies say he only received a reduced fare.
87. Pound, "What Is Money For?" and Heymann, *Ezra Pound*, p. 78.
88. See Pound letter to Wyndham Lewis, March 12, 1939, Department of Rare Books, Cornell University; Pound letter to Professor Ibbotson, July 14, 1939, in V. I. Mon-

dolfo and M. Hurley, ed., *Letters to Ibbotson 1935–1952* (Orono, Maine: University of Maine Press, 1978), p. 100; Pound letter to Odon Por quoted in Heymann, *Ezra Pound*, p. 97; and Pound letter to "Germany and You," July 1937, Beinecke Rare Book and Manuscript Library, Yale University.

89. Geoffrey Wagner, *Wyndham Lewis: A Portrait of The Artist as the Enemy* (New Haven: Yale University Press, 1957), p. 81. Also see Pound letter to Wyndham Lewis, February 7/8, 1939, Department of Rare Books, Cornell University.

90. Ezra Pound, "ABC of Economics," published in 1933, reprinted in *Selected Prose*, p. 262.

91. Pound, *Jefferson and/or Mussolini*, p. 67.

92. Romano Bilenchi, "Rapallo 1941," *Paideuma* 8(1979):431–442.

93. Pound, *Guide to Kulchur*, pp. 105–106. An excellent analysis of this aspect of Pound's thinking is provided in Flory, *Ezra Pound and the Cantos*, p. 17.

94. The information on *The Protocols of Zion* is taken from John Gwyer, *Portraits of Mean Men: A Short History of the Protocols of the Elders of Zion* (London: Cobden-Sanderson, 1938); John S. Curtiss, *An Appraisal of the Protocols of Zion* (New York: Columbia University Press, 1942); and Colin Cross, *The Fascists in Britain* (New York: St. Martin's Press, 1963).

95. Norman, *Ezra Pound*, p. 177.

96. Pound's "Kongo Roux" is reprinted in Clearfield, "Pound, Paris and Dada," p. 135. Young suggests that the poem is a pastiche of quotes from Pound's letters to Francis Picabia; see Young, *Dada and After*. The other Pound quotes are from "The Individual in his Milieu," in *The Criterion*, October 1935, reprinted in *Selected Prose*, p. 274; *Guide to Kulchur*, p. 336; and Pound's letter to Wyndham Lewis, February 7/8, 1939. Department of Rare Books, Cornell University.

97. Pound, "What Is Money For?" p. 299.

98. Gwyer, *Portraits of Mean Men*, p. 11.

99. See Hamilton, *The Appeal of Fascism*, p. xix; and Heymann, *Ezra Pound*, p. 78. In Canto 52 Pound attributes an anti-Semitic remark to Mussolini.

100. Cross, *The Fascists in Britain*, p. 122.

101. The Pound-Leese letters, including Pound's defense of his genetic stock, are in the Beinecke Rare Book and Manuscript Library, Yale University. See also Stock, *Life of Ezra Pound*, p. 437; and Cross, *The Fascists in Britain*, p. 122.

102. William Carlos Williams letter to Pound, March 1926, in John C. Thirlwall, ed., *The Selected Letters of W. C. Williams* (New York: McDowell and Obolensky, 1957), pp. 69–70. Williams letter to Pound, April 6, 1940, unpublished, in the Beinecke Rare Book and Manuscript Library, Yale University.

103. For the influence of *The Protocols of Zion* on Hitler and Himmler see Lucy S. Dawidowicz, *The War Against the Jews: 1933–1945* (New York: Holt, Rinehart and Winston, 1975), pp. 16, 71. The Stock quote is in *Life of Ezra Pound*, p. 441.

104. Ezra Pound, "The Revolution Betrayed," *British Union Quarterly* 2(1938):36–48.

105. Pound letter to Mike Gold, August 27, 1930, Humanities Research Center, The University of Texas at Austin.

106. Stock, *Life of Ezra Pound*, p. 441, quoting Pound.

107. Pound letters to Henry Swabey, March 3, 1935, and December 19, 1936, in Paige, *Selected Letters*, pp. 270, 285.

108. Pound, "The Individual in his Milieu," p. 273.

109. Pound, *Guide to Kulchur*, p. 256.

110. Goldring, *South Lodge*, pp. 71–72.

111. Pound letters to W. H. D. Rouse, December 30, 1934, and to Felix E. Schelling, April 1934, in Paige, *Selected Letters*, pp. 256, 262. See also Putnam, *Paris Was Our Mistress*, pp. 158–159.

112. Pound letter to Wyndham Lewis, February 8, 1939, unpublished, Department of Rare Books, Cornell University Library.

113. Pound letter to Wyndham Lewis, February 7/8, 1939, Department of Rare Books, Cornell University Library.

114. Pound letter to William Carlos Williams, February 8, 1936, unpublished, Poetry/ Rare Books Collection, State University of New York at Buffalo.

115. Ibid.

116. William Carlos Williams letter to Pound, February 27, 1936, unpublished, Beinecke Rare Book and Manuscript Library, Yale University.

117. Pound, *Guide to Kulchur*, p. 256. See also Flory, *Ezra Pound and the Cantos*, p. 33.

118. Records of physical examination, St. Elizabeths Hospital.

119. Norman, *Ezra Pound*, p. 78.

120. See Stock, *Life of Ezra Pound*, pp. 400, 413; Norman, *Ezra Pound*, p. 347; and Chace, *Political Identities*, p. 61.

121. See Phyllis Bottome's letter to President Roosevelt, 1935, promoting Social Credit, and Pound's letter to Albert Einstein, February 6, 1934, Beinecke Rare Book and Manuscript Library, Yale University. Also see Pound's letter to Robert McAlmon, February 2, 1934, in Paige, *Selected Letters*, p. 252.

122. See Harrison, *The Reactionaries*, p. 116; Stock, *Life of Ezra Pound*, p. 405; and Pound, "Murder by Capital."

123. Pound letter to Harriet Monroe, September 14, 1933, in Paige, *Selected Letters*, p. 247.

124. Pound letter to "Centrobus" (see Chapter 3, n. 13).

125. Horace Gregory and Marya Zaturenska, *A History of American Poetry 1900–1940* (New York: Harcourt, Brace, 1942), p. 163; Chace, *Political Identities*, p. 86; John Mayfield, *The Black Badge of Treason* (Washington: Park Book Shop, 1944), p. 12, quoting Philip Guedalla.

126. See Stock, *Life of Ezra Pound*, pp. 408–409, 413.

127. E. P. Walkiewicz, "Back to ABC: A Report on the Sixth International Ezra Pound Conference," *Paideuma* 10(1981):173–180.

128. Pound's defense of Mussolini's invasion is found in his letter to the Animal Defense Society, November 14, 1935, Beinecke Rare Book and Manuscript Library, Yale University. Pound's reference to Ethiopians as "black Jews" is reflected in Nancy Cunard's letter to Pound in which she discusses Pound's letter to her of December 25, 1935, in Hugh D. Ford, *Nancy Cunard: Brave Poet, Indomitable Rebel 1896–1965* (Radnor, Pa.: Chilton, 1968), pp. 359–361. There is in fact a very small group of Ethiopians, the Falashas, who claim to be the lost tribe of Israel, and it may be this group that led Pound to his conclusion. See also Stock, *Life of Ezra Pound*, p. 416.

129. Walkiewicz, "Back to the ABC."

130. Heymann, *Ezra Pound*, p. 77.

131. See Norman, *Ezra Pound*, pp. 294–295; and Pound, "Paris Letter," *Dial* 74(1923):278.

132. Pound, "Bureaucracy the Flail of Jehovah."

133. Stock, *Life of Ezra Pound*, pp. 408, 414. See also Pound's letter to Archibald MacLeish, November 22, 1934, Manuscript Division, Library of Congress, in which Pound praises Roosevelt.

134. Pound letter to Ford Madox Ford, January 31, 1939, unpublished, Department of Rare Books, Cornell University. Pound letter to Samuel Putnam, January 6, no year, unpublished, Humanities Research Center, The University of Texas at Austin.

135. For the comparison between Pound and the Old Testament prophets I am indebted to James J. Wilhelm, *"Il Miglior Fabbro"* (Orono, Maine: National Poetry Foundation, 1982), p. 91.

136. Heymann, *Ezra Pound*, p. 94, quoting Pound's letter to J. D. Ibbotson, November 4, 1939.

137. Pound letter to Archibald MacLeish, January 7, 1934, unpublished, Manuscript Division, Library of Congress.

138. Pound letter to Irita Van Doren, n.d., unpublished, Manuscript Division, Library of Congress.
139. Stock, *Life of Ezra Pound*, p. 260.
140. See Richard M. Ludwig, *Letters of Ford Madox Ford* (Princeton: Princeton University Press, 1965), p. 260.
141. Pound letter to Stanley Nott, n.d., unpublished, Humanities Research Center, The University of Texas at Austin. Pound letter to Wyndham Lewis, February 20, 1929, unpublished, Department of Rare Books, Cornell University Library.
142. Eric Homberger, ed., *Ezra Pound: The Critical Heritage* (London: Routledge and Kegan Paul, 1972), quoting Pound, "Reply," in *New English Review*, October 12, 1933. Pound, *Guide to Kulchur*, p. 186.
143. Norman, *Ezra Pound*, p. 322.
144. Pound letter to E. E. Cummings, April 6, 1933, in Paige, *Selected Letters*, p. 244.
145. Pound letter to Wyndham Lewis, March 30, no year, unpublished. Department of Rare Books, Cornell University Library.
146. H. L. Mencken letter to Pound, November 28, 1936, in Forgue, *Letters of H. L. Mencken*, pp. 410–411.
147. H. L. Mencken letters to Pound, November 15, 1934, and March 1, 1937, in Carl Bode, *The New Mencken Letters* (New York: Dial Press, 1977), pp. 328–329, 404–405.
148. Pound letter to Felix E. Schelling, April, 1934, in Paige, *Selected Letters*, p. 255.
149. Robert Frost letter to Louis Untermeyer, February 5, 1938, in Robert Frost, *The Letters of Robert Frost to Louis Untermeyer* (London: Jonathan Cape, 1964), p. 304.
150. William Carlos Williams letter to Pound, April 6, 1938, unpublished, Beinecke Rare Book and Manuscript Library, Yale University.
151. Ford Madox Ford letter to Pound, February 17, 1937, in Ludwig, *Letters of Ford Madox Ford*, pp. 270–272. Arthur Mizener, *The Saddest Story: A Biography of Ford Madox Ford* (New York: World Publishing Company, 1971), pp. 445–446.
152. Ford letter to Pound, March 9, 1938, in Ludwig, *Letters of Ford Madox Ford*, pp. 289–290.
153. Ford letter to Pound, March 16, 1938, in Ludwig, *Letters of Ford Madox Ford*, p. 292. Also see Brita Lindberg-Seyersted, "Letters from Ezra Pound to Joseph Brewer," *Paideuma* 10(1981):369–382.
154. William B. Yeats letter to Ethel Mannin, April 8, 1938, in Wade, *Letters of W. B. Yeats*, p. 851. Yeats's poem "The Second Coming" is found in *Yeats Selected Poetry* (London: Pan Books, 1974), pp. 99–100.
155. Pound letter to Wyndham Lewis, March 2, 1939, unpublished, Department of Rare Books, Cornell University Library. Pound also implied to friends he visited in America that the Fascists had paid for his trip. See, for example, Jordan, "The Last Trouba-dor," p. 126, and also the FBI file on Pound.
156. Norman, *Ezra Pound*, p. 357.
157. Stock, *Life of Ezra Pound*, p. 460. See also Jordan, "Last Troubador."
158. Pound letter to Wyndham Lewis, September 11, 1939, unpublished, Department of Rare Books, Cornell University.
159. Jordan, "Last Troubador," and Heymann, *Ezra Pound*, pp. 85–86.
160. Pound's suggestion of trading Guam for films of Noh plays can be found in Laughlin, "Gists and Piths." That it was a serious suggestion is confirmed by Pound's letter to the *Japan Times and Advertiser*, May 4, 1941, Beinecke Rare Book and Manuscript Library, Yale University. See also Stock, *Life of Ezra Pound*, pp. 454–455.
161. FBI file on Pound.
162. William Carlos Williams letter to Robert McAlmon, May 25, 1939, in Thirlwall, *Selected Letters of W. C. Williams*, pp. 177–178. Ford Madox Ford letter to Allen Tate, May 3, 1939, in Ludwig, *Letters of Ford Madox Ford*, p. 319.
163. Jordan, "Last Troubadour."
164. FBI file on Pound, interview by FBI agents of one of Pound's hostesses during his 1939 trip.

165. Jordan, "Last Troubadour."
166. William Carlos Williams letter to James Laughlin, June 7, 1939, in Thirlwall, *Selected Letters of W. C. Williams*, pp. 183–184.
167. FBI file on Pound.
168. Putnam, *Paris Was Our Mistress*, p. 58.
169. The original invitation from President Cowley to Pound, April 7, 1939, is in the Beinecke Rare Book and Manuscript Library, Yale University. Pound's letter to Ibbotson is in Pound, *Letters to Ibbotson*, pp. 94–95.
170. Norman, *Ezra Pound*, p. 368.
171. Ibid., p. 367; and Stock, *Life of Ezra Pound*, p. 415.
172. Accounts of the commencement luncheon may be found in Norman, *Ezra Pound*, p. 370; and in Stock, *Life of Ezra Pound*, pp. 466–467. President Cowley's letter to Pound suggesting that Kaltenborn had intentionally provoked him is July 11, 1939, Beinecke Rare Book and Manuscript Library, Yale University.

CHAPTER 6: TREASON

1. Stock, *Life of Ezra Pound*, p. 467. The letter from Jay Bradley to Pound, July 20, 1939, explaining Wiseman's background, is in the Beinecke Rare Book and Manuscript Library, Yale University.
2. Pound letter to Wyndham Lewis, September 11, 1939, unpublished, Department of Rare Books, Cornell University Library.
3. See Stock, *Life of Ezra Pound*, p. 470.
4. H. L. Mencken letters to Pound in Bode, *The New Mencken Letters*, pp. 452, 461; and in Forgue, *Letters of H. L. Mencken*, p. 438.
5. Pound quoted in files of the FBI.
6. Heymann, *Ezra Pound*, p. 97, quoting Pound letters to Odon Por.
7. Stock, *Life of Ezra Pound*, p. 490, quoting Pound's article in the *Japan Times*, August 12, 1940. Heymann, *Ezra Pound*, p. 96, quoting Pound's article in the *Japan Times*, July 22, 1940.
8. Pound letters to Mr. Philipps, American Ambassador to Italy, February 5, 1940, and March 1, 1940, Beinecke Rare Book and Manuscript Library, Yale University. The Italian article was in *Meridano di Roma*, March 24, 1940, and is summarized by Stock, *Life of Ezra Pound*, p. 490.
9. Pound letter to Ronald Duncan, March 14, 1940, in Paige, *Selected Letters*, p. 341; Corrigan, "Literature and politics," n. 60, quoting a letter from Pound to Henry Swabey, February 28, 1940; Pound letter to Henry Swabey, May 9, 1940, in Paige, *Selected Letters*, p. 345.
10. Pound letter to Henry Swabey, May 9, 1940, in Paige, *Selected Letters*, p. 345.
11. H. L. Mencken letter to Pound, April 15, 1940, in Bode, *The New Mencken Letters*, p. 461.
12. See Hall, *Remembering Poets*, p. 240; and Stock, *Life of Ezra Pound*, pp. 484–485.
13. Tim Redman, "The Repatriation of Pound, 1939–1942," *Paideuma* 8(1979):447–457.
14. Pound letter to Kitue Kitasono, October 29, 1940, in Paige, *Selected Letters*, p. 346.
15. C. H. Douglas letter to Pound, February 22, 1935, Beinecke Rare Book and Manuscript Library, Yale University. The encouragement of the Nazi officer is in Johnson, "Pound, Accused of Treason."
16. FBI files on Pound.
17. The assessment of the radio gift is in Wickes, *The Amazon of Letters*, p. 193. Pound's letter to Ronald Duncan, March 31, 1940, is in Paige, *Selected Letters*, p. 342. See also Heymann, *Ezra Pound*, p. 92.
18. Harry Meacham, *The Caged Panther: Ezra Pound at St. Elizabeths* (New York: Twayne, 1967), pp. 19–22.

19. Redman, "Repatriation of Pound," p. 450.
20. Norman, *Ezra Pound*, p. 384, quoting *The Philadelphia Record*, November 29, 1945.
21. Robert A. Corrigan, "Ezra Pound and the Italian Ministry for Popular Culture," *Journal of Popular Culture* 6(1972)767–781.
22. Ackroyd, *Ezra Pound and His World*, p. 83; Stock, *Life of Ezra Pound*, p. 499; and FBI files on Pound.
23. Corrigan, "Literature and Politics."
24. FBI files on Pound. See also Heymann, *Ezra Pound*, p. 109.
25. Ibid, p. 103.
26. Williams, *Autobiography*, p. 316. E. E. Cummings letter to Pound, October 8, 1941, in Frederick W. Dupree and George Stade, eds., *Selected Letters of E. E. Cummings* (New York: Harcourt, Brace and World, 1969).
27. Robinson, *H. D.*, p. 19.
28. Pound, Those parentheses, radio speech of December 7, 1941. In Doob, *Ezra Pound Speaking*, pp. 20–22.
29. Herman A. Sieber, "The Medical, Legal, Literary and Political Status of Ezra Weston (Loomis) Pound (1885–   ). Selected Facts and Comments" (Washington, D.C.: Library of Congress Legislation Reference Service, 1958), p. 31. This is usually referred to as the Sieber report.
30. Eleanor and Reynolds Packard, *Balcony Empire* (New York: Oxford University Press, 1942), pp. 250–251.
31. Redman, "Repatriation of Pound," quoting a Pound letter to Adriano Ungaro, December 9, 1941.
32. *Ibid.*, quoting a Pound letter to Adriano Ungaro, December 12, 1941.
33. Pound, "On Resuming," radio speech of January 29, 1942. In Doob, *Ezra Pound Speaking*, pp. 23–27.
34. Redman, "Repatriation of Pound." The fact that his daughter Mary did not have a passport, and presumably would have had difficulty getting one because of her illegitimacy, is thought by some to have played a significant role in Pound's decision to remain in Italy. See, for example, James Laughlin's letter to Dorothy Pound, January 6, 1972, in the Lilly Library, Indiana University. In early 1939 Pound had explored the possibilities of legally adopting Mary; see Pound's correspondence with Joseph H. Cochran, May 16, 1939, in the Beinecke Rare Book and Manuscript Library, Yale University.
35. Redman, "Repatriation of Pound," quoting Pound letters to Cornelio di Marzio December 28, 1941 and to Odon Por, December 29, 1941.
36. "Retirement," *Time*, January 26, 1942, pp. 53–54.
37. Pound, "On Resuming."
38. Pound radio broadcasts are reprinted from Heymann, *Ezra Pound* pp. 116–120, except the broadcast of April 9, 1942 which is from the FBI files on Pound. Transcripts of many of Pound's broadcasts are available at the Library of Congress.
39. Bilenchi, "Rapallo 1941." The interviews for the article actually took place in February and March 1942. See David Anderson, "Letter to the Editor," *Paideuma* 9(1980):401–402.
40. See Heymann, *Ezra Pound* p. 144; Doob, *Ezra Pound Speaking*, p. xi; and the Pound file of the Department of Justice. Pietro Squarcio is acknowledged to be Pound in the FBI files on Pound.
41. Stock, *Life of Ezra Pound*, p. 506.
42. Bilenchi, "Rapallo 1941."
43. FBI files on Pound, quoting an Italian friend.
44. The Pound files of the Department of Justice and FBI detail recording dates and receipts of money paid to Pound. See also Doob, *Ezra Pound Speaking*, pp. xi–xii.
45. Dorothy Pound letter to Nancy Cunard, August 21, 1948 or 1949, Humanities Research Center, The University of Texas at Austin.

46. Pound letter to William Joyce, July 18, 1941, Beinecke Rare Book and Manuscript Library, Yale University.

47. For references to Pound's letters using "Heil Hitler" and a swastika, see Chapter 5, n. 90. Pound's praise of *Mein Kampf* is found in an April 24, 1942, letter to "Pel" (probably Camillo Pellizzi) in the FBI file on Pound. His characterization of Hitler as a "saint and martyr" is in the interview he gave to the reporter from the *Chicago Sun;* see Johnson, "Pound, Accused of Treason."

48. Stock, *Life of Ezra Pound,* p. 491; Pound letter to Shakespear and Parkyn, October 5, 1945, in Cornell, *Trial of Ezra Pound,* p. 9; Corrigan, "Literature and Politics."

49. Notes made by Huntington Cairns following an interview with Pound in March 1949, in the Cairns file, Manuscript Division, Library of Congress.

50. Isaiah Berlin letter to Denis Goacher, June 16, 1953, Humanities Research Center, The University of Texas at Austin.

51. Dorothy Pound letter to Nancy Cunard, August 21, 1948 or 1949, Humanities Research Center, The University of Texas at Austin.

52. Shea and Romano, "The Pound-Williams conference."

53. Bilenchi, "Rapallo 1941."

54. David Anderson, "Review of A. Jung and G. Palandri, *Italian Images of Ezra Pound: Twelve Critical Essays,*" *Paideuma* 10(1981):439–443.

55. Pound file of the Department of Justice.

56. "Six on Radio for Axis Facing Indictments," *New York Times,* January 14, 1943, p. 1.

57. William Carlos Williams letter to Robert McAlmon, January 19, 1943, in Thirlwall, *Selected Letters of W. C. Williams,* pp. 211–213.

58. Dorothy F. Green, Memorandum on Ezra Pound to William E. Foley, May 10, 1956, in the Pound file, Department of Justice. The memorandum quotes interviews with Italian radio technicians.

59. Pound radio broadcasts are reprinted from Heymann, *Ezra Pound,* pp. 120–121, and also from the FBI files on Pound.

60. Heymann, *Ezra Pound,* p. 114.

61. Corrigan, "Pound and the Italian Ministry for Popular Culture," p. 774.

62. Heymann, *Ezra Pound,* p. 136.

63. Joseph Cary, reviewing Doob's *Ezra Pound Speaking, Paideuma* 9(1980):211–213.

64. See correspondence between George Biddle and Pound in the Manuscript Division, Library of Congress. See also George Biddle, *Artist at War* (New York: Viking, 1944), pp. 70–71.

65. William L. Shirer, "The American Radio Traitors," *Harpers,* October 1943, pp. 397–404.

66. Ibid. See also "Allies in Italy Hold George Nelson Page," *New York Times,* July 16, 1944, p. 17.

67. Heymann, *Ezra Pound,* pp. 136–138.

68. De Rachewiltz, *Discretions,* p. 187, 245.

69. For an account of Mussolini's rescue see William L. Shirer, *The Rise and Fall of the Third Reich* (New York: Simon and Shuster, 1959), p. 1304. The characterization of Mussolini's supporters is found in Denis Mack Smith, *Italy: A Modern History* (Ann Arbor: University of Michigan Press, 1969), p. 490.

70. For accounts of Italian Jews during the war see Nora Levin, *The Holocaust: The Destruction of European Jewry 1933–1945* (New York: Schocken Books, 1973), p. 465; Martin Gilbert, *Auschwitz and the Allies* (New York: Holt, Rinehart and Winston, 1981), p. 157; and Daniel Carpi, "The Origins and Development of Fascist Anti-Semitism in Italy, 1922–1945, in Yisrael Gutman and Livia Rothkirchen, eds., *The Catastrophe of European Jewry* (Jerusalem: Yad Vashem, 1976), pp. 292–297.

71. Brendan Jackson, "Seventh International Ezra Pound Conference, University of Sheffield, 11–14 April 1981," *Paideuma* 11(1982):157–166. See also Stock, *Life of Ezra*

Pound, p. 516; and Heymann, *Ezra Pound*, p. 153. Heymann's information came from Pound's daughter, Mary de Rachewiltz. The episode of the Italian girl is described in Barbara C. Eastman, "The Gap in the Cantos: 72 and 73," *Paideuma* 8(1979):415–427. See also Seelye, *Charles Olson and Ezra Pound*, pp. 69–70.

72. Heymann, *Ezra Pound*, p. 142.

73. Ezra Pound, *Impact: Essays on Ignorance and the Decline of American Civilization* (Chicago: Henry Regnery, 1960), p. 195. See also Pound, "An Introduction to the Economic Nature of the United States," published in Italian; translated, revised, and reprinted in *Selected Prose*, pp. 167–185.

74. Pound, "Introduction to the Economic Nature of the United States." Also Heymann, *Ezra Pound*, p. 143, quoting Pound's letter to Fernando Mazzasoma, November 1944.

75. Heymann, *Ezra Pound*, p. 149, quoting the FBI file on Pound. The reference to "Russian Jewocracy" is apparently an allusion to the belief held by Hitler and many top Nazis that the Jewish conspiracy outlined in *The Protocols of Zion* was being assisted by Communists in Russia. For a discussion of this see George L. Mosse, *Toward the Final Solution: A History of European Racism* (New York: Howard Fertig, 1978), p. 179.

76. Heymann, *Ezra Pound*, p. 145; Norman, *Ezra Pound*, p. 380. Ciano had been a friend of Pound's and the two had corresponded regularly in the 1930s; these letters are in the Beinecke Rare Book and Manuscript Library, Yale University.

77. Pound's call for Churchill's execution is found in the FBI file on Pound, quoting a 1940 Pound statement. His willingness to assist in the shooting of Norman is in his letter to James Farrell, February 23, 1934, in the Van Pelt Library, The University of Pennsylvania.

78. FBI file on Pound; and Pound's letter to Natalie Barney, December 25, 1943, Beinecke Rare Book and Manuscript Library, Yale University.

79. Heymann, *Ezra Pound*, p. 150; see also the FBI file on Pound.

80. Stock, *Life of Ezra Pound*, p. 519; Heymann, *Ezra Pound*, p. 140.

81. Heymann, *Ezra Pound*, p. 144; and Smith, *Italy*, p. 491.

82. The length of time during which Pound lived together with Dorothy and Olga varies according to the source. Mary de Rachewiltz, Ezra and Olga's daughter, says this arrangement existed for almost two years (*Discretions*, p. 258). Dorothy claims it was for only a year (Dorothy Pound letter to Ronald Duncan, July 15, 1945, Humanities Research Center, The University of Texas at Austin). A letter in the FBI file on Pound from "J. B." to Pound, May 25, 1944, states that "I am sorry to hear that you have to move," thereby supporting Dorothy Pound's dating of the move.

83. De Rachewiltz, *Discretions*, p. 258. See also Dorothy Pound's letters to Ronald Duncan, September 15, 1945, and to Rose Marie Duncan, November 28, 1947, Humanities Research Center, The University of Texas at Austin. See also Hugh Kenner, "D. P. Remembered," *Paideuma* 2(1973):485–493.

84. Stock, *Life of Ezra Pound*, p. 519. Also see "Allies in Italy Hold George Nelson Page," *New York Times*, July 16, 1944, p. 17.

85. William Carlos Williams letter to Robert McAlmon, January 19, 1943, in Thirlwall, *Selected Letters of W. C. Williams*, pp. 211–213.

86. Ernest Hemingway letter to Archibald MacLeish, May 5, 1943, in Baker, *Ernest Hemingway: Selected Letters*, pp. 544–545.

87. William Carlos Williams letter to Robert McAlmon, February 23, 1944, in Thirlwall, *Selected Letters of W. C. Williams*, p. 220.

88. Ernest Hemingway letter to Allen Tate, August 31, 1943, in Baker, *Ernest Hemingway: Selected Letters*, pp. 549–550.

89. Archibald MacLeish letter to Hemingway, July 27, 1943, in Winnick, *Letters of Archibald MacLeish*, p. 316. Hemingway's reply of August 10, 1943 is in Baker, *Ernest Hemingway: Selected Letters*, p. 548.

90. Ernest Hemingway letter to Allen Tate, August 31, 1943, in Baker, *Ernest Hemingway:*

Selected Letters, pp. 549–550. MacLeish's letter to Harvey H. Bundy, September 10, 1943, is in Winnick, pp. 317–318.

91. George H. Tichenor, "This Man Is a Traitor." *P. M.*, August 15, 1943, pp. 3–5.
92. Mayfield, *Black Badge of Treason*, pp. 5, 15.
93. Stock, *Life of Ezra Pound*, pp. 519–520. See also the FBI file on Pound.
94. Anthony J. Joes, *Mussolini* (New York: Franklin Watts, 1982), pp. 361–363.
95. De Rachewiltz, *Discretions*, pp. 241–242. See also Kenner, *Pound Era*, p. 470.

CHAPTER 7: THE NON-TRIAL

1. Ben D. Kimpel and T. C. Duncan Eaves, "More on Pound's Prison Experience," *American Literature* 53(1981):469–467.
2. "Poet Ezra Pound Flown Here to Answer Treason Charges," *Washington Post*, November 19, 1945, p. 1.
3. Seelye, *Charles Olson and Ezra Pound*, p. 45, quoting Caresse Crosby's recollection of Pound's statement, January 1946.
4. Dorothy F. Green memorandum to William E. Foley, (see Chapter 6, n. 58).
5. Kimpel and Eaves, "More on Pound's Prison Experience," quoting memorandum of Brigidiar General John M. Weir, July 3, 1945. "Seek Witnesses in Pound Case," *D.C. Times Herald*, October 29, 1945. D. M. Ladd memorandum to J. Edgar Hoover, October 29, 1945, FBI file on Pound.
6. Indictment of Ezra Pound by District of Columbia Grand Jury, November 26, 1945, in the Pound file of Department of Justice. Dorothy F. Green memorandum of April 27, 1950, quoted in Dorothy F. Green memorandum to William E. Foley, (see Chapter 6, n. 58).
7. William E. Peake, "Only Tried to Enlighten Us, Claims Ezra Pound, Who Became Benito's Boy," *Washington Post*, November 25, 1945; "Pound Reindicted by Jury on Traitor Charge," *Washington Post*, November 27, 1945.
8. Dorothy F. Green memorandum to William E. Foley, (see Chapter 6, n. 58).
9. Pound letter to Shakespear and Parkyn, October 5, 1945, in Cornell, *Trial of Ezra Pound*, pp. 7–11.
10. "Pound Refused Treason Trial Attorney Role," *Washington Post*, November 20, 1945.
11. Personal biodata on MacLeish, Fitts, Laughlin, and Moore was taken from published summaries; from the letters of MacLeish and Moore in the Manuscript Division of the Library of Congress; and from Henry W. Wells, *Poet and Psychiatrist: Merrill Moore, M.D.* (New York: Twayne, 1955).
12. Frost, *Letters of Robert Frost to Louis Untermeyer*, pp. 321–323, 345–346.
13. Archibald MacLeish letter to T. S. Eliot, November 1945, Manuscript Division, Library of Congress. This letter apparently was never sent.
14. Archibald MacLeish letters to the author, January 1981 and February 5, 1981.
15. Mrs. Merrill Moore letter to the author, September 28, 1981.
16. See the following letters from James Laughlin: to T. S. Eliot, December 23, no year, Humanities Research Center, The University of Texas at Austin; to Dorothy Pound, November 4, 1945, Lilly Library, Indiana University; and to Dorothy Pound, December 30, 1966, Lilly Library, Indiana University.
17. Seelye, *Charles Olson and Ezra Pound*, p. 77.
18. See FBI file on Pound case. In keeping with rules covering the release of these files under the Freedom of Information Act, the names of persons interviewed by the FBI are blacked out. However, sufficient biodata is often included in the interview so the identity of the person becomes obvious.
19. Ida Mapel letter to Dorothy Pound, November 27, 1945, Lilly Library, Indiana University. Julien Cornell letter to James Laughlin, November 21, 1945, in Cornell, *Trial of Ezra Pound*, p. 14.

20. Julien Cornell letter to James Laughlin, in Cornell, *Trial of Ezra Pound*, p. 14.
21. Ibid.
22. Affidavit in support of application for bail, *United States of America against Ezra Pound*, November 26, 1945, Pound file of the Department of Justice. In Cornell's book, *The Trial of Ezra Pound*, published in 1966, the term "violent insanity" was not included in the affidavit.
23. Cornell, *Trial of Ezra Pound*, p. 38, quoting the *New York Herald Tribune*, December 22, 1945. Also see "Ezra Pound Near Mental Collapse, Sent to Hospital," *Washington Post*, November 28, 1945.
24. Cornell letter to Dorothy Pound, January 25, 1946, in Cornell, *Trial of Ezra Pound*, p. 41.
25. Cornell letter to Arthur V. Moore, November 29, 1945, in Cornell, *Trial of Ezra Pound*, p. 26.
26. Cornell, *Trial of Ezra Pound*, p. 54, including quoting his letter to Pound of November 7, 1946.
27. Cornell letter to Dorothy Pound, January 25, 1946, in Cornell, *Trial of Ezra Pound*, p. 41.
28. Pound letter to Archibald MacLeish, September 1, 1956, unpublished, Manuscript Division, Library of Congress.
29. Peake, "Only Tried to Enlighten Us." Charles Norman, "The Case for and against Ezra Pound," *P.M.*, November 25, 1945, pp. 12–17.
30. Julien Cornell letter to Pound, November 29, 1945, Beinecke Rare Book and Manuscript Library, Yale University.
31. Marion R. King letter to the Department of Justice, November 28, 1945, in the Department of Justice file on Pound. See also Cornell, *Trial of Ezra Pound*, p. 124.
32. Merrill Moore, "Winfred Overholser, M.D., Sc.D., President 1947–1948. A biographical sketch," *American Journal of Psychiatry* 105(1948):10–14.
33. Interviews with two psychiatrists who knew Dr. Gilbert.
34. Winfred Overholser, M.D., now deceased, should not be confused with his son, Winfred Overholser, Jr., M.D., a practicing psychiatrist. Winfred Overholser, "Medical Insanity," *Medical Annals of the District of Columbia* 13(1944):382–383. Henry Weihofen and Winfred Overholser, "Mental Disorder Affecting the Degree of a Crime," *Yale Law Journal* 56(1947):959–981.
35. Winfred Overholser, "The Psychiatrist in Court," *George Washington Law Review* 7(1938):31–51. Overholser, "Medical Insanity," p. 382.
36. Overholser, "Psychiatrist in Court," p. 31.
37. Winfred Overholser, "Famous Madcaps of History," *Chicago Medical Society Bulletin* 42(1939):314–318.
38. Winfred Overholser, "Some Problems in Psychiatric Expert Testimony," *American Journal of Medical Jurisprudence* 2(1939):76–83. Overholser, "Psychiatrist in Court," p. 31.
39. Telephone interview with Dr. Maurice Platkin, July 1981.
40. Telephone interview with Dr. Winfred Overholser, Jr., May 2, 1981.
41. Moore, "Winfred Overholser, M.D."
42. The poem is in the Merrill Moore collection of letters in the Manuscript Division, Library of Congress. Mrs. Merrill Moore, in a letter to the author, March 25, 1982, doubts that her husband wrote it.
43. Telephone interview with Dr. Charles Dalmau, May 9, 1981.
44. They were not related according to J. Spencer Overholser, the Overholser family historian who kindly researched the question (letter of October 19, 1981, to the author). See also Pound, *Letters to Ibbotson*, p. 106, for evidence that Pound had written to Willis Overholser in 1940.
45. Article in the *Washington Star*, November 3, 1945, found in the Overholser file, Manuscript Division, Library of Congress.

46. Overholser letter to Charles Norman, January 8, 1960, St. Elizabeths Hospital file no. 1132.

47. Dr. Cody memorandum to Dr. Overholser, March 1, 1957, St. Elizabeths Hospital file no. 918.

48. Julien Cornell letter to Wendell S. Muncie, December 6, 1945, in Cornell, *Trial of Ezra Pound*, pp. 32–33.

49. Henry Weihofen, *The Urge to Punish* (New York: Farrar, Strauss and Cudahy, 1956), pp. 50–54. Dr. Weihofen was a personal friend of Dr. Overholser and co-author with him of other publications on law and psychiatry. For a good summary of the unfit plea see John H. Hess, Henry B. Pearsall, Donald A. Sliehter, and Herbert E. Thomas, "Criminal Law, Insane Persons, Competency to Stand Trial," *Michigan Law Review* 59(1961):1078–1100.

50. Richard C. Allen, Elyce Z. Ferster, and Jesse G. Rubin, eds., *Readings in Law and Psychiatry* (Baltimore: Johns Hopkins University Press, 1968).

51. Cornell, *Trial of Ezra Pound*, pp. 35–36.

52. Psychiatric examination of Ezra Pound by Dr. Marion R. King, December 13, 1945, St. Elizabeths Hospital file no. 1371. Also Marion R. King letter to Winfred Overholser, December 27, 1945, St. Elizabeths Hospital file no. 7.

53. Moore, "Winfred Overholser, M.D." It is of interest that Dr. Samuel Hamilton was another of the three investigators and was also at the time president-elect of the American Psychiatric Association; Dr. Overholser followed Dr. Hamilton in that post.

54. FBI interview with Dr. Wendell Muncie, February 20, 1956, in the FBI file on Pound.

55. Wendell Muncie telephone interviews with the author, September 4, 1980, and May 11, 1981.

56. For the definition of sociopathic personality disturbance used in 1945 see *Diagnostic and Statistical Manual of Mental Disorders* (DSM-I) (Washington, American Psychiatric Association, 1952), p. 38. See also Winfred Overholser and Winifred V. Richmond, *Handbook of Psychiatry* (Philadelphia: Lippincott, 1947), p. 185. Sociopaths continued to be held legally responsible for their actions even after the broadening of the definition under the Durham decision; see Abe Krash, "The Durham Rule and Judicial Administration of the Insanity Defense in the District of Columbia," *Yale Law Journal* 70(1961):905–952.

57. Muncie telephone interviews with author. See also FBI interview with Muncie.

58. Muncie telephone interview with author, May 11, 1981.

59. King letter to Overholser, December 27, 1945; Dr. Muncie letter to Overholser February 14, 1946, St. Elizabeths Hospital file no. 31.

60. Mullins, *This Difficult Individual*, p. 105, quoting Iris Barry in 1916. For good analyses of Pound's eccentric style of communication see Bill MacNaughton, "Pound, a Brief Memoir: 'Chi Lavora, Ora,'" *Paideuma* 3(1974):319–324; also Clearfield, "Pound, Paris and Dada."

61. Psychiatric examination of Pound by King.

62. Pound, Postscript to *Natural Philosophy*, p. 214.

63. Testimony of Dr. Gilbert, transcript of sanity hearing on Ezra Pound, February 13, 1946, in files of the Department of Justice, also reprinted in Norman, *The Case of Ezra Pound*, pp. 106–180.

64. Testimony of Muncie and King.

65. Drs. Gilbert, King, Muncie, and Overholser letter to the court as a report of their examination, December 14, 1945, in files of the Department of Justice, also reprinted in Heymann, *Ezra Pound*, pp. 189–190 as well as in most other Pound biographies.

66. The four systems of classification were the Standard, Armed Forces, Veterans Administration, and the International Classification of Disease. See Forward to the *Diagnostic and Statistical Manual*.

67. Overholser and Richmond, *Handbook of Psychiatry*, p. 156.

68. *The New Yorker*, August 14, 1943, p. 15.

69. "Ezra Pound Declared Insane, Mentally Unfit for Treason Trial," *New York Herald Tribune*, December 21, 1945.

70. Henry Weihofen, *Mental Disorder as a Criminal Defense* (Buffalo: Dennis, 1954), pp. 112, 446.

71. Department of Justice memorandum to FBI, December 3, 1945. Internal memorandum to U.S. Attorney General, December 18, 1945. Both are in the Pound file of the Department of Justice.

72. "Treason," *Time*, December 12, 1945.

73. "Ezra Pound," *Saturday Review of Literature*, December 15, 1945, p. 10.

74. Editorial, *Washington Post*, November 29, 1945; "Treatment of Traitors," *Detroit Free Press*, January 4, 1946; "Stern Justice Meted Out to Traitors in England," *Salt Lake City Tribune*, December 24, 1945. See also Frank Valery *et al.* letter to President Truman January 26, 1946, Department of Justice file; and anonymous letter to President Truman, December 9, 1945, FBI file.

75. Ernest Hemingway letter to Malcolm Cowley, November 14, 1945, in Baker, *Ernest Hemingway: Selected Letters*, p. 605.

76. Lion Feuchtwanger, Arthur Miller, Norman Rosten, and Albert Maltz, "Should Ezra Pound Be Shot?" *New Masses*, December 25, 1945.

77. De Rachewiltz, *Discretions*, p. 247.

78. Pound interview with Dr. Griffen, December 22, 1945, St. Elizabeths Hospital file no. 1368.

79. The clinical data in this section is taken from St. Elizabeths Hospital records on Pound, including psychiatric interviews of December 21, 1945 (file no. 1397); December 22, 1945 (file no. 1368); February 6, 1946 (file no. 1381); the report of Pound's Rorschach test January 10, 1946 (file no. 1385); and the report of the diagnostic case conference January 28, 1946 (file no. 1396), unless otherwise noted.

80. Pound interview with Dr. Harold Stevens, March 31, 1946, St. Elizabeths Hospital file no. 1397.

81. Pound interview with Dr. Winfred Overholser, February 7, 1946, St. Elizabeths Hospital file no. 1397.

82. Addison Duval telephone interview with author, September 12, 1980.

83. Carlos Dalmau telephone interview with author, May 8 and May 9, 1981.

84. Ezra Pound, "For a New Paideuma," *Criterion*, January 1958, reprinted in *Selected Prose*, p. 287.

85. Addison Duval telephone interview with author, September 12, 1980.

86. Diagnostic case conference records, January 28, 1946, St. Elizabeths Hospital file no. 1396.

87. Seelye, *Charles Olson and Ezra Pound*, p. 38.

88. Ibid., p. 45.

89. Albert Deutsch, "Sanity Trial of Ezra Pound Stirs Psychiatric World," *P.M.*, January 28, 1946.

90. Winfred Overholser, "Review of *The Mentally Ill in America* by Albert Deutsch," *American Bar Association Journal* 23(1937):982.

91. Wendell Muncie letter to Winfred Overholser, January 29, 1946, St. Elizabeths Hospital file no. 21.

92. Seelye, *Charles Olson and Ezra Pound*, p. 61.

93. James Laughlin letter to Winfred Overholser, January 24, 1946, St. Elizabeths Hospital file no. 22; Dr. Overholser memorandum to the Department of Justice, January 8, 1946, St. Elizabeths Hospital file no. 17.

94. Albert Deutsch, "Pound Gets Unsound," *P.M.*, February 14, 1946.

95. Addison Duval telephone interview with author, May 7, 1981.

96. "Impounded Records," *Newsweek*, January 7, 1946. J. M. McInerney memorandum to Isaiah Matlack, March 20, 1946, files of the Department of Justice.

97. Jerome Kavka interview with the author, July 28, 1981.

98. Harold Stevens interview with author, May 7, 1981; also Harold Stevens letter to author, June 2, 1981.

99. Kavka interview with the author.

100. "Miller Removed by Overholser at St. Elizabeths," *Washington Star*, August 24, 1945. See also "Doc Miller Blames Publicity Hangover on Alky 'bomb' Misquote," *Washington News*, August 14, 1945.

101. Julien Cornell letter to Dorothy Pound, January 25, 1946, in Cornell, *The Trial of Ezra Pound*, p. 41.

102. Telephone interviews by the author with Dr. Finner, May 6, 1981, and with Dr. Weisdorf, November 23, 1980 and May 11, 1981. Until recent years their psychiatric reports were classified "confidential" and were thus not available to Pound biographers. They were available, however, to the Department of Justice and the FBI.

103. J. Edgar Hoover telegram to FBI field offices, December 27, 1946, in the FBI file on Pound.

104. The meeting of Isaiah Matlack with Dr. Overholser is mentioned in a J. C. Strickland memorandum to D. M. Ladd, December 18, 1945, in the FBI file on Pound. Information on the possible Robert Frost contact with Dr. Overholser is from my telephone interview with Addison Duval, May 7, 1981. The allegation that Hemingway came to Washington to assist Pound is in Patmore, *My Friends When Young*, p. 100.

105. Carlos Baker letter to the author, September 8, 1981.

106. Lewis Carroll, *Alice's Adventures in Wonderland*, in *The Complete Works of Lewis Carroll* (New York: Modern Library), pp. 116–117.

107. Dr. Muncie telephone interview, May 11, 1981. The fact that Drs. King and Overholser had seen these records is established by King's letter to Overholser, December 6, 1945, in which he sent these records to him. See St. Elizabeths Hospital file no. 3.

108. Seelye, *Charles Olson and Ezra Pound*, p. 61.

109. Pound letter to Overholser, August 1, 1959, manuscript Division, Library of Congress.

110. Deutsch, "Pound Gets Unsound."

111. Cornell, *Trial of Ezra Pound*, pp. 42–43.

112. FBI file on investigation of circumstances surrounding Pound sanity hearing, December 1955 to March 1956.

113. The transcript of the sanity hearing on Ezra Pound is in the Pound file of the Department of Justice, and is also reprinted in Norman, *Case of Ezra Pound*, pp. 106–180.

114. Deutsch, "Pound Gets Unsound."

115. James Laughlin letter to T. S. Eliot, February 15, 1946, Humanities Research Center, The University of Texas at Austin. See also Laughlin's letter to Winfred Overholser, February 27, 1946, St. Elizabeths Hospital file no. 30.

116. Seelye, *Charles Olson and Ezra Pound*, pp. 72, 75.

117. Deutsch, "Pound Gets Unsound."

118. Fredric Wertham, "Road to Rappallo: A Psychiatric Study," *American Journal of Psychotherapy* 3(1949):585–600.

119. Dr. Dalmau telephone interview, May 9, 1981.

CHAPTER 8: ASYLUM

1. Robert J. Donovan, *Assassins* (New York: Harper, 1955), pp. 73–86.

2. Descriptions of Pound's room are from notes by hospital psychiatrists (Saint Elizabeths Hospital file no. 1415-A); and Carroll Terrell, "Saint Elizabeths," *Paideuma* 3(1974):363–379.

3. Wyndham Lewis letter to Pound, June 30, 1946, in Rose, *Letters of Wyndham Lewis*, pp. 394–395; William Carlos Williams letters to Pound, February 4, 1946, and March 29, 1946, unpublished, Lilly Library, Indiana University; Nancy Cunard letter to Pound in Ford, *Nancy Cunard*, p. 358.

4. Jacob Epstein, *An Autobiography* (London: Hulton Press, 1955), p. 56. Stock (*Life of Ezra Pound*, p. 562) says that Pound derived the title "rock drill" from a Wyndham Lewis review of Pound's letters, but the original source of the idea almost certainly was Epstein's work.
5. See Lee Bartlet and Hugh Witemeyer, "Ezra Pound and James Dickey: A Correspondence and a Kinship," *Paideuma* 11(1982):290–312; Wilhelm, *Later Cantos of Ezra Pound*, p. 87; Williams, "Penny Wise, Pound Foolish"; and William Carlos Williams, "Review," *Imagi* 4(1949):10–11.
6. Pound letter to Winfred Overholser, August 1, 1959, unpublished, Manuscript Division, Library of Congress. This is the letter that continues: "And some to King, whatever became of him. I thought he stuck his neck out possibly the furtherest." (See Chapter 7.)
7. See Stock, *Life of Ezra Pound*, pp. 544, 567, 569.
8. James Laughlin letter to Archibald MacLeish, September 11, 1957, Manuscript Division, Library of Congress.
9. Seelye, *Charles Olson and Ezra Pound*, pp. 56, 87.
10. See Clark Emery, "Saint Elizabeths," *Paideuma* 10(1981):407–409; Pound letter to "F. C.," unpublished, Cairns Collection, Manuscript Division, Library of Congress.
11. Pound letter to Huntington Cairns, July 21, 1949, unpublished, Manuscript Division, Library of Congress.
12. Pound letter to Wyndham Lewis, n.d., unpublished, Department of Rare Books, Cornell University Library.
13. Myrtle Istvan telephone interview with the author, February 25, 1981.
14. Psychiatric notes, March 12, 1948, and October 12, 1954, Saint Elizabeths Hospital file nos. 1399-a, 1414-a.
15. Sheri Martinelli, "Bulletin board," *Paideuma* 10(1981):469.
16. Huntington Cairns notes on interview with Pound, July 3, 1949, Manuscript Division, Library of Congress.
17. Heymann, *Ezra Pound*, p. 214; David Rattray, "Weekend with Ezra Pound," *The Nation*, November 16, 1957, pp. 343–349.
18. These descriptions are from Dr. Overholser's letters to Olga Rudge, May 4, 1948, and to Julien Cornell, December 6, 1948, Saint Elizabeths Hospital file nos. 201-a, 237.
19. Anonymous, interview with the author, May 27, 1981. The patient was admitted to the hospital for a behavioral disorder and was considered to be perfectly sane.
20. Dan Pinck, "A Visit with Ezra Pound," *The Reporter*, February 2, 1954, pp. 40–43. Also Rattray, "Weekend with Ezra Pound."
21. Stock, *Life of Ezra Pound*, p. 547, quoting a letter from Allen Tate.
22. William Carlos Williams letters to Pound, August 5–6, 1946, and April 26, 1950, unpublished, Lilly Library, Indiana University. See also the letters of Williams to Pound, April 6, 1946, and to Dorothy Pound, March 1, 1949, Lilly Library, Indiana University.
23. Psychiatric notes, March 12, 1948, September 30, 1948, and July 20, 1953, Saint Elizabeths Hospital files nos. 1399-c, 1399-d, 1411-c.
24. Pound letter to Wyndham Lewis, n.d., Department of Rare Books, Cornell University Library.
25. Seelye, *Charles Olson and Ezra Pound*, pp. 16, 43, 53.
26. Pound letter to Hayden Carruth, February 18, 1957, unpublished, The George Arents Research Library, Syracuse University. See also Bill McNaughton letter to Pound, May 26, no year, Beinecke Rare Book and Manuscript Library, Yale University.
27. Pound letter to Huntington Cairns, n.d., 1949, unpublished, Manuscript Division, Library of Congress.
28. Pound letter to Hayden Carruth, November 6, 1956, unpublished, The George Arents Research Library, Syracuse University.

29. Pound letter to Huntington Cairns, January 13, 1953, unpublished, Manuscript Division, Library of Congress.

30. Pound letter to William Carlos Williams, November 13, 1956, unpublished, Beinecke Rare Book and Manuscript Library, Yale University.

31. Michael Reck, Letter to the editor, *Paideuma* 3(1974):420–421.

32. James Laughlin letter to Archibald MacLeish, December 30, 1957, Manuscript Division, Library of Congress.

33. Seelye, *Charles Olson and Ezra Pound,* pp. 55, 93.

34. Psychiatric notes, October 17, 1947, Saint Elizabeths Hospital file no. 1398-a.

35. Psychiatric notes, March 18, 1949, Saint Elizabeths Hospital file no. 1399-c.

36. FBI interview with Dr. Overholser, February 23, 1956, FBI file on Pound.

37. Seelye, *Charles Olson and Ezra Pound,* p. 82.

38. Pound letter to Archibald MacLeish, June 7, 1956, unpublished, Manuscript Division, Library of Congress.

39. Robert Lowell's recollection of Pound's remark about "imbecilic mad niggers" in Ian Hamilton, *Robert Lowell: A Biography* (New York, Random House, 1982), p. 130. An example of a letter from London is Joseph Bard's letter to Pound, September 28, 1951, in the Humanities Research Center, The University of Texas at Austin.

40. John Kasper letter to Superintendent, June 14, 1950, Saint Elizabeths Hospital file no. 376.

41. Robert S. Bird, "Segregationist Kasper is Ezra Pound Disciple," four-part series in *The New York Herald Tribune,* January 30–February 2, 1957. The information in this section about Kasper is from this series unless indicated otherwise.

42. See Kasper's letters to Pound in the Lilly Library, Indiana University, and in the Beinecke Rare Book and Manuscript Library, Yale University, especially the letters of August 30, 1951, and October 30, 1951, at Indiana. See also Stock, *Life of Ezra Pound,* pp. 550–552; and Meacham, *The Caged Panther,* p. 63.

43. Pinck, "Visit with Ezra Pound."

44. The motto can be found rubber-stamped on some of Kasper's letters to Pound in the Beinecke Rare Book and Manuscript Library, Yale University. The similarity of Pound's and Kasper's writings was noted in Bird, "Segregationist Kasper." The information from John Chatel is in Rattray, "Weekend with Ezra Pound."

45. Kasper's Louisville quote is from Norman, *Ezra Pound,* p. 452. The flyers advertising the Charlottesville speech and his speeches in South Carolina sponsored by the Ku Klux Klan are in the Beinecke Rare Book and Manuscript Library, Yale University. Information on George Lincoln Rockwell's assistance is in the Kasper letters, Beinecke Rare Book and Manuscript Library, Yale University.

46. Accounts of Kasper's activities in Tennessee can be found in Anthony Lewis, *Portrait of a Decade* (New York: Random House, 1964), pp. 37–43; and in Benjamin Muse, *Ten Years of Prelude* (New York: Viking, 1964), pp. 94–103. The historical assessment is in Muse, p. 44.

47. See the Pound-Kasper correspondence in the Beinecke Rare Book and Manuscript Library, Yale University. The pamphlet is John Kasper, "Segregation or Death," Seaboard White Citizens Council, 1958, and is available in the Library of Congress.

48. Pound's quotes are from his letters to Archibald MacLeish, December 10, 1956, and December 18, 1956, in the Manuscript Division, Library of Congress. Bird, "Segregationist Kasper."

49. Meacham, *The Caged Panther,* p. 62. Pound letter to Wyndham Lewis, February 3, 1957, unpublished, Department of Rare Books, Cornell University Library. Pound letter to Brigit Patmore, September 19, 1956, unpublished, Humanities Research Center, The University of Texas at Austin.

50. Rattray, "Weekend with Ezra Pound." See also the correspondence between Pound and Wang, including Wang's "Bulletin," Beinecke Rare Book and Manuscript Library, Yale University.

51. Pound letter to Hayden Carruth, March 19, 1957, unpublished, The George Arents Research Library, Syracuse University.

52. Pound letter to Hayden Carruth, November 6, 1956, unpublished, The George Arents Research Library, Syracuse University. The advice to James Dickey is found in a August 8, 1956, letter to him in Bartlet and Witemeyer, "Ezra Pound and James Dickey."

53. Pound told Archibald MacLeish that he had expected to be released from the hospital and back in Italy in six months. See Pound letter to MacLeish, September 1, 1956, Manuscript Division, Library of Congress.

54. An outline of this legal strategy is drawn by James Laughlin in a letter to T. S. Eliot, February 15, 1946, Humanities Research Center, The University of Texas at Austin.

55. Robert A. Corrigan, "What's My Line: Bennett Cerf, Ezra Pound and the American Poet," *American Quarterly* 24(1972):101–113, n. 22.

56. See Dorothy Pound letter to Ronald Duncan, August 23, 1946, Humanities Research Center, The University of Texas at Austin.

57. Julien Cornell letter to Dr. Overholser, May 2, 1946, Saint Elizabeths Hospital file no. 53.

58. Motion for bail, *The United States against Ezra Pound*, December 2, 1946, Department of Justice file on Pound.

59. Albert Deutsch, "Ezra Pound, Turncoat Poet, Seeks Release from Federal Mental Hospital," *P. M.*, January 28, 1947.

60. Ibid. See also Donald Anderson's memorandum for the record, January 8, 1947, in the Department of Justice file on Pound.

61. Petition for writ of habeas corpus, no. 3345, filed February 11, 1948, in the District of Columbia. See also T. Vincent Quinn, assistant attorney general, letter to Dr. Overholser, March 3, 1948, in the Department of Justice Pound file.

62. Dorothy Pound letter to Julien Cornell, March 13, 1948, in Cornell, *Trial of Ezra Pound*, p. 67, pp. 60–61.

63. John Drummond letters to Ronald Duncan, April 19, 1948, and August 18, 1948, unpublished, Humanities Research Center, The University of Texas at Austin. Wyndham Lewis letter to D. D. Paige, October 25, 1948, in Rose, *Letters of Wyndham Lewis*, pp. 467–468. See also Lewis's letter to Felix Giovanelli, November 19, 1948, ibid., p. 467.

64. James Laughlin letter to Pound, n.d. (1948 or 1949), Lilly Library, Indiana University.

65. Olga Rudge letter to Ronald Duncan, October 2, 1948, Humanities Research Center, The University of Texas at Austin. Olga Rudge letter to Ernest Hemingway, n.d., 1950, in Baker, *Ernest Hemingway: Selected Letters*, p. 482.

66. Ernest Hemingway letter to Dorothy Pound, October 22, 1951, in Baker, *Ernest Hemingway: Selected Letters*, p. 742. Hemingway letter to Harvey Breit, October 27, 1955, ibid., p. 849.

67. See the correspondence between Ronald Duncan and John Drummond with Dorothy Pound and Olga Rudge, Humanities Research Center, The University of Texas at Austin.

68. Archibald MacLeish, *Riders on the Earth* (Boston: Houghton Mifflin, 1978), p. 120. James Laughlin in a letter to Pound, June 16, 1948, informed him of this meeting (Lilly Library, Indiana University).

69. Francis Biddle, *In Brief Authority* (Garden City, New York: Doubleday, 1962), p. 292. For a concise review of this award and its consequences for Pound see Corrigan, "Literature and Politics."

70. Robert Hillyer, "Treason's Strange Fruit: The Case of Ezra Pound and the Bollingen Award," *Saturday Review of Literature*, June 11, 1949, pp. 9–28; Hillyer, "Poetry's New Priesthood," *Saturday Review of Literature*, June 18, 1949, pp. 7–38.

71. Wertham, "Road to Rapallo."

72. The stories on the Wertham article were in *The New York Times*, November 27, 1949, p. 33; *Newsweek*, December 26, 1949, pp. 35–36; and a *Washington Post* editorial quoted in *The American Journal of Psychotherapy* 4(1950):130. This issue contains other reactions to Wertham's article as well.

73. Pinck, "Visit with Ezra Pound," quoting Pound.

74. De Rachewiltz, *Discretions*, p. 292. See also Putnam, *Paris Was Our Mistress*, p. 155; and Stock, *Life of Ezra Pound*, p. 374.

75. Terrell, "St. Elizabeths."

76. Pound's access to books is outlined in the following sources: Heymann, *American Aristocracy*, p. 372; Williams, *Autobiography*, p. 343; Louis Q. Mumford, Librarian of Congress, letter to Dr. Overholser, December 12, 1955, St. Elizabeths Hospital file no. 757; and Memorandum to Dr. Overholser, August 8, 1947, St. Elizabeths Hospital file no. 165.

77. See Stock, *Life of Ezra Pound*, pp. 547, 558; Rudd Fleming, "A Reminiscence of Ezra Pound," *The Washington Sunday Star and Daily News*, November 12, 1972, p. H-2; Heymann, *Ezra Pound*, p. 211; José Vazquez-Amaral telephone interview with author, April 24, 1981; Huntington Cairns notes on interview with Pound, January 10, 1949, Manuscript Division, Library of Congress; and Phil Casey, "Ezra Pound Was Charming Host at St. Elizabeths, Critic Recalls," *Washington Post*, July 11, 1961.

78. Robert Payne, "A Visit with the Poet at St. Elizabeths Hospital, Washington," *World Review* 3(1949):13–16.

79. Myrtle Istvan telephone interview with the author, February 25, 1981. Ms. Istvan is a former St. Elizabeths Hospital secretary who prepared replies for Pound.

80. See Corrigan, "Literature and Politics"; and Mullins, *This Difficult Individual*, p. 287. The letter from Omar Pound to St. Elizabeths Hospital is dated April 18, 1946, and Dr. Samuel Silk's reply is April 27, 1946, St. Elizabeths Hospital file nos. 54 and 55.

81. Pinck, "Visit with Ezra Pound."

82. See William Carlos Williams letter to Pound, January 7, 1957, Beinecke Rare Book and Manuscript Library, Yale University.

83. Nursing supervisor memorandum to supervisory physician, October 28, 1952, St. Elizabeths Hospital file no. 1409.

84. See Jordan, "Last Troubadour"; and Mullins, *This Difficult Individual*, p. 290.

85. Jordan, "Last Troubadour."

86. Patricia Hutchins, "Ezra Pound's Pisa," *Southern Review* (new series) 2(1966):77–93; Pound letter to George Biddle, n.d., Manuscript Division, Library of Congress. See also Pound's letters to Biddle of August 30, 1957, and October 4, no year, in this file; and Biddle, *In Brief Authority*, pp. 294–295.

87. Marcella Spann Booth, "Through the Smoke Hole: Ezra Pound's Last Year at St. Elizabeths," *Paideuma* 3(1974):329–334, is the source of the information on the caviar. Huntington Cairns acknowledged bringing it in his letter to Pound, December 8, 1958, and Pound thanked him in his letter to Cairns, December 16, 1958; both letters are in the Manuscript Division, Library of Congress. The quote about ants is from Pound's letter to Cairns, n.d., 1948, Manuscript Division, Library of Congress.

88. Rattray, "Weekend with Ezra Pound"; Assistant Superintendent memorandum to Dr. Overholser, November 26, 1957, St. Elizabeths Hospital file no. 1223.

89. Mullins, *This Difficult Individual*, p. 298.

90. Stock, *Life of Ezra Pound*, p. 563; Vazquez-Amaral telephone interview with the author; see also Rattray, "Weekend with Ezra Pound."

91. MacNaughton, "Pound, a Brief Memoir"; Stock, *Life of Ezra Pound*, p. 563.

92. Sheri Martinelli, "Duties of a Lady Female," *The Floating Bear* 32(1966):411–413. Written in 1959.

93. Sheri Martinelli letter to Archibald MacLeish, August 15, 1957, Manuscript Division, Library of Congress.

94. Rattray, "Weekend with Ezra Pound."
95. Clarence Holt interview with the author, June 2, 1981; and Terrell, "St. Elizabeths."
96. Pound note to Dr. Overholser, November 29, 1955, St. Elizabeths Hospital file no. 749.
97. Pound letter to Dr. Overholser, November 22, 1955, and Dr. Overholser's reply to Pound, n.d., Beinecke Rare Book and Manuscript Library, Yale University.
98. Stock, *Life of Ezra Pound*, p. 563.
99. Materer, *Vortex*, p. 142.
100. Flory, *Ezra Pound and The Cantos*, pp. 246, 253.
101. Frederic C. Porten letter to the author, May 18, 1981. Also anonymous (former hospital nurse) interview with the author, January 19, 1981.
102. Heymann, *Ezra Pound*, p. 235. Marcella Spann letter to Dr. Overholser, August 16, 1956, St. Elizabeths Hospital file no. 824. Sheri Martinelli letter to Archibald Mac-Leish, February 15, 1958, Manuscript Division, Library of Congress. Doolittle, *End to Torment*, p. 57. Sheri Martinelli was still furious with Pound after he returned to Italy; see letter from Gilbert Lee to Pound, September 21, 1959, Beinecke Rare Book and Manuscript Library, Yale University.
103. Note of senior St. Elizabeths Hospital official found inside front cover of Noel Stock's biography of Pound (*The Life of Ezra Pound*) in the hospital library.
104. Dorothy Pound letter to Dr. Overholser, June 5, 1954, St. Elizabeths Hospital file no. 565.
105. Ehrenpreis, "Love, Hate and Ezra Pound." Sophocles, *"Women of Trachis," A Version by Ezra Pound* (New York: New Directions, 1953), p. 25.
106. Heymann, *Ezra Pound*, p. 232; Olga Rudge letter to Dr. Overholser, April 18, 1948, St. Elizabeths Hospital file no. 198; Angelo Palandri, "Homage to a Confucian Poet," *Paideuma* 3(1974):301–311.
107. Nursing notes from Pound clinical record, St. Elizabeths Hospital file nos. 1279–1352.
108. This was clear to the Department of Justice as early as 1947; see Isaiah Matlack's memorandum for the record, October 20, 1947, in the Department of Justice Pound files.
109. The sources of the information on his failure to seek release are the following: FBI interview of Dr. Overholser, February 23, 1956, FBI file on Pound; de Rachewiltz, *Discretions*, p. 292; Wyndham Lewis letter to D. D. Paige in Rose, *Letters of Wyndham Lewis*, p. 274; Wyndham Lewis letter to Pound, September 9, 1952, ibid., p. 548; John Drummond letter to Ronald Duncan, May 29, 1951, Humanities Research Center, The University of Texas at Austin; T. S. Eliot letter to Archibald MacLeish, July 13, 1956, Manuscript Division, Library of Congress; and Reck, *Ezra Pound, A Close-Up*, p. 108. Many others also noted Pound's disinterest in getting released from St. Elizabeths; for example see Mullins, *This Difficult Individual*, p. 287; Moulik, "The 'Insane' Poet"; and Eileen Simpson, *Poets in Their Youth* (New York: Random House, 1982), p. 165.
110. José Vasquez-Amaral telephone interview with the author, April 24, 1981. Pound letter to Archibald MacLeish, August 7, 1957, unpublished, Manuscript Division, Library of Congress. Williams, *Autobiography*, p. 340.
111. Wyndham Lewis, "Doppelgänger," *Encounter*, January 1954, reprinted in Lewis, *Unlucky for Pringle: Unpublished and Other Stories* (New York: David Lewis, 1973). For an analysis of Doppelgänger see Timothy Materer, "Doppelgänger: Ezra Pound and His Letters," *Paideuma* 11(1982):241–256.
112. The recollection of Dr. Overholser's remark is in MacLeish's letter to Ernest Hemingway, June 19, 1957 in Winnick, *Letters of Archibald MacLeish*, p. 397. The letter from Dr. Overholser to Pound is August 29, 1959, Beinecke Rare Book and Manuscript Library, Yale University.
113. Pound notes to Dr. Overholser dated March 19, 1946, November 13, 1955, March

15, 1953, February 13, 1956, and October 25, 1954, St. Elizabeths Hospital file nos. 41, 750, 223, 788, 1257. Also Pound notes to Dr. Overholser, n.d., Manuscript Division, Library of Congress; and Pound note to Dr. Overholser November 22, 1955, Beinecke Rare Book and Manuscript Library, Yale University.

114. Copy of Clarence B. Farrar letter to Harvard University Press, April 4, 1956, Beinecke Rare Book and Manuscript Library, Yale University.

115. Winfred Overholser letter to Alexander M. Campbell, Department of Justice, November 23, 1948; Overholser letter to Stanley E. Krumbiegel, Department of Justice, August 18, 1953; Overholser letter to Edmund Baxter, Department of Health, Education and Welfare, June 6, 1955; Overholser letter to Myrl E. Alexander, Department of Justice, April 4, 1956; Overholser letter to Frank Loveland, Department of Justice, March 26, 1957; St. Elizabeths Hospital file nos. 224, 499, 698, 803, 929.

116. "Ezra Pound Won't Recover Completely, Overholser Says," *Washington Daily News,* October 26, 1947. The original article on Pound was in the newspaper two days earlier.

117. William F. Tompkins, Department of Justice, letter to Dr. Overholser, September 30, 1954, and Dr. Overholser's reply to Tompkins, October 13, 1954, St. Elizabeths Hospital file nos. 588, 590. Dr. Overholser's previous assertion that Pound had been doing Chinese translations is in "Poet Ezra Pound Not Fit for Trial, Psychiatrist Says," *Washington Daily News,* January 29, 1947. See also Flory, *Ezra Pound and The Cantos,* p. 234.

118. Winfred Overholser letter to Stanley E. Krumbiegel. Overholser letter to William Elliott, February 2, 1955, St. Elizabeths Hospital file no. 652. Dudek, *Dk / Some Letters of Ezra Pound,* pp. 105–107.

119. This fact was confirmed by a physician who worked closely with Dr. Overholser and also by Dr. Overholser's secretary.

120. Psychiatric note, July 20, 1953, St. Elizabeths Hospital file no. 1411.

121. Overholser letter to Stanley E. Krumbiegel.

122. Psychiatric note, May 31, 1955, St. Elizabeths Hospital file no. 1416.

123. Merrill Moore letter to Dr. Overholser July 18, 1955, St. Elizabeths Hospital file nos. 1377 (the original letter) and 1418 (annotation when entered onto Pound's record).

124. Pound letter to William Carlos Williams, July 11, 1955, Beinecke Rare Book and Manuscript Library, Yale University. Merrill Moore letter to William Carlos Williams, July 18, 1955, Manuscript Division, Library of Congress.

125. Pound letter to Archibald MacLeish, May 16, 1956, Manuscript Division, Library of Congress; Seelye, *Charles Olson and Ezra Pound,* p. 111; Reck, *Ezra Pound: A Close-Up,* p. 80; Pound letter to Wyndham Lewis, n.d., 1952, Department of Rare Books, Cornell University.

126. Dorothy Pound letters to Ronald Duncan, August 9, 1946, and October 5, 1947, Humanities Research Center, The University of Texas at Austin. Also Pound letter to Wyndham Lewis, n.d., Department of Rare Books, Cornell University.

127. Psychiatric notes, June 27, 1947, and March 18, 1949, St. Elizabeths Hospital file nos. 1397-m and 1399-e. Winfred Overholser letter to Olga Rudge, May 4, 1948, St. Elizabeths Hospital file no. 201.

128. Psychiatric notes March 31, 1946–February 7, 1956, St. Elizabeths Hospital file nos. 1397–1428.

129. Harold Stevens letter to the author, June 2, 1981.

130. Carlos Dalmau telephone interviews with the author, May 8 and 9, 1981. Freud's analysis of Pound's problem is in Robinson, *H. D.,* pp. 423 and 428. A recent attempt to understand Pound's personality using psychoanalytic constructs is Durant, *Ezra Pound: Identity in Crisis.*

131. The opinions of Pound's sanity are from the following sources: William Carlos Williams letter to Overholser, October 24, 1947, St. Elizabeths Hospital file no. 173;

Jordan, "Last Troubadour"; MacLeish, *Riders on the Earth*, p. 122; Katherine Anne Porter, *The Collected Essays and Occasional Writings* (New York: Delacorte Press, 1970), p. 300; Vasquez-Amaral interview; and Boveri, *Treason in the Twentieth Century*, p. 164.

132. Eric F. Goldman, *The Crucial Decade—And After: America, 1945–1960* (New York: Vintage Books, 1960).

133. See Krash, "The Durham Rule."

134. Stock, *Life of Ezra Pound*, p. 560. Ernest Hemingway letter to Pound, July 19, 1956, in Baker, *Ernest Hemingway: Selected Letters*, pp. 864–865. Hemingway apparently had second thoughts about sending the medal and never did. The Hemingway letter to a friend is to D. D. Paige, October 22, 1951, ibid., pp. 739–740.

135. Douglas Hammond letter to Dag Hammarskjöld, January 7, 1955, Manuscript Division, Library of Congress. Hammond letter to Hammarskjöld, January 23, 1955; copy is in the Beinecke Rare Book and Manuscript Library, Yale University. The Pound-Hammarskjold correspondence is in the Beinecke Rare Book and Manuscript Library, Yale University, as is Hammarskjöld's letter to Harry Meacham, November 23, 1957, in which he acknowledged that he was working with Archibald MacLeish to secure Pound's release. MacLeish's letter to Milton Eisenhower, January 11, 1957, is in the Manuscript Division of the Library of Congress. A summary of attempts to secure Pound's release is in Meacham, *The Caged Panther*, p. 116.

136. Sam Hynes, "The Case of Ezra Pound," *Commonweal* 63(1955):251–254. "An Artist Confined," *Life*, January 1956.

137. Meacham, *The Caged Panther*, p. 121. Archibald MacLeish letter to Overholser, November 26, 1957, St. Elizabeths Hospital file no. 1018. MacLeish letter to Pound, July 22, 1957, Manuscript Division, Library of Congress. Ernest Hemingway letter to MacLeish, June 28, 1957, in Baker, *Ernest Hemingway: Selected Letters*, pp. 876–877. Robert Frost letter to MacLeish, June 25, 1957, quoted in Heymann, *Ezra Pound*, p. 247.

138. Archibald MacLeish letter to Overholser, November 16, 1956; Overholser letter to MacLeish, November 21, 1956; MacLeish letter to Overholser, November 26, 1957; Overholser letter to MacLeish, December 5, 1957; St. Elizabeths file nos. 873, 874, 1018, 1019.

139. Archibald MacLeish letter to Douglas Hammond, January 24, 1955; Huntington Cairns notes on interview with Pound, May 9, 1949; James Laughlin letter to MacLeish, December 30, 1957; Pound letter to Overholser, December 28, 1957; all in the Manuscript Division, Library of Congress. See also de Rachewiltz, *Discretions*, p. 289; and Mary de Rachewiltz letter to Overholser, October 20, 1957, St. Elizabeths Hospital file no. 1002.

140. MacLeish's remark appears in a letter to Alexis Saint-Léger Léger, June 9, 1956, in Winnick, *Letters of Archibald MacLeish*, p. 383. Details of the mechanics of Pound's release are in Heymann, *Ezra Pound*, p. 242 ff. The petition is dated March 2, 1958, and is in the Humanities Research Center, The University of Texas at Austin. Information on Adams and Hauge is contained in James Laughlin's letter to Harry Meacham, August 4, 1963, Lilly Library, Indiana University; and also in Heymann, *Ezra Pound*, p. 240. The Christian Herter letter to Overholser, January 2, 1958, is in the St. Elizabeths Hospital file no 1034. A description of Pound's 1939 meeting with Herter is in the Beinecke Rare Book and Manuscript Library, Yale University.

141. Archibald MacLeish letter to Dr. Overholser, March 30, 1958, St. Elizabeths Hospital file no. 1076. Pound's horoscope reading predicting the date of his release can be found in a letter from John A. Csepely, an officer of the Washington Astrological Society, to Leona Elizabeth Schoyer, April 9, 1957, Lilly Library, Indiana University. Mr. Csepely said that his prediction was based on the position of the stars.

142. Information on Thurman Arnold at Wabash is in the James Rader Wabash file, Beinecke Rare Book and Manuscript Library, Yale University. The Affidavit of Dr. Overholser, notarized, April 18, 1958, is in the file of the Department of Justice.

The order dismissing the indictment signed by Judge Laws, April 18, 1958, is in the file of the Department of Justice.

143. The information on Dr. Overholser's warning to Pound came from Winfred Overholser, Jr., telephone interview with the author, May 2, 1981. The commendation of Overholser for protecting Pound is in a letter from Eustace Mullins to Overholser, April 27, 1955, St. Elizabeths Hospital file no. 682.

144. Recommendation for discharge, May 6, 1958, St. Elizabeths Hospital file no. 1427. The quote by a friend is in a Mario Praz letter to Peter Russell, April 9, 1958, Humanities Research Center, The University of Texas at Austin.

145. Elizabeth Bishop, "Visits to St. Elizabeths," in *Elizabeth Bishop: The Complete Poems* (New York: Farrar, Straus and Giroux, 1969). The poem assumes an added dimension when it is known that Bishop's own mother had been in a psychiatric hospital since the poet's childhood; see James Merrill, "The Clear Eye of Elizabeth Bishop," *Washington Post Book World,* February 20, 1983, pp. 1–14.

CHAPTER 9: AFTER THE FALL

1. Pound interviews quoted from Norman, *Ezra Pound,* pp. 456, 461. Pound had previously said many of the same things to visitors at the hospital; see, for example, Pinck, "Visit with Ezra Pound." See also "Ezra Pound," *The Observer,* May 4, 1958.

2. Norman, *Ezra Pound,* p. 461; also Mary McGrory, *Washington Star,* April 30, 1958, quoted in Norman, *Ezra Pound,* p. 456. On the day Pound was discharged from the hospital Ernest Hemingway sent him a check for $1,500; see Hemingway letter to Pound, June 26, 1958, in Baker, *Ernest Hemingway: Selected Letters,* p. 883.

3. James J. Kilpatrick, "A Conversation with Ezra Pound," *National Review,* May 24, 1958, pp. 491–493.

4. Whittemore, *William Carlos Williams: Poet from Jersey,* pp. 58, 346.

5. Stock, *Life of Ezra Pound,* pp. 574–575; Materer, "Doppelgänger."

6. Doolittle, *End to Torment,* p. 62.

7. "Pound, in Italy, Gives Fascist Salute; Calls United States an 'Insane Asylum,'" *New York Times,* July 10, 1958.

8. Pound letter to Brigit Patmore, December 28, 1958, unpublished, Humanities Research Center, The University of Texas at Austin.

9. Hall, *Remembering Poets,* p. 184.

10. Pound letters to Dr. Overholser August 14, 1958, and March 14, 1959; Overholser letter to Pound, February 27, 1959; St. Elizabeths Hospital file nos. 1102, 1037, 1115.

11. Meacham, *The Caged Panther,* pp. 134, 181, quoting Pound letters. John Kasper letter to Pound, October 21, 1958, Beinecke Rare Book and Manuscript Library, Yale University.

12. Meacham, *The Caged Panther,* pp. 166–167, quoting the Pound letter to Christian Herter, September 14, 1958.

13. Stock, *Life of Ezra Pound,* p. 577; Kenner, *Pound Era,* p. 540.

14. De Rachewiltz, *Discretions,* p. 305.

15. Kenner, *Pound Era,* p. 540.

16. De Rachewiltz, *Discretions,* p. 305.

17. Ibid., pp. 305–306; Kenner, "D. P. Remembered."

18. Pound letter to Dr. Overholser, November 14, 1958, St. Elizabeths Hospital file no. 1108.

19. Winfred Overholser letter to Pound, February 27, 1959; and Thurman Arnold letter to Pound, March 3, 1959; St. Elizabeths Hospital file nos. 1115, 1116. Pound letter to Dr. Overholser, November 14, 1959, Beinecke Rare Book and Manuscript Library, Yale University.

20. Kenner, *Pound Era*, p. 547.
21. Heymann, *Ezra Pound*, pp. 267, 356n. Mr. Heymann cites Eva Hesse as the source of this information.
22. Ibid.
23. Pound letter to Dr. Overholser, August 1, 1959; Pound letter to Archibald MacLeish, September 9, no year; Pound letter to MacLeish, December 16, no year; all are in the Manuscript Division, Library of Congress.
24. James Laughlin letter to Dr. Overholser, December 1, 1959, St. Elizabeths Hospital file no. 1126.
25. Pound letters to Huntington Cairns, October 29, 1959, and to Archibald MacLeish, October 10, no year; both are in the Manuscript Division, Library of Congress. See also James Laughlin letter to A. V. Moore, October 10, 1959, Lilly Library, Indiana University.
26. Stock, *Life of Ezra Pound*, p. 583.
27. Ibid., p. 584. Heymann, *Ezra Pound*, pp. 268–269, quoting *New York Herald Tribune*, January 18, 1960.
28. Desmond O'Grady, "Ezra Pound: A Personal Memoir," *Agenda* 17(1979):285–299. Cornelio Fazio, medical summary of Ezra Pound, April 15, 1966, sent to St. Elizabeths Hospital; Dr. Fazio was with the medical clinic at the University of Genoa; St. Elizabeths Hospital file no. 1160. Pound had had a fear of germs for many years; Yeats had commented on it as early as 1930; see Stock, *Life of Ezra Pound*, p. 365.
29. Doob, "Some Notes on E. P."
30. Ibid.
31. Fazio, medical summary. It has also been rumored in psychiatric circles that Pound received electroshock therapy for his depression in Italy. I was unable to find any validation of this rumor, and it is not mentioned in the available Italian medical summaries.
32. Hall, *Remembering Poets*, p. 192. See also Levy, "Ezra Pound's Voice of Silence"; he places this remark in 1965.
33. Reck, *Ezra Pound: A Close-Up*, p. 146.
34. Stock, *Life of Ezra Pound*, p. 559.
35. Oscar Wilde, *Picture of Dorian Gray*, (New York: Barnes and Noble, 1969), p. 3. First published in 1890.
36. Norman, *Ezra Pound*, p. 445.
37. Heymann, *Ezra Pound*, p. 269, quoting *New York Herald Tribune*, January 18, 1960. See also O'Grady, "Ezra Pound: A Personal Memoir."
38. Stock, *Life of Ezra Pound*, pp. 586–587.
39. Michael Reck, "A Conversation Between Ezra Pound and Allen Ginsberg," *The Evergreen Review*, June 1968, pp. 27–84. The wording of the quote is that of Allen Ginsberg, *Composed on the Tongue* (San Francisco: Grey Fox Press, 1980), p. 7.
40. Kazin, "Writer as Political Crazy." See also Surette, *Light from Eleusis*, p. 67.
41. Meacham, *The Caged Panther*, p. 183, quoting Dorothy Pound. Pound's selection of his early poems as his favorites is recounted in O'Grady, "Ezra Pound: A Personal Memoir."
42. Heymann, *Ezra Pound*, p. 271.
43. Stock, *Life of Ezra Pound*, p. 585. Richard Stern claimed that the *Poetry* prize was "enormously important" to Pound; see Richard Stern, "A Memory or Two of Mr. Pound," *Paideuma* 1(1972):215–219.
44. See Chapter 8, especially the correspondence of Dag Hammarskjöld. See also Stock, *Life of Ezra Pound*, p. 580; and Meacham, *The Caged Panther*, p. 116.
45. Doob, "Some Notes on E. P."
46. "Poets' Prize Softens Ezra Pound; He Hopes to Visit U.S. Again," *New York Times*, September 7, 1963, p. 4.
47. Heymann, *Ezra Pound*, pp. 309–310, quoting Daniel Bell. See also Levy, "Ezra Pound's Voice of Silence."

48. Heymann, *Ezra Pound,* pp. 273–274.
49. Hall, *Remembering Poets,* p. 160.
50. Ibid, pp. 178–179.
51. James Laughlin letter to Dr. Overholser, April 29, 1960, St. Elizabeths Hospital file no. 1140.
52. Hall, *Remembering Poets,* pp. 131–132, 148.
53. Jordan Bonfante, "An Aging Genius in Exile," *Life,* March 27, 1964.
54. Hall, *Remembering Poets,* p. 143.
55. Ackroyd, *Ezra Pound and His World,* p. 115.
56. Omar Pound letter to Dr. Overhloser, December 11, 1960, St. Elizabeths Hospital file no. 1151.
57. Doob, "Some Notes on E. P."
58. Meacham, *The Caged Panther,* pp. 188–189. For another account of Pound's memory loss see Stern, "A Memory or Two."
59. Hall, *Remembering Poets,* p. 556.
60. Dudak, *DK / Some Letters of Ezra Pound,* p. 140.
61. Doob, "Some Notes on E. P."
62. Fazio, medical summary of Ezra Pound.
63. Reck, *Ezra Pound: A Close-Up,* p. 149.
64. Doob, "Some Notes on E. P."
65. Fazio, medical summary of Ezra Pound.
66. Clemenceau's quote is in Claudius A. Hand letter to Pound, February 9, 1954, Beinecke Rare Book and Manuscript Library, Yale University.
67. Information on the prostate operations is in Fazio, medical summary of Ezra Pound. A reference to Pound's "new physical inconvenience" is also found in Stern, "A Memory or Two." Pound's comment to Williams is contained in a letter, February 2, 1921, Poetry / Rare Books Collection, State University of New York at Buffalo.
68. See Kenner, *Pound Era,* p. 260.
69. Hall, *Remembering Poets,* p. 184.
70. Cookson, Introduction to Pound, *Selected Prose,* p. 18.
71. Ezra Pound, "The Serious Artist." Originally published in 1913 in *The Egoist,* reprinted in *Literary Essays of Ezra Pound* (New York: New Directions, 1968).
72. James H. Thompson, "Ezra Pound: Letter to Elizabeth Winslow," *Paideuma* 9(1980):341–356. See also Marian Ottenberg, "Pound Bid Recalls Fate of 7 Charged with Him," *Washington Star,* April 13, 1958. The two who were convicted were Douglas Chandler and Robert H. Best, both of whom had broadcast over Radio Berlin; both eventually died in prison.
73. Henry Kamm, "Pound, in Silence, Returns to Paris," *New York Times,* October 30, 1965, p. 38.
74. Levy, "Ezra Pound's Voice of Silence." Heymann, *Ezra Pound,* p. 301.
75. For examples of the intermittent quality of Pound's silences see Levy, "Ezra Pound's Voice of Silence"; Doob, "Some Notes on E. P."; Kenner, "D. P. Remembered"; Schaffner, "Merano 1962"; and O'Grady, "Ezra Pound: A Personal Memoir."
76. Levy, "Ezra Pound's Voice of Silence."
77. Stern, "A Memory or Two"; Guy Davenport, "Ezra Pound 1885–1922," *Arion* (new series) 1(1973):188–196.
78. Levy, "Ezra Pound's Voice of Silence."
79. Hall, *Remembering Poets,* p. 186.
80. Under current American Psychiatric Association nomenclature (DSM-III) the narcissistic personality disorder and the cyclothymic personality disorder are 301.81 and 301.13. Although Pound clearly became severely depressed after returning to Italy, there is no evidence of depression earlier in his life. Heymann (*Ezra Pound,* p. 37) attributes "melancholia" to him in England, but his source for this statement is Reck (*Ezra Pound: A Close-Up,* p. 39), who said that Aldington found Pound "in a low." When the original Aldington reference is examined (*Life for Life's Sake,* p.

216), it is found that Aldington was not talking about Pound being depressed at all but rather angry. Thus there are no grounds for diagnosing Pound with bipolar disorder (also know as manic-depressive psychosis). There is also no reason to entertain a diagnosis of cerebral syphilis for Pound, as all his blood tests at St. Elizabeths Hospital were negative. The most appropriate diagnosis for his last years is depression with psuedo-dementia; in a true dementia the neurological symptoms do not fluctuate as they did in Pound's case.

81. Ackroyd, *Ezra Pound and His World*, p. 62.
82. Levy, "Ezra Pound's Voice of Silence"; Fazio, medical report on Ezra Pound; Longstreet, *We All Went to Paris*, p. 339.
83. Hall, *Remembering Poets*, p. 186.
84. Allen Ginsberg, "Allen Verbatim," *Paideuma* 3(1974):253–273; Ginsberg, *Composed on the Tongue*, pp. 3–16; MacNaughton, "Pound, A Brief Memoir."
85. Kenner, "D. P. Remembered."
86. Heymann, *Ezra Pound*, p. 301; Hall, *Remembering Poets*, p. 192.
87. Hall, *Remembering Poets*, p. 192.
88. Levy, "Ezra Pound's Voice of Silence."
89. Heymann, *Ezra Pound*, p. 309.
90. Hall, *Remembering Poets*, pp. 149, 160.
91. Stern, "A Memory or Two."
92. Ezra Pound, "The Poet Speaks," *Paideuma* 8(1979):243–247, (a translation of his 1963 interview with Grazia Livi). See also Hall, *Remembering Poets*, pp. 183–185.
93. Pound letter to Felix E. Schelling, July 8, 1922, in Paige, *Selected Letters*, p. 181.
94. Stern, "A memory or two."
95. Kamm, "Pound, in Silence, Returns."
96. Reck, "Conversation Between Ezra Pound and Allen Ginsberg."
97. Heymann, *Ezra Pound*, p. 312.
98. Edith Hamilton, *The Greek Way to Western Civilization* (New York: Norton, 1930), p. 165. Pound had listed Greek tragedies as one of the seven essential requirements for an education in the Postscript to *Guide to Kulchur*, p. 352. See also Reck, *Ezra Pound: A Close-Up*, p. 108; and Heymann, *Ezra Pound*, p. 215.
99. Heymann, *Ezra Pound*, p. 314. O'Grady, "Ezra Pound: A Personal Memoir." Stern, "A Memory or Two." For an account of Omar Pound's attempts to get to Venice in time for the funeral see Peter F. duSautory in *Paideuma* 4(1975):199. When I asked Mr. Pound why the funeral could not have been delayed until he arrived, he responded that Olga Rudge had been in charge of all funeral arrangements (Omar Pound letter to the author, August 18, 1981).
100. Pound, "Homage to Sextus Propertius," in *Personae*, p. 219.
101. Kenner, *Pound Ezra*, p. 259.
102. This poetic fragment was labeled Canto 120 and used as the final Canto by Pound's publisher, James Laughlin, in *The Cantos of Ezra Pound*, 1972 edition. It was said to have been written in 1969. Olga Rudge, however, has disputed that this was supposed to be the last Canto and says that they were really supposed to end with the last fragment of Canto 117, "To be men not destroyers." See James Laughlin, "Bulletin Board," *Paideuma* 11(1982):187–188. Ezra Pound was in fact unable to finish his Cantos because he could not write a Paradiso, and disagreements among his friends about what the ending should be may be the most appropriate ending of all.

CODA

Robert Payne, *Hubris: A Study of Pride* (New York: Harper Torchbooks, 1960), p. 301.

INDEX

The young poet in London, around 1913.

Ezra Pound in the garden of his Paris studio, 1923.
(THE BETTMANN ARCHIVE)

Pound in his early
thirties. (THE
BETTMANN ARCHIVE)

Pound arriving in New
York in 1939, for his first
visit to the United States
in eighteen years.
(WIDE WORLD PHOTOS)

In front of his hotel in Rome at the time of the radio
broadcasts, 1942. (WIDE WORLD PHOTOS)

Pound in the custody of U.S. Marshals, returning to the United States under indictment for treason, 1945. (WIDE WORLD PHOTOS)

Admission photo, St. Elizabeths Hospital, December 26, 1945. The *New Masses* cover story, "Should Ezra Pound Be Shot?" had appeared the previous day.

Outside District Court, Washington, D.C., the day the treason indictment was dismissed, April 18, 1958. (WIDE WORLD PHOTOS)

Pound gives the Fascist salute on arrival in Naples, July 9, 1958. (WIDE WORLD PHOTOS)

(*Above:*) With his grandchildren, Patrizia and Walter de Rachewiltz, Merano, Italy, summer 1958. (WIDE WORLD PHOTOS) (*Below:*) With daughter, Mary de Rachewiltz, summer 1958. (THE BETTMANN ARCHIVE)

Eighty-four-year-old Pound at the Spoleto "Festival of Two Worlds," July 1969. (WIDE WORLD PHOTOS)